After the Crisis

Also published by Bloomsbury

Rome after Sulla, J. Alison Rosenblitt
Triumphs in the Age of Civil War: The Late Republic and the Adaptability of Triumphal Tradition, Carsten Hjort Lange
War as Spectacle: Ancient and Modern Perspectives on the Display of Armed Conflict, edited by Anastasia Bakogianni and Valerie M. Hope

After the Crisis
Remembrance, Re-anchoring and Recovery in Ancient Greece and Rome

Edited by Jacqueline Klooster and Inger N.I. Kuin

BLOOMSBURY ACADEMIC
LONDON • NEW YORK • OXFORD • NEW DELHI • SYDNEY

BLOOMSBURY ACADEMIC
Bloomsbury Publishing Plc
50 Bedford Square, London, WC1B 3DP, UK
1385 Broadway, New York, NY 10018, USA
29 Earlsfort Terrace, Dublin 2, Ireland

BLOOMSBURY, BLOOMSBURY ACADEMIC and the Diana logo
are trademarks of Bloomsbury Publishing Plc

First published in Great Britain 2020
Paperback edition first published 2021

Copyright © Jacqueline Klooster, Inger N.I. Kuin and Contributors 2020

Jacqueline Klooster and Inger N.I. Kuin have asserted their right under the Copyright, Designs and Patents Act, 1988, to be identified as Authors of this work.

For legal purposes the Acknowledgements on p. ix constitute
an extension of this copyright page.

Cover design: Terry Woodley
Cover image © The Battle of Actium (detail) by Neroccio di Bartolomeo de' Landi.
Science History Images/Alamy Stock Photo

All rights reserved. No part of this publication may be reproduced or transmitted in any form or by any means, electronic or mechanical, including photocopying, recording, or any information storage or retrieval system, without prior permission in writing from the publishers.

Bloomsbury Publishing Plc does not have any control over, or responsibility for, any third-party websites referred to or in this book. All internet addresses given in this book were correct at the time of going to press. The author and publisher regret any inconvenience caused if addresses have changed or sites have ceased to exist, but can accept no responsibility for any such changes.

A catalogue record for this book is available from the British Library.

A catalog record for this book is available from the Library of Congress.

ISBN: HB: 978-1-3501-2855-2
PB: 978-1-3501-9368-0
ePDF: 978-1-3501-2856-9
eBook: 978-1-3501-2857-6

Typeset by RefineCatch Limited, Bungay, Suffolk

To find out more about our authors and books visit
www.bloomsbury.com and sign up for our newsletters.

Contents

List of Figures vii
Notes on Contributors viii
Acknowledgements ix

Part One   Crisis: Concepts and Ideology

1   Introduction: What Is a Crisis? Framing versus
    Experience   *Jacqueline Klooster and Inger N.I. Kuin*   3

2   (Not) talkin' 'bout a revolution: Managing Constitutional
    Crisis in Athenian Political Thought   *Tim Whitmarsh*   15

3   Security: Calming the Soul Political in the Wake of
    Civil War   *Michèle Lowrie*   31

Part Two   Crisis Traumas and Recovery: Greece

4   Tragedies of War in Duris and Phylarchus: Social Memory and
    Experiential History   *Lisa Irene Hau*   49

5   Changes of Fortune: Polybius and the Transformation of
    Greece   *Andrew Erskine*   65

Part Three   Crisis Traumas and Recovery: Rome

6   Coping with Crisis: Sulla's Civil War and Roman Cultural
    Identity   *Alexandra Eckert*   85

7   Alternative Futures in Lucan's *Bellum Civile*: Imagining
    Aftermaths of Civil War   *Annemarie Ambühl*   103

Part Four   Resolving Civil War

8   Caesar and the Crisis of Corfinium   *Luca Grillo*   121

9   Young Caesar and the Termination of Civil War
    (31–27 BCE)   *Carsten Hjort Lange*   135

10 Agrippa's 'Odd' Speech in Cassius Dio's *Roman History* Mathieu de Bakker 151

Part Five Civil War and the Family

11 The Fate of the Lepidani: Civil War and Family History in First-Century BCE Rome *Josiah Osgood and Andreas Niederwieser* 169

12 The Roman Family as Institution and Metaphor after the Civil Wars *Andrew Gallia* 183

Notes 199
Bibliography 237
Index 261

Figures

1. *RRC* 433.2: *denarius* of M. Iunius Brutus portraying his putative ancestors (photo courtesy of American Numismatic Society) — 174
2. *RRC* 415.1: *denarius* of L. Aemilius Lepidus Paullus, portraying his putative ancestor on the reverse (photo courtesy of American Numismatic Society) — 175
3. *RRC* 419.3a: *denarius* of M. Aemilius Lepidus depicting the Basilica Aemilia (photo courtesy of American Numismatic Society) — 176

Contributors

Annemarie Ambühl is Associate Professor of Classics at the Johannes Gutenberg-Universität Mainz, Germany.

Mathieu de Bakker is Assistant Professor of Greek at the University of Amsterdam, the Netherlands.

Alexandra Eckert is Assistant Professor of Ancient History at the Carl von Ossietzky University of Oldenburg, Germany. She is a junior fellow at the Alfried Krupp Wissenschaftskolleg Greifswald in the academic year 2019/20.

Andrew Erskine is Professor of Ancient History at the University of Edinburgh, UK.

Andrew Gallia is Associate Professor of History at the University of Minnesota, USA.

Luca Grillo is Associate Professor of Classics at the University of Notre Dame, USA.

Lisa Irene Hau is Senior Lecturer in Classics at the University of Glasgow, UK.

Jacqueline Klooster is Assistant Professor of Classics at the University of Groningen, the Netherlands.

Inger N.I. Kuin is Assistant Professor of Classics Academic General Faculty at the University of Virginia, USA.

Carsten Hjort Lange is Associate Professor of Ancient History at Aalborg University, Denmark.

Michèle Lowrie is Andrew W. Mellon Distinguished Service Professor of Classics and the College at the University of Chicago, USA.

Andreas Niederwieser is a 2019 graduate of Georgetown College at Georgetown University, USA.

Josiah Osgood is Professor of Classics at Georgetown University, USA.

Tim Whitmarsh is A.G. Leventis Professor of Greek Culture at the University of Cambridge, UK.

Acknowledgements

The After the Crisis-conference from which this volume derives was organized as part of the OIKOS Anchoring Innovation research initiative. We are grateful to OIKOS, Anchoring Innovation, the Rijksuniversiteit Groningen, Groninger Alumni Fund, Sustainable Society, Groningen Research Institute for the Study of Culture (ICOG) and the RUG Young Academy for generous funding of this project. We thank Alice Wright and Lily Mac Mahon at Bloomsbury for their expert advice and the anonymous reviewers for their helpful remarks. Jos Janssen helped with editing and Zachary Wang with preparing the indices and bibliography.

Part One

Crisis: Concepts and Ideology

Introduction

What Is a Crisis? Framing versus Experience

Jacqueline Klooster
Groningen University
and
Inger N.I. Kuin
University of Virginia

1. The term 'crisis' and its genealogy

The last month of 2016, when the conference on which this volume is based took place, felt like a period of crisis. '"After the crisis" looks like an enviable position to be in at the moment', wrote one of the participants to us in the days leading up to the conference; this remark captured the mood well. Many people were reeling from the Brexit-vote in Great Britain and Donald Trump's election as President of the United States of America. At the time of writing this sense of crisis has hardly abated, and the long-term outcomes of both events are difficult to predict. Both Donald Trump and the Brexit-campaigners rallied their voters by appealing also to a sense of crisis, in this case the 'crisis' of immigration, of disappearing manufacturing jobs, and of the influence of international trade and cooperation on national identity and sovereignty.

Current political developments illustrate that the crisis of one group can be the desirable 'normal' of another. Crises do not simply happen, but are in large part created when influential actors decide to present an event or a state of affairs as such. When such labelling is successful, the targeted audience will experience the events affecting them as a crisis. In this volume we are turning our attention to crises in ancient Greece and Rome. We aim to explore how crises were remembered in antiquity, and how communities reconstituted themselves after a crisis. Could crises serve as catalysts for innovation or change, and how did this work? And, what do crises reveal about the accepted state of order against which they were defined and framed?

As we set out to apply the concept of 'crisis' to the ancient world, it is necessary to reflect on its genealogy. Reinhart Koselleck, in his history of the term 'crisis' for the work *Geschichtliche Grundbegriffe*, suggests that the concept as we know it is a modern invention. Etymologically 'crisis', of course, has its roots in the Greek word *krisis* (from the verb *krinō*), but this vocabulary had a range of meaning quite different from our 'crisis'. Koselleck delineates three ancient uses of *krisis*. First, in a legal context it meant 'decision', both in the sense of objective outcome and of subjective choice. Second, in early Christianity 'crisis' as 'decision' came to be applied to the Last Judgement, and acquired apocalyptic connotations. In a medical context, finally, it described the time in an illness at which it is determined whether the patient will live or die (Koselleck 2006: 358–61). The most common modern meaning of crisis, then, a political or economic event, was entirely absent from the ancient notion of *krisis*.

Based on these three fields of meaning Koselleck traces the development of 'crisis' as a concept in early modernity. Between the fourteenth and sixteenth centuries the term 'crisis' entered into the French, German and English languages in the ancient, medical sense of the word. Starting in the seventeenth century 'crisis' was applied metaphorically to the body politic in an extension of this medical usage. In the eighteenth century this political, metaphorical use of 'crisis' became more common. Around the same time 'crisis' developed into a central term in the philosophy of history. According to Koselleck, it became 'an epochal concept pointing to an exceptionally rare, if not unique, transition period' (Koselleck 2006: 371). The use of 'crisis' in the philosophy of history incorporated the earlier theological implications of the term: a crisis now described a final, history-changing moment or phase. The word 'crisis' became pervasive in the field of economics only in the nineteenth century. Economic 'crises' were seen as recurrent and transitional and, in spite of their negative humanitarian consequences, as inevitable signs of progress (Koselleck 2006: 389–93). Koselleck concludes with the enormous increase of the application of the concept of 'crisis' in the twentieth century, particularly in public media, which, he writes, has had 'few corresponding gains in either clarity or precision' (Koselleck 2006: 397).

Koselleck's critical analysis of crisis-terminology underpins the approach of this volume: we understand 'crisis' as a concept with a history of its own, which needs to be taken into account whenever the term is used in the context of historical interpretation. At the same time we are more optimistic both about the explicative value of 'crisis'-terminology, and about its potential relevance to the study of the ancient world. Even if the word *krisis* did not do the same work as it does now, the ancients did use alternative vocabulary to capture and frame events as exceptional and epoch defining. One strong example of such alternative vocabulary is the word *stasis*, 'civil strife'. In ancient discourse this term was ominous with its connotations of destruction, internecine killing, collapse and, indeed, crisis – *stasis* was the enemy of the city, of community and order. The *locus classicus* for *stasis* as the embodiment of a cataclysmic collapse of civilization is Thucydides' famous Corcyra episode: there *stasis* completely redefines the community, redrawing the lines of history into a 'before' and an 'after'. In Rome terms like *res novae, discordia* and *bellum civile* would later come to play a similar role, both for the purpose of organizing history, and in order to distinguish political change and violence deemed legitimate from their illegitimate variants.[1]

2. Framing a crisis: Rhetoric and narrative

An important reason why the concept of 'crisis' is valuable for looking at upheavals in the ancient world is that it allows us to explore how epochal events were framed. Such an exploration, in turn, will also reveal much about the accepted state of order against which crises were defined. We have identified *stasis* as one important example of crisis-terminology in ancient Greek discourse. In the footsteps of Thucydides, among others, the second-century CE historiographer Appian uses *stasis* as a lens for looking at Roman history. Appian marks the 'crisis' of the Gracchan revolt at Rome in the second half of the second century BCE as pivotal:

> The sword was never carried into the assembly, and there was no civil butchery (φόνον ἔμφυλον) until Tiberius Gracchus, while serving as a tribune and introducing laws, was the first to fall victim to civil strife (ἐν στάσει); and with him many others, who were crowded together at the Capitol round the temple, were also slain. Civil strifes (αἱ στάσεις) did not end with this abominable deed.
>
> App., *B Civ*. 1.0.2

The event was extraordinary, because it entailed several firsts. The *novum*-motif marks this upheaval as a period of transition: if something is described as 'first', the second, third and umpteenth occurrence of the phenomenon are implied. Appian describes the death of Tiberius Gracchus as a watershed moment. Rome before Tiberius and Rome after Tiberius are two different worlds.

Appian applies the term *stasis* consistently both to the events leading up to Tiberius' death and to Gaius' activities and death. The Gracchan crisis as the 'original' *stasis* is marked as the beginning and even as the cause of the many *staseis* that were to plague Rome afterwards. Later on in *Civil Wars* Appian has Tiberius' detractors say that he 'opened a large fountain of *stasis* (στάσεως τοσήνδε ἀφορμὴν) in Italy' (*B Civ.* 1.1.13).² In Appian's plot the Gracchan crisis sets off a string of *staseis* that will ultimately lead to the end of the Roman Republic. The author constructs a teleological frame of civil strife from the Gracchi up to Octavian and Marc Antony.³

One brief remark shows that Appian was acutely aware of the consequences of his own *stasis*-frame. Following his short account of the suspicious death of Scipio Africanus Minor he adds: 'Even this event, of such importance in itself, happened as a by-product (πάρεργον) to the civil strife (στάσει) of Gracchus' (*B Civ.* 1.3.20). Because Scipio Africanus Minor died during the Gracchan *stasis* it was just a side note. If it had happened during another time, it might have been considered a crisis in its own right. Appian understands that the teleological, big history crisis-frame he has chosen to perpetuate undeservedly relegates Scipio to the margins. More alarmingly, it renders his alleged murder, because it is *not* a crisis, 'normal'.⁴

So far we have spoken of crisis as a narrative frame. The crisis narrative is a way of structuring a series of disjointed developments, and of reconstituting the arc of history. With a view to politics the rhetoric of crisis organizes the world into what is normal and what is not. Framing political resistance as a symptom of crisis can legitimate the status quo as 'order', and make change seem scary; the emotional appeal exercised by the rhetoric of crisis solidifies a society's investment in the status quo. But perhaps we can go even further and claim that crises are at the heart of the narrative structure of history and historiography. As is well known, Hayden White claims that no historian can escape from presenting the bare events of the past in a narrative structure that is to some extent consciously or unconsciously pre-determined by ideological convictions; there is no such thing as objective scientific historiography, he argues (White 1973). Even more importantly, history needs narrative form for it to be 'history' at all. In a 1980 article White demonstrates this by discussing two non-narrative alternatives to historiography: the annalistic account, and the chronicle. Lacking both causality and the sense of an ending, these forms are devoid of what White calls 'emplotment' or 'plot', a feature which he claims 'imposes a meaning on the events ... by revealing at the end a structure that was immanent in the events all along' (White 1980: 23). In the absence of narrative, he states, there is no history, only meaningless events.

But, what sort of events deserve recording? What is history made of? For the answer to this fundamental question White turns to Hegel, who says that *history*, in the sense of events that deserve recalling and recounting, can only really come into being in the context of a *state* (a community bound by laws) since the 'events' recorded by historians are typically the breaches of such 'laws'. In this sense, history is *always* the history of crises. Critical events threaten established order, and need to be reverted, or alternatively, helped along in order to reach a new status quo; they are watersheds or transitions (White 1980: 15, referencing Hegel, *Philosophy of History*, transl. Sibree 1956: 60–1).

3. Framing a crisis with Cicero

The Catilinarian conspiracy of 63 BCE has from antiquity onwards been cast as a crisis-event, and greatly differing interpretations have been offered.[5] The narrative forms this particular crisis receives, then, warrant attention in a general consideration of the phenomenon. It is beyond the scope of this chapter to go into all the versions of the Catilinarian crisis, but we will discuss one reflection on the process of its narrativization found in a letter by Cicero, *ad Familiares* 5.12, in order to identify and discuss recurrent elements in crisis narratives: the analysis of causes (agency), the proposed remedies, the narrator, the narrative point of view (teleological or otherwise), the form of the narrative (an episode in a larger work, a monograph), and its aims.

Cicero wrote the letter in 56 BCE to his friend, the historian and statesman Lucius Lucceius, urging him to write a historical account celebrating Cicero's heroic deeds as consul (5.12.1–2). The letter is notorious for the fact that its author, as he admits, 'impudently' (5.12.2–3: '*impudenter . . . impudentem*') asks Lucceius not to worry too much about the so-called 'laws of historiography' (*leges historiae neglegas*), but to give the glorious consul a *little* more credit than truth allows (*plusculum etiam quam concedet veritas largiare*, 5.12.3). Telling Lucceius that he desires an account of his consulship, Cicero gives an intriguing sketch of how he thinks this should ideally be done:

> If I prevail upon you to undertake the task, I persuade myself that the material will be worthy of your ready and skilful pen. I fancy a work of moderate length could be made up, from the beginning of the conspiracy down to my return from exile. In it you will also be able to make use of your special knowledge of political changes (*civilium commutationum scientia*), in explaining the origins of the revolutionary movement and suggesting remedies for things awry (*vel in explicandis causis rerum novarum vel in remediis incommodorum*). You will blame what you judge deserving of reproof and give reasons for commending

what you approve, and if, according to your usual practice, you think proper to deal pretty freely, you will hold up to censure the perfidy, artifice and betrayal of which many were guilty towards me. Moreover, my experiences will give plenty of variety to your narrative, full of a certain kind of delectation to enthral the minds of those who read, when you are the writer. Nothing tends more to the readers' enjoyment than varieties of circumstance and vicissitudes of fortune.

Cic., *Fam.* 5.12.4, transl. adapted from Shackleton-Bailey

Cicero explicitly has in mind a fully rounded story, what White would call 'emplotment' or 'plot'. He metaphorically speaks of a drama 'with various acts' (*varios actus*, 5.12.6), and remarks upon the pleasure of reading such a rounded story in the, as he wishfully thinks at this point, 'secure hindsight' (*secura recordatio*, 5.12.5) that everything turned out for the best, thereby demonstrating his awareness of the importance of a satisfactory closure (teleology) for structuring the events.

Lucceius' account must start with the beginnings of the conspiracy, and end, not with the averting of the conspiracy, but with Cicero's own return from exile: his personal happy ending. This shows that the narrative should identify the fate of the *res publica* with that of Cicero the statesman. The view that all had ended well was already obsolete some seven years after the writing of this letter, when the war between Caesar and Pompey broke out. This shows well the broader point that the hindsight with which an author writes always determines the way in which the crisis is told, because it influences what the *telos*, the end to which a crisis led, is held to be, and whether this *telos* is evaluated in a positive or in a negative way (Grethlein 2013; Powell 2013).

Lucceius is singled out as an authoritative narrator by Cicero (*auctoritas clarissimi et spectatissimi viri*, 5.12.7), with special knowledge of political changes, to be used 'in explaining the origins of the revolutionary movement and in suggesting remedies for things awry' (5.12.4). The phrasing (*vel* ... *vel*, see above) suggests that these are really two sides of the same coin, or parts of a narrative continuum. In identifying the cause of the evil, one may simultaneously point to remedies, and so affirm the satisfactory moral logic of the narrative world. To colour Lucceius' inquiry into the causes of the Catilinarian affair, Cicero furthermore suggests a personalized moralizing approach: as Lucceius analyses the causes and suggests remedies, he must also 'blame what he judges deserving of reproof and give reasons for commending what he approves' (5.12.4). He may go so far as to criticize some individual hostilities towards Cicero; an openly partisan approach.

This personal emphasis provides a clue to how Cicero views the 'causes and origins' of the crisis and reveals why he seems confident and happy about the ending of the affair: once you uproot the individual culprit, and rehabilitate the saviour of the Republic, the crisis should be over. This need not surprise us, considering the tendency among ancient historiographers to focus on individuals as the motors of the historical process. Of course Thucydides takes history to an abstract level and claims that human affairs, including crises, take place according to certain universal laws. And some historiographers actually have it both ways. Appian claims in his proem that he shows the excesses and cruelty to which 'boundless personal ambition of men, their dreadful lust of power, their unwearying perseverance' could lead (*B Civ.* 1.6). Yet he is not blind to the socioeconomical dynamics that drive the Roman civil wars he is describing, identifying inequality of land possession and the resulting social inequality as important factors in the process.

Often, various parties to a conflict express different opinions on its nature and causes. As we can glean from Sallust, for instance, the story Catiline himself seems to have broadcast in order to justify his cause, of institutionalized social injustice (in particular the debt system in Rome), was a different one from the Ciceronian narrative of Catiline as a destructive individual who wanted the ruin of Rome.[6]

Indeed, for all his talk of 'knowledge of political changes and their causes and remedies', Cicero's analysis does not see beyond a narrative of his personal experiences. This explains why he makes such a fuss about the format of Lucceius' envisaged work. He knows Lucceius to be working on a grand history of the Italic and the Civil Wars (5.12.2). While initially pretending not to care whether the account of his own deeds will form an episode in this larger history of Rome's Wars, or be described in a separate monograph, throughout it becomes clear that Cicero would prefer the latter. This has to do with his personal political situation at the moment of writing, which was still precarious because of the lingering insinuation of abuse of his consular powers in executing citizens without a trial. He needs a monograph, *now*. And, besides, a monograph has its benefits from a compositional point of view:

> The actual chronological record of events exercises no very powerful fascination upon us (*ordo ipse annalium mediocriter nos retinet*); it is like the reciting of an almanac (*quasi enumeratione fastorum*). But in the doubtful and various fortunes of an outstanding individual we often find surprise and suspense, joy and distress, hope and fear, and if they are rounded off by a notable conclusion, our minds as we read are filled with the liveliest gratification. So I shall be especially

delighted if you set my story apart from the main stream of your work in which you embrace events in their historical sequence ... (*in quibus perpetuam rerum gestarum historiam complecteris*).

Cic., Fam. 5.12.6, transl. Shackleton-Bailey

This final consideration illustrates Cicero's awareness of what White calls 'the value of narrativity for the representation of reality' (White 1980: 5–27). In order to have a history, one needs a narrative, one with a clear beginning, middle and ending, that makes moral sense of the events recorded.

The making of a crisis is, to a large extent, in the telling or framing. This, of course, entails the questions of who gets to tell the story and design the narrative of the crisis, at what point in time, and with what kind of intentions. It may be a story told immediately afterwards by the victorious party to incriminate the losers and promote its own propaganda. Or it might be a subversive account by the ones on the losing end, long after the fact. Reconciliation might be the aim of the story, and this may be reflected by a spreading of the responsibilities across several parties, while acknowledging the trauma, as we find, for instance, in poetic reflections of the experience of war like the *Aeneid* or Horace's *Roman Odes*.[7] Or, on the other hand, one could simply gloss over the most contested bits of the story. Crisis-narratives, then, can be a means of anchoring the changes brought about by the crisis in question. A crisis plot facilitates coming to terms with the post-crisis situation, because it roots the new, unknown world order in the past.

4. Experience

Although the linguistic turn in the philosophy of history precipitated by White's theory of emplotment made us aware of how the message of ancient crisis narratives depends on the medium, and on the narrator and his point of view, it has recently been challenged in important ways. Notably, the Groningen historians Frank Ankersmit and Eelco Runia have criticized White's work for taking us ever further away from 'history itself'. Ankersmit asked, instead: 'Can the historian enter into a real, authentic, and "experiential" relationship with the past – that is, into a relationship that is not contaminated by historiographical tradition, disciplinary presuppositions, and linguistic structures?' (Ankersmit 2005: 4). Ankersmit, and others with him, believe that it is at the very least incumbent upon us to try.

Through the concept of memory, which for Ankersmit takes the place of history, 'an experience or re-experience of the remembered past' can be achieved

(Ankersmit 2005: 5). Runia has proposed that objects can serve as carriers of memory, and can give us unmediated access to the past (Runia 2006, 2010). Recently David Carr has built on the work of Ankersmit and Runia by proposing a phenomenological approach to configure history as experience:

> Rather than asking: What *is* history? Or: How do we *know* history? a phenomenology of history inquires ... into the experience of the historical. How does history present itself to us, how does it enter our lives, and what are the forms of experience in which it does so? ... experience in this context connotes not just observation but also involvement and interaction.
>
> Carr 2014: 1

For these theorists the language of historiography builds up a barrier between past and present that can and must be broken down using the paradigm of experience.

Ankersmit's thought has influenced the study of the ancient world greatly, as can be seen in the so-called 'mnemonic turn' of ancient history,[8] and in, for instance, Grethlein's (2013) application of the experience paradigm to ancient Greek historiography. The history-as-experience movement provides a challenge to the concept of 'crisis' as we have discussed it so far. Crisis-terminology appears like an example of White's notion of emplotment, but can crises also exist outside of narrative? In other words, is a crisis something that can truly be experienced? Or do crises only arise once the rupture between past and present has been made, once the, even very recent, past has been captured in language? We have so far defined 'crisis' as a category of historiography and a category of ideology: in both cases the concept of 'crisis' organizes past experience, and serves as a framework for present and future experiences. On this understanding 'crisis' is a shared, intersubjective mode of interpretation. Perhaps, however, crisis can even be an aspect of experience: once we are familiar with the concept from its uses in historiography and ideology we may, individually, be able to know and feel crises as they happen. Whether or not such 'experienced' crises are subsequently affirmed by intersubjective framing or anchoring is another matter.

5. Crisis, anchoring and recovery

Crises turn the lives of individuals upside down, and they can leave marks on a community for many years after the event. We are interested in the aftermaths of crises precisely because of the changes that often accompany crises. People living in post-crisis societies have no choice but to adapt to the changes caused by crisis. Such adaptation entails the question of how the relationship between the pre-crisis situation and the new status quo is constructed, and by whom. It may involve revisions of historical narratives about communal pasts and of shared identities through diverse strategies of re-anchoring: the selection of new, additional anchors, the adaption of existing anchors, and sometimes even a discarding of old ones.

The After the Crisis-conference was organized under the auspices of the Anchoring Innovation research initiative of OIKOS, the national research school for Classical Studies in the Netherlands. The concept of 'anchoring' serves as a metaphor and a heuristic tool for the many different ways in which people connect the new to whatever is already familiar: the old, the known or the traditional. What is called or considered 'old' or 'new' is not always a matter of objective diagnosis: it is a judgement established through discourse and negotiation (Sluiter 2017). Because crises invariably force some form of change on the affected individuals and societies, the concepts of re-anchoring and anchoring are particularly well suited to promote a better understanding of ancient coping mechanisms after crises. Apart from the editors the contributors to the volume work independently from the Anchoring Innovation initiative. The following chapters will engage the topic of crisis recovery in terms of forging and re-forging connections between the pre- and post-crisis situation; some chapters will apply the concept of anchoring, but merely as one among several possible heuristic tools that can be used to study these connections.

Crises affect all areas of life, and crisis recovery likewise spans different spheres. We find traces of such recovery strategies in texts as well as visual representations; in literary as well as in documentary texts; in official ideology as much as in subaltern responses. Individuals and communities affected by violent upheavals will always have to find ways to cope with post-crisis realities and to adjust to life after the crisis. This book brings together the diverse testimonies for such ways of coping that have survived from antiquity.

In Part One, Crisis: Concepts and Ideology, the terminology and rhetoric of crisis discourses are investigated. Immediately following this introductory chapter Tim Whitmarsh's '(Not) talkin' 'bout a revolution: Managing Constitutional Crisis in Athenian Political Thought' examines how the modern concepts of 'crisis' and 'revolution' do and do not translate to ancient contexts. Both are frames for human experience, leading Whitmarsh to question whether people in antiquity experienced time *as such* differently than we do now, or whether there are ideological reasons why Athenians may not have seen a revolution where we would. In 'Security: Calming the Soul Political in the Wake of Civil War', Michèle Lowrie looks at another central modern concept: the metaphor of state security, or Latin *securitas*, first crops up in philosophical contexts to denote the tranquillity set out as the ultimate goal of human life by ancient philosophers. When, in the wake of crisis, tranquillity becomes a political imperative, it justifies imperial governance and encourages depoliticization. Lowrie shows how security discourses have always favoured hierarchical governance strategies, central power and trade-offs in citizen rights.

In Part Two, Crisis Traumas and Recovery: Greece, we move from concepts to consequences, specifically the individual and collective psychological traumas that result from crises. Lisa Hau's 'Tragedies of War in Duris and Phylarchus: Social Memory and Experiential History' investigates how the so-called 'tragic' historiography of the Hellenistic period simultaneously aimed at provoking empathy and producing a warning for future generations. These works, by telling the crisis from the perspective of the victims, aim to correct the dominant, victorious crisis plot, and provide an alternative space for working through the war traumas of the losing side. Andrew Erskine's 'Changes of Fortune: Polybius and the Transformation of Greece' looks at how Polybius uses the study of history as a way of coping with Greece's changed position in the Mediterranean. He argues that the emotional trajectory of Polybius as an individual parallels that of Greece under conquering Rome: going from apprehension and hostility to relief and optimism, to total obedience and rejection, and ending in resignation and acceptance, both the author and the people he describes struggle to find a way of coming to terms with the new reality of Rome's dominion.

Part Three, Crisis Traumas and Recovery: Rome, continues the theme of crisis trauma from Part Two, but shifts its focus to Rome, and to Roman civil war traumas specifically. Alexandra Eckert's 'Coping with Crisis: Sulla's Civil War and Roman Cultural Identity' argues that the continuous re-remembering of the atrocities of Sulla Felix was a way of working through the trauma of the proscriptions after the civil war with Marius. Annemarie Ambühl's 'Alternative Futures in Lucan's *Bellum Civile*: Imagining Aftermaths of Civil War' turns to the war between Caesar and Pompey. She asks whether the alternative outcomes of this war imagined in Lucan's *Bellum Civile* may constitute a counterfactual historical space for the losing side to cope with the war's outcome.

Part Four, Resolving Civil War, continues the subject of the crisis of the Roman civil wars. Instead of looking at the psychological aftermaths of crises, the chapters in this section focus on the legal and political strategies for ending a civil war, and moving on. Luca Grillo's 'Caesar and the Crisis of Corfinium' discusses how Caesar, by harkening back to the historiographical topos of *stasis*, tries to present himself as the solution to and the end of civil war, rather than as an instigator or even participant. Carsten Hjort Lange's 'Young Caesar and the Termination of Civil War (31–27 BCE)' focuses on the period from 31 to 27 BCE to analyse Octavian's successful strategy to break the cycle of civil war. Defining these years as a post-civil war process of 'normalization' Lange lays out both the practical and ideological dimensions of this process. Mathieu de Bakker, finally, takes as his starting point the fictionalized account of the famous 'Debate on the Constitution' in Cassius Dio (52.1–41). In 'Agrippa's "Odd" Speech in Cassius Dio's *Roman History*', De Bakker unravels Dio's reasons for choosing this particular format to present the crucial moment of transformation from Roman Republic to monarchy. By pointing out the historical intertexts with Herodotus and Thucydides De Bakker shows how the debate, set two hundred years earlier, in fact addresses contemporary issues under Commodus and the Severi.

In Part Five, Civil War and the Family, we turn to the impact of civil war on families, specifically in the Roman world. 'The Fate of the Lepidani: Civil War and Family History in First-Century BCE Rome', by Josiah Osgood and Andreas Niederwieser, looks at the aftermath of the so-called 'Rising of Lepidus', exploring the problems that being on the losing side in civil war posed for the families of M. Junius Brutus, L. Cornelius Cinna and M. Aemilius Lepidus. These families attempted to rehabilitate themselves and to reintegrate into society after civil war using family history, in particular by adapting how the family's past was remembered. Andrew Gallia's 'The Roman Family as Institution and Metaphor after the Civil Wars' analyses how the experience of civil war transformed Roman understandings of the family, both as an institution and as a metaphor for other kinds of social relationships. On the one hand the functioning of the family in times of crises could stand in for the (mal)functioning of society at large, while on the other hand the civil war could raise to prominence formerly nearly invisible dependent members of the family, such as wives, as the *Laudatio Turiae* demonstrates. These two tendencies later emerge as the pillars of Augustus' new order: the broken family as a metaphor for political dissolution, and increased pragmatic reliance on the family, and in particular on women, as a social institution. Together these two final chapters illustrate, once again, how crises and their consequences force people to adapt, on the level of the community, the political leadership, the family or the individual. Even if crises exist primarily as narrative frames to make sense of the world around us, they structure our understanding of the ebbs and flows of human experience, and thereby affect deeply how we are in the world, before, during and after the crisis.

2

(Not) talkin' 'bout a revolution
Managing Constitutional Crisis in Athenian Political Thought

Tim Whitmarsh
University of Cambridge
University of Pretoria

The controversial theorist Paul de Man, in an influential essay entitled 'The Crisis of Contemporary Criticism', argued that a crisis is only as critical as it feels:

> It can always be shown, on all levels of experience, that what other people experience as a crisis is perhaps not even a change; such observations depend to a very large extent on the standpoint of the observer. Historical 'changes' are not like changes in nature, and the vocabulary of change and movement as it applies to historical process is a mere metaphor, not devoid of meaning, but without an objective correlative that can unambiguously be pointed to in empirical reality, as when we speak of a change in the weather or a change in a biological organism. No set of arguments, no enumeration of symptoms will ever prove that the present effervescence surrounding literary criticism in France is in fact a crisis that, for better or worse, is reshaping the critical consciousness of a generation. It remains relevant, however, that these people are experiencing it as a crisis and that they are constantly using the language of crisis in referring to what is taking place.[1]
> De Man 1967: 42

Crisis is for de Man a phenomenological rather than a historical event; a matter of feeling rather than objective fact. Much the same is often said about political crises, or – to use a more loaded term (which I shall attempt to recuperate in this chapter) – revolutions. Modern studies of revolutions have turned away from essentialist typologies (or recipe lists) of revolution as a political phenomenon,[2] and towards analyses of revolutionary rhetoric and symbols.[3] Like a crisis in French literary criticism, a political revolution is a revolution when, and only when, it is persuasively proclaimed as such.

The Graeco-Roman world saw plenty of decisive political change that had a lasting impact: the advent of democracy, the 'world-empire' of Alexander the Great and its aftermath, the coming of Rome, the Christianization of the Empire. Scholars, however, have in general resisted calling these events 'revolutions', for reasons related to those we have mentioned. Greeks and Romans did not, it is claimed, *announce* or *receive* these events as revolutionary. In one of the very last essays he wrote, Moses Finley attacked (among others) Ronald Syme, author of *The Roman Revolution*,[4] for universalizing what is (he argues) a precisely culture-specific notion:

> Once it is acknowledged that the *modern* concept of revolution (and the idea itself) stems from the eighteenth century, and in particular from the French Revolution, then all 'universal-historical' attempts to bring events in the Graeco-Roman world, or generally in the pre-capitalist world, under a single rubric, 'revolution', must inevitably deprive the concept of any value for historical analysis.[5]
>
> Finley 1968: 49

Finley argues not only that the pre-capitalist world did not know (phenomenologically or intellectually) of revolutions, but also that this alleged absence rules out the possibility of speaking in such terms. Paul Veyne has argued along similar lines.[6] This avoidance of any language of revolution has been attributed in part to a general conservatism in the ancient mindset, thought to have seen change as inherently destructive. To quote Paul Cartledge:

> Political ideas and practices which we might want to label positively as 'revolution', such as the invention of democracy, they [the early Greeks] would habitually and automatically anathematize as 'new' or 'newer things', opposing them unfavourably to that which was traditional (*patrion*).... On the other hand, the Greeks did actually achieve revolutions or at any rate profound and lasting transformations in both their political practice and their political consciousness.
>
> Cartledge 1998: 381

Cartledge, more realist than de Man, allows that the Greeks achieved 'lasting transformations in both their political practice and their political consciousness', but equivocates as to whether these should be called 'revolutions', precisely on the grounds that the ancients lacked the terms and conceptual resources to allow them to evaluate revolutions in positive terms. There was thus (he proposes) a dissonance between theory and practice: the Greeks (by which he means those of the archaic and classical period) were more revolutionary (and more constructively revolutionary) in reality than the conservatism of their political discourse allowed them to recognize.

Underlying both Finley's and Cartledge's positions is a belief in the culturally constructed nature of the experience of time itself. Ancient Greece and Rome, according to this way of thinking, understood temporality in a radically different way: where the modern West might see change and sharp discontinuities, they saw different modulations within the same pattern. Revolutionary thinking, it is assumed is exclusive to the technologized modern West, with its narrow emphasis upon time as unidirectional and progressive. A contrast between 'cyclical' pre-industrial and 'linear' post-industrial temporalities has been asserted commonly in post-Durkheimian social anthropology: in particular, Edmund Leach has argued (building in part on the work of classicists) that the concept of cyclical time is fundamental to religion's role in denying mortality (the linear event par excellence).[7]

Even the shifting semantics of the word 'revolution' (which is common, *mutatis mutandis*, to most major European and Slavonic languages)[8] have been held to tell us something about circular and linear time. In early English, a 'revolution' was a 360-degree cycle, returning one to the same point. In the early modern period, however, the sense 'radical change' began to be prioritized ahead of the 'return to the same'.[9] The Glorious Revolution, the French, the Enlightenment, the Industrial Revolution: all were united by a sense that what follows the break was radically and irrevocably different to what preceded it. And this way of thinking was contagious: political revolutions have their own kind of intertextuality. Thus the French Revolution was cited and re-appropriated by Russian revolutionaries (some of whom adopted 'Le Marseillaise' as an anthem, Figes and Kolonitskii 1999: 66–7), and the Russian by the Chinese (Van de Ven 1995). In more recent years, revolutions have become part of the everyday language of art and leisure (David Bowie was a 'revolutionary'), personal politics ('the sexual revolution') and capitalist economics (a car may have a 'revolutionary new design'). In the hyper-accelerated global market, the present is ever poised between the equally rupturing forces of obsolescence and innovation. 'The prospect of one-way change', writes Noel Parker, 'is a specific feature of modernity: an epoch . . . turned to the future'.[10]

This supposed shift from a cyclical to a linear understanding of time has been variously explained. For some, it was Augustinian Christianity that created the 'myth of history as a redemptive drama', displacing an older view of time as repetitive (Gray 2018: 25). The modern concept of a revolution, however, long post-dated the advent of Christianity; and, as we shall see presently, pre-Christian antiquity itself had forms of providential history that saw political change as rationally planned amelioration, along a linear path. A more certain influence is the rise of capitalism, labour and the nation-state. Modern time, this argument runs, is tyrannized by the clock and the calendar, defining features of the nation-state: work-time, leisure-time, boredom and time-wasting are products of an industrialist algorithm that transforms the human experience into a resource to be managed effectively. At the macro-level, this modernist construction of time understands history as progress, defined in technological and economic terms, and driven by capitalism's need for expanding markets; it conceives of human society in terms only of primitive and progressing, Third World and First (Whitrow 1988).

There is, however, a fundamental paradox posed by all who posit a radical shift between a (broadly) ancient, cyclical mode of temporality and a (broadly) post-industrial, linear one: the argument that the modern experience of time is fundamentally different from what went before is itself predicated on and clearly illustrates the linear, revolution-based model of history. The modern West not only invents revolutionary thinking, it also instantiates it. In attempting to relativize the concept of the revolution, by claiming that *only* modernity thinks in this way, and in attempting to argue that different paradigms are needed for antiquity, its exponents in fact reinforce their fundamental commitment to the very model they seek to limit.

In fact, to ask 'when and why was circular time replaced by linear?' is to ask the wrong question. For sure, different cultures experience time in different ways; but the experience of time is never reducible to simple geometrical proxies. Thanks to language and memory, humans and human social groups are multi-temporal: they can experience the distant past as closer than yesterday, and the future as more real than the present; the same event can sometimes be felt as part of a general pattern of existence, and sometimes as the product of a different era.

If we change the angle of vision, indeed, it quickly becomes clear how implausible it is to argue that the ancient Greeks had no concept of linear, progressive change. As has long been recognized, from at least the fifth century onwards, Greek sophists explained human civilization in terms of a progressive emergence from a primitive to a developed state, via the discovery of a series of technologies (housing, medicine, writing, etc.).[11] Armand D'Angour has argued that the picture of the Greeks as pathologically conservative is simplistic: innovation was far from *verboten*, as was its praise; and indeed the fifth-century coinage *kainos* ('novel') may have been intended to articulate a more positive discourse of innovation (D'Angour 2011). Pauline LeVen has discussed the innovative practices enacted and explicitly paraded in late-classical poetics: thus Timotheus famously sings of the 'newly fashioned [or new-fashioning] Muse'.[12]

The celebration of innovation in literary creation, indeed, is to be found throughout Aristophanes and Euripides, and persisted at least to the Roman imperial era (Whitmarsh 2005: 54-6; cf. 87-9).

These revolutions are, admittedly, in the cultural rather than the political sphere; it is not uncommon to find scholars speaking of 'cultural revolutions'.[13] But is there really a firewall between culture and politics? States that believe they are capable of unprecedented developments in the fields of literature, art and technology tend to believe that their excellence in these fields is down to their superior socio-political set-up. This superiority might be attributed to the qualities of individual rulers in the city, and not to any political change as such; but, as we shall see, in democratic Athens it was indeed linked to a sense that the current political set-up was markedly better than what had preceded it – even if articulations of that sense could be complex and contradictory.

Indeed, it is notable that the Greeks *did* have a phrase that describes well a 'revolution', namely *metabolē politeias* (literally 'a change in political constitution'). This is not an obscure phrase: it is the subject of the fifth book of Aristotle's *Politics* (as we shall see below). It does not, to be sure, exactly map onto the modern 'revolution': in particular, it does not carry the same, predominantly positive (at least for revolutionaries) connotations, although it is certainly more neutral than the pejorative *katalusis* (marking the 'undoing' or 'destruction' of a political order, a word used primarily in counter-revolutionary rhetoric or legislation). Nor does it necessarily imply the speed, coherence of ideological purpose and total overhaul of all the state apparatus that we associate with modern revolutions. But this lack of exact fit is no reason to give up: after all, *no* English word translates any Greek word exactly, and nor would we expect it to.

None of this should surprise. Democracy was quite clearly considered by the Athenians to be a step forward in human history, and one moreover that could be forcibly imposed on others to their advantage (see further below). Analogously, it is well known (and easily illustrated: see e.g. Aristides' oration *To Rome*) that imperial Rome could be seen as the fulfilment of a providential plan, and that Roman imperial power, once consolidated in the figure of the *princeps*, guaranteed that harmonious peace would supplant the warfare that had preceded it. Both the Athenian democracy and the Roman Empire were thus imagined as progressive stages in a linear development of human society. So why the obdurate insistence that the Greeks had neither the language nor the experience of revolutions? It has more to do, I believe, with modern scholars' obsessive fixation upon a schematic distinction between 'ancient' and 'modern' time than with any sensitive reading of the evidence.

In this chapter I consider how political revolutions were processed in Greek political thought, taking the transition to democracy in classical Athens as my primary example. My contention is that classical Athenians were far from incapable of conceptualizing revolution. On the other hand – and this is my central point – their attitudes towards it were complex and contradictory, for reasons that we can trace clearly. Revolution was a knotty problem: central to Athens' understanding of itself in historical terms, but also problematic, indeed painful.

The complex, conflicted nature of Athens' approach to the idea of political revolution, I argue, was the result of the coexistence of four different ideological strains in Athenian thought. These are as follows.

1. The 'democratic-revolutionary'

Firstly, and most obviously, classical Athenians could think of their own history in terms of a democratic revolution. The revolution consisted not in Cleisthenes' reforms (which held very little interest for the Athenians)[14] but in the deposition of the sixth-century tyrants, which was commemorated in art and narrative alike. The obsessive focus upon the tyrants can partly be explained, as Robin Osborne has argued, by the ever-present threat that the democracy might be overthrown and tyranny return (Osborne 2010: 270–1). Legislation against tyranny (and rewarding tyrannicide) is widely attested, particularly from the late fifth century onwards (Teegarden 2014). But there is more to it than this: it seems to have been particularly important to Athenian ideology to present democracy as a transformative event in history that 'revolutionized' their society. Democracy was intellectually defined, and emotionally sustained, by shadow-boxing against tyranny.

This revolution was played out repeatedly – albeit allegorically – in tragedy, Athens' premier public media, which repeatedly stages the venality and ultimate implosion of royal households. Richard Seaford has gone so far as to define tragedy as an 'aetiological myth adapted to the needs of the *polis*', adding that 'tyranny ... belongs to the aetiological past' (Seaford 2003: 103, 104). Tragedy's most fundamental plot type – reflected in dramas such as *Agamemnon*, the Electra plays, *Antigone*, *Oedipus Tyrannus*, *Medea*, *Hippolytus* and *Bacchae* – tells not only of the collapse of tyranny but also of the unharmed survival of the collective, embodied in the chorus.

The emergence of democracy out of tyranny could be tied to a discourse of emancipation. Herodotus famously attributes the growth of Athenian military power to democracy (ἰσηγορίη): 'While they were under tyrants, the Athenians were no better in war than any of their neighbours, but once they had got rid of the tyrants they were far and away the first of all. This therefore shows that while they were oppressed they were willing to be cowardly, but once they had been freed (ἐλευθερωθέντων) each one was zealous to achieve for himself' (Hdt., 5.78; cf. 7.102–4). Crucial for our purposes is that the discourse of democratic freedom is linked to the idea of radical transformation through time: the verb ἐλευθερόω implies taking something that is not free and turning it into something free. It is reasonable to assume that Herodotus' depiction of Athenian freedom directly channels Athenian democratic ideology; but it also contributes to a distinctively Herodotean weft, the opposition between Greek freedom and Persian despotism.[15] Athens' own liberation from tyranny is thus implicitly placed in a relationship of analogy with the Greek world's liberation from Persia.

Like all ideological constructions, this temporal model, and the moral polarities that it embodies, could be deconstructed via a recursively Oedipal logic. If democracy was sired by tyranny, it could be presented not as its opposite but as its successor. Hence for example the traces of critique of Athenian imperialism in Herodotus' depiction of overweening Persian kingship (Moles 1996); or, more blatantly, in the description of Athens as a 'tyrant *polis*' in Thucydides.[16] This is not, however, a rejection of the revolutionary narrative so much as a second-order qualification of it: it is not that the shift from tyranny to democracy is undesirable, it is simply that Athens has failed fully to enact it.

Athens' optimistic narration of the democratic revolution fed a general belief that political change can create new, utopian possibilities. This appears in refracted form in several of Aristophanes' plays (notably *Acharnians, Peace, Birds, Lysistrata* and *Wealth*), comedies that envisage qualitatively better worlds, even as they satirize and debunk that aspiration. This is revolutionary democratic thinking transposed into the fictional realm: the inspiration for *Birds*' Cloud-cuckoo-land, for example, is not just the dream of recovering a mythical golden age, but also the democratically inspired hope that humans can create a better world in the future. It is precisely a *polis* that Peisetaerus and Euelpides want (Ar., *Av*. 48, 121, 826, 829, 1277, etc.), and they create a new community based – at least initially – upon a new political dispensation of peace and egalitarianism. *Birds* is not a straightforwardly pro-democratic play, but the urge to found a new, revolutionary political order based in justice is plausibly based in a democratic conception of transformative time as capable of driving human progress towards higher political ideals. At lines 227–262 the hoopoe sings a solo celebrating the prospects of the two men-turned-birds, celebrating 'the revolution' (τὰ νεώτερα:

literally 'the newer things'), and praising Peisetaerus as 'innovative in his thoughts' (καινὸς γνώμην) and 'an attempter of new acts' (καινῶν ἔργων ... ἐγχειρητής, 252–256).

2. The essentialization of democratic Athens

Set against the 'democratic-revolutionary' claim is the argument that Athens is, and always has been, essentially democratic. According to this way of thinking, the tyrannical phase was a short-lived interruption into an otherwise unbroken narrative of Athenian quasi-democracy. Solon is of course a crucial figure here (Osborne 2006: 10–14), but the narrative can extend further back, into mythical times. The democratic temper of Theseus in Euripides' *Suppliants*, for example, has often been noted.[17] Isocrates in his *Panathenaicus* explicitly contrasts other states, in which 'we see the people at war with other constitutions (πολιτείαις) that do not appeal to them, overturning them and slaying those at their head', with Athenian democracy, which has remained in place for 1000 years (!).[18]

Lysias' funeral speech (*Oration* 2) offers an excellent parallel: beginning with the myths of the Athenian defeat of the Amazons and of the intervention at Thebes to ensure the burial of the dead, the orator proceeds to the Athenian offer of sanctuary to the Heraclidae, in defiance of the Spartan king Eurystheus; he then, predictably, turns to the Persian Wars. All of these are examples of 'battles fought for justice' (17), from time immemorial. As Jonas Grethlein notes, 'the sequence of virtuous enterprises establishes a continuum that ultimately transcends the sequentiality ... Beneath the sequentiality, there is the continuity of virtue (ἀρετή)' (Grethlein 2010: 113). The effect of the speech is to create the idea of a timeless essence of Athenian (democratic) virtue, manifested in a consistent championing of the rights of the disempowered and resistance to tyrannical forces, 'preferring to do battle for the weaker on the side of right, rather than favour the powerful by giving up to them the men whom they had wronged' (12). This essentialism is implicitly linked to the purity and continuity of the Athenian stock, thanks to autochthony and resistance to intermarriage (17–20). The avoidance of hybridization ensures continuity.

This conception of Athens as in effect always-already democratic minimizes the revolutionary nature of the fifth-century state. By casting off tyranny and embracing democracy, Athens was simply exercising its ingrained instincts, and returning to its true, timeless state. It is no coincidence that the speech in which Lysias embeds these thoughts is an *epitaphios*. As Nicole Loraux has argued, the projection of history in these narratives is an 'immobile narrative': 'the perennial nature of Athenian merit is enough to give coherence to the narrative. In the historical excursus of the funeral oration we do not find the unfolding of a continuity, but the repetitive and exemplary enactment of a single *arete*' (Loraux 1986: 134). Indeed, the funeral oration, an annually recurring institution that commemorated both the recent dead and the autochthonous origins of the citizen body, embodied through ritual repetition this very timeless, eternal Athenianness.

3. The 'imperialization' of the discourse of revolution

Inseparable from Athens' belief in the superiority of its own political institutions was the belief that it had the right to impose these on others. This is a difficult phenomenon to assess, however, since we have very little direct evidence for the reasons behind or the practical implementation of this policy. The extent to which it was pursued has been debated, and a recent, thorough survey of the evidence casts doubt on the idea that any systematic agenda was followed.[19] Nevertheless, it is clear that Athens thought in principle that its institutions should be emulated by other states: this is, for example, the best interpretation of Pericles' claim in Thucydides Book 2 that fifth-century Athens saw itself as an 'education' (παίδευσις) to Greece: other states should reform themselves along Athenian lines (Thuc., 2.41.1; cf. 2.37.1, where Athens' laws are said to be a παράδειγμα).[20] Athenians were not always idealistic about the effects of democracy: they also stoked popular revolutions in opposing cities cynically, in order to destabilize them. Consider, for example, Thucydides' passing comment on the failure of Athenian policy vis-à-vis Sicily in the 410s:

> [the Athenians,] finding themselves unable to impose on them [the Syracusans] that discord by which they might have brought them over to their own side, either as a result of a change of government (*metabolē politeias*) or by means of a military force that was greatly superior ...
>
> ... οὐ δυνάμενοι ἐπενεγκεῖν οὔτ' ἐκ πολιτείας τι μεταβολῆς τὸ διάφορον αὐτοῖς, ᾧ προσήγοντο ἄν, οὔτ' ἐκ παρασκευῆς πολλῷ κρείσσονος ...
>
> Thuc., 7.55.2[21]

Thucydides' point here is that Athenian imperial ambitions are usually prosecuted either by military means or by political subversion, i.e. undermining oligarchies and tyrannies by promoting democracy among the people. In the case of the

Syracusans (who already had a democracy) neither was possible. *Metabolē politeias* in this case (at least in Thucydides' view) would have been used instrumentally by the Athenians to introduce 'discord' (τὸ διάφορον) into Syracuse. This looks, then, like a relatively straightforward example of an instance where political revolution is seen as antithetical to the interests of a state, and indeed beneficial to the state's enemies.

If we read under the surface of Thucydides' anti-democratic sheen, however, we can begin to glimpse a more positive ideology. Political machination does not preclude commitment to the cause; in fact, in many cases it presupposes it. What looks to others like cynical, manipulative or callous behaviour can be rationalized by its practitioner as consistent with ideological principles. It is not impossible, then, that those who were committed to democracy saw its imposition on oligarchic states not just as a destabilizing tactic to further Athenian power, but also as a positive strategic contribution to the general political health of the Greek world. Indeed, to speak of sincere and manipulative behaviour as antonymous or exclusive in this context is to misconstrue the psychology of the ideologue. Athenian democrats may well have considered their hegemonic tactics as simultaneously contributing to the same liberation from which they had benefited when they had deposed their own tyrants (see (1) above). The writer known to us as 'the Old Oligarch' captures the paradox: the Athenian *dēmos* 'wants to be free and to rule others' (Xen., [*Ath. pol.*] 1.8). What we see here, therefore, are the dim traces of a knotty paradox with which the Athenians grappled: to impose democracy was at once to subjugate and to liberate.

4. Counter-revolutionary discourse

Finally we turn to the deeply embedded belief that political revolutions are by their very nature deleterious and to be avoided – whatever their ideological content. This belief runs, for example, throughout Aristotle's analysis of revolutions in book 5 of *Politics*. I quote from the opening section of the book:

> Almost all the other subjects which we intended to treat have now been discussed. There must follow the consideration of the questions, what are the number and the nature of the causes that give rise to revolutions in constitutions (μεταβάλλουσιν αἱ πολιτεῖαι), and what are the causes that destroy (φθοραί) each form of constitution, and out of what forms into what forms do they usually change, and again what are the safeguards (σωτηρίαι) of constitutions in general

and of each form in particular, and what are the means by which the safeguarding (σῴζοιτο) of each may best be put into effect.

Arist., Pol. 1301a

Aristotle sees the *politeia* ('political constitution', 'form of government'), as the quiddity of a *polis*, a city: the two bear the same relationship as plot does to poem in the *Poetics*.[22] The *politeia* is what lends coherence and meaning to life in a *polis*. In our passage, he describes two alternatives for the *politeia*: salvation (σωτηρία) or destruction (φθορά). These are strong terms, and they carry with them emotional weight: if the *politeia* is saved, then the citizens are; if it is destroyed, then the consequences will involve loss of life.

This sense that revolution is likely to be bloody and destructive is widespread in early Greek thought, but in Athens it is likely to have been fed in particular by the two late-fifth-century revolutions, that of the Four Hundred in 411 and especially that of the Thirty Tyrants, the brutal military *junta* imposed by the Spartans after the end of the Peloponnesian War in 404. Xenophon, in his account of the rule of the latter, describes the successful attempt of Critias (the most notorious tyrant of them all) to have his rival Theramenes put to death under the pretext of incompetence, vacillation and conspiracy to subvert. In the course of his prosecution speech, as reported by Xenophon, Critias accuses the defendant of flip-flopping between sides:[23]

> It is true, of course, that all revolutions (*metabolai politeiōn*) are attended by loss of life (πᾶσαι μεταβολαὶ πολιτειῶν θανατηφόροι) but you, thanks to your changing sides so easily, share the responsibility, not merely for the slaughter of a large number of oligarchs by the commons, but also for the slaughter of a large number of democrats by the aristocracy.
>
> Xen., Hell. 2.3.32

Revolution, Critias says, is always deadly – that is a given – but Theramenes has made it even worse. Xenophon's behind-the-scenes ventriloquizing lends an acerbic irony to the episode: Critias' casual acceptance of bloodshed serves to characterize him as someone inured to killing. But that irony does not undercut the generalization; in fact it reinforces it. Even revolutionary killers, Xenophon implies, acknowledge that revolutions kill. And the oligarchic revolutions in Athens of the late fifth century were – as an objective historical fact – particularly destructive.[24]

But for all that they are undesirable, revolutions are, in Aristotle's view, inevitable. The *politeia* is the result of rational decision-making on the part of the collective about how best to achieve justice: 'many forms of constitution have come into existence with everybody agreeing as to what is just, that is proportionate equality' (*Pol.* 1301a). Achieving perfect justice, however, is impossible: 'All these forms of constitution then have some element of justice, but from an absolute point of view they are erroneous' (1301a). In other words, a *politeia* is a necessarily stochastic social programme that aims at the impossible task of enacting generally a particular view of justice that originates in the advantage of one particular group. Because virtue is arbitrarily distributed across the social classes, and because some claim superiority on the grounds of birth, any given *politeia* will never perfectly reflect the desires and aspirations of those on the ground (1301a-b). Revolutions are thus to be understood in principle as rational attempts, however unwelcome in practice, to rebalance justice within the city: 'the overthrow of constitutions ... usually responds to a deviation from justice in the very framework of the constitution' (1307a). Certainly, Aristotle gives the firm impression that the majority of *metabolai* occur because unruly or immoral characters gain a foothold, out of a desire for personal gain or disruption for its own sake (1302a–b). But they can also be caused by the correct perception that wealth and benefits have been distributed unjustly: 'for men revolt (στασιάζουσιν) both when they are themselves dishonoured and when they see others honoured; and the distribution of honours is unjust when persons are either honoured or dishonoured against their deserts, just (δικαίως) when it is according to desert' (1302b). Revolt against the established order, then, is rooted in *stasis*, in civil strife between the different factions, and can in certain circumstances be motivated by a rational attempt to restore justice to the polity; to recalculate, that is to say, the algorithm of justice that lies at the heart of the *politeia*.

Other structural features of society that can precipitate revolution include the hyper-dominance of one individual, the disproportionate growth of one sector (the poor or the rich), electoral fraud and inter-ethnic strife (1302b–1303a). In these cases, *metabolai* are founded not in subversive zeal, i.e. a negative character trait on the part of the factional, but in a rational judgement that power is at present inappropriately distributed in society. The preservation of the *politeia* is thus desirable for practical reasons, because it maintains harmony and stability and avoids violence and bloodshed; but the preserved *politeia* is no more perfect an embodiment of civic justice than the one that is proposed by the revolutionaries. It just happens to be the status quo. (Aristotle, incidentally, takes it for granted that all revolutionaries themselves have a clear vision for the *politeia* they would like to impose: there are no anarchists in the *Politics*.)

Aristotle therefore sees revolution as in some circumstances rational, in that it seeks to renegotiate a necessarily imperfect social contract, but undesirable in the sense that it causes instability and violence. But what is striking about this analysis of revolution, from a modern perspective, is that it downplays the revolutionary nature of the revolution itself, which is imagined as a mere recalibration within a stable system. Revolution is, essentially, the reallocation of power from one group to another: it never involves reimagining the philosophical principles that underlie society as a whole. It is the exchange of one *politeia* for another, but it can never consist in the wholesale revision of the concept of *politeia*.

According to this way of thinking, then, revolutions are not defined by the nature of the political change they effect: all they do is recalibrate the power balance between mass and elite within the city. Rather, their dominant feature is their tendency to cause disruption, violence and suffering. It is likely (as I have mentioned) that the fear of revolution intensified in Athens towards the end of the fifth century, after two violent coups; certainly, this is the picture painted by the counter-revolutionary legislation of the restored democracy (Teegarden 2014). The oligarchic revolutions of the late fifth century found no apologists: the traumatic memory of these events was managed carefully by a mixture of deliberate forgetting and actively remembering that one was forgetting (this is the paradox of collective amnesia/amnesty (*amnēsikakia*: 'not remembering bad things'), brilliantly dissected by Nicole Loraux in a late essay (Loraux 2002: 145–69). Nevertheless, the allergic reaction to oligarchic revolution is rooted in more than an allergy to oligarchy. Both Xenophon and Aristotle suggest that *all* revolutions are violent. And indeed this antipathy to civil discord is deeply rooted: the poetry of Alcaeus, for example, shows a similar preference for peace and continuity rather than civil violence.[25] Indeed, it probably reflects a traditional communitarian psychology, stressing the maintenance of social order as a counterpart to cosmic order, and reinforcing group solidarity through religious ritual.

Each of these four ideological-narrative forces pulls in a different direction. In brief, revolution could be understood as: the fundamental story of Athens' emergence out of tyranny into freedom; non-existent, given the strong continuity in Athens' essential state since time immemorial; a force for change for the subject states in the Athenian Empire, which however raised complex questions about freedom and subjugation; and as a phenomenon defined fundamentally by the presence of interpersonal violence and social instability (irrespective of the system replaced and the system introduced). Given these contradictions, it is unsurprising that the Athenians never developed a unified, uncontested conception of their own democratic revolution.

Where does this leave circular and linear time? Eric Csapo and Margaret Miller have argued that fifth-century Athens distinguished these in terms of political ideology (Csapo and Miller 1998). Aristocratic temporality, they argue, based in the fiction of dynastic renewal across the ages, was fundamentally repetitive and self-renewing. Democratic time, by contrast, presented the present as qualitatively different from the past. As we have seen, at least for the Athenian democracy, this is at best partially true: democracy claimed, if not simultaneously then within the same ideological space, that it was revolutionary and traditional at the same time.

It may, indeed, be a general truth that conceptions of time are messy and paradoxical rather than geometrically neat; they are phenomenological rather than mathematical. Even Edmund Leach – one of the architects, as we have seen, of the view that Greeks saw time as cyclical – did not claim that Greeks understood time as *merely* cyclical. His argument, rather, was that cyclical time constituted a wilful denial of linearity: 'People ... tend to think of time as something that ultimately repeats itself ... not because there is no other possible way of thinking, but because we have a psychological (and hence religious) repugnance to contemplating either the idea of death or the idea of the end of the universe' (Leach 1961: 126). However, not only am I unconvinced that particular cultures have exclusively 'linear' or 'cyclical' views of time; I am also unpersuaded that these diagrammatic metaphors do much to elucidate the experience of time. 'People usually confuse time and the measurement of time', writes Michel Serres.[26] One can certainly visualize time as a line when it is imagined as the aggregate of a series of distinct events, as say in a chronicle (like the Lindian chronicle or the *Marmor Parium*). Alternatively, one can imagine the repetition of the seasons in cyclical terms, as in the archaic metaphor ἐπιπλομένου δ' ἐνιαυτοῦ ('when the year wheeled round', Hes., *Theog.* 493). But these two-dimensional temporal metaphors are effective precisely because they are reductive narrative markers: their function is limited to, as Serres would put it, measuring. Most experiences of time are much more complex than this. Serres prefers what he calls a 'topological' model: time should be represented not in terms of distances on a plane surface, but rather as something like the pleats in a folded handkerchief: our relations of proximity to and distance from aspects of our past are complex, rucked up and unpredictable.

Let me conclude with a reflection on violence, with which the Athenians routinely associated revolution. Xenophon's Critias observes that revolutions always bring death; and indeed even the positively validated Athenian narrative of the emergence of democracy as a form of liberation is inseparable from an act of assassination. If it is right that tragedy endlessly replays the collapse of the royal house as the precondition for the emergence of democracy, it must also be right that tragedy sees the emergence of democracy as bathed in blood. Part of the ambivalence of the Athenian response to its revolution must be down to an awareness not only of past brutalities, but also the potential for future ones – whether in one's own state or in another's. It is much nicer and more comforting, at least for those who believe themselves to live in an enlightened polity, to imagine that that polity is as it is by virtue of its timeless, essential nature, rather than that its shape was improvised by human actors at the expense of other human actors. Ultimately, then, the explanation for the relatively muted nature of Athenian revolutionary rhetoric may lie not in the supposed poverty of their analytical tools or in the absence of any concept of linear time, but in the psychology of collective crisis-management. Conversely, we might add, the explanation for the centrality of revolution to modern political and cultural Western thought may lie in the greater willingness of modern Westerners, in an age of industrialized killing, to accept the sacrifice of fellow citizens (local and global) as a price worth paying for progress.

3

Security
Calming the Soul Political in the Wake of Civil War

Michèle Lowrie
University of Chicago

When Augustus came to power, monarchy provided the political solution to the civil wars that elevated him, and what is generally called the 'Augustan programme' forwarded a new ideology beyond practical measures to restore the symbolic wound to the Roman political imaginary. This period set in motion decisive features of Imperial ideology. Central to this ideology is a new concept first attested in Velleius Paterculus: 'the security of the Roman Empire' (*securitas . . . imperii Romani*, 2.103.4).[1] Modern 'national security' dampens the innovation of this phrase. When the word was invented, perhaps even by Cicero, *securitas* meant peace of mind in a strictly psychological sense. To transfer *securitas* from the soul to Empire implies the state has a metaphorical soul that inhabits its body politic. I call this implied metaphor 'the soul political'. When the phrase *securitas Augusti* circulates, the security of the emperor stands as synecdoche for the security of the Empire, which is itself a metaphor, since the Empire has no literal soul to feel tranquil.[2] The Romans used phrases such as *corpus rei publicae* ('body of the Republic', Cic., *Off.* 1.85) and *corpus imperii* ('body of Empire', Flor., 2.14.5–6), where the metaphorical dimension is transparent. But the discourse of security intimates that the political order has a soul without saying so directly. No metaphor for a collective soul has entered the political theoretical lexicon equivalent to the body politic. This latent metaphor arose as a coping mechanism in the wake of civil war. Unlike modern national security, which targets external threats, the fundamental task of Roman *securitas* is to keep civil war at bay.

Between Cicero and Velleius, civil war destroys the Republic and Rome reconfigures in a new Imperial form whose mandate was to keep the peace. A host of interrelated strands coalesce in the Roman political imaginary and produce a new way of thinking about physical safety, the quality of a citizen's attachment to politics, the leader's duties to preserve the state, and the state's duties not just to preserve the safety of its people, but also to safeguard their peace of mind. Security was forged in the conceptual crucible of political collapse and rebirth. By transferring philosophy's valorization of tranquillity as the soul's highest priority to the sphere of politics, the metaphor justifies suppressing Republican contestation in favour of Imperial peace. Civil war made contestatory politics too threatening to the blessed life. A new politics of *securitas* was the answer and the discourse emerges during the period of readjustment. Velleius is an important source for an ideology that uses the (largely) peaceful accession of Tiberius to claim the stability of Rome's new constitutional form.

1. *Securitas* and the *vita beata*

Ever since Plato's analogy between the city and the soul in the *Politeia*, the soul's condition has been available as an index of the community within political theory.[3] This analogy informs the expansion of *securitas*' semantic sphere from psychology to national security, from 'peace of mind', its consistent meaning in Cicero, to 'safety' under the Empire.[4] Cicero's gloss 'tranquillity' indicates the unfamiliarity of the word – he may have invented it.[5]

> However, the security of Democritus, which is the tranquillity of soul that they call contentment, ... that is itself the blessed life.
>
> Democriti autem securitas, quae est animi tranquilitas, quam appellant εὐθυμίαν ... ea ipsa est beata vita.
>
> Cic., Fin. 5.8.23

Cicero sets up a number of elements the post-Republican order will later link. Like *securitas*, *euthymia* also becomes a political good. In Appian's account, Augustus proclaims the end of civil war by announcing *eirenen kai euthymian* ('peace and good will', *B Civ.* 5.130). A contemporary of Augustus might translate this as *pacem et bonam voluntatem*, but a contemporary of Appian would surely reach for *pacem et securitatem*.

Cicero relates tranquillity of soul to basic animal and human drives that connect bodily integrity to social and intellectual needs (*Fin.* 5.9.24–17.46). *Salus* is the Republican word corresponding best to modern national security and this meaning persists under the Empire. Cicero establishes an analogy between *salus* and the *vita beata* of citizens:

> For just as a favourable journey has been set before the helmsman, health (*salus*) the doctor, victory the general, so has the blessed life of the citizens been set before the governor of the republic.
>
> ut enim gubernatori cursus secundus, medico salus, imperatori victoria, sic huic moderatori rei publicae beata civium vita proposita est.
>
> Cic., *Rep.* 5.8

The helmsman and the doctor are metaphors for the statesman and the general is his military analogue. With the analogy between *salus* and the collective *vita beata* here and with his equation of *securitas* with the *vita beata* itself in the *De finibus*, Cicero paves the way for making *securitas* the basis of the collective *vita beata*.[6] Still, these two clusters of thought have not yet joined: *securitas* does not yet pass over to the purview of the state. Neither *salus* nor *securitas* is a momentary condition for Cicero, but a disposition or habit of life that can be interrupted by disturbance. They contrast with illness, for *salus* a physical, for *securitas* a host of perturbations, including desire, fear, distress (*aegritudo*), excessive pleasure and anger. While *aegritudo* means illness in general for both body and soul, when it besets the soul, it can mean grief or sorrow more specifically, but also distress or anxiety more generally.[7] *Salus* and *securitas* represent a healthy unmarked condition at risk of degradation that therefore requires protection from harm. Once responsibility for *securitas* is attributed to the state, Cicero's equation of tranquillity with the *vita beata* that is philosophy's aim prepares for a further idea: that the state will need to provide not just protection for its citizens' material lives, but also a tranquil habit of living.

Beyond the difference in orientation, *salus* toward the body, *securitas* toward the soul, they differ essentially in their relation to the negativity that defines them. *Salus* is a condition of plenitude always in opposition to an implied lurking danger. Disease may be endogenous, but it does not arise conceptually from within *salus* itself. By contrast, lack inhabits *securitas* from within.[8] Security instantiates Roberto Esposito's theory of immunity: 'Life can be protected from what negates it only by means of a further negation' (Esposito 2011: 160). *Securitas* is a state of being devoid of care: the prefix *se-* (meaning 'apart'; the same as in 'separation'), the noun *cura* ('care'), and the suffix *-tas* that indicates an abstract noun.[9] Unlike *tranquillitas*, Cicero's dominant word for peace of mind, which turns toward the positive, *securitas* bears the traces of the worry it notionally forestalls.[10] By translating Democritus' *euthymia*, 'cheerfulness', into the negation of worry, Cicero introduces a dark element structurally parallel to the disturbance negated in *ataraxia* (alpha privative plus the nominal form of *tarasso* to disturb).[11] Both *securitas* and *ataraxia* are defined in terms of what they are not. One of the pressing questions about security is whether it can ever mean tranquillity in an absolute sense or whether it always carries worry along with it under negation.[12]

2. *Securitas imperii Romani*

Velleius Paterculus, that cheerfully blinkered supporter of Augustus and Tiberius, marshals a slogan with a bright future.[13] The full ideology of national security as the collective blessed life appears in his depiction of the citizenry's reaction to the news that Augustus has adopted Tiberius and made him his associate in tribunician *potestas*. Imperial succession will now proceed in a peaceful transition.

> The happiness of that day and the rally of the citizen body and the hands lifted almost into heaven and the hope conceived for the perpetual security and eternity of the Roman empire scarcely could we trace fully in that rightful work [I am planning to write], much less fill out here. Let us try to say this one thing: how it favoured all. Then the certain hope of offspring gleamed for parents, of marriage for men, of estates for masters, for all men of safety, quiet, peace, tranquillity, to such an extent that no more could be hoped for nor answer more happily to hope.

> laetitiam illius diei concursumque civitatis et vota paene inserentium caelo manus spemque conceptam perpetuae securitatis aeternatisque Romani imperii vix in illo iusto opere abunde persequi poterimus, nedum hic implere. temptemus id unum dixisse, quam ille omnibus faverit: tum refulsit certa spes liberorum parentibus, viris matrimoniorum, dominis patrimonii, omnibus hominibus salutis, quietis, pacis, tranquillitatis, adeo ut nec plus sperari potuerit nec spei responderi felicius.
>
> Vell. Pat., 2.103.4–5[14]

The *securitas imperii* envisioned here encompasses a safety that, linked to peace and quiet, implies the abeyance of military threats. To that extent, it resembles the *salus imperii* (safety of empire) Caesar mentions as its Republican predecessor: Caesar attempts to conciliate Scipio, a Pompeian, by saying that if he comes over to him, all will attribute to him alone 'quiet in Italy, peace in the provinces, and the safety of the empire' (*quietem Italiae, pacem provinciarum, salutem imperii*, *BCiv*. 3.57.4). But Velleius' security further entails the prosperous and more pointedly tranquil continuation of the social order. By putting his succession on a sure footing, Augustus has enabled the citizenry to go about the business of attending to their own succession, expressed via property, marriage and the production of heirs. Right order in the emperor's affairs entails the prosperity of all. The perpetuation of his house results in the perpetuation of the Empire, which in turn ensures the perpetuation of their houses. His wellbeing thereby has a causative relation to their wellbeing and that of the Empire as a whole.

Velleius' enthusiastic celebration of the happiness over the news re-enacts the jubilation attending not mere peace and safety, but the release from anxiety. With the topos of his inability to capture the mood's intensity, Velleius rhetorically concentrates attention on the most important point, how settling the succession favoured all. Succession looms so large because he identifies Augustus' prime accomplishment as the cessation of civil war.

> The civil wars were finished in the twentieth year, external wars buried, peace brought back, the fury of arms everywhere put to rest, force restored to the laws, authority to legal judgements, majesty to the senate, the magistrates' power to command brought back to its original limit, except two praetors were added to the existing eight praetors. Cultivation returned to the fields, honour to sacred rites, security to men, sure possession of private property to each; laws were emended for the public interest and carried for general wellbeing; membership in the senate was audited without harshness but not without rigour. The principal men who had won triumphs and the highest honours were enticed by the *princeps* to embellish the city.
>
> finita vicesimo anno bella civilia, sepulta externa, revocata pax, sopitus ubique armorum furor, restituta vis legibus, iudiciis auctoritas, senatui maiestas, imperium magistratuum ad pristinum redactum modum, tantummodo octo praetoribus adlecti duo. prisca illa et antiqua rei publicae forma revocata. rediit cultus agris, sacris honos, securitas hominibus, certa cuique rerum suarum possessio; leges emendatae utiliter, latae salubriter; senatus sine asperitate nec sine severitate lectus. principes viri triumphisque et amplissimis honoribus functi adhortatu principis ad ornandam urbem inlecti sunt.
>
> Vell. Pat., 2.89.3–4

Velleius amasses an extraordinary list of political, social and legal institutions, Roman values and salutary emotions. Brought together in brief compass and across spheres of meaning, all emphasize the restoration of order along with the proper hierarchies. The erasure of care encoded in the etymology of *securitas* governs the passage's logic: warfare and fury, civil war's affective signature, are explicitly negated. In their place return the positive qualities they had compromised in a precise economy of exchange. *Securitas* and 'sure possession of private property' occur as the fruits of peace among other panegyric topoi such as the 'cultivation ... of the fields' that return once Augustus has put civil war to rest. Transfers of power notionally threaten this peace with further internal disturbance.

Velleius sums up the Augustan restoration by imagining the rent limbs of a fragmented body reuniting at civil war's cessation.[15]

> With the civil wars buried, as we said above, and the limbs of the Republic coalescing, there †also coalesced† things which the long series of arms had lacerated.
>
> sepultis (ut praediximus) bellis civilibus coalescentibusque rei publicae membris, †et coram aliero†[16] quae tam longa armorum series laceraverat.
>
> Vell. Pat., 2.90.1

With the list of provinces that follows, Velleius knits together Imperial extension abroad with the Republic's body at home in an image of a greater Empire consisting of two parts. For Velleius, the body of the emperor serves as guarantor of security. His account of joyful celebration when Augustus names Tiberius his successor assumes the necessity of a living body to occupy the position of chief executive for continued *securitas ... imperii Romani* (2.103.4). Social order will be maintained so long as an appropriate heir may step into the emperor's shoes once he is gone. The solution to the succession problem anticipates the medieval distinction between the king's individual body natural and the body political of his majesty, which attaches to the office while its inhabitant may change.[17] For Velleius, all remains well provided a legitimate heir stands ready. Succession allows the founder to be replaced and charisma to become institutionalized.[18]

Velleius' narratives of Augustus' death and of Tiberius' accession enact security in the tension between expressed fear and the measures taken to restore calm.[19] The same operation occurs repeatedly in brief compass. Augustus on his deathbed wants 'all to remain safe (*salva*) after him' and knows whom he must summon (123.1); once Tiberius has arrived, Augustus feels 'himself secure' (*securum se*, 123.2) in his embrace. The reason for the fear does not need direct expression. 'When the body of the empire is indistinguishable from the mortal body of the emperor, the dissolution of the mortal frame of the one supreme man, the *unus homo* who holds *omnia*, may all too easily entail the disintegration of the body politic, resulting in a renewed plunge into the civil war out of which the principate had emerged.'[20] The arrival of Tiberius reassures because Augustus may now hand the state over to another singular leader of his choice.

Similar fear to Augustus' breaks out across the SPQR, similar calm attends its abatement when 'one man' assumes the majesty of leadership.

> What men then feared, what trepidation there was in the senate, what anxiety among the people, what fear in the city, on how narrow a margin we were between safety and disaster, neither do I have the time to express in my hurry, nor could anyone express it who did. I think I can say this one thing along with public opinion: the world whose ruin we had feared, we did not even feel disturbed, and such was the majesty of this one man, that neither on behalf of the good *** nor was there need for arms against the evil.
>
> quid tunc homines timuerint, quae senatus trepidatio, quae populi confusio, quis urbis metus, in quam arto salutis exitiique fuerimus confinio, neque mihi tam festinanti exprimere vacat neque cui vacat potest. id solum voce publica dixisse †habeo: cuius orbis ruinam timueramus, eum ne commotum quidem sensimus, tantaque unius viri maiestas fuit, ut nec pro bonis *** neque contra malos opus armis foret.
>
> Vell. Pat., 2.124.1

The contradiction between this account and the mutiny among Roman troops in Germany and Illyricum – a potential return to civil war – that follows on Augustus' burial may deprive Velleius of the approval of scholars expecting cool analytic judgement, but the representational processes of his text accord well with Roman strategies of political thought.[21] Velleius verbally enacts the erasure of cares in *securitas*' etymology by describing how the 'tumult' was quickly 'put to sleep' (2.125.1–4) with a common trope for peace of mind. His description of the cessation of fears at the successful transition does not use *securitas*, but performs fear's erasure with numerous phrases that negate psychic anxiety about the world among Senate and people and in the city. The textual repetition of the trope of security re-enacts its fundamental structure: the need to erase cares again and again. As with Augustus' worries, as with the state's fear, the 'tumult' is quickly 'put to sleep' (2.125.1–4). The security of the Empire is no static peace but a dynamic process of psychic repression transferred to and enacted in the political realm.

Velleius repeatedly returns to his production of this representation as its author: 'neither do I have the time to express in my hurry, nor could anyone express it who did'.[22] Security is a matter of safety, but also of feeling, of hope and the imaginative projection of prosperity into the future, and therefore it requires representation. Now, one might ask if the citizens were not going to go about their daily existence anyway. Peace certainly enables ordinary life, but the various contemporary military ventures at the edges of empire were no more threatening under Augustus or Tiberius than usual and the Roman way of life hardly lay in jeopardy.[23] What security accomplishes beyond safety per se is to forward safety's representation.

What goes missing here is as important as what is said. Velleius' account of the activities ensured focuses on the perpetuation of the household rather than of politics as a sphere for liberty, contestation and collective decision-making. The discursive Republican analogue might look like the conclusion to Cicero's fourth *Catilinarian* oration. In return for his custody of the safety of the city and his senatorial addressees, in return in short for his diligence in 'saving the state' (*ad conservandam rem publicam*, 4.23), Cicero asks for nothing but the continued memory of his consulship and for the Senate to watch over his son. Memory here is shorthand for glory, the best compensation for Republican virtue. There are many points of contact with Velleius. The context is no less imperial, but with a miniscule 'i': Cicero calls on Rome's empire, the army, the provinces and the whole apparatus of provincial clientage in his plea for recognition, which he valorizes even over his own physical safety. Inheritance and preserving the next generation are similarly at issue.

> But if the force of wicked men deceives and overwhelms my hope, I commend to you my small son, to whom there will be enough protection not only of his safety but also his dignity if you remember he is the son of one who has preserved all this at his own danger alone. Therefore make your decision with diligence and courage, as you have begun, concerning the highest safety, yours and that of the Roman people, concerning your wives and children, altars and hearths, shrines and temples, the roofs and seats of the whole city, the empire and freedom, the safety of Italy, the republic taken in its entirety.

> quod si meam spem vis improborum fefellerit atque superaverit, commendo vobis parvum meum filium, cui profecto satis erit praesidi non solum ad salutem verum etiam ad dignitatem, ei eius qui haec omnia suo solius periculo conservaverit illum filium esse memineritis. quapropter de summa salute vestra populique Romani, de vestris coniugibus ac liberis, de aris ac focis, de fanis atque templis, de totius urbis tectis ac sedibus, de imperio ac libertate, de salute Italiae, de universa re publica decernite diligenter, ut instituistis, ac fortiter. habetis eum consulem qui et parere vestris decretis non dubitet et ea quae statueritis, quoad vivet, defendere et per se ipsum praestare possit.
>
> <div align="right">Cic., <i>Cat.</i> 4.23–4</div>

The broader scope of Cicero's depiction of society jumps out. The Republican orator's picture spans the physical city, its geographic context, the monuments of religious institutions, in addition to family. Furthermore, Cicero refers to the decision-making capacity of the Senate, to liberty and the dignity beyond safety of his son, a dignity corresponding to the perpetuation of his father's glory through memory. These markers of Republican values are absent in Velleius. For the Imperial historian, the people's concerns have shrunk. The only one to make the decision is Augustus, whose succession reproduces himself and therefore the state in the next generation. Lying in the emperor's grant, general prosperity is no longer a shared object of active care. With anxiety now under wraps, the political sphere, comprising social concerns, family, religion and active governance, has transformed in Velleius' representation into the social sphere of family and property. General prosperity has been depoliticized among a people concerned with public affairs only to the extent that it mirrors their private affairs. The emperor now represents the people in a semiotic rather than a political sense.[24] The projection of prosperity onto the Empire and the emperor's person as notional compensation for restrictions in political action is a recurrent topos. This is both the benefit and the price of *securitas*.

Velleius' summary of the fruits of Tiberius' reign sounds just like Augustus' gifts to society. The remarkable correspondences between them speaks to security's function as a continually operative discourse that captures an ongoing political process. Both emperors usher in periods of restoration, expressed in a list of disturbances suppressed and values recalled within the civic places and institutions of Rome as well as across all the cardinal points of Empire.

> Credit was called back to the Forum, sedition removed from the Forum, bribery from elections, discord from the senate house; justice, fairness, and diligence, previously buried and overlain with decay were brought back to the city; authority accrued to the magistrates, majesty to the senate, weight to the judicial system; sedition in the theatres was suppressed, the will to do the right thing shaken into the citizens or the necessity imposed; right things are honoured, crooked set aside; the humble man looks up to the powerful without fearing him, the powerful walks before the humble without looking down on him. When was the price of grain more moderate, when was peace more fruitful? The Augustan peace, spread throughout East and West and whatever territory lies bounded by North or South, preserves all corners of the lands of the globe immune from fear of brigandage. The *princeps*' generosity claims as its own not only citizens' losses due to fortune, but those of cities. Restored are the cities of Asia, the provinces compensated for the predations of magistrates; honour is at the hands of those most worthy; punishment comes late against the wicked, but comes even so; favour is overcome by fairness, bribery by virtue; for the *princeps* – the best –

teaches his citizens through action and although he is the greatest in his capacity to give orders, nevertheless is still greater as an example.

revocata in forum fides; summota e foro seditio, ambitio campo, discordia curia, sepultaeque ac situ obsitae iustitia, aequitas, industria civitati redditae; accessit magistratibus auctoritas, senatui maiestas, iudiciis gravitas; compressa theatralis seditio; recte faciendi omnibus aut incussa voluntas aut imposita necessitas; honorantur recta, prava puniuntur; suspicit potentem humilis non timet, antecedit non contemnit humiliorem potens, quando annona moderatior? quando pax laetior? diffusa in orientis occidentisque tractus et quicquid meridiano aut septentrione finitur pax augusta per omnes terrarum orbis angulos a latrociniorum metu servat immunes. fortuita non civium tantummodo sed urbium damna principis munificentia vindicat: restitutae urbes Asiae, vindicatae ab iniuriis magistratuum provinciae; honor dignis paratissimus, poena in malos sera sed aliqua. superatur aequitate gratia, ambitio virtute: nam facere recte cives suos princeps optimus faciendo docet, cumque sit imperio maximus, exemplo maior est.

Vell. Pat., 2.126

Velleius does not imply things have fallen apart in Augustus' latter years – that would discredit his leadership.[25] Rather, the erasure of anxiety is always in process but never fully achieved. Restoration is a constant project not of peace, but of pacification, not of static tranquillity, but of security as a dynamic repression of continually simmering cares. The Romans tried 'at the succession of each new emperor to make *this* the definitive version of the Augustan settlement, the final return of the Golden Age, a dream of stability that never loses its potency at each new plunge into the maelstrom of history' (Hardie 1993: 58). Velleius' representational procedure enacts *securitas* verbally. Brigandage, colonial exploitation, institutional decay, sedition never simply go away, but demand constant intervention. *Securitas* measures the distance between political ideals and life's rough-and-tumble.

3. The peaceable kingdom

Horace showcases the ideology in the most fulsome expression before Velleius, whose account shares many aspects of Augustan age representations.[26] Even more explicitly than in Velleius, Augustus' safety guarantees social order in an intimate entanglement of prosperity, the feelings of the citizens, and the emperor's body.

For the cow wanders the countryside in safety, / Ceres and fostering good fortune nurture / the countryside, sailors fly over the waters / in peace, faith fears blame. Chaste houses / are fouled by no adultery, custom and law / have conquered tainted evil, new mothers / receive praise for bearing children / resembling their fathers, penalty attends / faults. Who would fear the Parthian, / who the frozen Scyths, who the offspring / shaggy Germany brings to birth / while Caesar Augustus is unharmed (*incolumi Caesare*)? / Who would worry (*curet*) about war with savage Spain?

> tutus bos etenim rura perambulat,
> nutrit rura Ceres almaque Faustitas,
> pacatum uolitant per mare nauitae,
>   culpari metuit fides,
> nullis polluitur casta domus stupris,
> mos et lex maculosum edomuit nefas,
> laudantur simili prole puerperae,
>   culpam poena premit comes.
> quid Parthum paueat, quis gelidum Scythen,
> quis Germani quos horrida parturit
> fetus, incolumi Caesare, quis ferae
>   bellum curet Hiberiae? ...
>
> Hor., *Carm.* 4.5.17–28

Because Augustus is safe, not only is the state safe from external enemies, but society prospers internally over land and sea, by custom and law, through all symbolic realms: georgic plenitude provides enough to eat; the economy thrives negatively and externally without pirates, positively and internally since morality (*fides*) grounds business dealings; chastity ensures children are born who resemble their fathers; no military threats cause fear from at least three points on the globe. The list's climax makes care's release (*quis ... curet?*) depend on Augustus' safety (*incolumi Caesare*, 27–8).[27] National and societal security join in holistic plenitude. It is not a question of the practical consequences of any policies Augustus might have enacted, however much these may have helped. Rather, his being holds together the moral as well as the political order.

Velleius brings back Horace's fruitful agriculture as a mark of Augustan prosperity.[28] Horace's implied negation of anxiety in *quis ... curet?* ('who would care?', 27–8) becomes explicit in Velleius' abstract noun *securitas*. Under the Empire, the concept circulates under its own name. Both authors conjoin security as an expression of the soul political with a metaphor for the body politic. For Horace, the safety of Augustus' own body stands as synecdoche for the social whole.

Horace extends security broadly in other ways as well. The poem ends with an image of prosperity, of combined emotional and economic wellbeing. The people's celebration, sober and after a glass or two, transforms the symposium, the carefree locus of private relaxation, into a communal event (*Odes* 4.5.37–40). The local meets the universal: the Italian peninsula is home in contrast to the foreign, Imperial foes of lines 25–8; Sun and Ocean order time and space on a cosmic scale. The question – who would fear the enemy, who would care about war – negates the supposition that anyone would. Horace's representation of a multiplicity sharing the negation of care is a step toward *securitas imperii*.

Augustus' symbolic role becomes more explicit at the end of *Odes* 4. As *custos* ('guardian', 4.5.2) of the race, Horace's Augustus watches over the people, but his governance surpasses pragmatic care: his safety embodies their security.[29] As in the king's two bodies traced by Kantorowicz (1957) through medieval political theology, Augustus' physical body bears the symbolic weight of the body politic. Horace intimates, however, that it is not just a question of the emperor's body, but of his moral disposition. *Odes* 4.14 intertwines the SPQR's care for honours due to his virtue with his guardianship of the state.

> What care of the fathers or of the citizens may immortalise your virtues for all time with gifts full of honours, Augustus, through inscriptions and memorial records

> quae cura patrum quaeve Quiritium
> plenis honorum muneribus tuas
>   Auguste, virtutes in aevum
>   per titulus memoresque fastus / aeternet
>
> <div align="right">Hor., <i>Carm</i>. 4.14.1–5</div>

> O present bulwark of Italy and mistress Rome
>
> o tutela praesens / Italiae dominaeque Romae
>
> <div align="right">Hor., <i>Carm</i>. 4.14.43–4</div>

Military might, carried out in this poem by Drusus and Tiberius as members of the Imperial family, combines with virtue, a matter of Empire with a matter of the soul. When delegates do the work of safeguarding the state, Augustus' role becomes fully symbolic.

Odes 4.15 redeploys a familiar scene in Augustan poetry to declare a new age and a commutation in the kind of poetry needed.[30] Apollo stops Horace from singing of 'battles and conquered cities' (*proelia ... victas et urbis*, 1–2) not because of generic decorum, as in the standard *recusatio*, but because the Augustan age has restored the blessed life, symbolized through a dense set of tropes that have built up over Horace's poetic corpus: agricultural abundance, the positive imposition of peace, negated war, negated licence, and the restoration of the arts that extended Roman empire and majesty from Latium through Italy to the whole world. Horace identifies Augustus' oversight with the cessation of civil war, expressed in Vergilian terms as *furor*, a disturbance of the soul, in addition to the physical threat that is force (*vis*).

> Your age, Caesar, has brought back rich crops to the fields and restored to our Jupiter the standards snatched from the proud doorposts of the Parthians and closed the temple of Janus, empty of war, and thrown reins on the license that evades right order and removed transgressions and called back the old arts through which the Latin name and Italian strength grew, and fame and the majesty of empire were extended to the rising sun from its Hesperian bedchamber.

>   tua, Caesar, aetas
> fruges et agris rettulit uberes
> et signa nostro restituit Iovi
>   derepta Parthorum superbis
>   postibus et vacuum duellis
> Ianum Quirini clausit et ordinem
> rectum evaganti frena licentiae
>   iniecit emovitque culpas
>   et veteres revocavit artis,
> per quas Latinum nomen et Italae
> crevere vires famaque et imperi
>   porrecta maiestas ad ortus
>   solis ab Hesperio cubili.
>
> <div align="right">Hor., <i>Carm.</i> 4.15.4–16</div>

Latin will eventually call confidence in the grain supply *securitas annonae* (e.g. Tac., *Ann.* 15.18.6). That and discipline weave military successes and political expansion into the image of prosperity of the Augustan programme. Memory of civil war still rankles as a disturbance of the soul to be negated. Horace builds on the negation of licence and transgressions to pull out the full force of negative definition in his formulation of how Augustus has earned the appellation *custos*. Passion defines civil war, negation defines the internal peace as well as foreign relations.

> With Caesar as guardian of public affairs, civil fury or force will not drive out peace, nor anger, which forges swords and threatens miserable cities; those who

drink the deep Danube will not break Julian edicts, nor the Getae, nor the Chinese and faithless Persians, not those born near the Tanais river.

> custode rerum Caesare non furor
> civilis aut vis exiget otium,
>   non ira, quae procudit ensis
>   et miseras inimicat urbis;
> non qui profundum Danuvium bibunt
> edicta rumpent Iulia, non Getae,
>   non Seres infidique Persae,
>   non Tanain prope flumen orti.
>
> Hor., Carm. 4.15.17–24

Horace's choice to define the suppression of civil war in terms of the negation of passions is instrumental to the development of *securitas* as an Imperial concept.

4. The soul political

In later Imperial ideology, it is not just the emperor's body, but his soul that becomes the symbolic vehicle for the collective. Seneca forwards an analogy between the body's obedience to the spirit of the individual and the populace's to the spirit of the one man whose life or soul they surround.

> Just as the whole body serves the spirit, ... so this great multitude surrounding the life of one man is ruled by his spirit, is driven by his reason, and crushes and breaks itself on its own strength, were it not upheld by his counsel.
>
> quemadmodum totum corpus animo deservit ... sic haec immensa multitudo unius animae circumdata illius spiritu regitur, illius ratione flectitur pressura se ac fractura viribus suis, nisi consilio sustineretur.
>
> Sen., Clem. 1.3.5

The body politic in question lies quiet or runs around disturbed depending on the command of the emperor as its soul political. His soul determines whether or not the state remains tranquil.

Beyond the governance of reason, the temperament and character of the emperor also come to suffuse the body of the Empire as its metaphorical soul. Seneca advances a striking image in which the security of the Empire comes to be understood as depending on the quality of the emperor's soul. He imagines the emperor's spirit spreading through Empire and makes it the mental and psychic centre of the body politic.

> The gentleness of your spirit will be handed over and diffused little by little through the whole body of empire, and all things will be formed in your likeness. From the head comes good health. From there all things are enlivened and upright or dejected in lassitude just as their spirit thrives or withers.

> tradetur ista animi tui mansuetudo diffundeturque paulatim per omne imperii corpus, et cuncta in similitudinem tuam formabuntur. a capite bona valetudo: inde omnia vegeta sunt atque erecta aut languore demissa, prout animus eorum vivit aut marcet.
>
> <div align="right">Sen., <i>Clem.</i> 2.2.1</div>

The organic metaphor differentiates the emperor out from the body politic as its head and spirit, but the organism itself is one. The Republic is the body politic to his soul political: 'you are the spirit of the Republic, it your body' (*tu animus rei publicae tuae, illa corpus tuum*, 1.5.1; *anima*, at 1.3.5).

Any distinction between emperor and Empire melts away in Florus, however much he has to apologize for the metaphor.

> The chief power passed to Octavius Caesar Augustus, who by his wisdom and skill set in order the body of empire, which was all overturned and thrown into confusion and would certainly never have been able to attain coherence and harmony unless it were ruled by the nod of a single protector: its soul, as it were, and its mind.

> quod potissimum ad Octavium Caesarem Augustum summa rerum redit, qui sapientia sua atque sollertia perculsum undique ac perturbatum ordinavit imperii corpus, quod haud dubie numquam coire et consentire potuisset, nisi unius praesidis nutu quasi anima et mente regeretur.
>
> Flor., 2.14.5–6

A protector's restoration of harmony in a disturbed state sets the emperor as the singular soul political of the Empire's body politic. The semantic fields of safety and of security fully conjoin in this trope even though Florus names neither *salus* nor *securitas*. The analogy of the *hegemonikon* ruling the body justifies sole rule; the emperor's control of the passions of the body politic depends not just on his mind's reason, but his quality of soul. The emperor's tranquillity is a prerequisite for his capacity to exert sovereignty over the passions of the Empire's body.

The emperor's state of soul is determinative for that of his people, but this does not mean that his tranquillity equals theirs. Rather, many Imperial passages conceptualize the emperor as a care*taker*. Seneca conjoins the emperor's taking cares with his function as the soul political. As the one 'to whom all things are a care ... he does not fail to nourish any part of the republic as if it were part of himself' (*cui curae sunt universa ... nullam non rei publicae partem tamquam sui nutrit*, 1.13.4). Whereas in Horace, the citizens' anxious care about the state of society and national security abates when Caesar's body is safe, here they all meld together. The direction of care reverses. But perhaps 'caretaker' gets it wrong: the emperor simply cares for himself since nothing separates his soul from the state's body. Such *cura tamquam sui* takes Foucauldian self-care, the spiritual exercises meant to ensure blessed life in a tranquil soul, into the political realm (Foucault 1988).

Securitas becomes the term for the people's tranquillity. Pliny quotes an edict of Nerva: 'I put the security of all above my own peace' (*me securitatem omnium quieti meae praetulisse, Ep.* 10.58.7). Again, the emperor's emotional state sits in relation to the security of the political entity in question. Pliny justifies sole rule on this basis: '[The emperor] who alone has taken on the cares and labours of all for the common good' (*qui pro utilitate communi solus omnium curas laboresque suscepit, Ep.* 3.20.12). But the paradox that the erasure of his quiet erases the cares of all – he must suffer distress to bring security to the people – is symptomatic of tensions in the ideology.

The soul political does not obey a single figuration, but rather revolves around a set of paradoxical entailments that cannot be put together logically: the emperor's soul inhabits the body politic; his care-taking erases the people's cares; the security of the state depends on the emperor's soul. But if his worried care-taking provides security to the Empire, then the tranquillity of the body politic comes at the expense of his own. Therefore, he cannot inhabit the body politic as its tranquil soul at the same time as taking on anxiety-producing labours to relieve the body politic's cares. No Roman author produces the full expression of this ideology because it defies reason. The care *securitas* erases consistently speaks to the notional threat of civil war, that is, of an internal split in the political order. The latent metaphorics of the soul political and security consistently crops up to ward off this threat, but the metaphorical system itself turns on an internal divide. In a first move, the emperor's singularity provides the solution to that divide by representing a unitary organism. But the internal division of the paradoxical figure – the emperor is the soul political of the body politic; he feels cares so the Empire may be carefree – symptomatically reproduces the very division that sole rule promises to overcome in the political sphere. Security compels as the ideological solution to civil war because it metaphorically captures and reproduces the structure of the problem it means to solve.

Part Two

Crisis Traumas and Recovery: Greece

4

Tragedies of War in Duris and Phylarchus
Social Memory and Experiential History[1]

Lisa Irene Hau
University of Glasgow
Universität Heidelberg

Duris and Phylarchus are shadowy figures. They are two of the hundreds of historiographers who wrote long and influential works of history in the early Hellenistic period, but whose texts are now lost. Nonetheless, their names are frequently mentioned in discussions of Greek historiography and are known by many who have never glanced at the fragments preserved of their texts. This curious state of affairs is due to the fact that the names of Duris and Phylarchus are closely connected with the idea of 'tragic history', or the idea that history in the Hellenistic era came under the influence of an aesthetic borrowed from tragedy and became more concerned with high drama and sensationalism than with a truthful account of the past. In a different paper, I have examined instances of 'tragic history' in Diodorus Siculus and have argued that this Hellenistic approach to history writing had a serious purpose, namely that of making the readers engage with the past by making them feel as if they were seeing or experiencing it.[2] In this chapter, I want to focus on the four fragments of Duris and Phylarchus most often connected with 'tragic history', of which three are concerned with the suffering of civilians or prisoners of war abused by victorious soldiers. I want to examine these fragments with fresh eyes and speculate about whether Duris and Phylarchus may have had additional purposes in mind, as historians of the losing side, that is historians of defeat and victimization.

First a few words about the theory of 'tragic history'. This theory originated with Eduard Schwartz in the late nineteenth century and held sway for at least the first half of the twentieth.[3] It held, on the basis of criticism of Duris and Phylarchus voiced by Polybius, Plutarch and Photius – i.e. the 'fragments' which we shall examine below – that these historiographers and others with them (although there was disagreement about which others) had followed a Peripatetic theory of history writing, which had deliberately assimilated historiography to poetry and specifically to tragedy. Ironically, the motivation for this assimilation was supposed to have sprung from Aristotle's famous dictum in the *Poetics* that 'poetry is more philosophical and more serious than history; for poetry tends to tell universal truths while history gives particular facts' (Arist., *Poet.* 9.1451b). The Peripatetic historians were thus thought to have tried to make historiography 'more philosophical and serious' by making it more poetic, that is less factual and, in modern terms, less historical.

These days, most scholars agree that the evidence for a Peripatetic school of history writing is too thin to bear the weight of this theory.[4] Nonetheless, most still consider Duris and Phylarchus 'less serious' historians than their classical predecessors and their Hellenistic successor Polybius, and it is common to describe their works as 'dramatic', 'rhetorical', and 'sensationalist'.[5] Recently, a counter-trend has sprung up, which argues that Duris and Phylarchus have been misrepresented by their critics and were in fact as serious as any ancient historian.[6] The unfortunate truth is that the question of the exact shape and character of the works of these two authors is unanswerable due to the scarcity and nature of their fragments. What interests me in this chapter is the possibility that the criticism of Duris and Phylarchus in Polybius, Plutarch and Photius indicates a difference in historiographical approach dictated not only by theoretical concerns (which I have discussed elsewhere and shall return to briefly below),[7] but also by the difference between writing history from the point of view of the victors and from the point of view of the defeated, i.e. by Duris and Phylarchus experiencing a crisis where those we consider mainstream historians only saw normality.[8]

1. Duris of Samos

We shall begin with Duris since he is the older of our two subjects and has often been posited as the first 'tragic' historian.[9] Duris lived in the late fourth and early third century BCE, but his actual dates are uncertain; he was most likely born during the Samians' exile 365–322 BCE while the Athenians occupied the island. At some point, probably in the early third century, he was tyrant of Samos, as his father may have been before him.[10] He was a prolific writer and is known to have written treatises on, among other subjects, Homer, drama, style, painting and engraving in addition to three historical works: the *Makedonika*, the *Samian*

History, and the *Agathocles* (of Sicily). It is reasonable to assume that a historian of such wide-ranging literary and artistic interests had consciously formed an idea of his own approach to historiography, and we shall see that at least one of the fragments relates to the genre in a theoretical way.

The 96 so-called fragments of Duris' historiographical works are collected in the *FGrH*.[11] These 'fragments' are mostly mere references to passages in Duris' works, with a few summaries or paraphrases of short passages, and the odd quotation. They are supplemented by 12 'testimonia', i.e. statements found in various authors about Duris or his work, which do not summarize its contents. Some of these references are very positive. Cicero, for instance, called Duris *homo in historia diligens*, 'a careful historian' (Duris, *FGrH* 76 T6 = Cic., *Att.* 6.1.8).

The fragments that interest us here are primarily F66 and F67, both pertaining to Duris' account of the Samian Revolt against Athens in the 440s BCE. We shall start with the longer of the two, F67, which is found in Plutarch:

> In the ninth month, when the Samians had surrendered, Pericles destroyed the city walls, seized their ships, and imposed a large fine, some of which the Samians paid immediately, and the rest they arranged to carry forward to a stated time, giving hostages as security. *Duris of Samos magnifies these events in the tragic style, accusing the Athenians and Pericles of savagery,* (Δοῦρις δ' ὁ Σάμιος τούτοις ἐπιτραγωιδεῖ πολλὴν ὠμότητα τῶν Ἀθηναίων καὶ τοῦ Περικλέους κατηγορῶν) although Thucydides, Ephorus and Aristotle do not include it in their narratives. But he does not appear to be telling the truth (in his claim) that he (i.e. Pericles) brought the trierarchs and the marines into the agora at Miletus and, after binding them to wooden boards and mistreating them terribly for ten days, gave orders to execute them by crushing their heads with planks, and then to abandon their bodies without funeral rites. *At any rate,* (T8) *since Duris does not usually keep his narrative based upon the truth even when he is not personally emotionally involved, he* (F67) *seems instead to have exaggerated the misfortunes of his native land to slander the Athenians.* (Δοῦρις μὲν οὖν [T8] οὐδ' ὅπου μηδὲν αὐτῶι πρόσεστιν ἴδιον πάθος εἰωθὼς κρατεῖν τὴν διήγησιν ἐπὶ τῆς ἀληθείας, [F67] μᾶλλον ἔοικεν ἐνταῦθα δεινῶσαι τὰς τῆς πατρίδος συμφορὰς ἐπὶ διαβολῆι τῶν Ἀθηναίων.)
>
> Plut., *Per.* 28, 1–3 (translation modified from Pownall in *BNJ*)

Plutarch disbelieves Duris' account of sadistic treatment of the Samian generals and marines by the Athenians under the leadership of Pericles and claims that Duris has 'magnified the events in the tragic style' (ἐπιτραγωιδεῖ). We shall save this idea of Duris' 'tragedizing' for a little later and focus for the moment on Plutarch's accusation of falsehood. Plutarch's justification for his statement that

Duris is telling lies is that Thucydides, Ephorus and Aristotle say nothing about this atrocity in their parallel narratives. But should Duris' version be so quickly discarded? Thucydides composed a narrative of moral decline where such savage brutality only later became a feature of Athenian behaviour, and so may well have ignored early instances.[12] Both Ephorus and Aristotle (probably in his *Constitution of the Samians*) are likely to have produced accounts that were based on the Athenian official version of events.[13] Moreover, it is clear from the rest of the *Life of Pericles* that Plutarch admired this Athenian statesman greatly, which undoubtedly made him loath to believe him capable of cruelty.[14] So perhaps Duris is right, and the Athenians did torture the Samian generals and marines for ten days before executing them by bashing in their heads with clubs or planks.

Or perhaps his was an exaggerated version of real, but less extreme, Athenian violence, based on social memory cultivated in Samos over the years between the end of the Samian Revolt in 439 BCE and Duris' time of writing, 140 to 150 years later.[15] The fact that Duris was a Samian does not just mean that he is likely to have been biased in favour of his homeland and prejudiced against Athens, but also that he had access to a rich tradition of social memory on the island, much of which was likely to centre on its fluctuating relationship with Athens. In the early third century when Duris was writing, the relationship between Samos and Athens had recently again been characterized by Athenian brutality and Samian suffering when the Athenians laid siege to the island and upon their victory depopulated the city and instated an Athenian cleruchy there. This initiated a 43-year long exile for the surviving Samians (365–322 BCE).[16] These events may well have coloured the islanders' collective memory of the earlier revolt. (It is unlikely that Duris referred to any written evidence for his version of events as Plutarch would then hardly have ignored it in his discussion of Duris' trustworthiness.)

Collective or social memory, of course, is not an accurate record of past events, but only of how those events are remembered and kept alive by a community.[17] Whatever the truth of the matter, it seems likely that the Samians remembered Athenian atrocities in the 440s, with greater or lesser accuracy, and that Duris, the Samian historian, decided to record their version of events rather than the canonical Athenian version. He was writing the history of the victims, not the victors.

Something similar seems to be true of F66, preserved in Photius' *Lexicon* to explain the meaning of a line in Aristophanes' lost play *Babylonians*: 'The Samian people, how marked with many letters/signs it is' (Σαμίων ὁ δῆμος ἐστιν ὡς πολυγράμματος). Photius first adduces two different possible explanations: (a) at some point, the Samians gave citizenship to slaves (for a price) when their citizen numbers had been depleted (and presumably these slaves were tattooed with letters or signs),[18] or (b) the original Ionian alphabet came from Samos. Then he adds a third explanation offered by Duris:

> But some (say that the phrase arose) because the Athenians tattooed the Samians who were taken prisoner in war with an owl, but the Samians (lacuna in text) with a samaina – a ship with two banks of oars first constructed by Polycrates, the Samian tyrant, as states Lysimachus in the second book of his *Returns*. But this is a fiction of Duris. Others (claim that) the samaina is a coin.

> οἱδὲ ὅτι᾿ Ἀθηναῖοι μὲν τοὺς ληφθέντας ἐν πολέμωι Σαμίους ἔστιζον γλαυκί, Σάμιοι <δὲ **> τῆι σαμαίνηι (ἔστι πλοῖον δίκροτον ὑπὸ Πολυκράτους πρῶτον κατασκευασθὲν τοῦ Σαμίων τυράννου, ὡς Λυσίμαχος ἐν βʹ Νόστων)· τὸ δὲ πλάσμα Δούριδος οἱ δὲ τὴν σάμαιναν νόμισμα εἶναι.
>
> Duris, *FGrH* 76 F66 = Photius, *Lexicon* Σαμίων ὁ δῆμος
> (translation modified from Pownall in *BNJ*)

Like Plutarch in the previous instance, Photius disbelieves Duris' account of abuse of prisoners during the Samian Revolt. Even if we are equally sceptical of the historicity of the mutual tattooing (and perhaps there is no need to be),[19] however, the most natural explanation for Duris' propagation of the story is not necessarily that he is lying: Duris was writing from within a community that may well have believed it to be true. It may even be possible to combine his explanation with the first one offered by Photius (on the evidence of Aristotle's *Samian Constitution*): if the Samians did indeed once give (or sell) citizen status to tattooed slaves, and if the Athenians during the Revolt did abuse their Samian captives (which is not in itself unlikely), the two events may well have become conflated in Samian social memory so that people at Duris' time believed that the tattooed citizens, in fact former slaves, had been former Athenian prisoners. In any case, Duris seems once again to have been writing from a Samian communal perspective with the express purpose of alerting his readers to the brutality of the conflict between Athens and Samos, which had largely been glossed over by the Athenian historiographical tradition (with which Duris presumably expected his early third-century audience to be familiar).

A third fragment of Duris is relevant to the investigation of 'tragic history'; indeed it is the fragment that has been used to connect Duris with Peripatetic literary criticism:

> In the first book of his *Histories*, Duris of Samos says the following: 'Ephorus and Theopompus are very inferior to the events (of their narratives). For they

adopted neither any *mimesis* nor any *hedone* in their narrative, but applied themselves only to the act of writing itself.'

Δοῦρις μὲν οὖν ὁ Σάμιος ἐν τῆι πρώτηι τῶν αὐτοῦ Ἱστοριῶν οὕτω φησίν· «Ἔφορος δὲ καὶ Θεόπομπος τῶν γενομένων πλεῖστον ἀπελείφθησαν· οὔτε γὰρ μιμήσεως μετέλαβον οὐδεμιᾶς οὔτε ἡδονῆς ἐν τῶι φράσαι, αὐτοῦ δὲ τοῦ γράφειν μόνον ἐπεμελήθησαν.»

Duris, *FGrH* 76 F1 = Photius, *Bibliotheca* 176, 121 a 41
(translation modified from Pownall in *BNJ*)

On the basis of this fragment, modern scholars have been quick to criticize Duris for apparently committing to such frivolous and un-Thucydidean qualities of historiography as *mimesis*, often translated as 'imitation' or 'dramatization', and *hedone*, pleasure.[20] In defence of Duris, Gray has argued forcefully that *mimesis* was used in Greek historiographical theory to mean not 'imitation' or 'dramatization', but 'appropriate/realistic representation', in the sense of presenting characters as acting and speaking in a realistic way.[21] Gray's arguments have been accepted by many, but it is perhaps significant that they have been rejected by Halliwell in his authoritative investigation of *mimesis* across antiquity. Halliwell argues that *mimesis* in fourth-century literary theory always carried a connotation of a 'certain kind or quality of representation, one that exhibits the objects of representation with imaginative directness or immediacy' (Halliwell 2002: 291). Ultimately, without the preservation of a sustained narrative by Duris himself, it is impossible to determine what exactly he meant by this term. It is clear, however, that he is contrasting the pleasure a reader will get out of his work because its narrative is either realistic or lively – or perhaps both? – with the lack of pleasure to be had from the works of Ephorus and Theopompus. What type of pleasure the reader was expected to get from Duris' works is a question we shall return to towards the end of this chapter.

Before we leave F1 behind, however, it is important to stress, because it has often been misunderstood, that Duris does *not* say that a realistic or lively narrative, or any aspect of his style to which *mimesis* may relate, should be preferred at the cost of a historically truthful account.[22] Truth was such an ingrained ideal of ancient historiography since the days of Herodotus that such a statement would have been unthinkable;[23] indeed, as Baron (2016) rightly notes, Duris may well have made an explicit claim to be telling the truth elsewhere in his preface. This did not, of course, prevent him from trusting specious sources, from patriotic bias, or even from inventing circumstantial detail as historians before him had done since Herodotus, but did he stray from the path of truth more significantly than that?

With this question, we come back to the issue of what Plutarch may have meant when he criticized Duris for ἐπιτραγῳδεῖν, 'magnifying in the tragic style'. Van der Stockt (2005) has analysed every instance of Plutarch's use of words from the root τραγ- and concludes that the basic meaning of ἐπιτραγῳδεῖν is 'to add tragic stuff to' an account, and that it is often connected with telling lies, but is separate from this charge. Pelling (2016) has elaborated on this and investigated what Plutarch might mean by 'tragic stuff', concluding that it sometimes has to do with pomposity and showiness, but at other times with great suffering. He goes on to argue on the basis of the narratives of Plutarch's *Lives* that Plutarch thought that a dramatic and tragically inspired narrative could be justified, but that such effects should not be applied to events that had in reality been less serious. Pownall's translation, which I adopted above, 'to magnify in the tragic style' is apt, as it captures both the idea of 'adding tragic stuff' to the account and the sense that Duris was thereby making the account less truthful. It seems that Duris had a way of telling (parts of) his story which corresponded to Plutarch's idea of the tragic. Certainly some of his fragments (especially F10 and F14) deal with showiness and pomposity (of Demetrios of Phaleron and Demetrios Poliorcetes respectively); but in the case of the Samians tortured and executed after the failed Revolt, the connotation of great suffering seems more likely. In other words, Plutarch thought that Duris had exaggerated the suffering of the prisoners of war and the brutality of the Athenians, and that this exaggeration devalued his use of a grand and dramatic style in the passage. Duris himself, however, may well have believed that he was telling the truth (and may indeed have been right) and consciously applied *mimesis* – regardless of whether it meant a realistic or a vivid quality – to this uncovering of an ugly historical moment.

Another possibility, which does not exclude the one just mentioned, is that Plutarch is detecting tragic emplotment of the historical events by Duris.[24] Plutarch himself used such emplotment in certain lives (notably the *Life of Antony*), but only when he felt that the historical events themselves had contained a tragic quality.[25] He clearly did not think that the events of the Samian Revolt had this quality, but it would not be strange if Duris, a Samian living much closer, geographically and temporally, to the events of the Revolt, and experiencing events of a similar nature in his own lifetime, were of a different opinion. Duris may well have felt that the heroic, but futile struggle of Samos for independence and the ultimately grim fate (as he believed) of her generals and marines warranted emplotment of the events on a tragic pattern. Emplotment does not automatically entail untruthfulness, though. As H. White noted when he coined

·the term, it is possible to emplot the same historical events in many different ways – e.g. as a tragedy, comedy or heroic tale[26] – which can each be equally true.

2. Phylarchus (of Athens or Naucratis)

Phylarchus' dates are unknown, but he probably died around the time when Polybius was born (*c.* 200 BC).[27] We do not know anything for certain about his life, not even his city of origin.[28] He wrote a history of the years 272–220 BCE with a particular focus on (and bias in favour of) Cleomenes III of Sparta. Like the works of Duris, this work is now lost except for scattered references (86 in total) in later authors, which show that Phylarchus was widely read, and much criticized. One of Phylarchus' critics was Polybius, who spends ten chapters of his *prokataskeue,* his two-book prologue to his main theme, polemicizing against Phylarchus' account of part of the Cleomenic War. Ironically, Polybius' criticism is our best indication of the character of Phylarchus' work – and it is not a very good indication since its one purpose is to destroy Phylarchus' credibility and posit Polybius' version of events as the authoritative one.[29] The part of this criticism that above all has connected Phylarchus with the theory of 'tragic history' is the following passage (categorized in *FGrH* as a testimonium rather than a fragment):

> Because he is eager to arouse the pity of his readers and make them share the suffering of which he tells, he puts on stage women embracing, tearing their hair and beating their breasts and, furthermore, the crying and wailing of men and women, children and parents, intermingled, as they are being led away to slavery. He does this throughout his whole history, [8] always trying to place the frightful events before our eyes in every detail. [9] I shall leave aside the vulgar and womanish nature of his disposition, and focus only on what is fitting and useful in a work of history. [10] The writer of history should not shock his readers by telling outlandish stories, seek out plausible speeches, and enumerate the circumstances concomitant with the events, like the tragedians (καθάπερ οἱ τραγῳδιογράφοι), but should mention the whole truth of what was said and done, even if it happens to be quite commonplace. [11] For the purposes of historiography and tragedy are not the same, but opposite (τὸ γὰρ τέλος ἱστορίας καὶ τραγῳδίας οὐ ταὐτόν, ἀλλὰ τοὐναντίον). For in tragedy it is fitting by means of the most believable words to shock and seduce the audience in the here and now, but in historiography by means of true events and speeches to teach and persuade for all time those who are eager to learn. [12] This is the case since, in tragedy, the main thing is the believable, even if it is untrue, because it aims at the

deception of the spectators, but in historiography it is the truth because it aims at benefitting those eager to learn. [13] In addition to these things, he narrates for us most of the violent changes of circumstance without giving the cause or detailed manner of the events, without which it is impossible to feel sensible pity or appropriate anger at anything that happens.

Phylarch., *FGrH* 81 T3 = Polyb., 2.56.7–13

This part of Polybius' barrage of criticism pertains to Phylarchus' narrative of the sack of Mantinea by the Achaean League in 227 BCE. The passage has been much discussed by scholars interested in 'tragic history', and to rehearse all the arguments in detail is beyond the scope of this article. The following discussion touches on many of the points raised in earlier scholarship and also adds a few new ones of its own.

Polybius' criticism of Phylarchus proceeds on several fronts: character (of the author), style (of the work), content, truthfulness and purpose, all summed up in the accusation that Phylarchus confused historiography and tragedy and thereby ruined the former. It pays to unpick his criticism and examine its constituent parts; but first we must face the problem of Polybius' terminology. It has seemed to many scholars, beginning with Zegers (1959), that Polybius is deliberately using Aristotelian terms to say the opposite of Aristotle, i.e. that historiography is a more serious and truthful genre than tragedy, and then categorize Phylarchus' work as a hopeless confusion between historiography and tragedy, i.e. tragic history. This confused sub-genre, Zegers and later scholars argued, had been created by the Peripatetics in order to make historiography more acceptable in Aristotelian terms. More recently, Marincola (2010) has convincingly demonstrated that the similarities between Aristotle's and Polybius' terminology are superficial, and that Polybius is using terms of literary criticism current at his time, but not in an especially Aristotelian or Peripatetic sense.

Secondly, we might dispense with the accusation of Phylarchus' 'vulgar and womanish' disposition. This is literary criticism akin to that levelled at Homer by Timaeus (according to Polybius himself), that he was a glutton because he portrays his heroes as always feasting (Polyb., 12.24), or by Dionysius of Halicarnassus at Thucydides, that he was ignoble for choosing an ignoble theme for his work (Dion. Hal., *Pomp.* 3). On the basis of this logic, Phylarchus portrays the 'vulgar and womanish' behaviour of women while their homes are being burned, their husbands killed, and their children abducted into slavery, and so his disposition must be 'vulgar and womanish'. It is tempting to think that it also means that he tends to focus on the experiences of the non-elite and of women, but this may be pressing the interpretation of essentially specious criticism too far.

More serious is Polybius' accusation that Phylarchus is untruthful. This seems to be the real kernel of Polybius' criticism, even if it is clothed in expressions relating to style; and, indeed, an examination of Polybius' use of words related to tragedy throughout his work shows that, to a greater extent than Plutarch, he tends to employ them to criticize other historians for telling fictions.[30] However, it is important to note that the untruths of which Polybius accuses Phylarchus are not on the macro-level: Polybius does not deny that the Achaeans sacked the city, but apparently thinks that Phylarchus made up many or all of the details about the distraught behaviour of the victims. One might argue that although Phylarchus may not have recorded the actual cries, screams and wails of the Mantinean population, it is reasonable to expect that crying, screaming and wailing did take place, because this is what happens when a city is being burned and pillaged and its population slaughtered, raped and abducted. We shall return to this difference between actual screams and imagined screams below.

This leads us to Phylarchus' attempt at shocking the readers and making them pity the Mantineans. It is important to read this criticism (2.56.7 and 10) with Polybius' statement in paragraph 13: 'In addition to these things, he narrates for us most of the violent changes of circumstance without giving the cause (αἰτίαν) and manner (τρόπον) of the events, without which it is impossible to feel pity or anger appropriately at anything that happens (οὔτ' ἐλεεῖν εὐλόγως οὔτ' ὀργίζεσθαι καθηκόντως δυνατὸν)'. The allegation of not giving the cause (αἰτία) is easy enough to understand: Phylarchus did not give the causes for the sack of Mantinea (or, allegedly, any other horrific event), and without knowing the causes behind such an event, the reader cannot know who is deserving of pity. The criticism for not giving the 'manner' (τρόπον) of the events is harder to unpick, and translators have had trouble with it. Shuckburgh (1889) translates αἰτίαν καὶ τρόπον as 'the causes which gave rise to them, or the course of events which led up to them', but it is hard to see how *tropos* can mean 'course of events'. Paton (1922) translates 'their causes or the nature of these causes', which is possible, but a bit odd. Walbank (1957 ad loc.) suggests that *tropos* here means 'direction' in a metaphorical sense, i.e. purpose, and this is followed by Marincola (2003: 297) and Waterfield, rendering 'cause or purpose of events' (Waterfield 2010). However, this meaning would not be in accordance with Polybius' use of *tropos* in the rest of his *Histories*. The word is used 295 times in the preserved text, always to mean 'manner' or, more rarely, 'direction', but never 'purpose'. Only one other time is it combined with *aitia*, namely in 1.57.3 where Polybius states that he does not have the space to enumerate the 'causes and manners (τὰς μὲν γὰρ αἰτίας ἢ τοὺς τρόπους) through which' Hamilkar and his Roman opponent in Sicily fought each other with ambushes and stratagems for months on end. This parallel is revealing. Polybius is surely not claiming to be unable to tell the purpose of the ambushes and stratagems – which would be obvious enough – but rather their 'detailed manner', or even 'technical details'. In the passage quoted above, he claims that Phylarchus gave his readers all the graphic and emotional details of the sack of Mantinea, but neglected the – in Polybius' eyes – more useful and historiographically suitable information about causes and technical, military details.[31] In other words, it is not the arousing of pity or anger in itself to which Polybius objects. He objects to the invoking of these emotions without giving the background causes for the suffering, which prevents the reader from deciding if the sufferers deserved their fate,[32] and without giving the technical military details of the operation, which might be useful to (a certain, ideal type of) readers.

If Polybius is right in this criticism and Phylarchus did throughout his work focus on presenting frightful events, even atrocities (τὰ δεινά, 2.56.8), in a visual and vivid – and realistic – manner without exploring the causes that led to those atrocities, do we have to agree that this is a bad thing? Might we not in the twenty-first century agree that such a laying bare of human cruelty and suffering has its own worth, no less than a history that investigates causes, but does not (often) linger on the human cost of war?[33] At the time of Polybius, the idea that such a narrative can have theoretical merit seems to have been propounded by another now fragmentary historian, Agatharchides of Cnidus, whose work and ideas we shall return to below.

In his criticism of Phylarchus, Polybius goes on to explain the causes for the sack, allegedly left out by Phylarchus. He concludes that we should, in fact, not pity the Mantineans: they had betrayed and massacred their Achaean garrison – a garrison for which they themselves had asked – and for this treachery they deserved their fate (Polyb., 2.57–58). This argument says more about Polybius than it does about Phylarchus. Polybius' narrator persona is a no-nonsense man of the world who has no pity for fools and who thinks that those who have committed crimes such as treachery deserve whatever they have got coming (see the continuation of this passage, 2.59, where he argues that the tyrant Aristomachus deserved to be tortured to death). Elsewhere I have investigated his use of the adjective ὠμός, usually translated as 'cruel', and have found that it is rare (27 instances across all of Polybius' preserved text) and mainly used when Polybius is criticizing other historians for using the term. Polybius himself very rarely sees any action as cruel, because he can usually explain the reasons for it (Hau 2016a: 68–71). Most twenty-first-century readers are unlikely to be so hard-nosed. For readers with post-Geneva Convention sensibilities, the sacking of a city is an atrocity regardless of that city's political allegiance. Whether or not Polybius' version of the events leading up to the sack of Mantinea is true,[34] present-day readers are likely to believe that it was wrong for the Achaeans and their Macedonian allies to respond by slaughtering men, enslaving women and children, and burning homes, that is by punishing the civilian population.

It is worth noting that Polybius can describe the suffering of civilians vividly and with pathos when he wants to – his account of Philip V's taking of Abydus and the mass suicide of the population is particularly harrowing (Polyb., 16.30–34) – but in the case of Mantinea, his sympathies are thoroughly on the side of the aggressors. The reasons for this are to be found in his own life and ideology.[35] Polybius had grown up in the leading circles of the Achaean League, in which he and his father had both held high-ranking positions in the years after the conclusion of the alliance with Macedon, before he was sent to Rome to await a trial that never happened.[36] Even his staunchest admirers (among whom I count myself) do not deny that his *Histories* is biased in favour of the Achaeans (e.g. Eckstein 2013). For our current purposes it matters little whether he was consciously whitewashing the actions of the League (so e.g. Schepens 2005) or merely reproducing the version of events with which he had grown up and/or which he had found in the memoirs of Aratus, the general in command of the Achaeans during the taking of Mantinea, which he admits to using as his main source for the events at 2.56.1. Phylarchus, on the other hand, was an admirer of Cleomenes (so Plut., *Arat.* 38.8), the Spartan king whose political programme of land-reform, debt-cancellation and conquest alarmed Aratus enough to ally the Achaean League with their previous enemy, Macedon, in order to stop him. Phylarchus may even have taken part in Cleomenes' campaigns personally (Africa 1960). For him it was important to tell the story of the victims of the Achaeans and Macedonians and to enlist the reader's sympathy for them.

Polybius' criticism implies that Phylarchus' history was, throughout, a very different reading experience from his own (see his repeated insistence in the quoted passage: 'throughout his whole history' [παρ'ὅλην τὴν ἱστορίαν] 2.56.7, 'always' [ἀεὶ] 2.56.8). It is impossible now to know if this was true or if they simply differed in which historical episodes they believed deserving of vivid and emotional treatment.[37] But if the two historiographers did disagree over how much attention to pay to violence and suffering, this difference in attitude to what history is or should be is closely connected with Polybius' criticism that Phylarchus 'enumerates the circumstances concomitant with events' (τὰ παρεπόμενα τοῖς ὑποκειμένοις ἐξαριθμεῖσθαι). As Schepens (2005: 163) acutely remarks: 'What may be termed "concomitant circumstances" from the point of view of the political and military strategists and decision-makers, may constitute the very essence of history for a historian who looks upon the facts from the perspective of the citizens who suffer as victims.'

The most notorious part of Polybius' criticism of Phylarchus is his comparison with 'the tragedians'. The main thrust of this comparison is clearly the accusation of fictionalizing historical events; since tragedy and historiography were both thought to deal with historical past events, it was vitally important for a historian to distinguish his own genre as the one characterized by truthfulness (Ruffell and Hau 2016). Another charge implied by the comparison is one of exaggeration, both of pomposity and of suffering as we saw in Plutarch. But a third charge implied by the term seems to be one of emplotment, namely that Phylarchus emplotted the events of Mantinea (which, according to Polybius, did not deserve it) as a grand tragedy, the same way Polybius himself had done with the events of Abydus. Essentially, both historians could employ this technique, but they disagreed over which episodes deserved such treatment, a conclusion which leads naturally to the question of Phylarchus', and Duris', purpose with their 'tragedizing'.

3. Purposes and motivations

I would hypothesize that Duris and Phylarchus were committed to 'telling it as it was', or at least how they believed it to have been on the basis of their sources, including social memory in the case of Duris and eyewitnesses likely to be emotionally and politically biased in the case of Phylarchus. They wanted to show people what had really happened, by offering an alternative version of past events to the canonical version written by the victors and their sympathizers.[38] Duris most likely wrote his history of the Samian Revolt as a counterweight to the Athenian version. That Phylarchus wrote his narrative as a counter-history to the Achaean version of Aratus is implied by both Polybius (2.56.1) and Plutarch (*Arat.* 38). They seem to have wanted to give the defeated a voice, but in a very specific way – a way which involved vivid and/or realistic descriptions of brutality and suffering, with plenty of circumstantial details (or 'circumstances concomitant with events', Polyb., 2.56.10), perhaps not all corroborated by sources. It is natural to ask why they chose this method, and not one closer to the methodical search for causes that we know from Polybius.

The explanation seems to have been connected with a desire to involve the reader emotionally in the narrative. Polybius (2.56.7 and 13) implies that a reader is supposed to feel pity and anger at Phylarchus' description of the sack of Mantinea. It is fair to imagine that these are the same emotions Duris was hoping to invoke in his narratives of the torture of Samian prisoners by the Athenians. But was the purpose of such emotional involvement really primarily pleasure as most scholarship on 'tragic history' would have us believe? It is hard to imagine that one could feel serious pity and anger at the same time as feeling what is commonly meant by pleasure, but it might be possible to find a clue to how this is possible in Aristotle. In his *Poetics* 1448b, he posits *mimesis*, by which he seems here to mean artistic representation, as an instinctive and quintessential human activity and states that 'mimetic objects' (τοῖς μιμήμασι) give everyone pleasure if they are well executed, even when they represent ugly topics. He goes on to explain that this is because we learn through *mimesis*:

> The explanation of this too is that understanding gives great pleasure not only to philosophers but likewise to others too . . . . This is why people enjoy looking at images, because through contemplating them it comes about that they understand and infer what each element means.
>
> Αἴτιον δὲ καὶ τούτου, ὅτι μανθάνειν οὐ μόνον τοῖς φιλοσόφοις ἥδιστον ἀλλὰ καὶ τοῖς ἄλλοις ὁμοίως . . . . διὰ γὰρ τοῦτο χαίρουσι τὰς εἰκόνας ὁρῶντες, ὅτι συμβαίνει θεωροῦντας μανθάνειν καὶ συλλογίζεσθαι τί ἕκαστον, οἷον ὅτι οὗτος ἐκεῖνος.
>
> Arist., *Poet.* 1448b 10–17, translation by S. Halliwell for Loeb

In other words, good *mimesis* even of unpleasant things leads to pleasure, but it leads to pleasure through understanding or learning, i.e. because it is didactic. It is worth considering whether this might not also have been part of what Duris meant by the *mimesis* in which he claimed to surpass Ephorus and Theopompus.

Intriguingly, the connection between a vivid narrative, the reader's emotion and didacticism is made explicit in a fragment of yet another lost work of history, by Agatharchides of Cnidus, who was contemporary with Polybius, but based in the library of Alexandria.[39] Agatharchides wrote a historical work *On Europe* and another *On Asia*, but most of what survives of his works comes from *On the Red Sea*, which was either a third work or part of *On Asia* which was later extracted. Like the works of Duris and Phylarchus, the works of Agatharchides are lost. But one of the surviving fragments is extraordinarily long and exists in two parallel versions in two different cover texts,[40] which are sufficiently similar for us to be able to imagine – more or less – what the original passage must have been like. The two cover texts are codex 250 of Photius' *Bibliotheke* and book 3, chapters 2–55 of Diodorus Siculus' *Bibliotheke Historike*. The Photius passage is 55 Budé pages long; the Diodorus version overlaps with the last 38 of them. (A less close paraphrase of this latter passage is in Strabo 16.4.5–20.) This long Agatharchides passage contains several vivid and emotionally involving descriptions of suffering and atrocities,[41] and he has often been included in the ranks of the 'tragic historians'.[42]

The explicit connection between vividness in description, emotionality and didacticism comes in F21, a long passage preserved only by Photius, and presented as a quoted extract from book 5 of *On the Red Sea*. The passage is introduced by the statement that 'many, he (Agatharchides) says, both of politically involved men and of those who write poetry, have been at a loss about how the extreme misfortunes of some people should be told in an appropriate manner by someone who is himself outside of danger'.[43] Then follow Agatharchides' thoughts on the matter. These include criticism of an orator for not sparing a thought for 'how to bring the suffering under the sight (of the reader) by means of vivid description' (πῶς τὸ πάθος ὑπὸ τὴν ὄψιν ἀγάγοι διὰ τῆς ἐναργείας, Agatharchides, F21 = Phot., cod. 250 446a), in which we recognize the expression 'to bring suffering under the sight/eyes (of the reader)' from Polybius' critique of Phylarchus. A little further on, Agatharchides praises Demosthenes for a fitting description of a sacked city (which city is unknown as the quotation does not match any preserved speech of Demosthenes), adding that 'for frightful events described with compassion usually arouse more harrowing pity' (τὸ δεινὸν γὰρ εὐνοίᾳ παρατεθὲν ἐμβριθεστέρους εἴωθε τοὺς οἴκτους ποιεῖν, Agatharchides, F21 = Phot., cod. 250 447a). τὸ δεινὸν recalls the τὰ δεινά which Polybius accused Phylarchus of always 'placing in front of our eyes'. Agatharchides seems to be calling for a description of such events which combines vividness with compassion (εὐνοίᾳ) for the specific purpose of invoking the reader's intense, even harrowing (ἐμβριθεστέρους), pity. In the same breath Agatharchides adds: 'Although he (Demosthenes) sharply, clearly, and concisely stripped each image of exaggeration, he did not forget the vividness that teaches the essence of the event' (τῆς διδασκούσης τὸ πρᾶγμα ἐναργείας, Agatharchides, F21 = Phot., cod. 250 447a). In this statement, Agatharchides explicitly connects vividness, ἐνάργεια, with didacticism, and on the basis of what he was saying a moment earlier, it is fair to assume that this vividness is supposed to involve the reader emotionally in the narrative, so that the didacticism works on an emotional level as well as, or instead of, an intellectual one.[44]

Employing a vivid description of atrocities in order to make the reader feel harrowing pity for the victims and anger against the perpetrators so that they learn something – this seems to me to be what Agatharchides is recommending and very possibly what Duris and Phylarchus (and Agatharchides himself) were attempting to do in practice. In aiming for greater vividness and greater realism, they may well have added circumstantial details to their narratives. A recent movement in contemporary history writing, experientialism, calls for greater vividness in narratives of the past, and its practitioners experiment with adding sounds, smells, and other circumstantial details to their accounts in order to make the reader feel like they experience the past.[45] There are affinities here with what the 'tragic' historians were doing. When they added emotional details like women crying and screaming as they see their children led off into slavery, they were recreating not the actual scene of a specific city being sacked, but a representative scene of any city being sacked. The details of screams and crying were the kind of things that happened *every time* a city was taken, even if they did not have reliable sources for them happening at this particular point in time, and narrating them in graphic detail made the readers feel like they were experiencing the catastrophe rather than just reading about it. And this emotional experience was supposed to be didactic.

But what was it supposed to teach? This question can be answered on two levels. On a practical level, such narratives were presumably supposed to teach solidarity with the victims of atrocities. This is a prominent topic in Diodorus Siculus, who also has numerous graphic descriptions of violence, and who often stresses what he calls 'the common weakness of mankind', which should make human beings look out for each other.[46] It is also likely that these passages were meant to teach the reader not to commit such crimes if he ever got the chance – it is worth remembering that Duris, Phylarchus and Agatharchides were writing in a world where sackings of cities and enslavement of populations were very much still happening, and their readers may have been expected to be not just potential victims, but also potential perpetrators.

On a less directly practical level, tragedy is also often considered a didactic genre.[47] For Duris and Phylarchus, as champions of the alternative history, the version sanctioned by the social memory of the victimized community rather than by the victors, one might say that writing a vivid and emotional account of the past was a response to crisis. It is perhaps not too far-fetched to think that writing – and reading – a vivid and emotionally absorbing narrative about past suffering may have been a way of working through the communal trauma, or reaching communal catharsis.[48] And the method through which this was achieved, or attempted, was by 'tragedizing' traumatic events, i.e. by emplotting the experiences of the defeated as a tragedy and narrating them in a grand and vivid style while keeping their essence: the screams, the suffering and the violence.

5

Changes of Fortune
Polybius and the Transformation of Greece

Andrew Erskine
University of Edinburgh

In the introduction to his *Histories* the Achaean politician and historian Polybius stresses how history is about change: the study of the disasters of others helps us cope with the changes that we have to face in the present. But Polybius' subject is not merely change but change that was totally unexpected, for he had witnessed the overthrow of the established order in the eastern Mediterranean during the course of the second century BCE. The great Hellenistic kingdoms that had been the dominant powers for so long were now replaced by the Italian city of Rome and the cities of the Greek world had to adjust to a new political landscape. This transformation was observed, described and analysed by Polybius in forty books, only the first five of which survive intact.[1] His *Histories* are both an account of Rome's rise to world power and his own personal response to these events, which had a major impact on his city and on himself.

Rome first crossed the Adriatic with an army in 229 BCE to make war on the Illyrians. In the century that followed, its dealings with mainland Greece were an often confusing mix of diplomatic interventions, apparent disinterest and outbursts of violence, notably the Second and Third Macedonian Wars of 200–196 and 171–168 BCE respectively. The changes that resulted were significant but the process was too drawn-out to constitute a crisis in itself; rather it generated a series of interconnected crises, separated by place and time, some local, others involving a large number of Greek states. 'Crisis', however, is a term that is necessarily (and usefully) imprecise; in everyday discourse it is so pervasive that it defies any theoretical claim upon it. If there is a fundamental feature, it is that a crisis involves a profound challenge to the status quo. It can be both something experienced and something historiographically constructed, as will be evident from a reading of Polybius' history.[2] Writing his history enabled Polybius to reflect on the extraordinary events that had happened but also as a historian to shape the memory of them.

From our perspective Roman expansion continued into the first century BCE and beyond, but Polybius believed that the year 168 was the point at which Rome realized its goal of world rule (3.4.1–3). This was the year that saw both the end of the Macedonian kingdom and the beginning of his own detention in Rome, something that put a stop to what should have been a great political career.[3] It was, therefore, in the aftermath of decades of war and disruption that Polybius settled down to write his history. Things would in fact get worse for his native Achaea but he was not (yet) to know that. His history is particularly appropriate for this volume, because it shows us how a leading figure, who lived through a time of crisis, sought to come to terms with what had happened. In exploring the Greeks' developing relationship with Rome he was also exploring his own. As he constructs the history of their subjection to Rome he not only picks out key points in the process of transformation, but he also gives an insight into the changing mood. In doing so he offers something more personal than a straight narrative of events. Faced with Rome, these Greeks are at various times apprehensive, hostile, suspicious and optimistic until finally they recognize that Rome requires obedience. But also, and significantly, Polybius repeatedly wonders about what might have been.[4] Could it have been otherwise? Was there another course of action that would have prevented this Roman takeover? His thinking here is ambivalent, but shows that, even though he is writing after the events, he is, on one level at least, still very much involved in them.

1. Introducing change

Change is a fundamental theme in Polybius' history, addressed in the opening sentences of the first chapter:

> If those who wrote on human affairs before me had omitted the praise of history itself, then perhaps it would have been necessary for me to encourage everyone to take up and look positively on works of this kind, on the grounds that there is no better corrective for men than knowledge of what was done in the past. But not a few historians and not in a limited way, but all of them, from beginning to end, so to speak, have made use of this (ἀλλὰ πάντες ὡς ἔπος εἰπεῖν ἀρχῇ καὶ τέλει κέχρηνται τούτῳ).[5] For they declare not only that the truest education and training for a political career is the study of history, but also that the most vivid, in fact the only, teacher of the ability to endure nobly the changes of fortune is

the recollection of the reversals of others. It is clear that no one, least of all myself, would think it appropriate to say again things already well said by many. For the very unexpectedness of the events (τὸ παράδοξον τῶν πράξεων) about which I have chosen to write is sufficient to challenge and prompt everyone young and old to study my work.

Polyb., 1.1.1–4⁶

Polybius may attribute these ideas to his predecessors but by beginning with them he is emphasizing their relevance to his own work.⁷ The educational importance of history had already been noted by Thucydides in the fifth century BCE, but significantly Polybius is the earliest surviving historian to draw attention to its value for coping with change.⁸ There are earlier extant expressions of the sentiment that knowledge of the disasters of others can help men bear their own misfortune but for those we have to look to discussions of the value of literature generally, in particular tragedy.⁹

Yet the rest of the introduction takes its cue from the last sentence in the passage quoted above: the extraordinary and unexpected success of the Romans. Although this was a history in Greek for a primarily Greek audience, the Greek angle is surprisingly absent here.¹⁰ There is no sense that all this meant change, often quite jarring change, for the Greek world. This is not history as crisis but history as success, a teleological history that will culminate in Rome's universal rule.¹¹ It is focused on Rome and how Rome confounds expectations by coming to dominate the known world; there is not even a throwaway remark that this meant change also for Greeks. Polybius was certainly not unaware of this, but he chose not to prioritize it at the beginning of his history. His purpose here is to highlight the exceptional character of his subject: Rome had acquired an empire on a scale never before achieved, something that had taken it less than fifty-three years (1.1.5). But it would be wrong at this point to look for comment on what this meant for the Greeks. That would detract from the universal character of the Roman achievement, which brought all the peoples of the Mediterranean under Roman rule. In the second preface to his history, which occurs at the start of the third book, he does reflect on these subjects of Rome, but again not directly on the Greeks. Here he explains his decision to extend his history beyond his original terminus, the fall of the kingdom of Macedon in 168. At this point teleology itself comes to an end and what follows is presented as an examination of the character of empire, taking into account the views of both ruler and subject.

But although it is Roman success that gives his history its narrative structure, the Greek experience is not ignored and it forms a kind of sub-structure within the history, as the reader engages with a series of episodes that in turn represent the changing status of the Greeks themselves in relation to Rome. Alongside the narrative of Roman success there is therefore an equally compelling narrative of Greek failure. These episodes, which will be discussed below, are at once turning-points and moments of strong emotion, a combination which might allow us to characterize them as crises. In doing this, however, it is important to recognize that it is Polybius who is presenting them in this way as part of his attempt to explain Rome's acquisition of universal power.

In his opening paragraph Polybius drew attention to the role of history in coping with the changes of fortune. *Tyche*, variously translated as fortune, fate or chance, is a constant presence in his history, one that has generated an enormous amount of inconclusive modern scholarship. Scholars puzzle over how such a pragmatic historian could pay so much attention to fortune.[12] To some extent this question misinterprets what Polybius is doing in so far as it gives too great a causal role to fortune. Rather, the emphasis on fortune is a consequence of his interest in change. It often reflects the perspective of the protagonists of the history and allows the readers to experience vicariously the uncertainty of the past.[13] These were not things that they expected to happen (and often not things they could have predicted). But just because something is unexpected does not mean it cannot be explained. Unexpected changes pose challenges for people and for Polybius the study of history is one way of coping with those challenges.[14]

2. Crisis and emotion

But change and crisis are not the same. Changes happen all the time without being held to constitute a crisis. Furthermore change or potential change can be experienced as a crisis by one group and not by another. What makes a situation a crisis, I would suggest, is not only the threat that it poses to the status quo but also the sense that it is in some way out of one's control. This idea is implicit in Polybius' phrase 'the changes of fortune', that is to say changes that are attributed, by some at least, to fortune and therefore out of their control and often unexpected. The initiators of change, on the other hand, are more likely to see themselves and be seen by others as in control and therefore less likely to experience the events as a crisis. There are, however, two levels to the construction of a crisis, first the contemporary experience and secondly the subsequent reflection on those events, as carried out by a historian such as Polybius, whose interpretation will be shaped by hindsight.[15] While both the participant and the historian may interpret the events as a crisis, for the participant it is on-going whereas the historian will have identified a beginning and an end. A crisis, therefore, becomes part of the narrative the historian is presenting.[16]

Polybius, although he might not have addressed the Greek response to the changes brought about by Rome in his introductory comments, did approach this theme in other ways. He clearly identifies certain key moments in the development of Roman power in the East and in each case presents the Greek reaction, a reaction that is as much emotional as it is rational. These can be interpreted as a series of connected crises, situations where a perceived loss of control led to an emotional response. The representation and structuring of these moments are the work of Polybius and, while it may well be that they were experienced as crises at the time, our understanding is guided by the historian, who has himself seen the effects of Roman power. The crisis-character of these moments reflects his interpretation, as he explores change that is unwanted and which challenges the status quo.[17]

But Polybius is sensitive to crises generally and the depiction of them helps give momentum to his narrative. The focus of this chapter is on the Greeks but it is useful to review first his treatment of a major Roman crisis, both as an example of the phenomenon and as an illuminating contrast with the Greek experience. In the early part of the Second Punic War the Romans suffered three devastating defeats at the hands of Hannibal in three successive years, culminating in Cannae in 216 BCE. Polybius could have treated this as straight military history, but shortly before his account of the battle of Cannae he breaks away from his military narrative to convey the situation in Rome. The paragraph that follows transforms the account, not merely because it gives us the Roman non-combatant perspective but also because it introduces a powerful emotional component:

> After the news had reached Rome that the armies were encamped near one another and that clashes between the forward troops of each were happening every day, the city was tense and extremely anxious. Most people dreaded the outcome of the battle on account of having been defeated on many occasions already and now foresaw and imagined what would happen if they were to be totally defeated. Every oracle they possessed was on everybody's lips, every temple was full of omens and portents, as was every house, as a result of which prayers, sacrifices, supplications and entreaties filled the city. For when there is a crisis the Romans go to great lengths to propitiate both gods and men and in such circumstances there is no ritual that they consider unbecoming or beneath their dignity (δεινοὶ γὰρ ἐν ταῖς περιστάσεσι Ῥωμαῖοι καὶ θεοὺς ἐξιλάσασθαι καὶ ἀνθρώπους καὶ μηδὲν ἀπρεπὲς μηδ' ἀγεννὲς ἐν τοῖς τοιούτοις καιροῖς ἡγεῖσθαι τῶν περὶ ταῦτα συντελουμένων).
>
> Polyb., 3.112.6–9

Here Polybius presents a city gripped by fear and anxiety as it waits helplessly for the outcome; the inhabitants of Rome attempt to mitigate that feeling of helplessness by excessive measures aimed at winning over the gods.[18] Defeat brings the Romans to their lowest point; they have lost much of Italy and now fear that Hannibal might seize Rome itself. But Polybius follows Roman anxiety and panic with Roman recovery. In narrative terms the greater the crisis is shown to be, the more impressive the recovery. Here by showing the Roman reaction to the events at Cannae, both before and after the battle, Polybius is shaping it as a crisis, but it is one that the Romans overcome and the beginnings of that recovery are there soon after the news of the defeat has reached Rome. In spite of the fear and uncertainty of the people the Senate plan for the future and deliberate as becomes men (*andrōdōs*). Rome's *politeia* and general good sense give it the resilience to take back control, a point made by Polybius in the immediate aftermath of the battle in book three (3.118.6–9). He repeats this observation at the beginning of book six, when he comes to discuss the strengths of the Roman *politeia*, a term which is often translated rather narrowly as 'constitution' but should be understood as embracing the whole character of the Roman state.[19]

In highlighting the emotional responses of his protagonists Polybius is adopting a practice common in ancient historiography. Plutarch, for instance, praises Thucydides for the vividness (*enargeia*) that he creates in his depiction of emotions, something that he believes is the mark of a good historian. The aim, however, is not merely to make the reader know what it was like to have been there but rather to go further than that and enable them to feel the same emotions as those who were there.[20] The reader thus has the experience of being there without actually being there.[21] This experience at a distance is one of the ways a reader can learn from history, but learning from history also means knowing where it leads. As Polybius says, there are two routes to self-improvement, one involves personal suffering, the other, which is much less painful, involves observing the suffering of others.[22]

3. Turning-points

Greeks, however, do not show the same resilience as the Romans when things go wrong. In so far as we are to see Polybius looking back at times of crisis for the Greeks, it is at events characterized by lack of control and a certain emotional component. His history offers a series of turning-points from which the Greeks emerge not stronger but weaker until they are entirely subservient to Rome.

Polybius can be seen to highlight at least three key moments in the process of transformation as he reflects on the Greeks' changing relationship with Rome: the Aetolian alliance with Rome in 212/211 BCE and the apprehension that it generates, the Isthmian Games of 196 BCE, where Greek anxiety turns to joy on hearing Flamininus' proclamation, and Rome's victory over Macedon at Pydna in 168 BCE that marks the point when the whole world is subject to Rome. This section of the chapter will consider each of these in turn.

a) The Aetolian alliance with Rome

Despite the fragmentary nature of the narrative it is clear that Polybius placed considerable emphasis on the alliance between Rome and Aetolia.[23] It was this treaty, directed against Philip V of Macedon, that enabled and legitimated Roman military activity in mainland Greece. At the time Rome was already in conflict with Philip as a result of the treaty he had made with Hannibal after the latter's victory at Cannae. This war, the so-called First Macedonian War (214–205 BCE), was never a priority for the Romans, who were preoccupied with fighting Carthage, but the involvement of the Aetolians and their allies made it more significant than it would otherwise have been.

In a series of three speeches, spread over some ten years, Polybius evokes the changing responses to Rome before and after the establishment of the Aetolian alliance.[24] The first is delivered at a peace conference held at Naupactus in 217 BCE with a view to negotiating an end to the Social War, which had seen the Aetolians in conflict with Philip and the Achaeans. The speaker, Agelaus of Naupactus, advocating peace, warns his audience about 'the clouds now appearing in the West' (τὰ προφαινόμενα νῦν ἀπὸ τῆς ἑσπέρας νέφη) that if ignored could deprive the Greeks of the freedom to conduct their own affairs (5.104.10–11). The winner of the struggle between Rome and Carthage, he suggests, would look East, so Philip and the Greeks need to be prepared. But, as long as they stop fighting among themselves, they will be able to deal with any offensive. Indeed when the time is right Philip himself might challenge for worldwide rule. This confidence is no longer there in the second speech, which is set in 210 BCE and is an unsuccessful attempt to stop the Spartans joining with the Aetolians and Romans. On this occasion the speaker is an Acarnanian ambassador named Lyciscus. He emphasizes the danger posed to the whole of Greece by these barbarians who threaten enslavement, draws attention to their ill-treatment of captured populations, and in an echo of the first speech says that 'such a great cloud from the West ... will be the cause of great evils for all the

Greeks' (τηλικοῦτο νέφος ἀπὸ τῆς ἑσπέρας ... πᾶσιν ἔσται τοῖς Ἕλλησι μεγάλων κακῶν αἴτιον).²⁵ The third speech dates from 207 BCE, and is an attempt to bring the war to an end and persuade the Aetolians to come to an agreement. The Aetolians are represented as having set in motion a situation over which they are losing control. The Romans, having been introduced by the Aetolians, are behaving as barbarians do:

> You yourselves [the Aetolians] when you gain possession of a city would not dare to violate the free men or burn the city, because you consider such conduct to be cruel and barbarous. Yet you have made a treaty by which you have given up all the rest of the Greeks to the barbarians to be subjected to the most shameful outrages and lawlessness.
>
> καὶ κυριεύσαντες μὲν αὐτοὶ πόλεως οὔτ' ἂν ὑβρίζειν ὑπομείναιτε τοὺς ἐλευθέρους οὔτ' ἐμπιπράναι τὰς πόλεις, νομίζοντες ὠμὸν εἶναι τὸ τοιοῦτο καὶ βαρβαρικόν· συνθήκας δὲ πεποίησθε τοιαύτας, δι' ὧν ἅπαντας τοὺς ἄλλους Ἕλληνας ἐκδότους δεδώκατε τοῖς βαρβάροις εἰς τὰς αἰσχίστας ὕβρεις καὶ παρανομίας.
>
> Polyb., 11.5.6–7²⁶

The Romans are now in Greece and doing visible damage. As evidence of what the Greeks are suffering the speaker cites the fate of the 'wretched Aeginetans', whose city had been captured by the Romans earlier in the war.²⁷

The escalating loss of control is evident in the verbal overlaps between the speeches. The first speech introduces the clouds from the West, something still undefined which the Greeks can handle with the right strategy, but by the second speech the cloud is becoming more real; it is Rome and it will be the cause (*aition*) of great evils for all the Greeks. By the third speech the fire started by the Aetolians needs to be put out. Now there is no mention of that cloud from the West, because it has already arrived. Instead the question is what will happen next and the prognosis is gloomy: the outcome of the war will be the beginning (*archē*) of great evils for all the Greeks as the Romans continue to intervene in the East. As the language shifts from talk of causes to beginnings, so the spectre of impending disaster moves closer.²⁸ The phrase 'the cloud from the West' is distinctive, but, while the reference to the beginning of great evils might be proverbial, it can also be read as an allusion to the two influential historians of the fifth century. Herodotus uses it of the Athenian assistance to the Ionian revolt that led to the Persian Wars and Thucydides of the Athenian refusal to negotiate before the Peloponnesian War.²⁹ These three speeches in Polybius set up the struggle in the Greek world that would lead to Roman domination, and they help to make it clear what is at stake for the Greeks. The Aetolian decision to make peace with Philip in 206 BCE is thus an attempt to take back control. This may not yet be a crisis, but elements of one are there; we can observe the fear of losing control and the increasingly emotive character of the speeches as they stress the terrible nature of a Roman sack.

There has been considerable debate about the authenticity of Polybius' speeches, but it is hard not to see these interconnected speeches as being, in part at least, the product of hindsight.[30] Across a period of ten years they succinctly sketch out the changing relationship between Greeks and Romans as the latter move from outsiders to allies in the politics of mainland Greece. Polybian hindsight reveals a series of missed opportunities, as each speech offers an alternative path.[31] The first speaker Agelaus urges the Greeks to put aside their differences and makes the case for unity. He envisages the Greeks united and safe from outside threats. That, however, was a path that was not taken. Then the lengthy speech of Lyciscus to dissuade the Spartans from joining with Aetolia and Rome encourages the reader to ask what would have happened if they had refrained from doing so. The final speaker addresses the question of foresight (*pronoia*) and implies that if the Aetolians had foreseen the consequences of their actions, then they would never have allied with Rome. Events have moved on so far that this speaker is rather like the historian himself looking back over what has happened. The advocacy of foresight here is itself a result of hindsight, the knowledge on the speaker's part of what has already occurred as a result of the treaty. But there is still an opportunity to change the direction of events. If the Aetolians were to make peace now, the speaker suggests, then Greece might be saved from ruin and allowed to enjoy freedom and security. At the same time, however, he predicts that the Romans will want to return in full force after they have defeated Hannibal. He leaves open whether they will treat the Greeks well or badly, but Polybius' readers will have their own ideas on this. The identity of this third speaker is unknown but if the suggestion that he is a Rhodian is correct, then that is an added irony, since Rome would return a few years later not at the invitation of the Aetolians but of the Rhodians.[32] The themes of enslavement and ruin in this last speech seem to reflect the circumstances of Greece after the Macedonian defeat at Pydna in 168, while the threat to Greek freedom is a recurring theme throughout the speeches.[33] All of this suggests that Polybius is interpreting the past through the present, his own experience of the events of the second century BCE moulding his representation of the Greek response in the early years of Roman intervention. While there were no doubt some prescient politicians observing Roman success in Italy, the speeches seem too uncannily prophetic to be an accurate reflection of debate in the late third century BCE. They allow readers to return to a time when things might have been different, while at the same time forcing them to contemplate why events turned out as they did.

b) The Isthmian Games of 196 BCE

The First Macedonian War was more of a proxy war on Rome's part, a necessary extension of their struggle with Hannibal, but the Second Macedonian War was a major undertaking. It ended with the defeat of Philip V at the battle of Cynoscephalae in 197 BCE, after which a settlement had to be negotiated and arrangements made for those Greek cities that had been subject to Philip. The Roman position was to be made clear at the Isthmian Games at Corinth in 196 BCE. The leading men from all over the Greek world gathered at the festival in anticipation; each would have been wondering how their city would cope in this new environment. Polybius tells us that the assembled crowds were alive with speculation:

> ... some claiming that there were certain places and cities from which it was impossible for the Romans to withdraw, others asserting that they would withdraw from those places that were considered to be famous while keeping hold of those that had less prestige but were able to serve the same purpose.

> ... τῶν μὲν ἀδύνατον εἶναι φασκόντων Ῥωμαίους ἐνίων ἀποστῆναι τόπων καὶ πόλεων, τῶν δὲ διοριζομένων ὅτι τῶν μὲν ἐπιφανῶν εἶναι δοκούντων τόπων ἀποστήσονται, τοὺς δὲ φαντασίαν μὲν ἔχοντας ἐλάττω, χρείαν δὲ τὴν αὐτὴν παρέχεσθαι δυναμένους καθέξουσι.
>
> Polyb., 18.46.2

Not content with this, they vied with each other at guessing which cities would be retained by Rome. The overwhelming impression here is uncertainty and importantly uncertainty among those who would be used to wielding power; indeed Polybius characterizes it as *aporia*, a term which captures the discomfort and confusion of these men.[34] Events are outside their control; instead they wait upon the decision of the Romans.

Polybius' account goes beyond the strict requirements of historical narrative and instead he offers a description so vivid as to make his readers almost experience the event itself;[35] not only does he convey what the audience hear and see, but also the emotions that they feel. When the herald reads out the Roman announcement that declares those cities that had been subject to Philip to be 'free, without garrisons or tribute and governed by their ancestral laws' (ἐλευθέρους, ἀφρουρήτους, ἀφορολογήτους, νόμοις χρωμένους τοῖς πατρίοις), the anxiety of the assembled crowds is replaced by astonishment (18.46.5). There is an air of unreality to the situation. Not only are they unable to believe it, they hear it as if in a dream. To comprehend it they need to hear it a second time and then their reaction is one of joy (*chara*), bordering on religious fervour as they hail the Roman commander Flamininus as their saviour. He goes on to say that what the Romans did in fighting for Greek freedom was truly remarkable. This, for Polybius, was an important moment, yet he acknowledges that any attempt to capture what the Greeks there experienced must fall short.

The joy felt among the Greeks at the announcement was due to their relief that what was feared by so many did not happen. Rather than taking over the garrisons of the defeated Macedonians the Romans had undertaken to withdraw their forces. But such freedom needed to be defended. Nevertheless, too many Greeks felt that protecting and maintaining it was something beyond their control. It was not long before voices were heard repeating the earlier warning that Rome was a threat to freedom, but even those who spoke out and encouraged resistance, such as Polybius' compatriot Philopoemen, did not really believe that it was possible to stop the Roman erosion of Greek liberty. The best that could be hoped for was that it could be slowed down.[36] What is striking, in contrast to the crisis that faced the Romans after Cannae, is the passivity of the Greeks, at least in Polybius' eyes. Whereas the Romans, faced with the possibility of submission to Hannibal, rallied together and did everything they could to defend their freedom, the Greeks were too often resigned to their fate and as a result surrendered their freedom to the Romans.

Polybius' description of the Isthmian Games must be read against the knowledge that both he and his readers had that 196 BCE did not mark an end and that this vaunted freedom would prove to be illusory. This does not prevent him saying, without any apparent irony, that what the Romans did there was remarkable. Again he is to be found looking back and considering what might have been, a world in which the Greeks were indeed free. His emphasis on the announcement of 196 BCE may even be a challenge to his Roman contemporaries to live up to their earlier promises.[37]

c) The battle of Pydna

Around twenty-five years after the Isthmian announcement Rome embarked on the Third Macedonian War, this time against Philip's successor Perseus, who would be defeated at the battle of Pydna in 168. The resulting abolition of the Macedonian kingdom marked a decisive change in the relationship between the Greeks and Rome. Polybius' full account of these events no longer survives but he leaves no doubt about their significance. In his second preface, as he reviews the structure of his history, he writes:

> The fifty-three-year period came to an end with these events [war with Perseus and end of Macedonian kingdom] and the increase and extension of the Romans' dominion was completed. It seemed, moreover, to be universally agreed as a matter of strict necessity that what remained was to hearken to the Romans and to obey their orders.[38]
>
> ὅ τε γὰρ χρόνος ὁ πεντηκοντακαιτριετὴς εἰς ταῦτ' ἔληγεν, ἥ τ' αὔξησις καὶ προκοπὴ τῆς Ῥωμαίων δυναστείας ἐτετελείωτο· πρὸς δὲ τούτοις ὁμολογούμενον ἐδόκει τοῦτ' εἶναι καὶ κατηναγκασμένον ἅπασιν ὅτι λοιπόν ἐστι Ῥωμαίων ἀκούειν καὶ τούτοις πειθαρχεῖν ὑπὲρ τῶν παραγγελλομένων.
>
> Polyb., 3.4.2–3

This is a key moment. From now on all must obey Roman orders, a very different prospect from the celebration of freedom that had taken place less than three decades earlier. In contrast to 196 BCE the anxiety that preceded Pydna is not assuaged afterwards.

Polybius' presentation of events both before and after the defeat of Macedon suggests that this was indeed a time of crisis for the Greeks generally. As the conflict developed, communities and confederations were sharply divided about their policy towards Rome. The Boeotian League was the first casualty, broken up by Rome after it attempted to align itself with Macedon. Polybius reports divisions in Achaea, Aetolia and Acarnania, together making up the bulk of central and southern Greece, as well as the island state of Rhodes.[39] Dealing with Rome could induce a sense of paralysis. In Polybius' own Achaean League there was hesitation and perplexity about what to say and do in the circumstances (28.3.5–6, 28.6). This uncertainty was a reflection of the Greek states' lack of control. All they could do was to anticipate what Rome might want or what it might be willing to accept, but that was not an easy matter and the consequences of getting it wrong could be serious. Nor do we have to rely only on Polybius for our knowledge of this awareness of Roman power; it can be found also in contemporary epigraphic evidence.[40]

The sense of crisis intensified after the Roman victory as Greeks witnessed enslavement and massacres at Romans' hands or purges at their own.[41] States sought to find ways of demonstrating their loyalty to Rome, which might mean sacrificing those politicians whose behaviour or policies were considered to have been suspect. The Rhodians, for example, had long been friends of the Romans but after an ill-judged attempt to broker a peace between Perseus and Rome they found themselves the object of Roman anger, which left their ambassadors 'completely demoralized and despondent' (εἰς ἀθυμίαν ὁλοσχερῆ καὶ δυσχρηστίαν, Polyb., 30.4–5).[42] As part of their efforts to restore good relations with Rome the Rhodians voted to execute all who had supported the Macedonian cause.[43] They had little choice but to do as the Romans wished. Achaea may have been less compromised, but pro-Roman politicians still handed over to the Romans around a thousand of their compatriots, whose support for Rome was alleged to have been too restrained. These men, with Polybius among them, were all then transported to Italy, where they would languish until the end of the next decade.[44]

The conclusion of the Third Macedonian War is the point where history and the personal come together for Polybius. His own career in some ways mirrors the Greek experience. He begins as an advocate for an independent Achaea and tries to maintain this position in the face of encroaching Roman power, then, like Greece, he loses his freedom and has to submit to Roman orders. In his case this means being taken as a detainee to Rome. That the conclusion of Rome's imperial quest and his own loss of freedom should occur at the same time is surely no coincidence. The longer his detention lasted, the more appropriate Pydna must have seemed as the terminal point for Rome's rise to world power.

It was in the aftermath of these events that Polybius began writing his history. His subject was the rise of Rome but it was also a reflection on and consequence of the trauma of the previous few years. As he sat in Rome working on the history, he mulled over how the Greeks ended up as subjects of Rome, obliged to recognize its authority. Far from writing a simple narrative, Polybius is constantly asking questions about the events he is narrating. He interrupts the narrative in book six to consider the nature of the Roman state: what was it about Rome that enabled it to survive the crisis of Cannae and go on to seize control of the world? But, as we have seen, he also ponders where it went wrong for the Greeks and whether different actions would have led to a different outcome. As his narrative approaches Pydna, however, the options available to the Greeks become fewer and fewer until all that most people can do is stay quiet and hope. Although Polybius does not say explicitly what his position was, he would seem to place himself among those who 'did not like seeing everything settled and power over the world falling into the hands of one empire, neither working together with the Romans nor opposing them in any way but entrusting the result to fortune' (τῶν οὐχ ἡδέως μὲν ὁρώντων κρινόμενα τὰ ὅλα καὶ τὴν τῆς οἰκουμένης ἐξουσίαν ὑπὸ μίαν ἀρχὴν πίπτουσαν, οὔτε δὲ συνεργούντων οὔτ' ἀντιπραττόντων ἁπλῶς Ῥωμαίοις οὐδέν, ἀλλ' οἷον ἐπιτετραφότων τῇ τύχῃ περὶ τῶν ἀποβησομένων, 30.6.6).[45] But such equivocation was not looked upon kindly by Rome. As a detainee in Rome Polybius reflected on his own actions but a certain caution must have been necessary in what he wrote in his history – he would not have wanted to implicate himself more than necessary. Some did take action and risk siding with Perseus; if they were prepared to take the fatal consequences of their failure, then they were, Polybius believed, noble and praiseworthy, but if they tried to avoid them as some did, they were contemptible.[46]

Pydna, along with the end of the Macedonian kingdom, is the point to which Polybius' history is heading, but although his history is teleological, it is not determinist; it is not portraying the inevitable. There had been alternative paths, but by 168 BCE there was no alternative. After Pydna obedience to Roman orders was 'universally agreed as a matter of strict necessity' (Ῥωμαίων ἀκούειν καὶ τούτοις πειθαρχεῖν ὑπὲρ τῶν παραγγελλομένων).[47] Polybius may not have wanted this and his political actions may have aimed at avoiding this outcome but in the aftermath of the Third Macedonian War he recognized that that was how things were.

4. Crisis renewed: Resistance in the 140s BCE

The 140s saw renewed opposition to Rome in Macedon and Achaea. In Macedon a usurper named Andriscus laid claim to the throne and for a while successfully fought off Roman attempts to suppress him. Further south the Achaean League refused Roman orders to divest itself of several cities including Sparta, Corinth and Argos, a refusal that led to a short war that ended with the Roman sack and destruction of Corinth. Polybius' original intention had been to conclude his history with the end of the Macedonian kingdom in 168, but he subsequently decided that he should extend it. So the disturbances of the 140s were not part of the original narrative plan. Indeed he began his history before they had even happened. They do, nonetheless, fit into the narrative arc and serve to demonstrate Polybius' original thesis that everyone now had no choice but to accept Roman orders. The year 168 had marked an end; for Polybius it was evident that henceforth there was no alternative to Roman rule. The Achaean leader Critolaus, however, is represented as pursuing a policy of an Achaea that was both independent and a friend of Rome, a policy that Polybius himself might have once espoused, but that time had passed (38.12.8). This opposition to Rome reflects a failure to grasp the new reality, a failure to see that other possible worlds were no longer possible.

So convinced was Polybius of the futility of resistance that he characterized those who resisted as possessed or mad. In Macedon it was a heaven-sent infatuation that had taken hold of the supporters of Andriscus and this despite Rome having saved them from all the disadvantages of monarchy (36.17.15). In Achaea it was only thanks to fortune that the mindlessness and madness of the leaders did not do more damage.[48] Polybius' decision to extend his history followed these events and was influenced by the need to explain what had occurred.[49] This was all the more pressing because what had happened was so terrible, so much worse than anything that had previously happened to the Greeks (38.1).

Polybius was not in Achaea during this 'mad' surge of anti-Roman feeling; instead he was present with the Roman general Scipio Aemilianus at the siege of Carthage in North Africa. On his return, however, he helped with the reconstruction of Greece, in effect acting as an intermediary between the Roman authorities and Greek cities (McGing 2010: 145–6). This must have been a difficult position to maintain, on the one hand justifying Roman decisions, on the other defending Greek interests (39.3–5). At this time Polybius was acting both as a politician and as an historian, each role requiring a different approach to political events. His comments on those two roles help to illuminate how the crisis of the 140s affected him:

> In times of crisis (κατὰ τοὺς τῶν περιστάσεων καιρούς) it is proper that those who are Greeks help the Greeks in every way, whether by giving support, by concealing faults, or by pleading for deliverance from the anger of those in power. This is something that I myself actually did at that very time. But the transmission of the literary record of past events to succeeding generations should be kept free from any falsehood, so that instead of the ears of readers being pleased for the present, their minds may be reformed in order to avoid further repetition of these mistakes.
>
> Polyb., 38.4.7–8[50]

For Polybius the Greeks were to blame for the catastrophe that engulfed them, but at the same time he recognized that the real world required pragmatism. As a leading figure involved in these events he would defend and protect his compatriots, but as a historian he was obliged to tell the truth, not merely because the truth was important but also in order that his readers would be able to learn the necessary lessons and so use them as a guide to their own future conduct. Yet maintaining this distinction may not have been quite as simple as he suggests; indeed it has been argued that the suggestion itself might be a rhetorical strategy to allow him to make a case to the Romans in defence of the Achaeans (Thornton 2013: 38–40).

The resistance of the 140s ends in defeat and resigned acceptance of Roman rule. The misfortune of the Greeks was complete, says Polybius.[51] One proverb in particular was being repeated throughout Achaea: 'If we had not perished quickly, we would not have been saved' (εἰ μὴ ταχέως ἀπωλόμεθα, οὐκ ἂν ἐσώθημεν, 38.18.12). Here we find not only relief at the shortness of war but also an end to resistance and an implicit recognition of Rome as the ruling power. Polybius himself by this stage accepts this, not only rationally but also emotionally, as his concluding reference to his own goodwill (*eunoia*) to Rome suggests (39.8.1–2).

5. Conclusion

Polybius' history was written in the aftermath of an extraordinary transition that affected the whole Greek world. He himself was not a neutral outside observer but a man heavily involved. Indeed he was writing his history while a detainee in Rome, a consequence of both Roman success and Greek failure. His own life was interwoven with these events and he himself experienced something very much on the lines of the emotional transitions he ascribes to the Greeks.

It might be tempting to think in terms of a 'Second-Century Crisis', but that would be too broad and unhelpful and would take the focus away from moments of real apprehension and uncertainty. If we were to identify a crisis for the Greek states, then it would be the time of the Third Macedonian War. Politically divided cities, feeling powerless in the face of forces beyond their control, sought to position themselves in relation to Rome. First they had to anticipate the outcome of the war, which may have required them to reconcile the tension between what their citizens wanted and what they thought was likely to happen, and once Roman victory was clear they had to ensure that Rome looked upon them with favour or at the very least did not take punitive action against them. These circumstances inform Polybius' history as he looks back on Rome's conquest of his world. The wars that decided the fate of the Greeks were fought primarily between Rome on the one hand and the Macedonian and Seleucid kingdoms on the other. These conflicts, however, had serious implications for the Greeks, whether individual cities or powerful confederations like Polybius' own Achaean

League. Speakers within the *Histories* often warn against what is coming, warnings that seem to reflect Polybian hindsight rather than sentiments expressed at the time. Moreover, a second crisis strikes while Polybius is writing his history, the Macedonian and Achaean resistance of the 140s, an irrational and hopeless attempt to change what Polybius had come to see as inevitable.

Polybius aimed to show how in fifty-three years the Romans brought the world under their sole rule, but he is also writing as a Greek for Greeks. As he was being deported to Italy, he would have asked himself: did it have to be this way? In his history he shows the choices that were made and the alternative paths that could have been taken but were not. At the same time he is offering lessons for the future. His readers should look at the choices and take care not to repeat these mistakes themselves. Here lies the educational value of history. Whether it also helped the reader to cope is not so clear. It might be expected to have provided a sense of perspective as they compared their own experience with those of their predecessors, but it is often difficult to attain that level of detachment in the present and Polybius may have been so involved that he too found it difficult. Strikingly, he believed that the Greek crisis of the 140s was so bad that it surpassed every previous Greek disaster from the Persian Wars onwards.[52]

Part Three

Crisis Traumas and Recovery: Rome

6

Coping with Crisis
Sulla's Civil War and Roman Cultural Identity

Alexandra Eckert
University of Oldenburg

1. Florus on Sulla's civil war: Bloodshed unheard of in Roman history

At the beginning of the second century CE, Florus' history of the Roman wars described how the Romans had risen to power through their victories over external enemies and by overcoming internal strife. In the second book of his work, Florus provides a remarkable statement regarding Sulla's civil war of 83/82 BCE. According to Florus, 'all the bounds of rage ... were transgressed' (*ultimo ... rabiem supergressum est*) and cruelty ruled until 'none remained to be slain' (*donec deessent qui occiderentur*, Flor., 2.9.5).

At first, it seems hardly imaginable that civil strife could become so extreme. Yet Florus lays bare to his readers the details of one of the worst internal conflicts in Roman history. Florus describes the enormous death toll of the civil war's final battles near Sacriportus and at the Colline Gate in October and November 82 BCE. According to Florus, a total of 70,000 Roman citizens were slain in these two battles.[1] However, the overall bloodshed was significantly higher. In the period between the arrival of Sulla's army near Brundisium in spring 83 BCE and the decisive battles near Sacriportus and at the Colline Gate in late 82 BCE, Sulla and his commanders had routed many legions of enemy forces in a series of battles such as those of Mount Tifata, Clusium, Faventia and Fidentia.[2] Diodorus Siculus' and Appian's reports testify to Sulla's civil war resulting in an overall death toll of 100,000 soldiers.[3]

To comprehend the enormity of these numbers, we have to put them into context. Census figures from the early first century BCE suggest that the Roman population of the Italian peninsula in 83 BCE amounted to between 900,000 and one million citizens.⁴ Thus, Sulla's second march on Rome exacted a very high price: about 10 per cent of all Roman citizens between the spring of 83 BCE and November 82 BCE.

Yet, as Florus emphasizes, the cessation of military campaigns by no means marked the end of the bloodshed (*nec idem tamen caedium, qui bello finis fuit*; Flor., 2.9.23). Sulla's victory in the civil war was followed by months of terror and indiscriminate slaughter. After the Battle of the Colline Gate, Sulla ordered the mass execution of 4,000 Roman citizens who had opposed him in the Villa Publica. This he did despite having promised to spare their lives if they voluntarily surrendered (Flor., 2.9.23). According to Florus, the Villa Publica massacre was followed by a period of utter anarchy in Rome: a time in which 'anyone who wished to do so, slew [others] in various parts of the city' (*quos in urbe passim quisquis voluit occidit*, Flor., 2.9.25). As a consequence of Sulla giving his soldiers and followers free rein to assassinate whomever they wanted, countless Romans died in the aftermath of the Villa Publica event. The death toll of these arbitrary killings reached such dramatic proportions that even Sulla's partisans recognized that Roman society was on the brink of self-destruction. Finally, one of Sulla's followers, a certain Fufidius, suggested that 'the lives of some ought to be spared in order that Sulla might have someone to whom to give orders' (*vivere aliquos debere, ut essent quibus imperaret*).⁵ Florus' statement that Sulla's civil war reached such an extreme that 'none remained to be slain' (*donec deessent qui occiderentur*) bears a striking similarity to Fufidius' words. Both statements express the fear that the *res publica* would cease to exist if the excessive bloodshed continued.⁶

During November 82 BCE, the Romans endured days and even weeks of arbitrary assassinations from which neither senators nor ordinary citizens were safe. It was only at Fufidius' prompting that Sulla decided to end the indiscriminate slaughter.⁷ He introduced proscriptions as a new punitive measure against members of the opposing faction among the Roman elite. However, as Florus points out, the period of the proscriptions saw more than just the cruel public murders of individual Roman noblemen. Sulla also collectively punished many Italian municipalities. The possessions of cities such as Spoletium, Interamnium, Florentia and Praeneste were sold; in the case of Sulmo, Sulla even ordered the destruction of the town (Flor., 2.9.25–27).

According to Florus, at least 10,000 Roman citizens died on Sulla's orders after Sulla's victory on 1 Nov 82 BCE.⁸ In order to comprehend the full extent of the terror and destruction, it is necessary to draw on other ancient sources that recount the Villa Publica massacre, the period of arbitrary killings in Rome, the surrender of Praeneste and the proscriptions. According to Livy, Valerius

Maximus, Plutarch and Orosius, Sulla's indiscriminate violence against his fellow citizens after the Battle of the Colline Gate added a further thirty to forty thousand Romans to the 100,000 soldiers who had already died during the battles of the civil war in 83/82 BCE.[9] In the end, Sulla's vengeance raised the already considerably high number of dead from his second march on Rome by at least a third.

The enormous death toll following the cessation of the civil war battles may have provoked Florus to ask the rhetorical question of whether 'the number of those slain in times of peace should not be rated higher' (*isti tot in pace non plures sunt?*, Flor., 2.9.25) than those killed in war. Every seventh Roman citizen perished during Sulla's civil war of 83/82 BCE and as a result of the violence he unleashed following his victory at the Colline Gate. The bloodshed and terror did not cease until the beginning of 80 BCE, when the Roman judicial system began functioning again, and trials, such as Cicero's famous defence of Sextus Roscius of Ameria, finally stopped Sulla's partisans from arbitrarily extending the proscription lists.[10] More than thirty months of terror across the entire Italian peninsula had come to an end.

2. The trauma of Sulla's civil war

This chapter will argue that Sulla's civil war and his acts of violence between 83 BCE and the beginning of 80 BCE constituted a fundamental crisis for Roman society. Sulla's responsibility for the first major civil war in Roman history and for the unprecedented death toll of about 14 per cent of all Roman citizens had profound consequences for Roman society and even changed Roman cultural identity.

This chapter will apply Vierhaus's concept of 'historical crisis' to Sulla's civil war and his acts of violence. It will also analyse the period of 80 BCE to the outbreak of the civil war between Caesar and Pompey in 49 BCE and illustrate how Roman society employed a particular coping strategy for dealing with the 'Sullan crisis'.

A striking example of the effects of this coping strategy is the civil war between Caesar and Pompey. Caesar had been one of the key persons to drive the process of coping with the effects of Sulla's civil war and Sulla's acts of violence. Yet, in 49 BCE, he saw himself in the role of being the initiator of yet another major civil war. The fact that he was faced with enormous pressure to distance himself publicly from Sulla – through his policy of *clementia* ('clemency') – may be seen as a consequence of how the Romans dealt with the 'Sullan crisis'. When the triumvirs Lepidus, Marc Antony and Octavian decided to inflict proscriptions on Roman society once again in 43 BCE, they – just like Caesar before them – had to distance themselves publicly from Sulla. It is highly significant that the triumvirs included a desperate attempt at explaining in an official document why their proscriptions were somehow 'milder' than those of Sulla: the edict on the proscriptions of 43 BCE. Yet, this attempt at justification failed and, infamously, the proscriptions of the triumvirs were to go down as the last in Roman history.

3. Scholarship on the concept of 'crisis'

The term 'crisis' has received renewed attention in the field of Classics during the last decade, in both the German and English-speaking worlds.[11] A broadly accepted assumption is the view of the German historian Reinhardt Koselleck that crises generally mark turning points in history.[12] The most common usage of the term crisis by ancient historians is the so-called 'Crisis of the Roman Republic'. A key publication on this is Christian Meier's book *Res Publica Amissa* (1966), which proposes that the years between 90 and 60 BCE should be perceived as a 'crisis without end'. Considering the ongoing debate his monograph provoked, it is a little surprising that Meier did not provide a definition of the term crisis until the second edition of his book in 1980.[13] In this edition, Meier drew on the 1978 article of the early modern historian Rudolf Vierhaus titled *Zum Problem historischer Krisen* (*On the Problem of Historical Crises*). Vierhaus's definition of historical crisis was quite influential. His ideas found their way into many publications on crises, among them Hölkeskamp's thorough evaluation of the term 'crisis' in the introductory chapter of his 2009 volume *Eine politische Kultur (in) der Krise?* (*A Political Culture in Crisis?*).

4. Vierhaus and his concept of 'historical crisis'

Vierhaus points out that, in contrast to the use of the term 'crisis' as a label for categorizing important historical events for the purpose of mere description, a concept of 'historical crisis' necessarily has to provide added value for historical analysis. In other words, a concept of 'historical crisis' must facilitate new structural insight into the preconditions, causes, main driving factors, key events and consequences of a crisis.[14] Vierhaus has identified several important criteria for a concept of 'historical crisis':

1. A historical crisis is caused by economic, social or political disruptions.[15]
2. A historical crisis severely affects a society at large or its fundamental subsystems, e.g. economy or political institutions. It may even endanger the existence of a society.[16]
3. A historical crisis has a beginning and an end, i.e. it is associated with a clearly demarcated period of time.
4. A historical crisis is a process with different stages or phases.[17]
5. In the course of a historical crisis, usual forms of economic, social or political regulation within a society are either no longer applied or are no longer capable of handling the severe disruptions which are occurring. As a consequence, social norms and values lose authority.[18]
6. A historical crisis encompasses times of great uncertainty in which small changes in the course of events may produce grossly different consequences for the society in question.[19]
7. In contrast to a medical crisis, where complete recovery may be the result, a historical crisis is irrevocable per se and encompasses substantial structural transformations affecting fundamental aspects of a society.[20]

The concept of a historical crisis as described by Vierhaus provides a comprehensive and convincing theoretical basis for analysing historical processes. Yet, when studying Sulla's civil war and his acts of violence, it seems reasonable to refine Vierhaus's terminology slightly.

In 2009, Hölkeskamp proposed greater specificity by taking 'internal conflicts', the 'collapse of institutions for conflict resolution' and the 'failure of procedures for establishing consensus' into account when discussing historical crises (Hölkeskamp 2009b: 8).

Another important aspect is the role of social norms and values. In his book *Crisis Management in the Roman Republic*, Golden defined 'crisis' as 'a perceived threat to core values' (Golden 2013: 4). This rightly points to the importance of conforming to or transgressing social values in times of historical crisis.

5. Vierhaus's criteria applied to Sulla's civil war and Sulla's acts of violence

The outbreak of the civil war of 83/82 BCE marked a major political disruption for the Romans and may be defined as a historical crisis according to Vierhaus's concept. In the course of Sulla's civil war, major political institutions that played a key role in conflict resolution – such as the Roman Senate and the courts – disintegrated or collapsed completely.

The historical crisis of Sulla's civil war and his acts of violence began in spring 83 BCE, when Sulla's legions landed at Brundisium, and ended at the beginning of 80 BCE, when juries convened again in Rome. Different phases are discernible. After a comparably moderate beginning with the Battle of Mount Tifata in 83 BCE, the civil war escalated rapidly after the failure of peace negotiations between the consul Lucius Scipio Asiaticus and Sulla.[21] In 82 BCE, Sulla's commanders routed many legions of the opposing side over several battles. The final battles of the civil war, at Sacriportus and at the Colline Gate, saw extremely high death tolls and ended with 100,000 Roman soldiers losing their lives in combat.[22] After his victory at the Colline Gate on 1 November 82 BCE, Sulla ordered the mass execution of enemy soldiers, who had voluntarily surrendered, thus violating the fundamental principle of *deditio in fidem*. This massacre marked the beginning of a total breakdown of fundamental social norms and values.[23] After the Villa Publica event, Sulla gave his soldiers – 23 legions all over Italy – free rein to kill whomever they wanted: personal enemies and non-partisan citizens alike.[24] The death toll skyrocketed, not least due to Sulla's orders to execute 12,000 inhabitants of the Italian town of Praeneste, who had surrendered to Sulla's commander Cethegus on the promise of being spared.[25] Finally, after nearly 30,000 Romans had already perished during the period of indiscriminate slaughter following Sulla's victory at the Colline Gate, Sulla introduced the proscriptions. This new punitive measure was directed against his enemies among the Roman nobility and had most severe consequences, not only for the affected individuals, but for their wives and children, too. Though Sulla's *Lex Cornelia de proscriptione* decreed an end of the proscriptions on 1 June, 81 BCE, Sulla's partisans continued to add the names of wealthy members of the Roman elite in order to enrich themselves. These arbitrary extensions of the proscription lists prolonged the time of terror and public homicide for many months. The period of cruelty came to an end only after the Roman judicial system began functioning again in early 80 BCE and after Cicero had won his case for Sextus Roscius of Ameria against Chrysogonus, one of Sulla's most prominent partisans at that time.[26]

The risk of Cicero and his client losing their case was high, as their opponent, Chrysogonus, was very influential and had engaged one of Rome's best lawyers at that time – Hortensius. Had Cicero lost his case, the proscriptions would have continued for many more months. Cicero's final appeal to the judges in his speech *Pro Sexto Roscio* pointed out how the persistent emotional strain caused by the ongoing public homicides of the proscribed threatened to eradicate one of the core values of Roman society – *humanitas* – from the hearts of even the mildest Romans (Cic., *Rosc. Am.* 154).

6. Cultural trauma: The social dimension of coping with a crisis

Undoubtedly, the 'Sullan crisis', the historical crisis of Sulla's civil war and Sulla's acts of violence, with its enormous death toll of around 14 per cent of all Roman citizens, had a severe impact on both the economic and military capacity of the Roman Republic. Yet, it is also important to investigate the social dimension of this historical crisis. The social structure of the Roman elite was irrevocably changed: many of its members had either died in battle or had lost their life, property or political rights during the proscriptions. Moreover, the Romans of all social strata who had been killed on Sulla's orders had been deprived of one of the fundamental rights at the heart of the Roman Republic – the right of appeal to court. In addition, Sulla's actions against the wives and children of proscribed Romans, and his collective punishment of Italian towns represented severe forms of kin liability. Here again, Sulla had violated core values and key principles codified in Roman law – the ideas of individual accountability and justice.[27]

While the criteria described by Vierhaus allow for a succinct categorization of the 'Sullan crisis' as a historical crisis, Vierhaus's 'crisis framework' does not provide the means for describing how Roman society responded to and coped with this crisis. In order to fill this analytical gap, this chapter will employ the concept of 'cultural trauma'. The American sociologist Jeffrey C. Alexander describes cultural trauma as follows:

> Cultural trauma occurs when members of a collectivity feel they have been subjected to a horrendous event that leaves indelible marks upon their group consciousness, marking their memories forever and changing their future identity in fundamental and irrevocable ways.
>
> Alexander 2004: 1

Alexander's model can be applied whenever a (not necessarily large) group of members of a society suffer from a horrendous event that human beings have inflicted on them. Alexander describes the consequences of such events for both individuals and the collectivity at large. He clearly distinguishes between persons being traumatized as individuals and societies experiencing cultural trauma as a whole. Persons exposed to a horrendous event often develop individual trauma as a direct and inevitable consequence. Yet, cultural trauma is not an immediate result of the horrendous event. Cultural trauma occurs on a societal level only if members of a society have gone through different phases of a 'social process of cultural trauma'. During the first phase, members of the society who recognize the importance of the horrendous event for both individuals and the community form 'carrier groups'. Carrier groups lobby to convince a majority of the society to acknowledge the overall relevance of the horrendous event and to actively participate in efforts to cope with its consequences. The ensuing patterns of communication and social interaction are called 'social mediation'.[28] A critical success factor for carrier groups and their attempt to win over a majority in a society in the course of the 'socially mediated process of cultural trauma' is the creation of a succinct 'master narrative'. A master narrative is a convincing and compelling description of the horrendous event. It conveys the names of victims, their suffering, the consequences for the society at large, and the responsibility of the perpetrators for violating fundamental social values. As such, the master narrative purposefully illustrates the relevance of the horrendous event for both individual members and the society. As soon as a majority of the members of said society accepts the plausibility of the master narrative, a consensus is reached that the horrendous event had traumatic effects on individuals as well as devastating consequences for the society as a whole. Said majority will cooperate to overcome the immediate and long-term impact of the horrendous event with a 'working through' in political, legal or other institutional 'arenas'.

According to Alexander, the final phase of the social process of cultural trauma has been reached and cultural trauma has been established successfully when the master narrative of the horrendous event has been adopted into a society's cultural identity and is preserved by institutionalized forms of remembering. These shared efforts in a society represent an attempt to prevent a reoccurrence of the horrendous event by reinforcing the social values that have been severely violated by the perpetrators.

7. A social process of cultural trauma: The case of the 'Sullan crisis'

The 'Sullan crisis' is a striking case from the perspective of cultural trauma. As a consequence of the enormous death toll, the large number of public homicides, and the fact that Sulla's punitive measures included far-reaching kin liability, many Romans had directly experienced suffering and severe personal losses. Most of the Romans – even if they counted themselves among Sulla's party – belonged to one or more of the following groups:

1. They had lost family members, relatives or friends in civil war battles or due to Sulla's violence after the Colline Gate.
2. They had witnessed massacres and public homicides in Rome and Italy, such as the massacre in the Villa Publica, the killings of Sulla's marauding soldiers and the public assassinations in the course of the proscriptions.
3. They were deprived of property and political rights due to the proscriptions.
4. They had experienced collective punishment as citizens of Italian municipalities.

Although the proscriptions were confined to members of the Roman elite, the civil war and Sulla's acts of violence had affected all strata of Roman society. It therefore seems plausible that a majority of Romans perceived the entirety of the 'Sullan crisis', i.e. both Sulla's civil war and Sulla's acts of violence, as a 'horrendous event'.[29]

As a consequence of Sulla's deeds, several carrier groups formed, most notably the children and friends of the proscribed, who wished to regain their political rights, members of the old senatorial elite whose political influence had been marginalized due to Sulla's reform of the Roman Senate, and citizens of Italian towns who were affected by Sulla's punitive measures, such as the inhabitants of Arretium and Voltaterrae. In the case of the 'Sullan crisis', the social process of cultural trauma could rapidly progress through its initial stages because those who had suffered from Sulla's deeds already represented a majority among the Romans. Close family members, relatives and friends of the almost 14 per cent of Roman citizens who had died as a consequence of Sulla's civil war and the violence in its aftermath were aware of key elements of the master narrative through personal experience, i.e. the suffering of the victims, the names of the perpetrators and their responsibility for the violation of fundamental social norms. The carrier groups needed little to no lobbying to have a majority of their fellow citizens acknowledge the grave consequences of Sulla's terror and bloodshed for both individuals and Roman society at large. Hence, in the case of the 'Sullan crisis', the phase of working through in public arenas, most notably the legal arena, started as early as 80 BCE. This is illustrated by the trial against Sextus Roscius, which took place while Sulla still held the office of dictator.[30]

In his speech *Pro Sexto Roscio*, Cicero eloquently presented key elements of the master narrative of the 'Sullan crisis' and addressed the dictator's responsibility for the current situation – yet without naming Sulla explicitly. By relating the Battle of Cannae and the Battle of Lake Trasimene to Sulla's civil war and the Sullan proscriptions, Cicero achieved a twofold effect. First, he illustrated that the death toll of the 'Sullan crisis' equalled or even surpassed that of the worst military defeats in Roman history. Secondly, by placing Hannibal's campaign in Italy during the Punic Wars and the 'Sullan crisis' side by side, Cicero demonstrated that Sulla had brought Roman society to the brink of destruction. Yet, Cicero did not stop at outlining the relevance of the 'Sullan crisis' for Roman society at large. With the moving question, 'Who was not injured there by Phrygian steel?' (*quis ibi non est uulneratus ferro Phrygio?*), Cicero addressed the many Roman citizens who had lost family members, relatives and friends as a consequence of the 'Sullan crisis'. By referring to the swords from Phrygia that Sulla and his soldiers had captured during the First Mithridatic War, Cicero singled them out as the perpetrators and attributed responsibility to them for the deaths of so many fellow citizens.

Winning over the judges in this trial was a remarkable achievement for Cicero. The acquittal of his client Sextus Roscius the Younger prevented an outrageous injustice. Otherwise, the child of the illegally proscribed Roman citizen Sextus Roscius the Elder would have suffered the death penalty for the false accusation of parricide. Moreover, Cicero and his supporters prevented one of Sulla's most influential partisans, Chrysogonus, from seizing the property of yet another wealthy Roman by arbitrarily and illegally extending the proscription lists. The outcome of the *Pro Sexto Roscio* speech was, therefore, a wide and clear signal that the period of arbitrary bloodshed that had threatened to destroy social bonds in Roman society was over.

The year 80 BCE saw another important step in working through the injustice of Sulla's acts of violence. Young Cicero successfully reclaimed Roman citizenship for a woman of Arretium, an Italian town whose inhabitants had been deprived of Roman citizenship by Sulla's punitive measures.[31]

Just one year later, Lepidus' election as consul in 78 BCE sent a signal to the political arena that the working through of the consequences of the 'Sullan crisis' held broad support in Roman society. In his election campaign, Lepidus addressed key points of the injustice resulting from Sulla's acts of violence. Lepidus promised to return the auctioned property of proscribed Romans to their lawful owners, to bring back those that Sulla had exiled and to reinstate Italian municipalities as owners of the land that Sulla had deprived them of.[32] Lepidus' claims were popular, but he was unable to realize them.

In 77 and 76 BCE, shortly after Sulla's death, the young Caesar pressed charges of extortion against three prominent Sullan partisans. The conviction of Cn.

Cornelius Dolabella, the praetor of 81 BCE, forced him into exile. Cn. Cornelius Dolabella, a relative of the praetor and consul of 81 BCE, and Antonius Hybrida, one of Sulla's commanders in Greece during the First Mithridatic War, were acquitted by juries.[33]

The 70s BCE also saw a decade-long initiative to restore the rights of the tribunes of the plebs. In the end, one of Sulla's main political measures directed against both the Roman people and members of the old senatorial elite was rescinded. A first step, the *Lex Aurelia de tribunica potestate* (law on the restoration of tribunician powers) of 75 BCE, lifted Sulla's ban preventing former tribunes of the plebs from applying for other magistracies in the *cursus honorum*.[34] Yet, it took until 70 BCE for the rights of the tribunes of the plebs to be restored completely.[35]

In the same year, further activities for coping with the consequences of the 'Sullan crisis' demonstrated that the working through had gained momentum. The standing of the old senatorial elite of pre-Sullan times was strengthened substantially by two measures. The *Lex Aurelia Iudicaria* restored the position of Roman knights as jurors in the Roman court system.[36] The expulsion of seventy senators from the Roman Senate by the censors of 70/69 BCE was most likely directed against Sulla's followers.[37] Prominent Sullan partisans who lost their seat in the Senate were Antonius Hybrida and P. Cornelius Lentulus Sura.[38]

In 70 BCE Caesar successfully lobbied to stop the prosecution of proscribed Roman citizens who had escaped Sulla's bounty hunters in the years 82 and 81 BCE. While this measure did not restore to these Romans their former property and rights, it did guarantee their personal safety (Cass. Dio, 44.47.4).

In the same year Cicero prevailed in court against one of the most hated of Sulla's partisans, Gaius Verres, who was accused of extortion in the province of Sicily. The plethora of evidence Cicero presented in the first speech of the first hearing led Verres to go into exile voluntarily. Although this prematurely ended the trial, Cicero decided to publish the speeches of the second hearing and present all the evidence to a wider public. In the third speech of the second hearing, he succinctly summarized important points of the master narrative of the 'Sullan crisis' in order to delegitimate Verres' position as one of Sulla's most faithful partisans.[39] According to Cicero, Sulla was the first man in Roman history to possess such exceptional power that he could dispossess, disenfranchise and even execute many Roman citizens. When Sulla publicly auctioned the property of proscribed Romans, he would even declare that he was selling his booty (*se praedam suam vendere*), thereby openly expressing the fact that he saw no problem in treating Roman citizens like foreign enemies (Cic., *Verr.* 2.3.81).

Cicero's highly emotional plea, 'May the immortal gods grant that there may never be another [Sulla]!' (*di immortales faxint, ne sit alter!*), signalled the extent to which Sulla had perverted his victory in the civil war and how a majority of Romans never wished to experience such a crisis again.[40]

The year 70 BCE became the prelude to a decade that saw the most progress in coping with Sulla's atrocities. From 66 BCE onwards, legislative initiatives were proposed to reclaim funds embezzled from the Roman state treasury by Sulla and his partisans during his dictatorship. Although none of these initiatives were successful, they became the focal point of public attention.[41] Several remarkable court decisions in 64 BCE repealed the immunity that Sulla's *Lex Cornelia de proscriptione* had granted those who had killed proscribed Romans. As a consequence, Cato the Younger and Caesar initiated trials that sought to sentence some of Sulla's bounty hunters to death for the assassination of Roman citizens.[42] The Roman public perceived these trials as a substitutionary punishment of Sulla himself, who had already died in 78 BCE (Plut., *Cat. Min.* 17.7).

In 64 BCE Cicero campaigned for the consulship of the following year. In his speech *In toga candida* he severely attacked the opposition candidate for the consulship, Catiline, for having been one of Sulla's cruellest bounty hunters in the years 82 and 81 BCE. Cicero announced that if he should become consul, he would prosecute Catiline for having committed one of the most outrageous crimes to occur during Sulla's reign of terror: the public torture and assassination of the praetor M. Marius Gratidianus.[43] Cicero's plans to prosecute Catiline were quashed by the Catilinarian conspiracy. Eventually, Catiline and many of his followers perished in battle at the end of 63 BCE.[44]

A notable number of Catiline's partisans were children of the proscribed, who, utterly frustrated in their attempts to regain their right to run for public office, had decided to support their former archenemy Catiline. As a consul, Cicero played a major role in the public debate on the issue of the rights of the descendants of the proscribed. While he publicly declared in his speech *De proscriptorum liberis* ('On the Children of the Proscribed') that the claims of the children of the proscribed to have their rights reinstated were justified, he nevertheless argued for declining the initiative out of *raison d'état*.[45]

With the exception of the issue of the rights of the children of the proscribed, which Caesar resolved in 49 BCE, Roman society had mostly concluded the working through of the 'Sullan crisis' during the 60s BCE.[46] Intense debate on Sulla's cruel deeds and their consequences for both individuals and Roman society at large had sharpened public awareness of how gravely Sulla had violated fundamental social values. Thereafter, any Roman who attempted to repeat

Sulla's offences against Roman core values was confronted with enormous social pressure to justify himself and risked loss of legitimacy in Roman society. This social response represented the Romans' coping strategy to prevent members of their society from following in Sulla's footsteps.

8. The 'Sullan crisis', cultural trauma and Caesar's civil war

During the twenty years from 80 BCE to 60 BCE, Caesar played a major role in the working through of the 'Sullan crisis'. He probably involved himself so deeply in this process, because he had been proscribed under Sulla and had only narrowly escaped his bounty hunters.[47]

When, nearly thirty years after Sulla's death, Caesar initiated another civil war in 49 BCE, the cultural trauma of Sulla's civil war and acts of violence resulted in enormous pressure on him to distance himself from Sulla as far as possible, so as not to lose the backing of his supporters. Caesar's policy was therefore not only a response based on his own experience under Sulla, but also a consequence of the working through of the 'Sullan crisis'. In February 49 BCE, Caesar demonstrated that his policy of clemency was not mere propaganda. After the sack of Corfinium, Caesar granted mercy and liberty to the defeated enemy soldiers and refrained from any punitive measures against the inhabitants of the Italian town, even though they had openly sided with Pompey.[48] Shortly thereafter, he wrote a letter intended for wider circulation to Oppius and Cornelius Balbus, two of his political supporters in Rome, in which he distanced himself from Sulla:

> I am very glad that your letter expresses such strong approval of what happened at Corfinium. I shall be glad to follow your advice and, all the more so, that I spontaneously resolved to display the greatest clemency and to do my best to reconcile Pompey. Let us try by these means to win back the goodwill of all and enjoy a lasting victory, seeing that others have not managed by cruelty to escape hatred or to make their victories endure, except only L. Sulla, whom I do not propose to imitate. Let this be the new style of conquest, to make mercy and generosity our shield.
>
> Cic., *Att.* 9.7.C1; transl. Shackleton-Bailey, adapted

In this letter, Caesar openly declares that he aims to continue the policy of clemency he had just demonstrated at Corfinium and that he will try to achieve reconciliation with Pompey. Caesar also explains that he will employ clemency in an attempt to win over a large majority of Romans and establish a stable political situation after the civil war. He contrasts his own policy of clemency with the cruelty of others that had provoked such hatred and which led to their victories proving short-lived. Caesar emphasizes that he will not imitate Sulla's deeds, despite Sulla having been the only civil war commander whose political measures had lasted for several years. Caesar's letter implies that he wished for an end to the civil war and for a stable political situation, without repeating Sulla's deeds.

In a letter to Atticus, dated 26 March 49 BCE, Cicero informs his friend that he had commended Caesar for his clemency at Corfinium (*clementiam Corfiniensem*). Cicero quotes a short passage from Caesar's answer to him. According to Cicero, Caesar had written the following: 'You [Cicero] characterize me [Caesar] correctly (you know me quite well), as nothing is more foreign to my nature than cruelty.' (*recte auguraris de me (bene enim tibi cognitus sum) nihil a me abesse longius crudelitate*; Cic., *Att.* 9.16.1–2). So, Caesar once again confirms his policy of clemency and assumes a firm stance against cruelty. Moreover, Caesar declares his firm will to continue showing clemency towards his enemies, despite knowing that some of Pompey's commanders, whom he had granted mercy at Corfinium, had decided to continue the military campaign against him (*neque illud me movet, quod ii, qui a me dimissi sunt, discessisse dicuntur, ut mihi rursus bellum inferrent*; Cic., *Att.* 9.16.2). Hence, Caesar once more draws the very same line of distinction between Sulla and himself, as he had in his letter to Oppius and Cornelius Balbus earlier that month – yet without naming Sulla directly.

More than one year later, Caesar again proved that his former declarations had not just been vain words. In August 48 BCE, immediately before the battle of Pharsalus, he ordered his soldiers to spare their fellow citizens on the enemy side whenever possible.[49] After the battle, Caesar pardoned those of Pompey's troops who had surrendered.[50]

Unlike Sulla, Caesar did not proscribe defeated enemy commanders. He even supported some of the survivors in successfully applying for political office. Caesar also treated favourably the wives and children of his opponents who had died in battle: he reimbursed widows their dowry and granted a portion of the inheritance to their children.[51] Caesar continued his policy of clemency while he pursued Pompey, who had fled to Egypt. When Caesar arrived in Alexandria shortly after the Egyptians had killed Pompey, he dealt with the corpse of his dead enemy with respect. He also had Pompey's murderers executed and he pardoned Pompey's partisans in Egypt.[52]

In autumn 47 BCE, Caesar returned from Egypt to Rome. Up until that point, Caesar's leading role in the working through of Sulla's deeds and his policy of clemency had saved him from coming into conflict with the cultural trauma of the 'Sullan crisis', despite having initiated another major civil war. However, Caesar then made a decision that damaged his legitimacy among Romans: he auctioned Pompey's property in public.[53] When Caesar did this, the Romans confronted him with a collective groan of rejection. Both the masses and Caesar's followers refused to bid, until finally Antony purchased Pompey's possessions.[54]

Another point that proved problematic for Caesar's legitimacy was his decision to use the dictatorship to institutionalize his position as the most powerful man in Rome. Caesar's first dictatorship in 49 BCE lasted only a few days and, therefore, did not evoke strong memories of the Sullan crisis. However, when Caesar was appointed dictator for ten years in 46 BCE and then even became lifelong dictator in 44 BCE, he stirred up memories of the cruel deeds that Sulla had committed as dictator.[55]

In late 82 BCE Sulla had forced an assembly of the Roman people to appoint him dictator with unprecedented power for an unspecified term.[56] Sulla abused his dictatorship in an attempt to legalize his acts of violence during and after the civil war. Hence, when Caesar successively extended the duration of his time in office as dictator, he demonstrated that he no longer respected the working through of the 'Sullan crisis' and its outcome, to which he himself had so substantially contributed with his initiatives in the 70s and 60s BCE. Consequently, Caesar's decision initiated a strong social response and the office of dictatorship was abolished in 44 BCE, shortly after Caesar's assassination.[57]

9. The proscriptions of the triumvirs in 43 BCE

One of the most striking testimonies to how profoundly Roman society had responded to the breach of fundamental social norms during the 'Sullan crisis' has come down to us through Appian in the form of the proscription edict of the Second Triumvirate, which dates to 43 BCE. When crafting this official document, Octavian, Marc Antony and Lepidus put great effort into distancing themselves from Sulla's deeds. They justified the proscriptions of 43 BCE as a means of preventing an era of terror and the killing of innocent citizens by marauding soldiers. Furthermore, the triumvirs of 43 BCE promised that they would prosecute only their fiercest enemies to minimize the number of fellow citizens whom they had to kill and to keep the total number of names on their proscription lists as low as possible. In their edict, the triumvirs referred to Sulla's surname *Felix* ('the Fortunate'), which he had adopted – as the first Roman ever – at the end of 82 BCE, and ensured that they would not repeat Sulla's cruelty:[58]

> We [the triumvirs] shall not deal harshly with any multitude of men, nor shall we count as enemies all who have opposed us or plotted against us, or those distinguished merely by their riches, their abundance, or their high position; nor shall we slay as many as another man who held the supreme power before us, when he, too, was regulating the commonwealth in civil convulsions, and whom you named *Felix* on account of his success; and yet necessarily three persons will have more enemies than one. We shall take vengeance only on the worst and most guilty.
>
> App., *B Civ*. 4.10; transl. Horace White, adapted

The power of the cultural trauma of Sulla's deeds and the ensuing reinforcement of social norms in Roman society proved stronger than the triumvirs' propaganda. Their attempts to exculpate themselves from repeating Sulla's cruelty remained futile. Seneca the Younger addresses how problematic the proscriptions of 43 BCE proved for Emperor Augustus. Moreover, according to Pliny the Elder, Augustus' part in the proscriptions of 43 BCE led him to becoming an object of hatred (Sen., *Clem*. 1.11.1–2; Plin., *HN* 7.147).

Emperor Tiberius also saw himself confronted with the effects of the cultural trauma of the 'Sullan crisis'. The arbitrariness and terror of his treason trials provoked the memory of Sulla's cruel deeds. Suetonius informs us of verses circulated on the streets of Rome warning Tiberius not to imitate Sulla (Suet., *Tib*. 59–60). The imperial era saw the reoccurrence of civil strife. Yet, it is remarkable that none of the parties involved resorted to proscriptions again.

10. Conclusion

The 'Sullan crisis', i.e. the civil war of 83/82 BCE and Sulla's acts of violence between 2 November 82 BCE and the beginning of 80 BCE had grave consequences for Roman society at large. To cope with this crisis, the Romans initiated a social process of cultural trauma. This coping strategy aimed to strengthen the social values that had been violated by Sulla's cruel deeds. This social response represented an attempt at preventing such a crisis from occurring again.

During the 70s and 60s BCE the Romans undertook a working through of the 'Sullan crisis' in the judicial and political arenas, and established cultural trauma. The effects of these shared efforts in Roman society were already visible in the civil war between Caesar and Pompey. Caesar managed to distance himself from Sulla with his policy of clemency, despite having initiated a major civil war. Yet, when he stirred up memories of the proscriptions and Sulla's reign of terror by publicly auctioning Pompey's property in 47 BCE and by declaring himself lifelong dictator in 44 BCE, he lost legitimacy and could not prevail. The desperate attempts of the triumvirs to justify their measures illustrate that after Roman society had concluded the working through of Sulla's deeds, Romans were confronted with an enormous social pressure not to repeat Sulla's acts of violence. The proscriptions of 43 BCE reactivated the effect of the cultural trauma of the 'Sullan crisis' and were thus the last in Roman history.[59]

Alternative Futures in Lucan's *Bellum Civile*
Imagining Aftermaths of Civil War

Annemarie Ambühl
University of Mainz

1. Introduction: Alternative futures, narratology and virtual history

Lucan's *Bellum Civile* (*BC*), the epic on the civil war between Caesar and Pompey composed by a highly talented young poet who tragically fell victim to Nero's wrath, has provoked many different readings in the history of scholarship. During the past few decades, the long prevailing Stoic and Republican readings have been superseded by deconstructivist readings; accordingly, the narrator of the *Bellum Civile* is no longer identified with the historical author Lucan nor simply seen as a champion of Republicanism or anti-Neronian resistance. Yet this has only led to another interpreters' dilemma, as a polyphony of multiple textual voices now seemed to vie with a nihilistic authorial stance, which eventually resulted in the postmodern image of a text waging a civil war against itself.[1] Recent narratological studies have refined this picture once more by pointing out the sophisticated and innovative literary techniques that make up the fabric of Lucan's epic.[2] Moreover, fruitful attempts have been made to apply memory studies and trauma theory to the *Bellum Civile* in order to explain its unique literary form and its shifting perspectives; in this view, beyond trying to revive the lost Republic or representing a counter-memory from the viewpoint of the defeated party, Lucan's poetic re-enactment of the civil war conjures up an unfinished past that never comes to an end, an eternal present that still haunts the descendants of all the civil war participants.[3]

The present chapter, on the contrary, does not look at the past as embodied in Lucan's epic but at the future or rather at various potential futures – although paradoxically these futures have already become part of the past or present of the historical author and his audience. The *Bellum Civile*, however, not only alludes to the historical future of the Neronian principate, but also sketches a wide range of alternative futures that could have resulted from the civil war. Even the possibility that the civil war might have been prevented altogether is hinted at. Such passages where the narrator or characters of his epic envisage an alternative course of events can be interpreted within the narratological framework of 'If not-situations', 'Beinahe-Episoden' or 'Ungeschehenes Geschehen' as defined by Irene de Jong (2004: 68–81) and Heinz-Günther Nesselrath (1992).

Lucan's narrator repeatedly insinuates that the civil war could have been stopped or at least delayed at crucial turning points, and along with it the unfolding of the epic plot (also in the sense of Hayden White's 'emplotment'; cf. Klooster and Kuin in this volume).[4] What if the personified Patria had been able to convince Caesar not to cross the Rubicon (*BC* 1.183–203), what if the mutiny of Caesar's soldiers had been successful (5.237–373), or what if Caesar had been killed in the storm at sea (5.476–702) or at Pharsalus – by none other than his future murderer Brutus (7.586–596)? What if Pompey had not listened to his advisors and declined to fight the fatal battle (7.45–130)? What if after his defeat he had turned to the Parthians to form an alliance instead of sailing to Egypt, where he was to be murdered treacherously (8.159–471)? What if Caesar had stayed forever on his Egyptian holiday with Cleopatra and given up the civil war in order to discover the sources of the Nile (10.188–192)?

Yet, in the case of an historical epic dealing with a real civil war that had a huge impact on the course of history, such alternative constructions gain a larger significance beyond the structure of the epic. What would have happened if Pompey instead of Caesar had won the civil war? Would in this case the Republic really have been restored (as Caesar's heir Augustus paradoxically claimed to have done), or would it have resulted in just another brand of 'tyranny'?[5] Would Rome have been able to defeat the Parthians and establish a true world empire, were it not for the losses suffered because of the civil wars (see below § 3)? Or could the civil war have been prevented altogether if the triumvir Crassus or Julia, Caesar's daughter and Pompey's wife, had not died prematurely (*BC* 1.98–120), or if the soldiers on both sides had refused to fight their brothers in arms (see below § 3)?

Such methodological questions have been posed as a thought experiment in the historical sciences, known as 'virtual history' with its variants of alternative or counterfactual history.[6] This approach has been applied to ancient history, too;[7] here usually either the fates of 'great men' such as Alexander, Hannibal or Augustus and major turning points of Roman history such as the battle of Cannae or the

Teutoburg Forest serve as virtual case studies, whereas the civil war between Caesar and Pompey does not get much attention.[8] In addition, text-oriented studies have emphasized the tension between teleology and contingency that is enacted through narrative techniques such as hindsight or 'futures past', 'sideshadowing' and counterfactual narrative, and strategies of narrative re-experience aimed at making the past present for the audience.[9] Such dealings with the 'semantics of historical time' have been studied from a philosophical point of view by Reinhart Koselleck in his *Futures Past* (2004; German original: *Vergangene Zukunft*).[10] In his recent monograph on experience and teleology in ancient historiography, Jonas Grethlein refers to Koselleck's term but defines it in a different, more specifically narratological way as the entwining of retrospect and prospect, which results from the asymmetry between the characters' and the historian's perspectives: 'the stronger the future in a given narrative's "futures past", the stronger its focus on experience; the more the "futures past" is treated as past, on the other hand, the more prominent becomes its teleology' (Grethlein 2013: 8; cf. 13–14).

These studies have focused mainly on Greek and Roman historiographers, especially on Polybius (see Andrew Erskine in this volume), Livy or Tacitus, whereas the genre of (historical) epic has drawn relatively little attention so far.[11] As a notable exception, Robert Cowan (2010) has identified a 'poetics of contingency' as a hallmark of Silius' *Punica*, the historical epic on the Hannibalic War, which was composed shortly after Lucan's *Bellum Civile*. Indeed, Cowan argues that Silius in his re-enactment of the Second Punic War as a crucial turning point in Roman history engages intertextually with Homer's, Vergil's and Lucan's strategies of 'sideshadowing', the signalling of possible alternative outcomes (Cowan 2010: 328–39; cf. Cowan 2018 on Horace and Lucan).

In general, however, Lucan has not often been considered in this context, although a poetics of 'dramatic presentification' ('dramatische Vergegenwärtigung', Schlonski 1995: 159) has long been identified as one of the characteristics of his innovative narrative style.[12] The present chapter argues that such phenomena in Lucan's civil war epic go beyond matters of narratology or poetics. By proposing various 'alternative futures', the narrator and his characters address wider psychological, social and political issues connected with the aftermath of a civil war. Some of these scenarios are clearly counterfactual, but others take up actual strategies that were employed in the various historical Roman civil wars by projecting them onto the war between Caesar and Pompey. Lucan's visions of potential and/or not realized aftermaths of the civil war thus constitute an experimental laboratory against which the actual strategies of dealing with the crisis of the first century BCE can be tested.[13] In Lucan's poetic imagination, the crisis of the Late Roman Republic was not a crisis without alternative ('Krise ohne Alternative' according to the historian Christian Meier (1997: 201)).[14] Such a close connection between the concepts of crisis and alternative history has likewise been suggested by Koselleck (2006: 370), who defines 'the multiplicity of mutually exclusive alternatives' as constituents of the concept of crisis in modern philosophy of history.[15] But before considering such larger issues in connection with the civil war depicted in Lucan's epic, first some modes of alternative futures as they are reflected in the text itself will be sketched briefly.

2. Narrative possibilities in moments of crisis: *liceat sperare timenti*

In an historical epic the exact degree of fictionality is hard to pin down and can only approximately be gauged by comparing and contrasting the epic narrative with extant historiographical accounts, which however have themselves been shaped by literary strategies sometimes closely resembling the epic ones. Nevertheless, the poet finds himself in a situation similar to that of the tragic poet as defined by Aristotle in his *Poetics* (1453b22–26), where the basic outline of the myth is more or less fixed, but the poet can demonstrate his inventive skills by introducing unexpected turns, even if they do not lead to a different ending. Earlier (1451a36–b7) Aristotle differentiates between the historian, who tells what has happened (τὰ γενόμενα), and the poet, who tells what may have happened (οἷα ἂν γένοιτο); in his view, what Herodotus put into verse (what we probably would call a historical epic) still has to be classified as history, which is concerned with particulars, whereas poetry is more 'philosophical', precisely because it addresses universal issues. From a modern narratological perspective, Irene de Jong has coined the term 'semi-fiction' (2004: 81) with regard to the Homeric epics, which claim to present a reliable account of the past but actually consist of a mixture of tradition (or 'historical facts') and invention. Interestingly, Lucan himself seems self-consciously to reflect on such issues of historicity and fictionality by introducing various prophets or seers and having them talk about the possibility of predicting or even changing the future course of events, among them the Etruscan seer Arruns and the astrologer Nigidius Figulus (*BC* 1.584–672) or the necromancer Erictho, who admits that she is able to change lesser fates but not the causal chain of world events (6.605–615). Such figures can be interpreted as analogues of the poet who shapes the fictional plot within the constraints of his historical subject matter.[16]

Here is not the place to review Lucan's complex concepts of *fatum* and *Fortuna*, whose narrow definitions in terms of Stoic determinism have recently been superseded by more open-minded readings.[17] Instead the connection of 'fate' or the future with Lucan's poetics can be concisely illustrated by adducing three parallel passages from the points of view of the narrator, a character of his epic and the implied perspective of the readers. In all three of them, the speaker places himself at a certain point within the action when the future course of events is still open and thus provokes various emotional responses wavering between fear and hope.[18] From the auctorial perspective, at the beginning of the civil war the narrator appeals to Jupiter to allow fearful humans at least a chance to hope (2.14–15: *sit subitum quodcumque paras; sit caeca futuri / mens hominum fati; liceat sperare timenti.* – Whatever you intend, let it be sudden; let men's minds be blind to future disaster; let the fearful have hope!).[19] From the point of view of a character, this is exemplified in the last words of the dying Domitius (one of Nero's ancestors), which he addresses to Caesar at Pharsalus (7.610–615). He proclaims that he is dying as a free man because he sees Caesar at this moment uncertain of his fate in battle (*dubium fati*) and therefore can still hope (*sperare licet*) that Caesar will be defeated. In an earlier passage of book 7 this same open perspective is applied to the anticipated reception of the epic by its future readers, not coincidentally in the context of a vision by an anonymous augur, who witnesses the battle of Pharsalus simultaneously from a great distance:[20]

> ... will stir both hopes and fears together
> and useless prayers when the battle is read;
> all will be stunned as they read the destinies, as if
> to come, not past and, Magnus, still they will side with you.

> ... cum bella legentur,
> spesque metusque simul perituraque vota movebunt,
> attonitique omnes veluti venientia fata,
> non transmissa, legent et adhuc tibi, Magne, favebunt.
>
> Luc., 7.210–213

The grip of the events narrated in Lucan's epic will be so strong that for a while readers will forget the historical outcome of the war and become totally immersed in the fiction of the moment by empathizing with the protagonists.[21] When interpreting *adhuc* as referring not to the historical present of the audience but to the fictional present as experienced in the act of reading ('up to this point of the action'), their favouring of Pompey is probably not to be read in the sense of a political statement but as a response to the tragic feeling of doom surrounding

Pompey at this stage. Through such narrative strategies Lucan's narrator creates for his readers the illusion of being a participant in the middle of the unfolding action, which at crucial turning points could still take a different course from the historical outcome.[22]

At the same time, this comes close to the ancient roots of the modern concept 'crisis' as defined by Koselleck (2006: 358–9): 'Κρίσις ... meant ... "decision" in the sense of reaching a crucial point that would tip the scales.... But "crisis" also meant "decision" in the sense of reaching a verdict or judgment ...'[23] In Lucan's epic, too, the 'crisis' of the civil war unfolds as a series of individual or collective decisions at crucial points *and* as a series of verdicts or judgements on these decisions. This is indicated by the frequent use of terms such as *discrimen* (e.g. in 7.108–109: *gladio permittere mundi / discrimen*; translated by Susan Braund as 'to surrender to the sword the crisis of the world'; cf. 4.192, quoted below in § 3). Caesar's famous dictum upon crossing the Rubicon, 'The dice is cast' (*Iacta alea est* according to Suetonius, *Iul.* 32), is not quoted literally, but alluded to at a later stage of the civil war on the eve of the decisive battle at Pharsalus, when Caesar wishes for the fatal hour soon to approach (6.7: *placet alea fati* – 'he chooses the gamble of Fate'), and shortly afterwards repeated by Sextus Pompey (6.603: *quo tanti praeponderet alea fati* – 'which way the gamble of such great destiny inclines'). Before, Lucan had Caesar at the Rubicon state his allegiance to his patron goddess Fortuna (1.226: *te, Fortuna, sequor* – 'Fortune, it is you I follow') and leave the judgement to the war (227: *utendum est iudice bello* – 'now war must be our referee'). This echoes the famous phrase *quis iustius induit arma / scire nefas: magno se iudice quisque tuetur; / victrix causa deis placuit sed victa Catoni* (1.126–128: 'Who more justly took up weapons is forbidden knowledge; each has on his side a great authority: the conquering cause the gods, the conquered Cato'). That judgement in a civil war is indeed a highly subjective matter is demonstrated time and again, as both parties claim to fight for the better cause (*causa melior*: e.g. 4.259 vs. 7.349) and put the blame on their respective opponents.[24] Nevertheless both leaders are aware that the issue who is to be judged guilty in a civil war and the measures that are to be taken against the defeated party will eventually be decided by the victor. Caesar makes this pragmatic statement at the eve of the battle at Pharsalus (7.263): *nulla manus, belli mutato iudice, pura est* ('once the judge of war is changed, no hand is clean').

From the point of view of its characters and sometimes also through auctorial comments, the *Bellum Civile* thus addresses crucial issues raised by the aftermath of a civil war, although the action ends in the midst of the Alexandrian war long before any closure has been reached. The much-debated issue of the epic's ending need not be discussed here, particularly since the speculations about the various possibilities (Cato's suicide at Utica, Caesar's murder, the battle of Philippi, even Actium) ultimately only serve to demonstrate the potential endlessness of civil war.[25] All these historical consequences of the civil war between Caesar and Pompey up to the Neronian principate are indeed alluded to in the *Bellum Civile*, and it is idle to speculate whether such prolepses were intended to be internal or external.[26]

The following selection of passages will focus on different scenarios that sketch either counterfactual aftermaths or alternative solutions to the actual events of the civil war. Due to the limited scope of this chapter a preliminary overview rather than an exhaustive discussion of every single statement within its narrative context is intended. However, it will be important to pay at least some attention to the respective speakers and their intentions, for often precisely the ironic or cynical comments are used to sketch alternative outcomes.

3. Imagining (counterfactual) aftermaths and alternatives to civil war

In the *Bellum Civile*, the alternative scenarios span the whole range from crisis averted to total and catastrophic crisis. Nevertheless, among this wide variety a few overarching topics can be identified that are brought up in different contexts and that can provisionally be classified under eight categories (with some overlap), whereby the first four (**A** to **D**) represent an hyperbolical aggravation of the crisis and the remaining four (**E** to **H**) possible solutions to or aftermaths of the crisis: end of the world (**A**); desolation of Italy (**B**); global desolation / extinction of the Roman people (**C**); world war / fall of the Roman Empire (**D**); end of the civil war because of the death of one of its leaders (**E**), through their reconciliation (**F**), or through the initiative of the soldiers (**G**); dealing with the defeated party through a politics of either revenge or clemency (**H**).

To start with the most destructive scenario (**A**), the civil war is repeatedly compared to the destruction of the world through fire (*ecpyrosis*) or flood (e.g. 1.72–80).[27] Of course for Lucan and his audience it was evident that the world had not ended, but in ancient thought cosmic catastrophes anyway led to a cyclical rebirth, and at least in the praise of Nero in the proem (1.33–66), the Neronian principate is indeed seen as such a utopian rebirth leading to a future state of world peace (1.60–62). Still, on a more local scale (scenario **B**), the civil wars have left deep scars in the landscape of Italy, as the images of the desolated towns of Latium in books one (1.24–32) and seven (7.391–399) illustrate. Critics are divided as to whether these are basically realistic criticisms of a historical socio-economic crisis (Hunink 1992: esp. 200–1) or counterfactual vignettes that intertextually project images from the civil war poetry of Virgil and Horace onto an imaginary contemporary future (Groß 2013: 90–103).

Even worse, in the hyperbolical visions of book seven (scenario **C**), the global bloodbath at Pharsalus almost results in the extinction of mankind or at least of the Roman people. The losses will be so massive that the surviving population of the whole world will fit into the single city of Rome:

> To what has the multitude of humankind
> been reduced! We peoples born in all the world
> are not enough to fill with men the town-walls and fields;
> a single city holds us all.
>   ...and Rome, crowded
> by no citizen of her own but filled with the dregs of the world,
> we have consigned to such a depth of ruin that in a body so immense
> civil war cannot now be waged. The cause of such a great catastrophe
> is Pharsalia.

>   generis quo turba redacta est
> humani! toto populi qui nascimur orbe
> nec muros implere viris nec possumus agros:
> urbs nos una capit.
>   ...nulloque frequentem
> cive suo Romam sed mundi faece repletam
> cladis eo dedimus, ne tanto in corpore bellum
> iam possit civile geri. Pharsalia tanti
> causa mali.
>
> Luc., 7.399–408

In his cynical comment on the multicultural character of Neronian Rome, Lucan's narrator assumes the literary mask of a xenophobic satirist.[28] At the climax of the battle, he reformulates the same thought in a more positive sense and prays that the foreign troops from all over the world be spared, for after the civil war these will form the Roman people (7.542–543: *nam post civilia bella / hic populus Romanus erit*). The paradox conveys the bitter truth that ultimately civil war at Rome can only be stopped when there are no Roman citizens left.

The other side of the coin (scenario **D**) is the fear that as a consequence of the civil war Rome and the Roman Empire will be plundered by foreign enemies, either by Gauls and Germans or by Eastern peoples taking advantage of Rome's internal conflict. This responds to inveterate Roman fears: on the one hand the *metus Gallicus*, symbolized by the defeat at the Allia and the sack of Rome by the Gauls in 390 BCE and the invasion of the Cimbri and Teutones at the end of the second century BCE, actualized in the counterfactual image of Gallic hordes following in the wake of Caesar's legions (e.g. 1.481–486), on the other hand the *metus Punicus*, the fear of Hannibal, likewise revived in the figure of Caesar crossing the Alps (e.g. 1.183 and 303–305); in view of more recent history the *metus Parthicus* is added, as the Parthian question was to vex Roman politics from Caesar to Nero and beyond.[29] But again, Lucan gives these old anxieties a new twist by introducing them not as worst-case scenarios but as the preferable alternative to civil war. He has the men who at the beginning of book 2 are about to be conscripted for civil war wish that all the borders of the Empire be attacked by foreign enemies so that they will not have to fight in a civil war (2.45–56, esp. 52–53: *omnibus hostes / reddite nos populis: civile avertite bellum* – 'make us again the enemies of all the peoples, only ward off civil war').

This idea is developed further throughout the epic and culminates in Pompey's revolutionary – or utterly delusional – plan to form an alliance with the Parthians in order to attack Caesar and Rome with their help. The way he presents this plan to the Parthians (8.237–238: *Pompeio vincite, Parthi, / vinci Roma volet* – 'Conquer for Pompey, Parthians: willingly will Rome be conquered') differs tellingly from the version he presents to his Roman followers:

> Rome, favour my plans! What greater joy could the gods
> have ever given you than for you to wage a civil
> war with Parthian soldiers and exhaust a race so mighty
> and embroil it in our misery? When Caesar's armies
> clash with the Medes, then Fortune must avenge either me or the Crassi.

> Roma, fave coeptis;[30] quid enim tibi laetius umquam
> praestiterint superi, quam, si civilia Partho
> milite bella geras, tantam consumere gentem
> et nostris miscere malis? cum Caesaris arma
> concurrent Medis, aut me Fortuna necesse est
> vindicet aut Crassos.
>
> Luc., 8.322–327

Would this have resulted in the defeat of the Parthians by Caesar, in the defeat of Caesar by the Parthians, in utter catastrophe for Rome or even in a joint Roman-Parthian world empire?

We will never know, for Lentulus persuades the Pompeians to abort the plan and turn to Egypt instead, so that the epic plot is realigned with the historical course of events. Interestingly, Lentulus considers the Parthian plan as absurd as the possibility of a reconciliation between Pompey and Caesar (8.439–441: *ire per ista / si potes, in media socerum quoque, Magne, sedentem / Thessalia placare potes* – 'If through such scenes, Magnus, you can go, then you can also placate your father-in-law, seated in the midst of Thessaly').

The image of Caesar gazing at the heaps of the civil war dead (cf. 7.786–796), which is strikingly juxtaposed with the alternative of a reconciliation even at this point, may for our purposes serve as a transition from counterfactual scenarios on a global scale, where the civil war can only be ended by a world war or the end of the world, to more limited political scenarios. In this context two further counterfactual solutions are to be considered, first, that with the death of one of the leaders the civil war would come to its natural end (scenario E), and second, the possibility of an individual or collective reconciliation between the opponents (scenario F).

Lucan's epic throughout emphasizes the fact that Caesar and Pompey are father-in-law and son-in-law (*socer* vs. *gener*) in order to characterize the civil war as a parricidal war among relatives in the tradition of Romulus' fratricide (cf. 1.92–97) and further tragic models (on family and civil war, see also Gallia and Osgood in this volume). In line with this, the possibility of either Caesar being killed by Pompey or – more often – Pompey being killed by Caesar is frequently entertained (E). Thereby it is regularly (and counterfactually) assumed that the death of one of the leaders would put an immediate end to the civil war. Moreover, at various points in the war the civil war generals consider a voluntary retreat by flight or suicide in order to put an end to the fighting and to spare the lives of the Roman soldiers on both sides.[31] Some of these strategies were successfully employed in Republican warfare against foreign enemies, when either the self-sacrifice (*devotio*) of a Roman consul or the death of the opposing commander in a duel guaranteed Roman victory.[32] Yet in the new reality of civil war, these strategies no longer work. The civil war goes on after Pompey's flight from the battlefield at Pharsalus and also after his death, as his soldiers continue to fight under his sons' and Cato's command. Cato's suicide does not end the war either, and Caesar's murder only provokes a new civil war.

The counterpart to the possibility of one opponent being killed at the hands of the other is the chance of a private reconciliation between father-in-law and son-in-law (F), a possibility hinted at several times, for instance when the Massilians offer their city as a neutral place for peace negotiations (3.333–335), or in an auctorial comment on the fraternization of Pompey's and Caesar's soldiers that we will return to shortly (4.187–188: *iam iam civilis Erinys / concidet et Caesar generum privatus amabit* – 'soon, soon will civil war's Erinys cease and Caesar, as a private citizen, will love his son-in-law'). Also in their neighbouring camps in Epirus Caesar and Pompey almost come face to face (5.468–475, esp. 469–471: *miserique fuit spes irrita mundi / posse duces parva campi statione diremptos / admotum damnare nefas* – 'and futile was the miserable world's hope that the leaders might, when parted by the plain's tiny area, renounce the crime now brought so close').

But in fact the two generals never meet in the *Bellum Civile* while still alive. Caesar's belated attempt at a reconciliation while holding Pompey's head at the end of book 9 is sarcastically commented upon by the narrator in advance (9.1047–1049: *huncine tu, Caesar, scelerato Marte petisti / qui tibi flendus erat? nunc mixti foedera tangunt / te generis? nunc gnata iubet maerere neposque?* – 'Did you, Caesar, chase this man with wicked warfare, a man for whom you had to weep? Does the pact of families united touch you now? Do your daughter and your grandson bid you grieve now?'). In his ensuing speech, Caesar nevertheless paints a sentimental picture of a chance at mutual forgiveness forever lost:

> The one reward of
> civil war – to grant survival to the conquered – we have lost.
> ...
> The nations have been deprived of a day of happiness, our reconciliation
> has been lost to the world. My prayer has found no favouring gods –
> my prayer that, after laying down successful weapons, I might embrace you
> and ask from you your old affection and your staying alive,
> Magnus, and to be your equal, satisfied with a reward
> quite worthy of my toils. Then in lasting peace
> I could have helped you in defeat forgive the gods;
> you could have helped Rome forgive me.
>
> unica belli
> praemia civilis, victis donare salutem,
> perdidimus.
> ...
> laeta dies rapta est populis, concordia mundo
> nostra perit. caruere deis mea vota secundis,
> ut te complexus positis felicibus armis
> affectus a te veteres vitamque rogarem,
> Magne, tuam dignaque satis mercede laborum
> contentus par esse tibi. tunc pace fideli
> fecissem ut victus posses ignoscere divis,
> fecisses ut Roma mihi.
>
> Luc., 9.1066–1068, 1097–1104

The counterfactual scenarios of a quick solution either through reconciliation or because of the death of one of the civil war generals confirm *ex negativo* that in a civil war there can be no easy closure. What may have started as a family matter – but so did Romulus' murder of his twin brother Remus, that is seen as the ultimate cause of the Roman civil wars – has become a collective crisis involving various agents with different agendas that can no longer be solved in a private meeting.

Therefore some more sustainable alternatives to civil war need to be considered. The crucial role played by the masses or collective actors such as the soldiers in Lucan's epic has already been pointed out in scholarship.[33] Indeed, at various points in the epic scenarios are played through whereby groups of soldiers almost (but of course not quite) succeed in bringing the civil war to an end (scenario **G**). Notably these are the scenes of fraternization or mutiny in books 4, 5 and 9.[34] In this context the late Republican buzzword '*Concordia*', as we have seen just before in Caesar's discourse, is introduced in the narrator's prayer as a remedy against the discord of civil war:

> Now come, O Harmony, embracing all with eternal bond,
> the salvation of nature and the muddled universe
> and the sacred love of the world: now our age controls
> the great decision of what is to come.
>
> nunc ades, aeterno complectens omnia nexu,
> o rerum mixtique salus Concordia mundi
> et sacer orbis amor: magnum nunc saecula nostra
> venturi discrimen habent.
>
> Luc., 4.189–192

But this happy picture of fraternization is soon to be destroyed by a bloodbath made even worse by the brief prospect of peace. In his typical manner, Lucan's narrator undermines the whole concept of Concordia in the related episode of the mutiny of Caesar's soldiers: If *concordia* no longer helps, then let *discordia* come to the rescue (5.297–299: *sic eat, o superi: quando pietasque fidesque / destituunt moresque malos sperare relictum est, / finem civili faciat discordia bello* – 'So be it, O gods: since duty and since loyalty fail and the only hope remaining is in wicked ways, let discord bring an end to civil war')!

Notwithstanding this paradoxical wordplay, the whole issue of the soldiers' role in a civil war is given serious consideration in Lucan, as also emerges from the last topic to be discussed here, namely the controversial issue of how to deal with the defeated party in a civil war, either through revenge or through a politics of reconciliation (scenario **H**). Seemingly Lucan here telescopes different responses by civil war generals from Sulla to Octavian, by projecting them onto the one civil war between Caesar and Pompey. The alternatives are on the one hand the proscriptions that were initiated by Sulla at the end of the 80s BCE and reinstated by Mark Antony and Octavian in 43 BCE, and on the other hand the *clementia Caesaris* that was also claimed by his heir Octavian-Augustus (cf. *Res Gestae* 3 and 34).

While the historical Caesar during the civil war against Pompey and after his victory in most cases exercised *clementia* in his dealings with his former enemies, in Lucan's epic this practice is viewed from contrasting perspectives.[35] For instance, in his exhortation speech addressed to his soldiers before the battle at Pharsalus, Caesar warns them not to kill any fleeing Romans (7.319: *civis qui fugerit esto* – 'treat the man who flees as a citizen'), but after the battle, Lucan has him take personal revenge on the fallen Pompeians by denying them burial, precisely because in his wrath he remembers that they were his own fellow citizens who fought him (7.802–803: *sed meminit nondum satiata caedibus ira / cives esse suos*). However, the whole ensuing episode in which the narrator as it were enters into a discussion with Caesar about the issue of burial seems to be a counterfactual fiction invented by Lucan, as in other writers the issue of the unburied civil war dead is connected not with Pharsalus but with Philippi (e.g. in Suet., *Aug.* 13.2).[36] This can thus be seen as an example of the telescoping strategy.

Another such example is the practice of taking revenge on political enemies by having them proscribed.[37] From their perspective within the evolving events several characters assume that the eventual victor in the civil war will take cruel revenge on his fellow citizens by ordering proscriptions. The most extensive passage is the eyewitness account by an anonymous old man in book 2 (64–233), who vividly remembers the terrors of the civil war between Marius and Sulla. This is introduced as a warning of worse to come, for Caesar and Pompey have reached such an amount of power that they will not be content with the excesses of their predecessors (2.223–232, esp. 231–232: *neuter civila bella moveret / contentus quo Sulla fuit*). Yet the expectations raised by the old man's speech that Caesar's March on Rome will end in a bloodbath worse than Sulla's is contradicted by his unbloody takeover of the city at the beginning of book 3.

In the context of the battle at Pharsalus images associated specifically with the proscriptions reappear in the exhortation speech by Caesar. Here he imagines his own fate and the fate of his supporters at the hands of a potentially victorious Pompey:

> Picture the crosses, picture the chains for Caesar's side,
> this head of mine placed upon the Rostra, my limbs flung far and wide,
> crime committed in the Saepta, and battles in the closed-in Campus:
> we are waging civil war with a general of Sulla.
>
> Caesareas spectate cruces, spectate catenas,
> et caput hoc positum rostris effusaque membra
> Saeptorumque nefas et clausi proelia Campi.
> cum duce Sullano gerimus civilia bella.
>
> Luc., 7.304–307

In this case the imagined outcome is part of Caesar's battle rhetoric and serves to motivate his soldiers through fear of the consequences if they lose, as well as to put his enemy Pompey in the worst light possible by associating him with the terrors of the Sullan regime, such as the massacre on the Campus Martius (cf. 2.196–206).[38] But the passage not only recalls the image of the Roman forum littered with the mutilated corpses of proscribed citizens in the old man's tale from book 2 (2.160–173). Caesar's prediction also anticipates his own murder, although not quite in the form it was actually to happen. The counterfactual image of Caesar's beheaded and lacerated body (*et caput hoc positum rostris effusaque membra*) fuses with the fates of other men involved in his downfall, among whom the innocent Cinna, who was torn to pieces by the angry mob right after Caesar's improvised cremation on the forum (Plut., *Brut.* 20.11: διεσπάσθη).[39] The specific detail of Caesar's severed head on the rostra might even evoke an iconic image from the civil war narrative, namely that of Cicero's head and hand(s) displayed on the rostra on the orders of Antony (e.g. Livy, *Per.* 120: *caput quoque cum dextra manu in rostris positum est*; cf. Sen., *Suas.* 6.17).[40] In the subsequent books, the counterfactual image of Caesar's severed head subtly blends into the historical image of Pompey's cut-off head that was presented to Caesar at Alexandria.[41]

However, what is at stake here is not only the fate of the leaders but also the treatment of the veterans, especially the ones of the losing side, and the related topic of amnesty, which has a high political and sociological relevance in post-civil-war societies up to the present day (see Lange in this volume). The issue is explicitly addressed in the capitulation speech by the Pompeian commander Afranius, who surrenders to Caesar at Ilerda (4.344–364). He claims that he and his legion did not fight as civil war partisans (348: *non partis studiis agimur* – 'we are not driven by party enthusiasm') but only fulfilled his duty as a Roman officer; accordingly, Caesar should forgive them their capitulation (355–356: *hoc hostibus unum, / quod vincas, ignosce tuis* – 'pardon your enemies for this alone – that you are victor'). Indeed, Caesar grants them amnesty (363–364: *at Caesar facilis voltuque serenus / flectitur atque usus belli poenamque remittit* – 'but Caesar favourable and with unclouded face relents, exempting them from punishment and war-service'). The narrator praises the fate of the Pompeian veterans who return to their farms and are no longer bound by loyalty to either one of the civil war generals (4.382–401, esp. 399–401: *... sollicitus menti quod abest favor: ille salutis / est auctor, dux ille fuit. sic proelia soli / felices nullo spectant civilia voto* – 'their minds are without uneasy bias: one is the giver of their safety, one had been their leader. So they alone are happy, watching civil battles with no prayer'). Their comrades who after Pompey's death try more or less the same arguments with Cato are less fortunate (9.227–951). Their wish to lay down their arms after the death of their leader (238–239: *sub iura togati / civis eo* – 'I pass into the power of a citizen in toga') and to appeal to Caesar's amnesty (246–247: *clausa fides miseris, et toto solus in orbe est / qui velit ac possit victis praestare salutem* – 'for us losers, confidence is limited – in all the world he is the only one who could, if he would, offer safety to the conquered') is denounced by Cato as cowardly treason, and they are forced to join him on his march through the snake-infested Libyan desert. In these two corresponding scenes, contrasting responses to the issue of amnesty in a civil war are explored.

4. Conclusion

Lucan's *Bellum Civile* not only stages competing memories of the actual events, but also offers a wide range of possible aftermaths and alternatives to the historical civil war between Caesar and Pompey. Rather than being obsessed with an (anyway far too simplistic) opposition between the lost Republic and the contemporary principate that emerged from the civil wars, the epic meditates on the lasting effects of civil war in society. On the one hand it projects actual political issues from the whole series of civil wars that were fought in the first century BCE from Marius and Sulla to Antony and Octavian onto its subject matter, the civil war between Caesar and Pompey, such as the choice between a politics of revenge or of clemency. On the other hand it sketches wholly counterfactual scenarios ranging from apocalyptic catastrophes to hopeful utopias of reconciliation and fraternization that would both in contrasting ways have resulted in bringing the civil war to an end. While the most obviously counterfactual scenarios such as the end of the world usually remain limited to imaginary sketches that are not worked out on the level of the epic plot, the more realistic and at the same time more controversial political issues are developed at length in various scenes and debated in direct speeches. But notwithstanding all these possible alternative futures, in the end Lucan's bleak vision of total civil war without alternative still prevails.

Part Four

Resolving Civil War

8

Caesar and the Crisis of Corfinium

Luca Grillo
University of Notre Dame

The first book of Caesar's *Bellum Civile* (*BCiv.*) gives a selective account of his march through Italy (*BCiv.* 1.12–23)[1] and dwells heavily on the events at Corfinium (*BCiv.* 1.16–23). This detailed account, along with those of other sources (especially Appian and Cassius Dio) and of various contemporary letters (from Cicero's correspondence), provides so much information that Shackleton Bailey called the battle at Corfinium 'the best recorded episode in Roman warfare' (1956: 57).[2] Such a wealth of information puts us in a privileged position to evaluate Caesar's narrative, both in historical and in historiographical terms. Accordingly, in the first part of this contribution I will conduct a brief comparison between sources to isolate the peculiarities of Caesar's account and to assess them within the narrative of the *Bellum Civile*. In the second part, I will argue that Caesar's language alludes to two famous crises and that these allusions represent one more way to reinforce the grand ideology of his work.

1. The crisis at Corfinium: *cedant arma togae*

After crossing the Rubicon and officially starting the civil war in January 49 BCE, Caesar tried to pursue Pompey, who left Rome and headed toward Brundisium. According to the *BCiv.*, Caesar marched south until he reached Corfinium, where his enemy Lucius Domitius Ahenobarbus had found refuge (*BCiv.* 1.15.6) and had asked Pompey for support (*BCiv.* 1.17.1). Waiting for a response, Domitius makes preparations against Caesar's siege and buys the loyalty of his soldiers with promises of land (*BCiv.* 1.17.3–4). Pompey in his response refuses support (*BCiv.* 1.18.6), yet Domitius tells his soldiers that Pompey is on his way nonetheless, while secretly plotting to flee with a few friends (*BCiv.* 1.19.1–2).

But rumour goes out, the soldiers despair of Pompey's rescue and quarrel with each other (*BCiv.* 1.19.3–20.1) until they learn about Domitius' escape plan (*BCiv.* 1.20.4). They capture him, make contact with Caesar, and promise to open the gates and turn Domitius in (*BCiv.* 1.20.5). Caesar lets Domitius and the other officials go free and unharmed, he returns their money to them (*BCiv.* 1.1.22.3–4), and welcomes the soldiers into his ranks (*BCiv.* 1.22.5).

Appian's brief account closely resembles Caesar's: he confirms the siege, Domitius' failed attempt to escape and subsequent capture, and the merciful response by Caesar, who welcomes the soldiers into his ranks and lets Domitius go with the money.[3] Cassius Dio does not mention Domitius' attempt to flee, but he adds some other details: Pompey asked Domitius to leave, and he accepted, even if his promises of land had managed to buy the soldiers' favour. While he was making preparations to depart, however, his associates refused what looked like an escape and defected to Caesar, who let Domitius and the other senators go free.[4]

Both Appian and Cassius Dio hint at internal problems, but they partially disagree on their nature and neither provides much detail. Appian registers no internal *stasis*, until the locals 'captured Domitius at the gate, while he was escaping, and brought him over to Caesar' (*BCiv.* 2.38).[5] According to Cassisus Dio, however, it was Domitius' staff, 'those with him', who refused to follow his plan to flee and joined Caesar (41.11.2).[6] In a letter to Atticus, written days after the event (on 23 February), Cicero gives yet another version: 'Rumour has it that Domitius and those with him, once they got the news [that Pompey would not come to their rescue], turned themselves in to Caesar' (*Att.* 8.8.2).[7] I will return to these differences in the next section.

The crisis of Corfinium figures prominently also in other contemporary letters by Cicero, Pompey, Domitius and Caesar himself, which have survived in Cicero's exchange with Atticus. From these letters, we can reconstruct the following sequence of events. On 10 February Pompey believed that Domitius would leave Corfinium and join him (*Att.* 8.11a), but on the following day he expressed disappointment upon learning that in fact Domitius was planning to stay and he invited him to leave as soon as possible (*Att.* 8.12b). On 16 February he wrote again to urge Domitius one more time to leave Corfinium (*Att.* 8.12c.2) and restated his refusal to come to his rescue (*Att.* 8.12c.4). In the meantime, a letter from Domitius reached Pompey to request his intervention, and on 17 February Pompey replied with another refusal to march against Caesar, who had arrived, and demanded that Domitius leave at any cost and join him (*Att.* 8.12d).[8] On the following day, while writing to Atticus (on the night of 18 February), Cicero himself was informed that Caesar was just outside Corfinium, and that

Domitius was inside with a strong army, ready to fight (*Att.* 8.3.7). At this point Cicero still hoped that Pompey would join Domitius, since he did not know about Pompey's letters of refusal. While Cicero's hopes were still high on or around 18 February, Pompey had complained to the consuls Marcellus and Lentulus, blaming Domitius for the crisis at Corfinium (*Att.* 8.12a.1). On 20 February Pompey invited Cicero to leave and join him (*Att.* 8.11c). Cicero learned about Pompey's intentions and on 22 February he informed Atticus about Pompey's plan to leave both Domitius and Italy (*Att.* 8.4.4).[9] On the following day, in another letter to Atticus, Cicero expressed his disappointment at Pompey's decision and reported that 'they say that, having heard the news [that Pompey would not bring aid], Domitius and those who were with him turned themselves in' (*Att.* 8.8.2). This is the only insight from Cicero's letters about what happened *inside* Corfinium.

We can draw a few conclusions from this quick comparison between these sources.[10] Cicero and Caesar agree in presenting the outcome of the siege at Corfinium as particularly consequential, indeed Cicero even confesses to Atticus that 'I am in suspense waiting for the outcome at Corfinium, from which it will become evident if the republic can be saved' (*Att.* 8.5.2).[11] Cicero's letters and other sources also agree in presenting the Pompeians as every bit as unprepared, fearful and undecided as Caesar claims (*Att.* 8.8.1; cf. *Att.* 8.11d.1), while Caesar displays all the organization, determination and speed the Pompeians lack (*Att.* 8.9a.2).[12] Equally, all sources mention Caesar's mercy approvingly.[13] Cicero and Caesar, however, disagree on the characterization of Domitius: Cicero did not think highly of Domitius ('there is no one more stupid than Domitius', *Att.* 8.1.3, written on 15 or 16 February), but he was hopeful about his attempt to stop Caesar (cf. *Att.* 7.26.1) and never blamed him for the undesired outcome of this attempt, for which he blamed Pompey instead (8.8). Caesar, however, makes Domitius into a model of treachery and selfishness: he lies to his soldiers and attempts to flee secretly with a few friends (1.19.1), and as a result he is distrusted by his troops (1.20.5).

Caesar's longstanding animosity toward Domitius,[14] and the discrepancies between his account and the other sources suggest that here his literary embellishment, *exaedificatio*, may have affected the narrative significantly.[15] Moreover, Caesar's portrayal of Domitius perfectly fits his characterization of Pompeian leaders: an isolated but powerful group of individuals, a 'faction of a few individuals', *factio paucorum*, who are deceitful warmongers, moved by personal animosity or ambition, and hence disunited, disorganized and unprepared.[16] And in turn, this characterization of the Pompeians in the *BCiv.*

epitomizes the values that define its main players. Caesar, in contrast, is a reasonable and merciful leader, open to negotiations and more interested in sparing than killing his enemies, whom he sees as fellow citizens.[17] Borrowing some language from Cicero, one may state that Caesar presents himself as a 'proconsul wearing a toga' (as opposed to one wearing armour), a *(pro)consul togatus*, and that he uses the crisis at Corfinium to advertise his successful solution to an internal *stasis* without shedding blood. Weapons and civil strife yield to Caesar's diplomacy, according to his proclaimed ideal of *clementia*. His army is loyal and motivated, and, of course, he enjoys the support of the towns of Italy and of most of the Pompeian soldiers, who have been forced to fight against him by their crooked leaders.

According to the *BCiv.*, Caesar's dealings with other *municipia* occupied by the Pompeians follow the same pattern: Caesar arrives earlier than his enemies deemed possible, and his arrival polarizes them. As a rule, a few leaders try to stick to their opposition, while the people and the majority of the soldiers would rather side with him. Upon learning their will, Caesar makes a show of his mercy: without shedding blood, he spares and dismisses the Pompeian leaders and welcomes in his ranks the soldiers, who were already Caesarian at heart. Repetition of formulaic language designs a pattern, which exemplifies Caesar's characterization of himself, his soldiers and his enemies (Grillo 2012: 134–6). Thus Caesar's *exaedificatio*, which is particularly evident in his characterization of Domitius, contributes to shaping a uniform narrative about the Pompeian leaders, whose base motifs and evident failures are opposed to Caesar's noble ideals and successful policies.

2. A literary allusion to a famous narrative of crisis

As noted above, other sources also differ from Caesar on the account of the *stasis* that took place within the walls of Corfinium. Cicero does not mention any disunity between Domitius, his soldiers and the inhabitants of Corfinium, but focuses on the relation between him and Pompey. Similarly, Appian does not dwell on the internal crisis, but simply states that the inhabitants capture Domitius at the gates and turn him over to Caesar, who spares him and lets him go with his money (2.38). Dio Cassius stresses Domitius' willingness to obey Pompey and evacuate (41.11.1), but this plan displeases his associates and they turn to Caesar, who welcomes them and lets the rest go unharmed (41.11.2–12.1). Thus, a comparison with other sources does not allow us to assess accurately the scope and degree of Caesar's *exaedificatio* of the internal crisis, but it does throw into relief his choice to dwell on it.

Caesar opens the description of the internal strife by stating that 'early in the evening, the soldiers who were at Corfinium rebelled' (*milites qui erant Corfini prima vespera secessionem faciunt*, *BCiv.* 1.20.1). This language is charged. The soldiers' withdrawal and refusal to obey their commander's orders amounts to nothing less than a mutiny, and Cynthia Damon rightly translates 'the soldiers at Corfinium became mutinous' (Loeb 2016). And yet, Caesar does not use *seditio*, the normal word for mutiny, but *secessio*. *Secessio* is a rare noun, which scores only two other occurrences in the *BCiv.*, and is nowhere else used in the entire *corpus Caesarianum*; in the *BCiv.*, it indicates a secession by the plebs in the middle of civil strife. In particular, the first occurrence of *secessio* refers to an unidentified episode in Roman history, when plebeians were fighting for their rights and retired to occupied temples and heights (*BCiv.* 1.7.5).[18] Having withdrawn, the (mutinous) soldiers at Corfinium talk about abandoning Domitius, but the Marsi disagree, *dissentire incipiunt*, and, significantly, the first thing they do in their disagreement is to occupy the best fortified position in town (*ab his primo Marsi dissentire incipiunt eamque oppidi partem quae munitissima videretur occupant*, *BCiv.* 1.20.3). The situation is at risk of degenerating, the disagreement seems irreconcilable, and the soldiers try to fight it out, 'such was the difference in opinion among them that they tried to engage and fight with arms' (*tantaque inter eos dissensio existit ut manum conserere atque armis dimicare conentur*, *BCiv.* 1.20.3). Caesar's choice of *dissentire* and *dissensio* continues to present the disagreement among soldiers as a civil strife: indeed, *dissensio* occurs only three other times in the *BCiv.* and always means 'civil war'.[19] Caesar's insistence on the vocabulary of *stasis* is remarkable for at least two more reasons: surprisingly, this vocabulary is rare in the *BCiv.*, as Caesar tends to avoid words directly indicating civil war; and Caesar excelled in *elegantia*, that is, the willingness and ability to choose the proper words.[20]

I would argue that, in describing the mutiny at Corfinium as *stasis*, Caesar follows the model of Thucydides' famous description of the crisis at Corcyra.[21] *Mutatis mutandis*, each crisis takes place in a similar context: two parties are at odds, democrats versus oligarchs in Thucydides, and the people and soldiers versus the 'faction of a few individuals', *factio paucorum*, or 'very few close friends', *perpauci familiares*, in Caesar (*BCiv.* 3.70, 1.19.2). Both in Thucydides and in Caesar, either faction enjoys external support: at Corcyra, the democrats look to the Athenians, while the oligarchs look to the Corinthians, and at Corfinium, soldiers and people look to Caesar, while the officials in charge look to Pompey; for all these parties, however, contact with the outside supporters is far from smooth. They clash, and one side takes the upper part of the city (*BCiv.* 1.20.3); in Thucydides, the oligarchs seem to win and summon an assembly (3.71.1 and 1.20.3), but their attempt to reconcile the other party fails; and similarly, in Caesar, the *factio paucorum* fails to reconcile the people, who reunite only to oppose Domitius (1.20.4–5).

From this point on, however, the two narratives part ways: the situation disastrously degenerates at Corcyra, but at Corfinium Caesar succeeds in putting an end to the *stasis* and avoiding disaster.[22] In his words, he intervenes 'in order to set himself and the Roman people free, who were oppressed by a faction of a few individuals' (*ut se et populum Romanum factione paucorum oppressum in libertatem vindicaret*, *BCiv.* 22.5).[23] Caesar's choice of the pointed and rare vocabulary of internal strife highlights the similarity.

After the description of the events at Corcyra, Thucydides suspends his narrative for two chapters to provide a general reflection on the nature of *stasis*: his analysis encapsulates many motifs found also in Caesar. Specific textual echoes are rare, but Thucydides offered Caesar a model and various topoi that could be conveniently redeployed.[24] Thucydides writes that this *stasis* was most savage and had a domino effect in all other states (3.82); and Caesar equally presents Corfinium as a model, within his march through Italy and within the *BCiv.* as a whole. For instance, in Book 2 Curio reminds his soldiers of the events at Corfinium as a touchstone (*BCiv.* 2.32); and internal references in Book 3 invite the readers to recognize the same model in the serial surrenders of Greek towns, where Caesar cures internal divisions, preventing the tragedy of *stasis*. Precisely in the context of Caesar's march through Greece, where many towns welcome him, *factio* occurs for the second and last time in the *BCiv.*[25]

Thucydides also specifies the causes and characteristics of *stasis*: 'the cause of all these evils was the desire to rule which greed and ambition inspire'; and 'while they pretended to be devoted to the common weal, in reality they made it their prize' (3.82.8, trans. Smith, Loeb). As a result, no one can remain neutral, 'the citizens in the middle were continually destroyed by either party', and people forge party associations, which 'are not entered into for the public good in conformity with the prescribed laws, but for selfish aggrandizement contrary to the established laws' (3.82.6).

To be sure, motifs of degeneration are not limited to the episode of Corfinium, but they apply particularly well to Domitius: it was Domitius who was assigned the province of Gaul 'without any regard for the law or correct procedure' (*BCiv.* 1.65), and Caesar's comment that 'all divine and human things are turned upside-down' (*omnia divina humanaque iura permiscentur*, *BCiv.* 1.6.8) recalls Thucydides' statement that *stasis* also means breaking oaths and every law: 'their pledges to one another were confirmed not so much by divine law as by common transgression of the law' (3.82.7; cf. Cic., *Sest.* 1.3). Further, according to the *BCiv.*, it was Domitius who at Pharsalus quarrelled with Lentulus and Scipio over taking Caesar's priesthood (*BCiv.* 3.83.1). It was also Domitius who, on the same occasion, suggested taking action against those who remained neutral (*BCiv.* 3.83.3), and this suggestion resembles Thucydides' statement that in *stasis* neutrality is not an option: 'neutral citizens died killed by both factions, either because they did not get involved or because they elicited hatred by evading death' (3.82.8). Caesar concludes 'in short everyone was concerned with offices for themselves' (*BCiv.* 3.83.4). Thus, throughout the *BCiv.* Caesar characterizes Domitius as a quintessential representative of leaders' behaviour in situations of *stasis*.

However, the most prominent feature of Domitius' conduct at Corfinium in *BCiv.* is his proclivity for lies and deceit, a proclivity not found in other sources,[26] but which in Caesar's account produces suspicion and mistrust:

> After reading the letter through, Domitius, concealing (*dissimulans*) its content, announced to his war council that Pompey would come quickly to their support. He urged them not to lose heart, and to prepare whatever would be useful for the city's defense. 2. He himself spoke secretly with a few friends and decided to plan an escape (*arcano cum paucis familiaribus suis*). 3. But Domitius' face did not fit his words (*vultus Domiti cum oratione non consentiret*) and his whole behavior was more fearful and timid than had been his habit in days past. Plus, his advice-taking conversations with friends were held in secret (*secreto*), contrary to custom, and he avoided meetings and crowds (*concilia conventusque hominum fugeret*). So the matter could not be covered up (*tegi*) and concealed any longer.
>
> *BCiv.* 19.1-3, Trans. Damon, Loeb.

The vocabulary insists on Domitius' falsity and secrecy: expressions like 'concealing', 'Domitius' face did not fit his words' and 'conceal' repetitively assert his deceitfulness; and equally repetitive language proclaims his vain attempt at concealment, 'in secret with few of his friends', 'in secret', 'he avoided meetings and crowds' and 'cover up'. These details, which no other source mentions, follow the protocol set by Thucydides: in *stasis* lying and deceit rule: 'the ordinary acceptance of words in their relation to things was changed as men thought fit' (3.82.4), and as a result, no one trusts anyone; even the stronger 'were rather disposed to take precautions against being wronged than able to trust others' (3.82.3).[27]

In conclusion, a comparison with other sources demonstrates that Caesar offers his account of events at Corfinium and magnifies the treachery of Domitius and the disunity it causes. Specifically, his portrayal of Domitius seems to owe much to his personal animosity, and his description of the *stasis* it generates redeploys some topoi and language from Thucydides.

By emphatically using language typical of civil strife and by evoking the spectrum of Corcyra, Caesar sets the stage for a quintessential situation of *stasis*: two armed factions remain at odds within the same community, each is supported by powerful external allies, and internal tension increases, along with treachery and concealment. Unsurprisingly, the tension escalates toward an open fight, in Caesar's words: 'so strong was the difference of opinion among the soldiers that they tried to engage and fight it out' (*BCiv.* 1.20.3). But surprisingly, the *dissensio*, which so closely points toward a *stasis* does not degenerate. Caesar's presence and everybody's distrust toward Domitius solve it, and the language dramatically emphasizes the difference: in a few lines the *tanta dissensio* evaporates, and 'so all, of one mind, surrender Domitius who was brought into the open' (*itaque omnes uno consilio Domitium productum circumsistunt, BCiv.* 1.20.5). Caesar's presence offers a better alternative and transforms Domitius from the cause of *stasis* to its end.

Once again, the vocabulary is charged: *omnes, uno consilio* and *circumsistunt* feature the mental and physical reunification of the soldiers. Specifically, *omnes* underscores the reunification between the Marsians and the other soldiers (*ab his . . . Marsi, BCiv.* 1.20.3); *uno consilio* directly opposes *dissentire* and *dissensio* (*dissentire incipiunt* and *tantaque inter eos dissensio exstitit, BCiv.* 1.20.3); and *circumsistunt* illustrates the reunification which brings an end to the division between parties (*inter se, BCiv.* 1.20.1, *inter eos, BCiv.* 1.20.3). Remarkably, two compounds from the same verb, *sisto*, highlight the complete transformation, from *dissensio exstitit* to *circumsistunt*, and give one more sign of Caesar's *elegantia*. From this point onwards, the soldiers and the people of Corfinium act in concert and together seek to make contact and to side with Caesar: 'they sent envoys from their ranks to Caesar, to inform him that they were ready to open the gates and follow his orders' (*legatos ex suo numero ad Caesarem mittunt: sese paratos esse portas aperire quaeque imperaverit facere, BCiv.* 1.20.5).

In other words, a comparison with other sources and Caesar's vocabulary (e.g. *secessio, dissentio* and *dissentire*) highlights his choice to describe the crisis at Corfinium as a potential *stasis*. Some references to motifs immortalized by Thucydides in his famous description of the events at Corcyra further contribute to Caesar's depiction of an essential situation of *stasis*. And yet, once the elements are all in place, once the *stasis* is ready to explode with Thucydidean violence, the divisions between parties are healed, which leads to a completely reversed situation of harmony. Thus, Thucydides helps Caesar to describe the crisis of

Corfinium as a non-*stasis*, a *stasis* manqué. As Caesar offers a peaceful alternative to the expected explosion, he crowns himself Mr After-the-Crisis.

Given that the dates of composition and publication of the *BCiv.* remain uncertain,[28] we can only speculate on the target audience and reception of Caesar's self-portrayal as a quintessential peace-maker and crisis-solver. Whichever the date of publication, Cicero's letters leave no doubt that Caesar's clemency, both during and after the civil war, appealed to his contemporaries: indeed, his mild attitude toward the Pompeians won him more approval and supporters than Pompey's threats and cruelty toward the Caesarians (cf. e.g. *Att.* 7.7 and 7.11).[29] And even after the civil war, Cicero would lavish praises on Caesar's *clementia* (e.g. *Marcell.* 7–8 and *Lig.* 15).

Similarly, we can only speculate on a readership's capability to see Caesar's allusions to Thucydides and to the Social War: admittedly, many missed them. And yet, I remain convinced that at least some Roman readers were able to appreciate them, especially given that their training in rhetoric was heavily based on imitation of Greek and Roman models and that Thucydides was undoubtedly part of the 'canon'. Perhaps, different readers managed to afford rather different levels of engagement with this rich text (not unlike today); and perhaps, Caesar's realistic sense of his multi-layered audience invited him to broadcast the same message through multiple media, in an attempt to reach as broad an audience as possible. For instance, in March 49 BCE, Caesar wrote a letter to Cicero about his 'new way of winning' (*nova ratio vincendi*, *Att.* 9.7c.1), which confirms his self-representation in the *BCiv.*; in 45 BCE the (Caesarian) Senate announced the construction of a temple to the *Clementia Caesaris*;[30] and the following year, Sepullius Macer, one of his followers (*RCC* 480.21), minted a coin with a sketch of the temple encircled by the inscription CLEMENTIAE CAESARIS. In other words, letters (*Att.* 9.7b and 9.7c), coins, monuments and the *BCiv.*, just to mention some examples, come together to advertise the same image: Caesar's campaign thus witnesses his intention (and anxiety?) to construct a desired narrative of the civil war; to use Hayden White's terminology, his 'emplotment' displays a strikingly consistent message through strikingly different media, in an attempt to frame the crisis in his own terms.[31]

3. A historical allusion to a famous civil crisis

Corfinium was not a neutral location. In the Roman imagination, it recalled the Social War; indeed the allies who rebelled from Rome located the capital of their resistance nowhere else than in Corfinium, which they renamed Italica. In Corfinium they instituted a federal assembly of the various communities, represented by a senate of 500 people, and in Corfinium they kept their treasure, minted coins and elected their annual magistrates, two consuls and twelve praetors. As a result, in Corfinium the resistance to Rome proved particularly stubborn, and once the Romans managed to take it, in the summer of 89, the war in northern and central Italy was practically over.[32] Caesar and Pompey may have retained personal recollections of Corfinium and the Social War, also because of the direct involvement of members from their families: both Gaius Marius, Caesar's uncle, and Pompeius Strabo, Pompey's father, led Roman troops in the area around Corfinium.[33]

I contend that the evocative power of Corfinium and Caesar's choice to cast the crisis and the soldiers' rebellion as a *stasis* produce an allusion to the Social War. As noted above, Caesar includes details that are absent in the other sources: just as the allies did in the Social War, the mutinous soldiers maintain a well-organized and well-defined structure to communicate with various parties within the town. The first effect of their *secessio* is that they find intermediaries and confer successfully and in an orderly manner. They function like separate states within the walls: 'they rebelled and communicated among each other thus, through military tribunes, centurions and the highest-ranking members of the staff' (*secessionem faciunt atque ita inter se per tribunos militum centurionesque atque honestissimos sui generis colloquuntur, BCiv.* 1.20.1; cf. 'after messengers were sent back and forth', *internuntiis ultro citroque missis, BCiv.* 1.20.4). Moreover, these soldiers withdraw for the same reason and with the same goal that lead the allies to rebel: having been let down by their Roman leadership, they realize that they need to look after themselves ('hope and confidence in our leader Domitius kept us here, but he has forsaken us all and planned his escape. We ought to consider our own welfare', *ducem suum Domitium, cuius spe atque fiducia permanserint, proiectis omnibus fugae consilium capere; debere se suae salutis rationem habere, BCiv.* 1.20.2).

Along with the location of the *secessio*, the similarity of some details in the context of internal strife evokes the spectrum of the Social War. In Caesar's narrative, the first rupture comes from a group of soldiers, the Marsi. Caesar almost never identifies Italian soldiers by their native region, and this exception made for the Marsi marks another meaningful choice.[34] During the Social War, the Marsi had been among the most active peoples opposing Rome: one of the two supreme commanders of the allied forces was the Marsian Poppaedius Silo; the Marsi blocked a Roman army along the *Via Valeria* on its way to Corfinium;

and the Romans managed to take Corfinium, only after defeating the Marsi (Gabba 1994: 124). In short, Caesar chooses to provide many details which are absent from other sources: Marsian soldiers oppose Domitius, a former consul and Roman general, and they give themselves a typically Roman organization, with military tribunes, centurions and most highly regarded staff (*tribuni militum, centuriones* and *honestissimi sui generis*); these details and his language come together and call to mind the Social War.

Before drawing some conclusions, I wish to discuss two implications triggered by these allusions to the Social War. Thanks to these references, Caesar rewrites history and stages the specific episode of the crisis at Corfinium within a broader and more universal context. In this broader context of the Social War, his peaceful solution to a potential *stasis* becomes a universal model for how best to defuse an internal crisis. The position of the episode of Corfinium within the structure of Book 1 enhances this universal claim, in several ways. Corfinium represents the apex of Caesar's mercy in his march through Italy (1.12–24); and formulaic language stresses the repeatability of his peaceful solution to conflict. Moreover, the sequence of his successes during his march presents a general test for his solution of the crisis in Spain, at Ilerda, which concludes Book one. At Ilerda, just like at Corfinium, the Pompeian leaders try to act secretively (*BCiv.* 1.19 and 1.84.1), the soldiers fight against their will (e.g. *BCiv.* 1.20 and 1.86) and show themselves reluctant to fight Caesar (*BCiv.* 1.20.5, 1.74 and 1.87); so that the entire blame falls on a few leaders, who are also spared (*BCiv.* 1.23 and 1.85.3). Here also Caesar displays incredible generosity with money (*BCiv.* 1.23.4 and 1.87.1) and takes care to protect the Pompeian soldiers after their surrender (1.21.2–6, 1.23.3 and 1.86.4). Lastly, both at Corfinium and at Ilerda Caesar gives a speech to restate his policy of mercy (*BCiv.* 1.22.5 and 1.85), to explain how he had been wronged (*BCiv.* 1.22.5, 1.85.5–10), and to argue that he had been forced to undertake a civil war against his will (*BCiv.* 1.22.5 and 1.85.2). Thus, the model of Corfinium provides both a memorable example of Caesar's peaceful march through Italy and a blueprint for the conclusion of Book 1. In turn, this conclusion offers a blueprint for the best way to conclude the entire civil war, according to the *BCiv.*[35]

The references to the Social War, however, carry also a second implication. The Social War put an end to the rebellion of the allies, but it did not eradicate the debate about granting Roman rights and privileges. In fact, the debate turned particularly hot at the opening of the civil war, and the disagreement represented one more way to divide Caesar from his opponents: throughout his career Caesar promoted an ongoing effort to enfranchise Italians by passing laws, founding colonies and by inviting members of the Italian aristocracy to be part of his staff.[36] This effort, however, had been challenged just before the beginning of the civil war. In 51 BCE, after Caesar had established the new Roman colony of Novum Comum (in Cisalpine Gaul), M. Marcellus, who was then consul, arranged a public flogging of one of its citizens. Roman citizens could not be flogged, and there is no doubt that Marcellus meant to express his disregard for the legitimacy of Caesar's foundation and, accordingly, he orchestrated the public punishment 'in order to insult Caesar' (App., *B Civ.* 2.26).[37] Marcellus went as far as inviting the man to show his scars to Caesar (cf. Gruen 1974: 461) and suggesting that the new colonists at Novum Comum be deprived of the Roman citizenship they had just been granted. Remarkably, at the beginning of the *BCiv.*, the same Marcellus who flogged a Roman colonist from Novum Comum declares in the Senate that 'levies should be held throughout Italy and armies summoned' (*BCiv.* 1.2.2). At Corfinium, however, those who had been levied and summoned by the Pompeians defect to Caesar: accordingly, at Corfinium Caesar reaps the fruit of his assimilating attitude toward provincials, and the Pompeians reap the fruit of their policies too.[38]

In other words, Caesar casts his solution of the crisis at Corfinium as a successful assimilation of Marsian soldiers, who break away from the deceitful command of Domitius and peacefully rejoin other soldiers and the Corfinians: the reference to the Social War, and, by implication, to the then contentious debate about granting Roman citizenship to Italians weaves various threads into a single narrative. This narrative coheres both with Caesar's policy of enfranchising allies and with the ideology of the *BCiv.*, perhaps hinting at his successful foresight.

In short, Caesar broadcast the same message through various means: personal letters, the *Bellum Civile*, coins and monuments come together to tell the same story, and this story strives to write the crisis' plot and to define its beginning, nature and end. Equally, the multiple layers of allusions which I tried to tease out display a variety of echoes, but these echoes work toward the same coherent narrative. The references to a long past episode from Greek history, as immortalized by Thucydides, resuscitate the spectrum of *stasis* to advertise Caesar's success in avoiding it, and Caesar avoided it precisely when it seemed unavoidable. The references to a much closer episode from Roman history create one more way to tell the same story: Caesar extols his peaceful assimilation of Marsian soldiers and his peaceful solution of the crisis of Corfinium setting it against the bloody fights which took place there between Romans and Marsians during the Social War.

It must be admitted that, for all Caesar's multimedia effort and literary sophistication in the *BCiv.*, his emplotment was only partially successful: his version of the civil war, with its specific beginning and conclusion of the crisis, did not go unchallenged. The suicide of Cato argued that what Caesar had called 'mercy' was in fact 'enslavement', that this 'mercy' was only *one* way to frame and 'solve' the crisis and that this way could and should be resisted and refused. Accordingly, some beneficiaries of his *clementia* followed suit and murdered him. In styling themselves 'liberators' they put forth a competing emplotment, which contested Caesar's narrative, reinterpreting his policies as the core rather than the end of the crisis. According to their emplotment, then, the end of the crisis coincided with Caesar's death, not with his victory and mercy. Or were they parricides, who killed their saviour, undoing Caesar's successful solution and thus precipitating the state back into another crisis?[39] In 46 BCE, that is, between various deeds of Caesar's mercy and his death, Cicero famously predicted 'a civil war' of emplotments (*magna dissensio, Marcell.* 29) dividing future generations and their assessment of Caesar: 'some will praise your achievements to the stars, but some perhaps will find that something is lacking' (*alii laudibus ad caelum res tuas gestas efferent, alii fortasse aliquid requirent, Marcell.* 29). More than two thousand years of reception demonstrate that this *dissensio* remains open: both Brutus' and Caesar's emplotment, to mention two, still enjoy supporters.[40]

4. Conclusions

In a letter to Atticus, Cicero voices some contemporaries' worst suspicions: Pompey may have abandoned Domitius and Corfinium intentionally and cynically, hoping that a slaughter by Caesar would cause such an uproar in public opinion that those who were still lukewarm would finally make up their mind and oppose Caesar actively (*Att.* 8.9a.1). Regardless of Pompey's intention, Caesar did not take the bait; on the contrary, he transformed Corfinium into a spectacular chance to advertise the defining traits of the two competing sides. According to his ideal of mercy and his proclaimed attempt to prevent a civil war, Caesar solves the crisis and avoids a disaster. His literary genius helps him to make the most of the occasion: in his narrative, the crisis at Corfinium represents the culminating point of his march through Italy, an archetype of his values and of his enemies' shortcomings, and an appealing model which formulaic language presents as repeatable and hence a touchstone throughout the *BCiv.*

The episode of Corfinium, however, demonstrates Caesar's literary genius also thanks to two allusions triggered by his language of *stasis*. Caesar borrows some Thucydidean motifs and reshapes them into his narrative to fit his specific purpose.[41] By weaving his narrative in Thucydidean terms, Caesar also plugs into the tradition of Greek thought which considered forgetfulness and 'forgiveness' as the best means to interrupt the bloody chain of *stasis*.[42] Thus, Caesar, tells the story of the non-*stasis* at Corfinium; and rather than portraying himself as a reluctant player in a *stasis* he wanted to avoid, he locates himself just outside it: in his account, Domitius is the cause, and he is the solution to the internal strife that rules among his opponents and that threatens to take over the Republic.

Caesar's decision to detail the internal events at Corfinium and his selection of vocabulary of civil dissension, rather than of mutiny, call to mind also the Social War. The setting at Corfinium, the allusions to the *stasis* caused by Domitius and the Marsi's armed *dissensio* sort at least two effects: they contribute to remap the specific episode of Corfinium within the larger framework of the Social War, thus magnifying both the potential extent of the crisis and of Caesar's unexpected solution. And in turn, this unexpected solution exemplifies some challenges that Caesar met throughout his career, demonstrating the foresight of his attitude toward assimilating provincials.

9

Young Caesar and the Termination of Civil War (31–27 BCE)

Carsten Hjort Lange
Aalborg University

Peace has all but disappeared from political discourse today; war is accepted as the normal condition (Bacevich 2016: 37). This was also the case for the Romans, whose success as conquerors inspired Polybius to write his history: we are reminded of Polybius' famous assessment that the Romans used violent force for all purposes (1.37.7). But how did the Romans respond to the proliferation of civil discord between their own citizens? I have recently argued that this and similar questions challenge the modern perception of civil conflict as an anomaly or aberration, and force us to consider the extent to which civil war became a 'normal' feature – in as much as civil war in some ways assumed the role formerly performed by foreign wars – of Roman political and social life. Civil war was long part of the Late Republican reality. Given the permeating influence of decades of civil conflict upon Republican political and societal culture, civil war could become 'normal' (Lange 2016). The language of foreign and civil war was similar, also because the civil war period used a language echoing that used in foreign wars.[1]

In (civil) war justification is essential, but this was only ever part of the equation. For a 'peace' settlement to work more is needed: that is, 'phase IV' operations (Crane 2005), activities conducted after combat in order to stabilize and reconstruct the former arena of war. For our purposes here, the 'phase IV' operations implemented by Augustus after his victory against Antonius and Cleopatra pose especially rich questions, and they will be the topic of this article. My focus is consequently less on the winning of wars, and more on the winning of the peace: in modern terms, this can include the restoration of administration and the political system, the organization of security measures, and the demobilization or neutralization of guerrilla groups (Crane 2005).

A large proportion of modern wars are in fact civil wars and their most likely legacy is renewed civil war (Armitage 2017: 6). Or put differently, the first answer to the question of how civil wars are brought to an end is that they are often not. In view of this truth, then, the question of precisely which civil war was ended by Augustus in the period between 31 and 27 BCE seems a legitimate one. In conceptualizing the civil wars of the Late Republic, it may be helpful to approach the war from roughly 91/88 to 29 BCE as one continuous war, preceded by flash points of strife in domestic politics and warning-signals from 133 BCE onwards.[2] Accordingly – to use the phrase coined recently by Holguin – the civil war itself is in fact a bag of several wars (Holguin 2015: 1770), including in this case the war against the *Socii* (see now mainly Dart (2014); Tac., *Hist.* 1.2 describes civil war as hybrid war). To approach the civil wars of the Late Republic as a single conflict emphatically means thinking about civil war as something beyond big battles. Essentially, the end of civil war only came with the accomplishment of the triumviral assignment, viz. the ending of a civil war and constituting of the *res publica* (Lange 2009). Augustus even went one further, at least when writing the *Res Gestae*: he suggests at chapter 34.1 not only that the civil wars had ended, but had in fact been *made extinct* (*in consulatu sexto et septimo, postqua[m b]el[la civil]ia exstinxeram* ('in my sixth and seventh consulship, after I had put an end to civil wars'). Note that civil war is in the plural here: this was a necessity, since Young Caesar had claimed that they had been ended already in 36 BCE (see below), and later reignited by Antonius when he aided Cleopatra.

Approaching war and civil war will always be like walking a tightrope. If we take our cue from modern ancient historians, then at least three different approaches are possible, recently sketched by Börm (2018: 56–7) in relation to Greek *stasis* but clearly identifiable in the Roman civil war context too. Firstly, *stasis* or civil war as a by-product of interstate war; secondly, class struggle as represented in economic inequality and social tensions; and finally, civil war as a product of power struggles among the elite (cf. Gehrke 1985). This third possibility will be the focus of this article – and, as we will see in greater detail later, approaching the Roman civil wars through the lens of elite power struggles also reflects modern approaches to internecine conflict.

As I have already mentioned, the Romans always expected warfare, expansion and victory; but they also expected the civil war to end. *Pax* is naturally related to the end of civil war (Lange 2009; Ginsberg 2017: 64–75; Cornwell 2017), but it must also be remembered in relation to victory. True Roman peace was not pacifism; rather, it was peace after victory in war (*RG* 13: *terra marique es]set parta victoriis pax*, 'when peace had been achieved by victories on land and sea', trans. Cooley 2009). Augustus' advertisement of his 'Peace' may seem a novel message in view of Roman militarism and imperialism, but Augustus' *pax* necessarily equated to Roman conquest. External peace meant Roman victory in war, and internal peace meant the end of civil war, the end of internecine conflict, and the resumption of Rome's capacity to successfully wage external war. 'Peace' simply sounds better than victory after a civil war (Lange 2009: 11).[3] *Pax* was thus part of the justification and self-stylization of Young Caesar, but we should not doubt that the ending of civil war was the actual task at hand. This article consequently examines potential approaches to Roman history from Actium to the Settlement of 28–27 BCE, defining the period from 31 to 27 BCE as a process of normalization in the wake of civil war; a transitional period from Republic to Principate, no less.

1. Approaching civil war

The language adopted by modern theoretical approaches enables us to form and articulate wholly new questions for evidence already well known to us. As historians we are traditionally conscious of the uniqueness of historical events, but war – civil as well as external – is nonetheless a repetitive and distinct form of human behaviour. While the manner in which wars are fought changes, the nature of war itself does not (Howard 1962: 6). In the Late Republic as well as during the Later Roman Empire, civil war was the dominant form of war. It has been a constant occurrence in Europe ever since, and these civil wars all include factional conflicts.[4] This article thus proposes to use certain modern approaches in order to rethink the nature of civil war, and thereby raise fundamental questions regarding ancient civil wars. Accordingly this article is concerned as much with the ways in which we approach and conceive of civil war as with the phenomenon of civil war itself.

Approaches to modern civil war are numerous. Firstly, there is the process of conclusion. Civil wars are hard to end: the average duration since 1945 has been 10 years (Fearon 2007).[5] Hartzell (2016: 122) soberly emphasizes that all civil wars end with a settlement of some kind. During the Cold War period the majority of civil wars ended via military victory, but this has now changed in favour of negotiated settlements (125). Then there is the aftermath. Regardless of whether civil war ends with a peace settlement or a decisive military victory, there is always the question of who gets what and when they get it, as recent work by Kathman and Shannon (2016: 113) and Hartzell (2016: 125: 'Who gets what and when') has raised. A large part of that aftermath moreover concerns what to do with rebel leaders and forces. One way of replacing and replicating the power of those leaders and securing a durable peace is to establish institutions which enforce the balanced distribution and practical cooperation of powers (Hartzell 2016: 125).

There is no need to claim that civil wars today and in the ancient world are exactly the same. But there are fundamental structures which repeat themselves throughout history – chief among them the actual process of 'winning the peace'. One possible approach we might deploy in seeking to better understand the civil wars of the Late Republic is to make a straightforward comparison between the phenomenon in the ancient and modern worlds. In identifying the trends shared by both contexts, we may move beyond the 'local'—that is, context-specific factors— and consider broader questions about the nature of civil war in general (cf. Scheidel 2015: 3–4). The recent analysis put forward by Blair in connection with the American Civil War (Blair 2015) may help to provide that, and some of the analysis below is informed by his approach. It is not my intention to compare straightforwardly the American Civil War with that of Rome in the Late Republic – although they do have some things in common – but the questions Blair poses are highly relevant for Rome during the Late Republic. These and similar approaches serve to reflect on the issue of civil war and how we as scholars approach and perceive it. These questions relate to generic features in civil war, as exemplified by Thucydides' description of the *stasis* at Corcyra (see esp. Thuc., 3.81–85; cf. Lange 2017).

First, however, a focus on the wider context of the last phase of the Late Republican civil war is in order. At Bononia in October 43 BCE the triumvirs set out to constitute the *res publica* and to set the state to rights, including the ending of the civil war and punishment of the assassins of Caesar.[6] This assignment was completed at Philippi; as a result, further justifications were needed in order for the triumvirs to justify the retention of their powers beyond their assignment. Consequently the settlement of Brundisium extended the triumvirs' assignment: the new task given to Young Caesar was to deal with Sextus Pompeius and thus to conclude the civil war.[7] Appian (*B Civ.* 5.65) refers to the task of eliminating Sextus Pompeius: 'Young Caesar was to make war against Pompeius unless they should come to some arrangement, and Antonius was to make war against the Parthians to avenge their treachery toward Crassus' (πολεμεῖν δὲ Πομπηίῳ μὲν Καίσαρα, εἰ μή τι συμβαίνοι, Παρθυαίοις δὲ Ἀντώνιον, ἀμυνόμενον τῆς ἐς Κράσσον παρασπονδήσεως).[8]

After the war in 36 BCE against Sextus Pompeius, Young Caesar was given an honorific column on the Forum, with *rostra*, a golden statue, and an inscription:

'Peace, long disrupted by civil war, he restored on land and sea' (App., *B Civ.* 5.130; cf. 5.132; Cass. Dio, 49.15.3): τὴν εἰρήνην ἐστασιασμένην ἐκ πολλοῦ συνέστησε κατά τε γῆν καὶ θάλασσαν). The enemy is left unmentioned (Lange 2016: esp. 119; cf. 125–53), because mentioning a Roman enemy would have been in clear breach of triumphal conventions. In principle, no triumph should be awarded after a civil war. Instead an ovation was given to Young Caesar *ex Sicilia* – conveniently solving the discrepancy.[9] At the same time Young Caesar wanted to claim to have accomplished the triumviral assignment, including the ending of the civil war. This way, by saying very little about the actual enemy, he could claim both: as restorer of *pax* after civil war and *triumphator ex Sicilia*, Young Caesar successfully created two separate and distinct, but not mutually exclusive, narratives.

This was not, however, the end of the civil war: it was later reignited by Antonius when he aided Cleopatra. The triumvirs could not keep a lasting peace, and in 32 BCE Young Caesar and the Senate in Rome declared war on Cleopatra. Cassius Dio underscores the official narrative of the Augustan regime when he states that the war was declared against Cleopatra, but was in reality against Antonius (50.4.5). Helping her, Antonius began a new phase of the civil war, which was finally brought to an end in 31/30 BCE. Antonius was deprived of all of his powers and of the consulship, which he was due to hold in 31 BCE (Cass. Dio, 50.4.3; Plut., *Ant.* 60). Antonius was now a *privatus*; and if he were to take up arms against Young Caesar and the *res publica*, he would declare war on the state and thus declare himself a *hostis*. This last phase of the civil war was finally brought to an end in 30 BCE, followed by the triple triumph in 29 BCE. Traditionally, the ultimate proof of the ending of the war and pacification of the enemy territory was the capture of the enemy leaders and their humiliating parade through Rome in their captor's triumph. At Actium however, there is no enemy. Through this lens, as I have written elsewhere, it is possible to see Actium as the latter phase in both a foreign and a civil war (Lange 2009; 2016). The triumviral assignment, including the issue of the ending of the civil war, was a vital part of Young Caesar's justification from early 43 BCE onwards. Again, Young Caesar could claim to have ended the civil war, begun by his opponent (*RG* 34, etc.).

We can also consider the final phase of the civil war, ending at Alexandria following the decisive battle at Actium (Lange 2011), through the lens of approaches to modern conflict – and here we return to Blair's discussion of the American Civil War. The most common way to end a civil war is third-party intervention (Blair 2015: 1754). But of course a third-party intervention in our period was clearly out of the question. This being the case, the alternative means of ending a civil war might involve a 'permanent' settlement, agreed upon by all parties, either by means of a decisive military victory (Blair 2015: 1754), or a negotiated peace (Blair 2015: 1756).

Blair (2015: 1756) claims that a negotiated settlement was impossible in the American Civil War due to non-negotiable issues, specifically the problems of Union and slavery. The question naturally following from this is whether any such negotiated settlement would have been feasible in the Roman context. Harris has recently hit the nail on the head by emphasizing that '... if Sextus ever, after Philippi, imagined that the Republican political system could be restored (and there is no evidence to that effect) he would be dreaming' (Harris 2016: 99); *contra* Welch (2012). Alston (2015: 149) adds that there could never really be a negotiated settlement, due to the violence of the proscriptions: the triumvirs had simply killed too many people. Where does that leave us? Does it logically follow, then, that the warring groups fought principally for survival? And if nothing was non-negotiable and this was only a civil war about power, whose participant factions struggled not for the dissolution of the *res publica* but rather for dominion over it, why was there no peace settlement? Perhaps, in fact, there was – but as I shall discuss in more detail later, we may find such a settlement only if we look for it.

Carrying this idea further, in principle all warring groups naturally aim to emerge on the winning side (Christia 2012: 3). But *changing* sides at the opportune moment can mean survival, especially if there is no credible guarantee that the victor will not strip his allies of power after the victory. As some recent work has emphasized, there is no such thing as an impossible alliance (Christia 2012: 4, 149–96). The straightforward answer might be that in Rome, without third-party intervention and without a permanent settlement, the third route, i.e. of decisive military victory, was the only possible outcome. In this regard the trajectory pursued by Augustus would not be dissimilar from those of his predecessors: indeed, the earlier settlements of Sulla and Caesar among others all came after military victory and enemy defeat. The violence and personal animosities associated with civil war do of course not help this process of reconciliation either.[10]

A further question essential for understanding the feasibility of a negotiated settlement on the one hand and the relative merits of a decisive victory on the other is whether there even were any peacemakers at all. After all, the impossibility of neutrality is a theme reiterated time and again in ancient accounts of *stasis*, from Thucydides to Aristotle and Cicero to Dio.[11] Peacemaking was unlikely – or perhaps it could only come with victory, as epitomized in Caesar's famous *clementia* or Augustus' more elaborate overtures to the conquered. Still, this does not truly explain why Augustus was successful in the end.

And how to negotiate a settlement, in any case? To return to our modern example, the American Civil War ended with a discussion about whether or not there was going to be an 'unconditional surrender' (Blair 2015: 1758). In Rome, on the other hand, the practice of political and military agreement normally came after a Roman victory, in a world in which Rome's resources overshadowed most of its enemies' from the fourth century BCE onward (Harris 2016: 304). During the Late Republic the civil war can be seen assuming the role previously performed by foreign wars (Lange 2016: 9): Rome, having 'made a conquest of itself', had imposed upon itself not a negotiated settlement, but a forced settlement.

The American Civil War did not end with the 'surrenders'; violence and insurgency continued after the war proper (Blair 2015: 1761). This is equally characteristic of Roman civil war. One example will suffice. Owing to the problem of brigandage and raiding in Italy in the wake of Sextus Pompeius' defeat – a phenomenon Italy had seen before, in the aftermath of Sulla[12] – C. Calvisius Sabinus (*cos.* 39 BCE) was appointed to restore order in the Italian countryside (App., *B Civ.* 5.132; cf. Cass. Dio, 49.15.1). Violence – experienced or witnessed from a distance – during (civil) war shatters a community's sense of normality, evident in this case in the changed landscape of Italy itself and the steps necessary to repair it (Hutchison and Bleiker 2015).

The American Civil War ended at some point between 1865 and 1871, without a negotiated settlement or a third-party intervention (Blair 2015: 1765). There is every reason to assume with the ancient evidence that Actium and Alexandria could be considered as either one or two wars, depending on the context. There were two triumphs, but at times the evidence uses *bellum Actiacum* to describe the whole war, not just the Actian campaign.[13] In Virgil (*Aen.* 8.675) there is talk of *Actia bella*, the plural envisaging the whole of the campaign. Similar issues are also evident in Cassius Dio: he is inconsistent on the precise date for the return to monarchy. Dio identifies the restoration of monarchy both with the battle of Actium[14] and the settlement of 27 BCE.[15] It is a neat coincidence that in Augustan times, the triumphs in 29 BCE would also have been the symbol of the ending of war – and with it a Roman victory. Perhaps 29 BCE is the year in which the civil war finally was at an end, the new settlement logically following in 28–27 BCE.

For Augustus, marking the end of civil war was not dissimilar to a traditional foreign war: that is, by monumentalizing the occasion with a triumph or an ovation. Approached in this way, we can conceive of Augustus connecting his claim to have ended such a war at least twice, if not four times, with a triumph or triumphal celebration: Philippi, Naulochus, the joint ovation with Antonius in 40 BCE for avoiding civil war, and Actium (ovation 36, triumph 31, no triumph was given after Philippi, although not much later one was awarded to Decimus Brutus after Mutina, a civil war victory in Italy). Similarly as for a traditional foreign war these triumphs displayed that the (civil) war had ended.[16] Augustus also closed the Temple of Janus twice (decreed three times).

Josiah Osgood has recently in an impressive article focused on how Roman civil war ended: constitutional change was normally part of this process, as well as *post eventum* justifications on the part of the victorious party of what had happened and their conduct in the encounter. However, he may in spite of his solid approach be mistaken, after all, in asserting that there was no '... immediate boast that the victor had ended civil war, certainly not by Augustus' (Osgood 2015: 1690). His analysis emphasizes that there was no connection between the closing of the Temple of Janus and the ending of the civil war. But is that so?

The slogan *pace parta terra marique* ('peace obtained by land and sea') is connected by several Latin authors to Augustus' closure of the Temple of Janus as well as to his peaceful settlement after the civil war against Antonius; this is clearly reflected by Livy, who, mirroring Augustus' boast to have ended *bella terra et mari civilia externaque* (*RG* 3.1: 'wars by land and sea, civil and foreign', cf. 4.2, 13), writes of a period 'after the battle of Actium, when the emperor Caesar Augustus had brought about peace on land and sea' (Liv., 1.19: *post bellum Actiacum ab imperatore Caesare Augusto pace terra marique parta*; cf. 30.45.1; *Laudatio Turiae* 2.25; Sen., *Clem.* 1.9.4; *Apocol.* 10.2). In remarkably similar fashion, Suetonius writes that Augustus 'closed three times the temple of Janus Quirinus, which had been closed but twice before his time since the founding of the city, in a far shorter period, having won peace on land and sea' (Suet., *Aug.* 22: *Ianum Quirinum semel atque iterum a condita urbe ante memoriam suam clausum in multo breviore temporis spatio terra marique pace parta ter clusit*). The slogan *pace parta terra marique* is also used on the Victory Monument at Actium (built before 27 BCE), emphasizing that peace had been secured on land and sea. No enemy is mentioned, which in turn does point to a civil war (Lange 2016: chapter 6). Mentioning a foreign enemy would of course have been entirely unproblematic. Young Caesar did not! Most importantly, in 36 BCE, as mentioned above, after the war against Sextus Pompeius, Young Caesar was given an honorific column on the Forum Romanum, with an inscription displaying a similar slogan to that found in the *Res Gestae* (App., *B Civ.* 5.130). This most likely goes back to the laurelled letter sent by Young Caesar in 36 and again in 31 BCE to the Senate (cf. *RG* 34.1).[17] There thus seems to be ample evidence connecting the Temple of Janus and the slogan *pace parta terra marique* with civil war. We should therefore approach Osgood's contention, that Augustus made no immediate boast to have completed the civil war, with some legitimate caution.

Where Osgood is certainly correct, however, is in his interpretation of the importance of the blurred distinction between foreign and civil war as an essential component of the 29 BCE narrative (Osgood 2015: 1690). He suggests that the boast in *RG* 34.1 about ending the civil war is late (Osgood 2015: 1691), but the contemporary evidence seems to tell a different story. There are indeed two narratives used by Young Caesar during this period, one connected to triumphs, partly in response to foreign victory, in this case against Cleopatra, and one to the triumviral assignment, including the ending of the civil war.[18] Osgood concludes with the following statement: 'hostilities generally were ended only through efforts by the victor, and Roman society more broadly, to find political solutions to underlying problems and to frame communal memory and understanding of recent warfare as constructively as possible, with an eye on the present and the future' (Osgood 2015: 1695). This contention seems more broadly acceptable.

In the end, to paraphrase the recent assessment of Neufeld (2015: 1710) on the resolution of the English Civil War, the internecine struggles of the Late Republic only ended when the issues over which the Romans were willing to kill each other were resolved, and when former combatants could work together. Or perhaps the simplest answer as to why the civil war ended is to be preferred: that they had just had enough. In any case, Augustus created a new settlement, a peace settlement – that is, a settlement after civil war had ended. And it is to that which we now turn.

2. The Settlement of 28–27 BCE

The process of change between Republic and Principate is well known, albeit poorly understood.[19] We may look at the 28–27 BCE Settlement as the accomplishment of the triumviral assignment,[20] and/or as the beginning of monarchy. Augustus in *RG* 34 claims to have handed back power after the extinction of the civil war(s). Unsurprisingly, many powers were then handed back to him at once. The triumviral assignment then became the model for Augustus' retention of the powers needed to carry out the assignments presented to him by the Senate and the people (establishing peace at the borders). Fixed-term tasks became the standard way for Augustus to justify his monarchy.[21] But apart from the poorly understood continuation from triumvirate to Principate, this long-term process often makes us forget one important aspect: the Settlement was (also) about the termination of civil war, about a peace settlement – pointing to the future – after the victory of Augustus.

Ando has accurately described the nature of public power under Augustus: regular terms of service and taxes used to pay salaries and discharge bonuses, all resulting in a hiatus between periods of military service and a 'performance of citizenship', as well as a separation between the soldiery and the individual commander; in other words 'the performance of citizenship, effectively transforming the soldiery into a servant of the state' (Ando 2008: 44). The result may not quite have been a state monopoly on violence, as Ando claims, writing of 'the state's monopoly on legitimate violence' (43) – whether legitimate or not – but a *containment* of violence certainly did ensue: the *lex Iulia de vi publica*, either Caesarian or Augustan in origin, even forbade men to collect and use arms at home except for hunting and on journeys (*Dig.* 49.6.1). There is however another aspect to this return to normality after the end of hostilities: the reintegration of enemy forces (see below). In modern scholarship the term *DDR* is used: Disarmament, Demobilisation and Reintegration (Berdal and Ucko 2009: 2). An infamous example – showing how it is not to be done – is the *CPA Order* 2, 2003, dissolving most of Iraq's security related structures (Ucko 2009: 90, 109).

The major weakness of the Roman state during the Late Republic explains the Settlement of 28–27 BCE: as I have already mentioned, Augustus retained his military might. The promise of securing the provinces from internal as well as external enemies justified the division of the provinces and enabled Augustus to retain most of the legions under his command. A recurring issue during civil war periods is low legitimacy, when state actors do not have the capacity to overcome challenges. State failure seems a fitting description of the Late Republic: dynasts and factions became the source of security and Late Republican Rome certainly lacked a monopoly on the legitimate use of force, or state violence (Lange 2016: 23). If the definition of state failure by Zartman (1995: 1) is accepted, in that state failure 'refers to a situation where the structure, authority (legitimate power), law, and political order have fallen apart, and must be reconstituted in some form, old or new', then Republican Rome may indeed be described as a failed state. But this all changed with the Principate.

The reconstitution of the Roman state was a process. Having defeated Rome's enemies in 31–30 BCE, Augustus finally returned to Rome in 29 BCE, in triumph. After a transitional pause he returned the triumviral powers to the *res publica* in 27 (*RG* 34.1). The transitional nature of the intervening period seems confirmed by contemporary evidence and by later literary sources: an *aureus* of 28 BCE displays on the reverse a togate Young Caesar, seated on the *sella curulis* and holding a scroll; the legend reads LEGES ET IVRA P R RESTITVIT ('he restored the statutes and legal rights of the Roman People'). This legend, *leges et iura*, must refer to statutes and laws and reflects the annulment edict of previous illegal and unjust triumviral ordinances (Rich and Williams 1999; Rich 2012: 89–105) and Young Caesar's restoration of laws in 28 BCE, as Tacitus and Cassius Dio write.[22]

Young Caesar had accomplished the assignment; he had ended the civil war; and he now reconstituted the state. Velleius Paterculus (2.89.2–6) emphasizes restoration, but his vague account makes no mention of Augustus' powers:

> The civil wars were ended after twenty years, foreign wars suppressed, peace restored, the frenzy of arms everywhere lulled to rest; validity was restored to the laws, authority to the courts, and dignity to the Senate; the power of the magistrates was reduced to its former limits, with the sole exception that two were added to the eight existing praetors. The old traditional form of the *res publica* was restored.
>
> *finita vicesimo anno bella civilia, sepulta externa, revocata pax, sopitus ubique armorum furor, restituta vis legibus, iudiciis auctoritas, senatui maiestas, imperium magistratuum ad pristinum redactum modum, tantummodo octo praetoribus adlecti duo. prisca illa et antiqua rei publicae forma revocata.*
>
> Vell. Pat., 2.89.3

According to Velleius Paterculus the civil war ended in 29 BCE with the closing of the Temple of Janus and the triumph of Young Caesar, having begun twenty years earlier with the crossing of the Rubicon.[23] The triumphs are awarded for victories in wars that are 'partly civil', as they were also dubbed in Cassius Dio's assessment (50.4.5). The war declared against Cleopatra was in reality against Antonius, although the spear rite in 32 BCE made the war initially foreign in nature. Later Antonius' decision to help Cleopatra against Rome turned the foreign war into a civil war.[24] On Velleius Paterculus two further comments are needed. In the first instance, as emphasized by Woodman, his was not a narrative of the restoration of the *res publica*, as this was never claimed by Augustus (see above). Secondly, Velleius' account is, rather, a description of the return to normality: in other words, this is an account of the ending of civil war. The passage 2.90.1 is vital, suggesting in its own words – rather similarly to the *Res Gestae* (34.1) – that 'the body of the state has been badly injured by the attacks of civil wars, but now that its adversary is dead and buried, its limbs can start to recover from their wounds' (90.1: *sepultis, ut praediximus, bellis civilibus coalescentibusque rei publicae membris, et coaluere quae tam longa armorum series laceraverat*; Woodman 1983: 262). Velleius Paterculus' written narrative is transparently close to the ideological narrative of the regime, suggesting that civil war is extinguished, while at the same time describing the settlement after the end of the civil war. Like the *Res Gestae*, it does not mention the new tasks at hand for Augustus after 27 BCE. Similarly, Livy (*Per.* 133) states that after the triple triumph in 29 BCE the civil wars ended after twenty-two years: 'Caesar returned to Rome to celebrate three triumphs, one for the campaign in Illyricum, a second for his victory at Actium, and the third over Cleopatra. He made an end to the civil wars in their twenty-second year' (*in urbem reversus tres triumphos egit, unum ex Illyrico, alterum ex Actiaca victoria, tertium de Cleopatra, imposito fine civilibus bellis altero et vicesimo anno*).[25]

As for the sense of an ending (see Westall 2014), the kind of equation drawn by the Latin authors – Augustus himself chief among them, of course – between the end of civil war and victory and triumph is also evident in the *fasti*. The *feriae* on the anniversary of the capture of Alexandria are recorded on four inscribed calendars. The Arval Fasti entry reads: *feriae ex s(enatus) c(onsulto), [q(uod) e(o) d(ie) Imp(erator) Caesar Divi f(ilius) rem pu]blic(am) tristiss(imo) p[e]riculo [libera]vit*.[26] The *fasti* of Praeneste and Amiternum have very similar entries, citing the reason for the celebration, most likely from the original senatorial decree. The Senate's decree of that year renaming the month Sextilis in Augustus' honour includes among the reasons for the choice that in that month Egypt was conquered and the civil wars were brought to an end.[27]

3. Veteran settlements

To turn to a final aspect of the process of ending a civil war – and to a very different and more literal kind of 'settlement' – a key aspect of the return to normality in the wake of the civil wars was the settlement of veterans in *coloniae*.[28] Even if we limit the discussion to the aftermath of the death of Caesar,[29] there is a clear pattern emerging: there were major settlements after Philippi, after Naulochus and after Actium.[30]

It becomes evident that – unsurprisingly – the ending of civil war involves numerous factors, often including the predictable roll-call of major decisive battles, the celebrating of victories and the granting of triumphs; but discharging soldiers and settling them after the close of operations appears to have been an equally significant factor. Even if the period from the death of Caesar is portrayed as one of continued civil war, Philippi, Naulochus and Actium were major turning points, especially if we look at the context of the minor victories, such as Perusia and Mutina, notwithstanding that many veterans from the former had already been settled (see Keppie 1983: 69). These battles were important, but they certainly did not end any conflicts; and consequently, no major settlements followed these victories.[31]

After Philippi the veterans were settled in accordance with the *Lex Titia* (App., *B Civ.* 4.7; Cass. Dio, 47.2.1, on the establishing the triumvirate). Eighteen cities were singled out for settlements (App., *B Civ* 4.3: selected as future colonies). There may have been trouble regarding the veteran commissioners.[32] For this reason it was agreed that Young Caesar should return to Rome to settle the situation and arrange land distributions for the soldiers. Antonius would deal with affairs in the East.[33] After Naulochus more soldiers were sent to veteran settlements.[34]

After the battle of Actium the army of Antonius was abandoned by its commander Canidius Crassus and the legions changed sides (Plut., *Ant.* 68.1–3; Cass. Dio, 51.1.4). They had been ordered into Macedonia by Antonius (Plut., *Ant.* 67.5) and remained intact for seven days (*Ant.* 68.3). As for changing sides, what else should they have done after their commander left the still raging battle? Later there was an amalgamation of the two armies (Keppie 1983: 74). Antonius' army was incorporated into the forces of Young Caesar and some were disbanded (Cass. Dio, 51.3–4; Plut., *Ant.* 73; Tac., *Ann.* 1.42; Suet., *Aug.* 17.3). If Dio is to be believed, it appears that Young Caesar's troops received land, but those of Antonius only money.[35]

Augustus mentions colonies for soldiers twice in the *Res Gestae*, and both mentions are highly significant in terms of understanding the new *princeps'* policy of normalization after the turmoil of internecine conflict. He writes first, at *Res Gestae* 15.3, that 'as consul for the fifth time [29 BCE] I gave to the colonists who had been my soldiers 1,000 sesterces each out of plunder; about 120,000 men in the colonies received this handout to mark my triumph' (*et colon[i]s militum meorum consul quintum ex manibiis viritim millia nummum singula dedi; acceperunt id triumphale congiarium in colonis hominum circiter centum et viginti millia*). Here the settlements are connected to the triumph of 29 BCE: this event and its generous aftermath is thus made to mark the official end of the civil war. In *RG* 28 Augustus continues: 'I settled colonies of soldiers in Africa, Sicily, Macedonia, both Spains, Achaea, Asia, Syria, Gallia Narbonensis and Pisidia. Moreover Italy has twenty-eight colonies settled under my authority, which have been in my lifetime very busy and densely populated' (*colonias in Africa, Sicilia, [M]acedonia, utraque Hispania, Achai[a], Asia, S[y]ria, Gallia Narbonensi, Pi[si]dia militum deduxi. Italia autem XXVIII colonias, quae vivo me celeberrimae et frequentissimae fuerunt, me[a auctoritate] deductas habet*). What springs to mind is that the colonies are outside Italy. This arrangement is not only about the end of civil war; it is about the settlement *after* war, at home and within the Empire more broadly. This fits the idea of the nature of public power under Augustus, as described by Ando (see above): Augustus retains the army under his command and at the same time makes sure that soldiers could not be misused to fight another round of civil war in Italy.

There is debate about whether the figure given in *RG* 15 is too large; but it may not just refer to the forces under arms at Actium (Keppie 1983: 74–5). Brunt (1971: 338) suggests that the figure involved soldiers from Philippi, Naulochus and Actium. Keppie however thinks it odd to pay out the *congiarium*, marking a triumph, to soldiers who had not actually fought in the campaign earmarked for memorialization (75).[36] Where does this leave us? There is indeed good reason for believing that this figure involves soldiers who fought in the civil war of 44–31 BCE. After all, the war was over; the triumph signified the end of the civil war as well as the conquest of Egypt. That is why Augustus wrote 'at the time of my triumph': Young Caesar had accomplished the triumviral assignment. As a result of victory and peace (*RG* 13) money was paid to all the troops who had fought the war.[37] Not only the soldiers but also the plebs received their share. Keppie (1983: 75) rightly concludes: 'This was a distribution to loyal subjects to mark the successful conclusion of civil war.'

Brunt (1971: 333, 338) commenting on Cassius Dio (51.4.6) adds that some soldiers were deported. Keppie's grounds for disagreement on this point seem sober: such a policy would not help Young Caesar to win them over, at all (Keppie 1983: 76).[38] But Brunt's idea may find some support in Dio, who writes the following of the new *princeps*' interactions with the soldiery in that year:

> Consequently he was making no headway, and he furthermore learned by actual experience that arms had no power to make the injured feel friendly toward him, and that, while all those who would not submit might perish by arms, yet it was out of the question for anyone to be compelled to love a person whom he does not wish to love.

> καὶ διὰ ταῦτα ἐπειδὴ μήτε τι ἥνυε, καὶ προσέτι καὶ ἐξ αὐτῶν τῶν ἔργων ἔμαθεν ὅτι οὐδὲν τὰ ὅπλα πρὸς τὸ τοὺς ἀδικουμένους εὐνοϊκῶς οἱ ἔχειν ἐδύνατο, ἀλλὰ ἀπολέσθαι μὲν πᾶν τὸ μὴ ὑπεῖκον δι' αὐτῶν οἷόν τε ἦν, ἀναγκασθῆναι δέ τινα φιλεῖν ὃν μὴ βούλεται ἀδύνατον ὑπάρχοι.

> Cass. Dio, 48.8.4

Surely, these were pertinent lessons for a future emperor.

4. Conclusion

Ultimately Augustus ended the civil war(s) after a century of turmoil. Contributing factors may simply have been chance or fatigue; the phrase 'last man standing' springs to mind. If so – and if fatigue alone were really the principal factor underlying the resolution of the conflict – then that aspect may render the question of how to end a civil war successfully absurd in this case. Nevertheless, it is quite clear that the Settlement of 28–27 BCE finally brought to an end the problematic Late Republican relationship between soldiers and their commanders, which had been played out time and again through Roman history, from Marius' reforms onwards, if not earlier. This is of course not a novel conclusion. However, focusing on the period from Actium (31 BCE) to the Settlement of 28–27 BCE, it becomes apparent that the regime used different layers of justification on the one hand, and general activities meant to stabilize Rome after civil war – that is, implementing 'phase IV operations' on the other hand.

One component was the actual winning of the war, through a decisive victory; but apart from that, in practical terms the Settlement of 28–27 BCE (or even 29–27 BCE, concluding with the closing of the Temple of Janus and the triumph in 29 BCE), the settling of veterans, and the moves toward power sharing and rehabilitation played their part too. The veteran settlements happened, unsurprisingly, after major victories, thought to have ended the civil war. Osgood (2015: 1685) is right to point out that major horrific battles did not (or not always) end civil wars, but Actium and its postscript Alexandria did. Until 69 CE that is. After that Augustus initiated a return to normality, a programme of reconciliation through *clementia* and power sharing. But at the same time a monarchy, with Augustus in charge of most armed provinces, was put in place to keep him in power, famously summed up by Tacitus (*Hist.* 1.1): *postquam bellatum apud Actium atque omnem potentiam ad unum conferri pacis interfuit, magna illa ingenia cessere...* ('But after the battle of Actium, when the interests of peace required that all power should be concentrated in the hands of one man, writers of like ability disappeared...'). In any case, the civil wars were difficult to quell; Young Caesar had to try more than once, succeeding only with the death of Antonius and Cleopatra. He thus forcefully brought to an end the civil war(s) of the Late Republic. But there is more, all depending on how we approach ancient civil war. Applying the lens of modern theories and approaches of conflict, we can conclude that some features of ancient civil wars are indeed regular features of any civil war. Accordingly, we can compare Augustus' settlement with other civil war settlements, ancient as well as modern.

10

Agrippa's 'Odd' Speech in Cassius Dio's *Roman History*[*]

Mathieu de Bakker
University of Amsterdam

1. Introduction: Debate, crises, antecedents

After his narrative of Octavian's victory over Antony and Cleopatra, the historian Cassius Dio (ca. 164 to after 229 CE) inserts a debate in which Agrippa and Maecenas offer advice to Octavian about the future Roman constitution. First, Agrippa argues on behalf of a restoration of 'democracy' and a return to the Roman republican government such as it existed before the civil wars (52.1-13).[1] Maecenas replies with a longer speech and sets out the parameters of the principate, adding a list of practical recommendations to guarantee smooth government of the emperor in cooperation with the Roman elite, both in the city and in the provinces beyond (52.14-41).

The debate on the Roman constitution is remarkable for its length (an entire book) and position in Dio's *Roman History*.[2] Dated in the year 29 BCE, it accompanies a watershed, as the first fifty books are devoted to Rome's origins, kings and republic, and the last thirty to the principate up to Dio's own time. The pivotal nature of Octavian's victory and subsequent constitutional reforms may explain why he adds such an elaborate scene. It allows him to highlight topics relevant for his work as a whole and, by its antiphonal form, bring to the fore divergent considerations in relation to the institution of the principate as well as its practical implementation. Furthermore, it has a dramatic function in characterizing the heavyweights within Octavian's administration. Meanwhile, Octavian himself is offered two different types of constitution, and, in picking the one that in retrospect leads to peace and restoration, confirms his foresight as a ruler.

Scholars have framed the debate as a text of crisis. It accompanies the narrative of the critical transition from republic to principate at the end of the first century

BCE after turbulent decades of civil war, but its content also reflects problems in the governance of the Roman Empire at the beginning of the third century, when Dio himself was a member of the Senate and twice fulfilled the consulship.[3] He witnessed the reigns of no fewer than eleven emperors, and served as adviser to some of them. In particular Maecenas' speech is considered to have been based upon contemporary developments; it has been read as an antidote against the crisis that Dio saw emerging in the principate under Commodus and the Severan dynasty, a crisis that would worsen after his death, presumably around 230.[4]

Dio is not the first to incorporate a passage with constitutional recommendations within the context of such crises. The tradition goes back to Herodotus' debate on the future Persian constitution, held amongst three prominent conspiring nobles after the overthrow of the Magi (3.80–82). It is picked up by Thucydides, who embeds constitutional theory in his funeral oration and in the speeches that accompany the Mytilene and Melos crises, as well as the decision to attack Sicily (2.35–46; 3.37–48; 5.85–113; 6.9–23).[5] Another example is Polybius' essay on the Roman constitution, which follows the narrative of the great crisis of the Second Punic War (6.1–18).[6] Unlike Polybius, however, Dio makes his characters voice these ideas, as he in general seems less reluctant to ascribe speeches to his characters than Polybius did. And whereas Herodotus makes Darius himself settle the debate in his favour, Octavian, the winner of Dio's debate, merely listens and does not make a contribution.[7] Dio departs also from Thucydides in presenting a debate within a private, confidential setting, which may raise questions as to its authenticity.[8] In fact, as various scholars of Dio point out, the debate in its particular form can hardly have been historical, not in the least because various elements are more at home in a third-century context than in that of the Late Republic.[9] Rather, the debate reflects a tradition in ancient historiography of marking great political turnovers with some form of debate. Historically, this is entirely self-evident: major changes in stateforms do not occur without serious discussions. Although the content of such debates may be anachronistic, their presence in a narrative of such a pivotal moment in history can be considered perfectly natural.[10]

This chapter will be concerned with Agrippa's contribution to the debate, i.e. his recommendation to Octavian to restore the Republic, couched as it is in terminology familiar from the Greek historiographical tradition.[11] In contrast to the detailed analyses of Maecenas' advice (see above, n 4), Agrippa's shorter and more idealistic speech is often assessed only in general terms.[12] Some take it as a rhetorical set-piece that serves as a springboard to Maecenas' longer and more practical advice, whereas others argue that the two speeches are complementary, and each in their own way reflect aspects of the Roman constitution as it took shape under Octavian.[13] Furthermore, there is the issue of the Greek affinities within Agrippa's speech: it is thought that Dio makes his speaker imply, or include, a Hellenic *polis* model of democracy.[14]

The main problem with this speech however concerns the incompatibility that is felt between speaker and content. Why would Agrippa, who operates throughout as Octavian's most loyal supporter, recommend him to lay down power and restore the Republic?[15] Although Dio's use of different sources may account for the perceived oddness of Agrippa's speech (Schmidt 1999: 108–9), it makes more sense to look for clues *within* the text that may explain why he makes Agrippa reject monarchy. In his study of the speeches in the *Roman History*, Van Stekelenburg follows the lead that the speech is meant to underline Agrippa's unconditional support to Octavian in spite of their disagreement about the Roman constitution (Van Stekelenburg 1971: 108). Indeed, both after the speech (52.41.2) and in Agrippa's obituary, Dio observes his loyalty, arguing that 'he helped him [Octavian] in setting up the principate *as if he truly desired autocrat rule*' (ὡς καὶ δυναστείας ὄντως ἐπιθυμητὴς, 54.29.3, my italics). Through this particular phrasing Dio implies that Agrippa acted against his personal preferences, but set them aside for the benefit of Octavian's interests, general peace and the common good.[16]

In this contribution I will further explore this intra-textual approach. Rather than seeking a historical explanation or defining Agrippa's seemingly odd speech exclusively in relation to Maecenas' subsequent advice, I will assess it within the wider context of Dio's reconstruction of the crisis of the Roman Republic, and evaluate it in relation to the themes and techniques that he employs in his narrative.[17] This approach entails a closer look at Dio's characterization of his protagonists, and an assessment of Agrippa's rhetoric against the backdrop of recent events. In particular in the books that precede the debate 'frankness of speech' (παρρησία) and 'freedom' (ἐλευθερία) are repeatedly thematized, which raises questions regarding the debate itself. I will argue that the relation of power between Octavian and his confidants, as well as the dynamics of the debate, with Agrippa speaking first, qualify these concepts, in spite of Octavian's gratitude for his adviser's 'frankness of speech' afterwards (52.41.1). Agrippa's approach may then be defined as a 'crisis'-strategy: afraid of falling victim to the mechanisms of civil strife opportunism and enmity, he sets aside his love for the Republic in favour of his loyalty to Octavian.

2. The wider context I: Dio's characterization of the Caesars

Recent studies have sought to analyse Dio's techniques of characterization. Although Dio as a narrator is described as 'overt and intrusive', presenting himself 'as a circumspect, trustworthy, and well-informed guide' (Hidber 2004: 198), he turns out to be surprisingly reticent in discussing aspects of the characters who are staged in the *Roman History* (Pitcher 2018b: 226). Pitcher observes a contrast between Dio's frequent use of generalizations about human behaviour and his restraint in offering 'snap judgments on individuals' such as found in the work of his predecessor Thucydides.[18] In Dio's history, characters are usually constructed through their deeds and words, an approach by which, in Pitcher's words, '[Dio's] reader is compelled to become an interpreter'.[19]

Narrative strategies encouraging the involvement of readers and appealing to their interpreting faculties are, in fact, an important aspect of ancient historiography that has only recently received more attention in scholarship.[20] In the case of the characterization of individuals, a reader is 'empowered' to construct a portrait based on the words, thoughts and deeds ascribed to that individual, and the ways in which they interrelate with those of other characters as well as with more general statements found in the narrative.[21] This is a linear process, in which individual pieces gradually offer themselves in the course of the narrative so that an increasingly complete – and often complex – picture emerges that can be matched against a reader's preliminary assumptions and (fore)knowledge about the presented individual.

Dio's narrative of the Roman civil wars can be considered a treasure trove in this respect. The episodes of the first and second triumvirates and the rise of Octavian at the expense of Antony and Lepidus are rich in detail and paint a haunting picture of the poisonous atmosphere in civil war Rome and beyond, which needs to be taken into account when evaluating Agrippa's performance and the nature of his advice to Octavian. The typical feature of this period – as of any civil war – is that no one can be trusted, or, as Dio himself phrases, 'no one apart from Cato took part in public life in a way that was honest and free of some form of private material interest' (37.57.3), and, as he makes Philiscus say to Cicero, 'those who lust after power ... exchange even their dearest friends and closest relatives for their worst enemies' (38.29.4).[22]

In characterizing Caesar, Dio selects and arranges the material assembled from his sources in such a way that an unflattering portrait emerges. He blames Caesar for pretending to defend the interests of the state, but in reality seeking to become sovereign ruler (41.17.3; 56.1).[23] For this purpose, he sets constitutional laws aside, for instance by enlisting senators without appropriate background (43.47.3-6) and by allowing convicted exiles to return home (43.27.2-3). Dio explains Caesar's success as resulting from his ability to hold his composure (e.g. 38.11.1-2), hide his intentions and wait for the right moment to strike (τοῦ ... καιροῦ διεσκόπει, 38.11.4).[24] After his death, Dio makes Antony praise these abilities of Caesar in his eulogy:

> He understood well how to discern shrewdly what was concealed, to dissimulate plausibly (πιθανῶς ψευδαγνοεῖν) what was evident, to pretend (προσποιήσασθαι) to know what was hidden, to conceal (ἀποκρύψασθαι) what he knew, to adapt occasions to one another and to draw the proper inferences from them ...
>
> Cass. Dio, 44.38.7-8, transl. Cary

Dio, however, also highlights more ruthless aspects of Caesar's character. During his campaign in Thessaly Caesar inspires fear by murdering the inhabitants of Gomphi (41.51.4-5) and during his campaign in Africa he orchestrates the killing of some suspected followers at the hands of their own comrades (43.13.1-2).

Dio characterizes Octavian as even better at calculating and pretending than his adoptive father, whose tactics become increasingly transparent in the latter stages of his career.[25] Upon hearing about Caesar's murder, Dio writes that he 'felt great pain ... but did not dare to revolt straightaway' (45.3.1). He quickly returns from Greece to Italy and enters Rome as a private citizen, pretending that the sole purpose of his visit is to claim his inheritance (45.5.2, observe ὡς). He pays court to Antony, although the latter had stolen from his possessions (45.5.3). He also practises strategic reticence when he discovers that his attempts to run for tribune are obstructed, calculating that the Romans will support him anyway because of his relationship with Caesar, and funding the festivals that the latter had instituted (45.5.4-6.4).[26] Later, the same calculation and pretence dominate Octavian's dealings with his fellow-triumvirs. Octavian and Antony understand each other's intentions perfectly but initially consider it inopportune (ἄκαιρον, 45.8.2, cf. 45.11.1; 47.1.1; 50.1) to put them to the test. Instead they arrange a 'feigned agreement' (προσποιητὸν ὁμολογίαν, 46.54.4) and take measures to hide their ambitions of ruling the entire Empire (46.55.2-56.1). Octavian for instance marries the daughter of Antony (46.56.4),[27] publicly celebrates the latter's successes in war (49.18.6-7) and conceals his defeats (49.32.2). Meanwhile, however, he secretly forges alliances with Antony's opponents. In this he goes so far as to befriend Decimus Brutus, one of Caesar's assassins (45.14.3; 46.36.4-5). Dio reflects here again on opportunism in times of civil war (48.29.3), echoing Philiscus' words to Cicero (see above). Finally, once Octavian has secured power for himself, his character is contrasted with that of Caesar in his rejection of the kind of honours that the latter had gladly accepted when they were offered to him in Rome (49.38.1, cf. 49.15.3–5, 51.20.4). Although Dio does not judge these actions in his own voice, he implies that Octavian acted more considerately in his attempts to avoid being in the limelight.

Importantly, however, Octavian is portrayed as more ruthless and violent than his adoptive father, in particular as he takes part in the proscriptions of powerful, wealthy Romans (e.g. 47.2.2: ἐβιάζοντο). Dio underscores the cynical nature of these killings, pointing out that the triumvirs agree to trade off their personal friends against one another (47.5.4–6.3) and that they do not allow the Romans to mourn the dead (47.13.2, cf. 48.13.6). Although Antony and Lepidus are singled out for their cruelty (51.15.1), Octavian is not exculpated, as it is merely his relatively young age that causes his killing list to be shorter than that of his fellow-triumvirs (47.7.1–5). In particular the wealthy classes are vulnerable, many of whom are killed so that the triumvirs can pay off their armies (47.4–5.3; 6.6–7). Octavian also uses public funds to hire soldiers (46.46.5; 48.1–2), who help him in forcing his political agenda upon the Romans, and they also plunder the countryside (47.14) whilst assisting the triumvirs in large-scale confiscations (47.16–17, cf. 48.6.3).[28] Thus in the triumvir Octavian nothing of Caesar's clemency is left. The siege of mutinous Perusia ends in its destruction along with the deaths of many senators and knights, with Antony's brother Lucius among them (48.14). Equally harsh are Octavian's killing of the nobility that had served under Sextus Pompeius (49.12.3–5) and his slaying of the young Caesarion and Antyllus after the battle of Actium, of whom Dio notes that they are his own relatives (51.6.1–2; 15.5). Father and son Florius Aquilius have to draw lots to decide who is to be slain (51.2.4–6). Dio also mentions a strikingly cruel incident in Octavian's private life, when he leaves his wife Scribonia for Livia on the very day that the former gives birth (48.34.3). Finally, unlike Caesar, Octavian does not fall under Cleopatra's spell, but only pretends to be interested in her to orchestrate Antony's suicide (51.10.4–9, cf. 51.6.6; 8.3–7; 9.5–6).[29] We conclude, then, that up to the debate between Agrippa and Maecenas, Octavian is portrayed in the *Roman History* as a calculating ruler, acting against his opponents in more cruel and unforgiving ways than his adoptive father.

3. The wider context II: Speeches in the *Roman History*

Apart from describing the deeds of his protagonists and encouraging his readers to compare and evaluate them, Dio uses the device of incorporating speeches to illustrate the poisonous atmosphere of the civil wars. Thus we find many instances of disingenuous speech on the part of the triumvirs, who hide their intentions in order to manipulate their audience. An example is Caesar's speech to his – partially – mutinous soldiers at Placentia (41.27-35), in which he denies aspirations to sovereignty (41.35.4), whereas he is immediately afterwards installed as dictator (36.1-2). It is ironic that Caesar censures his soldiers for their greed (41.28), and praises them for the very virtues that are lacking on his part in his behaviour to the Roman state (41.29). Elsewhere, too, Caesar does not speak his mind, for instance in addressing his officers at the time of the war against Ariovistus in Gaul (38.36-46). Here, Caesar claims that men with possessions are inevitably plotted against, and should therefore anticipate with a pre-emptive strike (38.40.2). His words succeed in deflecting attention from the fact that he wages war without Rome's authorization.[30] Dio lays bare the emptiness of the claims that Caesar and Pompey make in their speeches, each calling the other a tyrant and himself a liberator, and appealing to the loyalty and solidarity amongst the troops, while ignoring that they themselves are tied by bonds of kinship. Instead, they fall out with one another, as Dio alleges in his own evaluation, because of their 'insatiable lusting for power' (ἀπλήστῳ τῆς δυναστείας ἐπιθυμίᾳ, 41.57).[31]

Disingenuous elements are also found in the few speeches ascribed to Antony and Octavian, most notably their harangues before the battle of Actium, where each leader belittles his opponent (Antony: 50.18.1-3; Octavian: 50.24-27), plays down the other's resources and fighting power (Antony: 50.16.2-3; Octavian: 50.29), and praises himself as the best man to finish the job, with exaggerated references to earlier successes (Antony: 50.17; Octavian: 50.28). Antony, like Caesar and Pompey before, presents himself at the end of his oration as a liberator and his opponent as a sovereign (50.22.4), whereas Octavian keeps his cards to his chest where it concerns the future, and points at the great spoils that will fall to his troops if the battle is won (50.30.4).

Dio's orations delivered by individuals other than the triumvirs mostly revolve around the theme of 'frankness of speech' or 'outspokenness' (παρρησία). To which degree is the speaker able to speak his mind? This is illustrated in an ambiguous manner in the way Dio stages Cicero, whose terrified performance on Milo's behalf in Pompey's presence (40.54) is contrasted with his *Philippica* after Caesar's murder. Dio represents Cicero's famous set of orations by way of one speech, in which he makes Cicero claim that not being entitled to free speech would force him to leave Rome (45.18.2). His invective against 'tyrant' Antony is rounded off with the ironic statement that he does not fear death as a result of this instance of 'frankness of speech' (παρρησία, 45.46.3). The effect of Cicero's speech is diminished by Calenus' subsequent apology for Antony (46.1–28), which slanders Cicero (46.1–28), and the latter's insults against Calenus further abate his authority (46.29.1). During the proscriptions he pays the ultimate price for his outspokenness (47.8.3–4; 11.1–2).

A more authoritative outspokenness is presented in the case of Cato, whom Dio, following Sallust, reports as standing up against Caesar in the debate on Catiline's conspiracy (37.36.2–3), and in refusing him a triumph (37.54.2). Cato also opposes Caesar on the issue of the installation of a commission to redistribute the land (38.3), and prefers honourable suicide to subservience to Caesar, claiming that he is 'raised in freedom and with the right to frankness of speech' (ἔν . . . ἐλευθερίᾳ καὶ ἐν παρρησίᾳ τραφείς, 43.10.5). Other instances of outspokenness take place exclusively in private conversations, such as Philiscus' consolatory speech to Cicero (38.29.1), and Caesar's soldiers who jest freely about his relationship with Cleopatra and his position as a ruler (43.20).

4. Agrippa's role in the *Roman History*

It is against this background of war, oppression, murder, greed, deceit, pretence, distrust and the lack of frankness of speech that the nature of Agrippa's advice to Octavian should be evaluated. In the narrative that precedes the debate Agrippa plays a relatively modest role. Dio does not hint at the origins of his friendship with Octavian, but introduces Agrippa when he is sent out to defend Italy against the attacks of Sextus Pompeius (48.20.1–2). By this stage he is already an important man in Rome, where he sponsors the equestrian 'Trojan Games', and prides himself for being a close friend of Octavian (ἅτε καὶ πάνυ φίλος ὢν τῷ Καίσαρι, ἐλαμπρύνετο, 48.20.2). After a brief reference to his successful capture of Sipontum (48.28.1), Agrippa re-enters the narrative when Octavian summons his return from Gaul, where he is engaged in quelling a revolt across the Rhine, and entrusts him with assembling a fleet against Sextus Pompeius. By this stage Agrippa holds the consulship (37 BCE), and is offered a triumph, which he tactfully refuses 'as he considered it shameful to make a show whilst Octavian had experienced setbacks' (48.49.4). Dio expresses his admiration for Agrippa's construction of an artificial harbour near Puteoli, stating that he 'conceived of a magnificent task and also brought it to completion' (ἔργον μεγαλοπρεπὲς καὶ ἐνενόησε καὶ ἐξεποίησεν, 48.49.5). In the subsequent battle of Mylae, Agrippa defeats Sextus (49.2–4.1) but does not pursue the ships that flee. Speculating about the admiral's possible motives, Dio points out Agrippa's awareness that Octavian did not want anyone to outshine him:

> For he used to say to his close friends that most men in positions of power (ἐν ταῖς δυναστείαις) do not want anyone to be superior to them, but take care of most cases, at least those that provide easy victory, by themselves, and assign others to the less glamorous and more unusual tasks. And if they are at any moment compelled to entrust one of the more prestigious enterprises to them, they are irritated and displeased when their subordinates gain a good reputation from them. For they do not pray for them to suffer defeat and fare badly, but neither do they prefer them to obtain a great reputation upon securing a total victory. He therefore recommended that the man intent on being kept alive (τὸν ἄνδρα τὸν σωθησόμενον) should take the burdensome tasks from his superior's shoulders, whilst preserving their accomplishment for them. I know that this is the way it naturally works and that Agrippa took care of it ...
>
> Cass. Dio, 49.4.2–4, transl. loosely based on Cary

This passage, which may be based upon Dio's own experiences with various emperors,[32] can be considered crucial for his presentation of Agrippa's role and the explanation of his ultimate success in Roman politics. First, Agrippa – in contrast to many contemporaries – remained loyal throughout to his superior and never, in spite of his military victories and his popularity with the soldiers, considered competing with him. But more importantly, he was also aware that he should under no circumstance *give the impression* of being able to compete, and he therefore abstained from personal glory, keeping the spotlights upon Octavian at all costs. Acting otherwise could make a difference between life and death, as becomes clear from the phrase 'he who is intent on keeping himself alive' (τὸν σωθησόμενον).[33] Agrippa is thus presented as making a political choice in his support of Octavian, and devising a strategy that seeks the avoidance of even the slightest form of mistrust. One may assess his choice against the backdrop of the recent proscriptions, which had claimed the lives of many innocent Romans who were murdered merely for their wealth, potential ambitions or popularity, and also in light of the behaviour of two other talented admirals of his age, Sextus Pompeius and Menas, whose shifting allegiances did not guarantee them success in the long term.[34] By using them as foils, Dio presents Agrippa's behaviour as unconventional in this period, and highlights Octavian's awareness of the precariousness of his position in relation to this powerful adviser, to whom he donates the unparalleled gift of a golden crown adorned with beaks of ships (49.14.3–4).

It is Agrippa's unwavering loyalty that Dio praises in his obituary, too.[35] He calls him the 'best' man of his time, and the one who used his friendship with Augustus to the greatest advantage for the emperor and for the state. For the more he defeated the others in virtue, the more he voluntarily subjected himself to him, and while he provided him with all his wisdom and courage to the most profitable ends, he spent all the honour and power that he returned to him upon the benefactions to others.

Cass. Dio, 54.29.1-2 transl. loosely based on Cary

Dio observes that as a consequence of his loyalty to Octavian, the monarchy, and the Roman people he did not incur envy or hatred from either side (54.29.3). From this, we can conclude that he saw in Agrippa's choice an essential cause of Octavian's success and the period of peace that resulted from it.

It is important to note here that Maecenas, who opposes Agrippa in the debate, also remains faithful to (and trusted by) Octavian throughout his career.[36] However, his background as *eques* makes him a less plausible rival to Octavian. Though he does take part in the actual warfare, he is not commanding armies or ships, but fulfilling administrative functions in Octavian's government. In the books that precede the debate he is mentioned a few times as caretaker of Italy during Octavian's absence in the East (49.16.2), and Octavian later sends Agrippa to back up his authority (51.3.5). Maecenas' position, then, differs from that of Agrippa in that he never poses a threat to Octavian in the first place and, because he is liked, can always speak freely to him. This is one of the aspects that Dio singles out in Maecenas' obituary, claiming that it was the 'frankness' (παρρησία) of friends like him that restrained impulsive behaviour on Octavian's part (55.7.3).

For Agrippa, however, frankness of speech is qualified, and this should be borne in mind when evaluating his debate with Maecenas in book 52. Whereas the latter's contribution can be compared to that of Philiscus in his private speech to Cicero (38.18-29), Agrippa must remain circumspect, although he has gained his superior's trust. He may have been earnest in recommending that Octavian step down and reinstall the Republic, but the language in which he couches his advice differs greatly from Maecenas' more open-minded, practical lecture on the governance of the Empire. His phrasing shows that he is consciously avoiding any offence that may be felt to reside in his words. It is to the actual words of his speech, then, that we should finally turn.

5. Agrippa's advice

In a noteworthy article on speeches in Herodotus, Pelling points at Herodotus' awareness and dramatization of the pitfalls of giving advice to a powerful king or tyrant, observing that advisers tend to tread 'tactfully', and often express themselves in oblique ways, with the use of generalizations and language that is deliberately 'shrouded'.[37] This 'distorted' language of advice may not have escaped the notice of Dio, a connoisseur and avid imitator of his classical Greek predecessors, and may account for the odd nature of Agrippa's recommendations, certainly when compared with the more practical, matter-of-fact approach of Maecenas afterwards.[38]

An important and so far unnoticed aspect of Agrippa's advice is that it responds to the intention of Octavian to lay down his arms and return the state into the hands of the Senate and the people and effectively restore the Republic (52.1.1). Although Dio does not report this intention as part of an actual speech, the context makes clear that Agrippa and Maecenas had been made privy to his plans:

> He made his decision together with Agrippa and with Maecenas – for he shared all his secrets with them
>
> Cass. Dio, 51.1.2

The debate, then, differs from its antecedent in Herodotus in that the starting point is not the question of which constitution should be chosen after the crisis, but the question of whether Octavian's intention to restore the Republic is sensible. Agrippa's speech should be seen as a direct response to an actual political plan, and not as a theoretical reflection on a constitution that has long gone.

The opening words of Agrippa's speech ('do not be surprised, Caesar, if I will dissuade you from monarchy') make clear that he wants to confirm Octavian in his intention.[39] The wider context of the debate raises the question of whether Agrippa could have spoken differently without endangering his position. Dio has staged him as an adviser once before in the narrative, when he dissuaded Octavian, before the engagement at Actium, from capturing Antony and Cleopatra by a stealth attack upon the rear (50.31.2). This recommendation was purely military, and Agrippa could speak with authority as a man of arms. In this political discussion, however, Octavian's intention may not have left him with another choice but support.

In the remaining part of the *exordium* Dio makes Agrippa appeal to his own *ethos*, underlining that he will under all circumstances put the interests of Octavian first, even though he himself would benefit much from a situation in which Octavian remains at the helm (52.2.1–2). This ties in with Dio's own observations on Agrippa's relationship with Octavian (see above) and with the qualities by which he had become his closest confidant. Making Agrippa, then, explicitly confirm his loyalty here is an indication that Dio shows him aware of the pitfalls in the discussion, the sensitivity of the subject and the importance of keeping his addressee foremost in his mind throughout his speech.

Next, Agrippa begins his argument, requesting of his addressee to make 'reasoning' (λογισμός) lead the way, a reasoning that has to be followed 'at ease' (καθ' ἡσυχίαν), as if they are taking part in a philosophical discussion (52.2.3). With this phrasing Dio anticipates Agrippa's further approach, which is mostly theoretical, in that he opposes to one another – in generalizing terms – the extremes of monarchy and democracy, without much allowance for nuance or differentiation between, for instance, the freedom of the Romans themselves and that of their subjects, or the relative autonomy that certain classes of citizens could enjoy under a monarchy.[40] In choosing a theoretical approach, and pretending to make both himself and his addressees subject to reasoning, Agrippa at least in the larger part of his speech avoids a recourse to arguments from recent history that might give offence to Octavian, such as the fact that those who killed his adoptive father were staunch supporters of the Republic. Instead, his abstract discourse offers Octavian the ideological theory with which he can back up his intention in front of the public bodies in Rome.

Another noteworthy element is the frequent use of the first person plural in Agrippa's speech, which indicates that Dio makes him avoid addressing Octavian in an overly direct way. His main concern is Octavian's reputation, which he believes will receive a blow if monarchy is chosen, regardless of whether such a decision were based upon progressive insight or had been premeditated all along. Agrippa explains these consequences in terms that resemble gnomic wisdom (52.2.4–3.3), reasoning from human behaviour in general, and claiming that Octavian will not be able to endure his reputation to be tarnished (52.2.7), a situation that would boil down, in effect, to a resumption of proscriptions and civil war, although Agrippa leaves this consequence unmentioned.

Generalizations continue in Agrippa's idealistic praise of *isonomia* ('equality of rights', 52.4). Implicit in this passage is the warning that monarchy will diminish the responsibility that citizens feel for the wellbeing of the state, and that coercion by a ruler will cause him to be hated. Under a 'tyranny', one is not willing to contribute to the collective, but only has individual interests in mind (52.5.1–2). This resembles the behaviour of the triumvirs and many of their opponents during the civil wars, although Agrippa sensibly remains silent on this. Instead, he points at practical problems that make the subjection of the city to a monarch problematic, such as Rome's traditional taste for 'freedom', and the autonomy that the Romans had granted to parts of the Empire that had traditionally been governed in democratic ways (52.5.4). He continues with an argument that he presents as 'most insignificant' (βραχυτάτου, 52.6.1), but that appears to be crucial in light of the preceding history: the funds that the monarch needs to realize his ambition of subjecting Rome and its Empire. This is a sensitive issue for Octavian, who survived several mutinies of his troops, struggled in his politics on redistributing the land (e.g. 48.6–11), and only managed to pay off his debts once he had laid his hands on Egypt. Such funds, Agrippa argues, will fall short in a monarchy, as citizens are not willing to contribute, but would expect the king to pay for everything, whilst hating the taxes that he imposes upon them.[41] Most notably, his troops will be in constant need of money since they are hired (a continuous source of worry for the triumvirs), whereas in a democracy, Agrippa argues, those who serve in the army are the very same who pay taxes and thereby benefit from the system (52.6.2–5).

After reflecting, again in general terms, on the compromised position of the monarch in a juridical system (one can think of Pompey's presence at Milo's lawsuit here, 40.54) and emphasizing the negative result for his reputation (52.7), Agrippa pauses on the position of the nobility, which will be needed for the governance of Rome's vast Empire, but will not accept being subjected to a monarch unless violence is applied and recourse is sought to murder (cf. 52.8.2 – again Agrippa leaves the proscriptions unmentioned). The alternative, to rely upon people of lower classes for governance, will be equally impossible, as their authority will not be accepted (52.8.6–8), with disastrous consequences for the cohesion of the state. This detail may hint at Dio's own time, when emperors increasingly by-passed the Senate and relied upon the military to conduct their policies,[42] but Octavian is also reported to have acted on the same assumption by sending Agrippa to Italy to support Maecenas in his administrative duties (51.3.5). In democracies, Agrippa goes on, 'love of honour' (φιλοτιμία) amongst the nobles will always benefit the state, as the involvement of the people increases the state's strength, whereas the subjection to a monarch makes the people weaker – an idea at least as old as Herodotus, who voices it in his narrative of the foundation of Athens' democracy (cf. Hdt., 5.78). Agrippa adds the risk a monarch runs of being overthrown by his own people, for which he uses Roman history as an example (52.9.3–5), and thereby indirectly warns Octavian not to follow such a course.

In what follows, Agrippa hints at the personal troubles for Octavian in becoming a monarch, presenting the burden of governance as almost insurmountable: 'Those in power have many troubles and in possessing vast wealth they are forced to spend vastly' (52.10.4).[43] Again, benefaction is prominent in Agrippa's reasoning, as he argues that the privilege of a king to grant favours in fact leads to envy amongst his citizens, all of whom will find a reason to consider themselves eligible, and many of whom will be disappointed. This inevitably leads to a hatred of the monarch and a weakening of his position, even if his intentions in granting favours are upright (52.11–12). Agrippa keeps reflecting on this theme in abstract terms, but the recent past of Rome lurks in the background, where Caesar was murdered in spite of his clemency and his generosity in handing out favours. By following a theoretical line of reasoning, Agrippa is able to present the deterioration of morals as an inevitable result of the king's position, even if he is of good nature.[44]

Agrippa adds references to Rome's recent past to the conclusion of his speech. In praising Caesar, Octavian's adoptive father, as one of the men whose superior had never been found (52.13.4), his words seem at odds with those of Dio, who praises Caesar for his military talents, but reproaches him (as well as his opponent Pompey) for pursuing autocracy at all costs and thereby undermining the state (e.g. at 41.57.4, and compare above). Yet even Caesar, as Agrippa points out, was not able to maintain his position, as his murder demonstrates.[45] Agrippa can only point at Sulla, the man of the first proscriptions (cf. 47.3.3–5), as a suitable alternative example for Octavian to follow (52.13.5): first assume dictatorship, and then step down. At the end of the speech Agrippa therefore recommends Octavian to postpone his plan to step down and restore the Republic until he has, like Sulla, put adequate and sufficient measures in place.

Thus Agrippa follows a mostly theoretical line of inquiry to support Octavian's intention, stressing his worries for his wellbeing and reputation and denying vehemently that he might himself benefit from a restoration of the Republic. Maecenas, who speaks from a position that is less compromised, strongly urges against this, and follows the arguments on behalf of monarchy that Dio himself expounds in his narrative.[46] The result is that Octavian reconsiders his intention and adopts Maecenas' proposal, in which he is seconded by Agrippa 'as if he had made these proposals himself' (52.41.2). Ironically, however, Octavian reiterates his original intention to restore the Republic in the Senate by way of pretence, so as to manipulate his audience, which begs him to remain in place as a monarch (53.11.4–5).[47]

6. Conclusion

For a long time, constitution debates in Greek literature tended to be studied in isolation. In the case of Herodotus' debate of the Persian constitution, this trend was countered by several scholars, who sought to place the debate in its immediate and wider context.[48] In the case of Dio's debate between Agrippa and Maecenas, in particular Van Stekelenburg and Ruiz looked for an assessment that included the wider context of the *Roman History* (see above). In this chapter I have elaborated upon their approaches and focused specifically upon Agrippa's speech, which is often considered odd, certainly from a historical perspective.

Agrippa's attitude as described by Dio contrasts with that of triumvirs like Pompey and Caesar, whom Dio portrays in earlier books. 'Both of them', in the words of Dio, 'claimed to fight wars on behalf of the common good, but only advanced their own interests and thereby ruined the former' (41.17.3). Agrippa acts contrariwise, and in subjecting himself to his friend, but de facto ruler, finds a parallel in the historiographical tradition in the case of Herodotus' Otanes. The latter idealizes 'equality of rights' (*isonomia*) in his contribution to the debate on the future Persian constitution (Hdt., 3.80), but when the Persians settle for a monarchy under his opponent Darius, he serves as a loyal general to his armies and conquers Samos (Hdt., 3.141–149).[49]

Agrippa, however, cannot speak his mind as freely as Maecenas does. The context of the debate reveals that already his very position as a powerful admiral may be felt as a threat to the interests of Octavian, who often keeps his cards close to his chest and does not reveal his plans. Dio shows his awareness of the sensitivity of Agrippa's position by couching the speaker's support for Octavian's intention in words of a theoretical, generalizing nature, which seek to admonish its addressees in oblique ways, and are far removed from the concrete political situation in Rome and the Empire. The use of this kind of rhetoric as a strategy to avert crisis must have been familiar to Dio himself. From what we know about his career, he appears to have aspired to a position of *adiutor imperii*, too, although, unlike Agrippa, he would not succeed in averting the crises that plagued the principate during the latter decades of his life.

Part Five

Civil War and the Family

11

The Fate of the Lepidani
Civil War and Family History in First-Century BCE Rome

Josiah Osgood and Andreas Niederwieser
Georgetown University

In the mid-second century BCE, Roman history was essentially the history of its great families.[1] When a man who held high office died, he passed out of living politics and into collective memory through a carefully orchestrated ritual, the *pompa funebris*.[2] This parade – headed up by actors wearing wax masks of the deceased's ancestors, then featuring the dead man himself on a bier, and ending with his living relatives – represented to the community the family's contributions to Rome. The masks of the ancestors, when not being used at a funeral, were stored in the *atrium* of the family's house and were labelled with names, political offices and achievements, and so familiarized the great stories of the past to the citizens who poured in each morning. Of course, in different houses one would find different stories, and one might even raise an eyebrow at the claims some families made for their early forebears – 'false triumphs, too many consulships' in Cicero's famous words.[3] No one family owned the past, but collectively the nobles to a large degree did.[4] Successes in war abroad and the elaborate funerary rituals reinforced each other.

Internal violence from the 130s began to fracture this culture of remembering and the full-scale civil war of the 80s nearly shattered it.[5] For the first time, leading Roman nobles were declared enemies of the state. Their houses were demolished, they were denied funerals, and the display of their images was banned. Sulla's proscriptions went even further: in exhibiting the severed heads of his enemies in the Forum, he cruelly inverted the tradition of the aristocratic funeral.[6] The memory of the dead was to be destroyed, and their familial prestige ruined. Noble families had gaping holes in their own histories – and so, to an extent, did the Roman People in its history. The lengthy and boastful memoirs

Sulla left unfinished at his death in 78 did nothing to bring Romans back together.[7] Instead, the decades that followed were to be marked by debates, even armed conflict, over Sulla's actions.[8]

In the rest of this chapter, we first briefly explore the uprising that broke out after Sulla's death in 78, generally associated with one of the year's consuls, M. Aemilius Lepidus. The uprising sheds light on how Romans understood political crisis and how they tried to end it – questions that are closely interrelated. Mostly, though, we focus on the aftermath of the uprising, looking at its main leaders or their surviving relatives, 'the Lepidani' of our title. Being on the losing side of what later, anyway, would be called a civil war posed a great problem for them. Each of their families' memory cultures was interrupted, and so their own prestige was under threat. Civil war, we will argue, led to new and aggressive strategies by all three families to rehabilitate themselves. In its new manifestations, family history offered a means of restoring cohesion after civil war. At the same time, though, familial desire for revenge was a lingering issue. In the second half of the chapter, we look at how the return of full civil war in 49 BCE revived old memories, raised new questions about the relationship of one's family to the *res publica*, and ultimately altered practices of fashioning family history.

1. The so-called 'Revolt of Lepidus'

To understand how aristocratic families tried to recover from the violence unleashed, first we must understand the violence itself.[9] It once was conventional among historians to regard Lepidus himself as more or less personally responsible for a renewal of civil war after Sulla's death.[10] The view goes back to ancient authors, for example Orosius, who wrote: 'after the death of Sulla, Lepidus, defender of the Marian party, rose up against the Sullan general Catulus and rekindled the ashes of civil war'.[11] The metaphor of fire recurs in the ancient accounts, and sometimes contributes to a more nuanced analysis of the violence. Appian wrote that after Sulla's abdication 'the Romans ... gradually fanned the flames of new seditions'.[12] Florus vividly suggested that 'the brand of this disturbance was lit by the funeral pyre of Sulla itself'.[13] While fire was an appealing metaphor to describe war (e.g. the Romans' 'fiery war' in Celtiberia in the second century BCE), it had particular appeal for describing civil conflict: fire suggested how easily – in the absence of 'external' enemies – such a conflict could spread; it conveyed the devastation brought to civil society; and the way a banked fire might prove not to be extinguished was particularly suggestive.[14] To varying degrees, then, most authors suggest that the rising of 78 must be understood as a flare-up in ongoing civil war that went beyond the ambitions of Lepidus alone.[15]

In fact, there was widespread and deeply held dissatisfaction with the policies of the dictator Sulla. Many resented the ban on the sons and grandsons of the proscribed from holding political office.[16] Those who lost land in the confiscations made on behalf of Sulla's veterans were still seething. The *plebs urbana* resented the curtailment of tribunician power.[17] It all boiled over with the death of Sulla. There were demands to restore the tribunate.[18] Inhabitants of Faesulae violently attacked the estates of Sullan colonists, reclaimed their land, and made a plea to the Senate.[19] In response, the two consuls for the year, one of whom was Lepidus, were assigned an army and instructed by the Senate to set off for Etruria.[20] Once there, Lepidus began championing the cause of the dispossessed (just as he had spoken earlier on behalf of the children of the proscribed). This widened an already-existing breach with his fellow consul, Q. Lutatius Catulus. In an effort not to let the quarrel escalate, in late 78 the Senate assigned both consuls *provinciae* for the next year and made them swear an oath not to make war on one another.[21] This was an innovative way for the Senate both to recognize the danger of what we would call a 'crisis' and to try to end it; significantly, the Senate did not yet invoke the so-called 'ultimate decree' that made a threat to the *res publica* more explicit. To end the crisis, it was better not to speak of crisis.

But the effort failed. When recalled to Rome to preside over elections, Lepidus requested a second consulship, perhaps primarily to protect himself. The Senate turned against him and passed the ultimate decree. Just outside Rome, Lepidus was defeated in battle and declared a *hostis*. He fled to Etruria and then Sardinia, where, after more fighting, he died. As his pyre burned, we are told, his body was dislodged by the force of the flames and had to be incinerated bare with a fresh supply of wood.[22] This curious story underscores how far removed from the aristocratic pomp of the Forum his funeral was. It also brings us back to the imagery of fire – a sense that with Lepidus' death, civil war was extinguished (perhaps?) or that civil war cruelly engulfed Lepidus too.

Given the widespread bitterness against Sulla and his policies, it is not surprising that Lepidus had some key supporters, members of aristocratic families that had sided with the Marians against Sulla in the 80s. These included L. Cornelius Cinna, son of Sulla's foe of the same name, and M. Junius Brutus, tribune of the plebs in 83.[23] A very important Lepidan was the *Scipio Lepidi filius* mentioned by Orosius – who can be identified as the biological son of Lepidus himself, adopted out to L. Cornelius Scipio Asiagenus (cos. 83).[24] Scipio Asiagenus fought Sulla after the latter's return to Italy and was later proscribed, meaning Lepidus' biological son could have no political future.

After Lepidus' defeat, many of his supporters, including Cinna, fled to the breakaway state of Sertorius in Spain – where the fire of civil war had been burning for some years. If they were not already proscribed, they had become *hostes publici* because of their support of Lepidus.[25] Others, meanwhile, had died during the fighting in Italy, including Lepidus' biological son. Brutus, who had been holding Cisalpine Gaul for Lepidus, was killed by the Senate's general Pompey, despite surrendering of his own accord.

The case of young Julius Caesar is also important to note here. Upon learning of the death of Sulla, Caesar raced back to Rome from Cilicia where he was on military service. Suetonius tells us that he was motivated by 'the hope of the new dissension which M. Lepidus was stirring up' (*spe novae dissensionis, quae per Marcum Lepidum movebatur,* Suet., *Iul. 3*). The lexical choices are pertinent to understanding ancient ideas of crisis, but Suetonius, in making Lepidus the prime mover of the trouble, probably was looking too much from hindsight. In any event, ultimately Caesar 'refrained from an alliance with Lepidus, although he was offered generous terms, because he lacked confidence both in Lepidus' capacity and even more his prospects, which he discovered were less promising than he had been led to believe.'[26] Still, Caesar would be an important figure in the aftermath, to which we now turn.

2. After the crisis: Reinventing family history

Let us begin with Cornelius Cinna and the restoration of his family.[27] Cinna remained with Sertorius in Spain until Pompey's final victory. Aside from M. Perperna, Sertorius' treacherous assassin, and a few of Perperna's collaborators, all Romans were then spared.[28] Pompey also burned the correspondence of Sertorius – a gesture of amnesty that made clear that old quarrels must be forgotten, the symbolism here being reinforced by the metaphor of extinction latent in burning (Osgood 2015: 1686–7). Cicero in his *Verrine Orations* of 70 described how Pompey did his best to secure the safety and wellbeing of all soldiers who sought pardon, but that was only the first step (Cic., *Verr.*, 2.5.153). A law was passed in Rome, in 71 or 70, the *lex Plotia*, that gave full restoration to the Sertoriani, including Lepidus' followers.[29] (Most likely, though, those Sertoriani who had been proscribed by Sulla were only offered asylum rights in certain cities.[30]) Thus the year 70 could be seen as the real end of civil war, as

Cicero suggested in his *Verrines*: 'Our civil dissension or madness or bad luck or calamity – whatever you choose to call it – has a not unhappy end, insomuch as those remaining citizens who survived are allowed to live on without harm.'[31] To use the terms of Klooster and Kuin in the Introduction to this volume, this was a reframing of the 'crisis plot', one in which destroying – and preserving – the lives of Roman citizens became a central theme. This is not to say that there were no other ways of framing recent history. For example, the prosecution of several men who had carried out murders in the Sullan proscriptions could appear to be the true end of 'Sullan tyranny'.[32]

Another important strand in the politics consisted of ideas surrounding the family. Cinna's brother-in-law Julius Caesar was a key advocate of the *lex Plotia*. He gave a public speech in support of it, one fragment of which survives: 'To me it seems that as our kinship demanded, I have not failed in toil, in effort, or in dedication.'[33] The quotation shows how Caesar was trying to win support from his listeners by covering himself in the prized Roman quality of *pietas*, devotion to one's family. Civil war, he was suggesting, had challenged the ability of family members to help one another.

It had also broken down families' ability to honour their dead and assert their collective prestige. The reintegration of the Lepidani – who at least to some degree encompassed earlier supporters of Sulla's great foe Marius – would prove a step in healing the ruptures in the traditional rule of the nobility and their public displays of family history. Just a year after the *lex Plotia* was passed, Caesar made a point of staging lavish funerals first for his aunt Julia, the widow of Marius, and then his own wife, Cinna's sister Cornelia.[34] Both women were given funerals in the Forum, with *laudationes* spoken by Caesar. *Imagines* of Marius were displayed for the first time since Sulla's dictatorship, and almost certainly the *imagines* of the patrician Cornelii Cinnae were shown too. The funeral of Cornelia was thus also a step in the rehabilitation of Cornelius Cinna. It is critical to note that it was unprecedented for a young woman to have received such a lavish public funeral. Now Caesar's love for his wife certainly must be given its due, but the public funeral was also aimed at reviving the family.

Now let us turn to the Junii Bruti. M. Brutus was probably around eight years old when his father died. No funeral was held for the elder Brutus of course.[35] But young Brutus could, and did, play up his remote paternal ancestor, L. Junius Brutus, Rome's first consul.[36] He also could play up his mother's ancestor, the tyrant-slayer C. Servilius Ahala.[37] This maternal lineage had appeal because it was much less doubted. L. Junius Brutus famously had killed his sons for plotting against the nascent *res publica* and so it could be asked how our Brutus was descended from him. Also, Ahala had further resonance after Brutus was adopted into his mother's family and took the name Q. Servilius Caepio Brutus.[38]

That name was just one of many strategies Brutus had for promoting personal and familial prestige. As a mint official in the mid-50s, he issued coins showing the goddess Liberty on the obverse and on the reverse the first consul Brutus walking between lictors with *fasces* (RRC 433.1). A second issue paired the head of L. Brutus with that of Ahala – a juxtaposition that helped paper over doubts about Brutus' paternal lineage (fig. 1, RRC 433.2). Brutus could not show his father's mask in the *atrium* of his house in Rome (since the father had had no funeral); but at a villa he had a painted family tree featuring again the Servilii along with the Junii Bruti (Cic., *Att.* 13.40.1/SB 343). Brutus' friend T. Pomponius Atticus created this family tree, and he also wrote a book at the request of Brutus that 'set out, in order, the members of the Junian family, from its origin to the present day, recording who was whose son, what offices he held, and when'.[39] Brutus was a master at finding ways of doing family history beyond the Forum and *atrium*.

Ultimately, Brutus' efforts went beyond using the glory of ancestors to compensate for the disastrous defeat of his father. He was intervening in contemporary politics (Gotter 2000: 332–3). Even as a relatively young man who had not held office, he gained through familial prestige a platform from which to attack Pompey's alleged autocratic leanings, as he did in 52.[40] Of course, attacking Pompey also helped Brutus answer the need for familial revenge. Note, too, that Brutus published a fictitious speech of defence for Milo in 52, arguing that it was right to kill a bad citizen and that the bad citizen's murderer should not be punished.[41] Brutus was starting to meld with the image he was promoting of his distant ancestors and, as we shall later see, this opened him up to be morally blackmailed.

Fig. 1 RRC 433.2: *denarius* of M. Iunius Brutus portraying his (putative) ancestors.

The patrician Aemilii employed a strategy similar to Brutus', playing up the memory of earlier generations, almost to the point of overkill.⁴² M. Aemilius Lepidus, the disgraced consul of 78, left two sons. One, L. Aemilius Lepidus, added the extra *cognomen* 'Paullus' to his name, falsely claiming descent from the conqueror of Macedon. As mint official, he issued coins in the name of 'Paullus Lepidus' that showed on their reverse the great Aemilius Paullus (fig. 2, *RRC* 415.1). Next to a tall trophy he swaggers, while the defeated Perseus stands with his hands bound and his pitiful children before him.

Paullus' brother, M. Aemilius Lepidus – the future triumvir – also served as mint official and issued his own coins that focused on another mighty ancestor, the M. Aemilius Lepidus who was twice consul, censor in 179/78, *pontifex maximus* and *princeps senatus* for thirty years until his death in 152. One issue shows the statue erected on the Capitoline to this M. Aemilius Lepidus to commemorate precocious gallantry during the Second Punic War (*RRC* 419.1). As a teenager he went into battle, killed an enemy, and saved a fellow citizen's life. Another coin shows the Basilica Aemilia, built by Lepidus as censor along with his colleague (fig. 3, *RRC* 419.3). The consul of 78, we are told, decorated the Basilica with shields showing portraits of his ancestors – and these shields are visible on this coin.⁴³

The Basilica was essential to the family's efforts at reintegration. By the mid-50s, Lepidus Paullus was refurbishing it. Cicero wrote to Atticus in the summer of 54 that the roof was nearly finished and that Paullus had reused the original columns.⁴⁴ Cicero also indicated that Paullus was at work on another basilica, to be constructed in the most lavish style.⁴⁵ Peter Wiseman has suggested that this

Fig. 2 *RRC* 415.1: *denarius* of L. Aemilius Lepidus Paullus, portraying his putative ancestor on the reverse.

Fig. 3 *RRC* 419.3a: *denarius* of M. Aemilius Lepidus depicting the Basilica Aemilia.

incipient work was destined to become the Basilica Julia, on the southern side of the Forum (Wiseman 1998: 108–10). In 50 BCE, according to Plutarch, Caesar drew from the streams of Gallic wealth and gave 1,500 talents to Paullus, serving as consul, to help finance his basilica (Plut., *Caes.* 29.3). As Wiseman suggests, it may be that the 1,500 talents was actually a payment for the southern site. Paullus had gotten into financial trouble with his expensive building projects, and wanted at least to make the old Basilica Aemilia as splendid as possible. The enormous bribe shows not that Paullus was easily bought. Rather it reveals how important the Basilica, and the glories of earlier Aemilii, had become to Paullus.

Like the funeral for Cornelia or Brutus' coins, the Basilica helped to knit a family on the wrong side of civil war back into Roman society and, to a degree, to knit Roman society back together. There were, though, as we have seen, ongoing strains and tensions: still painful memories, lingering anger over Sulla's disenfranchisements, anxiety over one-man rule. To return to our earlier metaphor, the fires of civil war had not been entirely extinguished.

3. Experiencing crisis in the family: Private relationships versus public obligations

Down to 50 BCE, our three families had similar goals in reintegrating their families into Roman communal memory while also navigating fresh political challenges. With the resumption of full-scale civil war in 49, the story becomes more dramatic. Political crisis now induced individual crises of conscience. At different moments, members of our families struggled with tensions between obligations to family and family tradition, on the one hand, and the desire to serve the *res publica* on the other. The divisions of civil war threatened to split their own families apart. Our evidence for this period is richer, and allows us to examine more deeply how Romans actually experienced a crisis similar to that of the 80s and 70s.[46] We shall also see that, as the long years of conflict unfolded, traditions of family history were contested and ultimately altered.

In 49 itself, memories of earlier civil war had sudden urgency, and there was much reflection on Sulla's methods and legacy in particular. Julius Caesar, famously, repudiated Sullan cruelty, writing in an open letter: 'let this be a new style of winning: to make mercy and generosity our defense'.[47] But he also saw the outbreak of war as a chance to settle some unfinished business – to see justice fully done for the victims of Sulla. After his victory over Pompey's generals in Spain in 49, Caesar had legislation passed allowing the sons and grandsons of the Sullan proscripts to serve in public office.[48] Cicero wrote that he had a report that Caesar was 'seeking punishment for Cn. Carbo, M. Brutus, and all the other victims of Sulla's cruelty, in which Pompey, as he says, was a partner'.[49] Was Caesar in fact little better than a new Sulla? Caesar himself had been dropping some hints that if he failed to get sufficient support from respectable senators, he might have to rely on harsher methods (Gelzer 1968: 207–8). Likely, though, Cicero was exaggerating. But the letter does point out how the question of where justice ended and revenge began vis-à-vis the last civil war was still a live one. Another sign of this: when news of Caesar's victory at Pharsalus reached Rome statues of Pompey and Sulla were overthrown (Caesar later had them restored).[50]

L. Cornelius Cinna embodied Caesar's politics of restoration in this period. In 44 BCE, he held office as praetor. As we shall see, he would later state that he gained this honour as a gift from Caesar, and it is true that Cassius Dio says that Caesar effectively appointed all the magistrates for 44 (App., *B Civ* 2.121; Cass. Dio, 43.47.1). The apparently long lag in time between Cinna's return in 70 and his acquisition of office has suggested that Cinna might actually have been proscribed and so was only eligible to stand for office in 49 (Hinard 1985: 343–4). But no source makes this clear, and it could be that he simply needed Caesar's direct help to gain his magistracy. One way or another, though, his holding the praetorship symbolized the restoration of Sulla's victims and the full rehabilitation of Cinna's own family.

We are better informed on how Brutus and the two Aemilii confronted the onset of civil war. Brutus might have been expected to take the chance finally to avenge his family on Pompey, as Caesar allegedly was claiming might be possible.

But Brutus decided to fight on the side of Pompey, 'thinking it his duty to put public affairs ahead of his own'.[51] Plutarch's language here likely reflects Brutus' rhetoric at the time – and indeed, a rhetoric that others could invoke in civil war.[52] Having Brutus was a huge boost for Pompey. It absolved him of the stains of earlier wars and also lent him the prestige not just of Brutus, but Brutus' ancestors. Brutus himself, in putting the *res publica* ahead of the honour of his immediate family, was honouring those ancestors too; Lucius Junius Brutus, after all, had had his sons executed. Brutus' prestige was shown when he arrived in Macedonia; Pompey 'rose from his seat and embraced him as a superior with everybody looking on'.[53]

As for the Aemilii, Lepidus, serving as praetor in 49, stuck with Caesar and became a key supporter, one Caesar could rely on nearly more than any other.[54] Paullus was thought likely to support Pompey but in the end did not – perhaps because of the 1,500 talent 'bribe'. Supporting Caesar, of course, was in harmony with any desire the brothers had to avenge their father, and Lepidus probably also saw active aid to Caesar as a path to advance his own career. But there are some hints that Paullus (who had achieved the top office of consul in 50) had misgivings similar to those of Brutus. There is no evidence that Paullus actually did anything actively to help Caesar in the civil war. And after the Ides of March, he supplied Cicero with political news and then during the war at Mutina went on an embassy to Sextus Pompey.[55]

After Pompey's defeat at Pharsalus, Brutus made his peace with Caesar, and turning Brutus to his side was of great value to the victor (Plut., *Brut.* 6.1–5). But the moral weight of family tradition bore down on Brutus, especially as Caesar looked more and more like a tyrant. According to Plutarch, Cassius appealed to Brutus to act against Caesar on the grounds that abolishing tyranny was a debt he owed his lineage (Plut., *Brut.* 10.6). Cicero was only slightly more veiled in his dialogue the *Brutus*.[56] Appeals were made to Brutus by other means too. Pamphlets circulated taunting Brutus for not truly being the consul's first descendant. But many, according to Dio, did at least pretend to accept the relationship, crying out: 'Brutus! Brutus! We need a Brutus!' and scrawling out the graffito 'Brutus, you are sleeping!' (Cass. Dio, 44.12.2–3). This last taunt recalled how the first Brutus seemed to be lethargic for far too long in the face of King Tarquin's tyranny, only stirring himself when Lucretia was raped by the king's son. In addition to all this, the heroic suicide of his uncle Cato affected Brutus. He asked Cicero to write a memorial of the man, he then contributed his own, and in the summer of 47 he married Cato's daughter, Porcia.[57]

Family history, recent and ancient, pointed inevitably to the need to kill the tyrant: it was Brutus' destiny.[58] As Cicero wrote after the Ides, 'Brutus is ours, and always will be ours – a man born for the benefit of the Republic, thanks not only to his surpassing courage, but also a sort of destiny that arises from the family and name of both his father and his mother'.[59] Ultimately Brutus was able to reconcile the need to honour his family and serve the *res publica*.

Cinna also had a crisis of conscience, akin to those experienced by Brutus and (probably to some degree) Paullus. The first hint of a possible moving away from his relative Caesar came with Cinna's marriage in 46 to Pompeia, the daughter of Pompey.[60] More dramatically, while not participating in the plot to kill Caesar on the Ides, he did appear later the same day in the Forum with the assassins.[61] He threw off his praetor's robe and told the crowd before him that Caesar was a despot and the assassins were tyrannicides in the best tradition of their ancestors. Cinna's speech was all the more powerful because everybody knew what Cinna owed his old brother-in-law. It was an inversion of Caesar's speech on the *lex Plotia*, almost even a reverse *laudatio*.[62] Like Brutus in 49, Cinna was placing *res publica* over family – although he could possibly say that he was acting in the best traditions of his family. Had not his father, after all, stood up to the first tyrant, Sulla? It was Caesar the Dictator who had abandoned the old Marians, not *vice versa*.

On 17 March, a furious crowd nearly stoned Cinna to death on his way to a Senate meeting.[63] He was only saved by Lepidus, the son of his old political ally. One might guess that in speaking out on behalf of the assassins, Cinna really aimed to prevent their destruction – to reach a compromise and preserve peace in the city.[64] Significantly, Cinna had put his praetor's robes back on for the Senate meeting on 17 March. As the victim of an earlier civil war, he would be a compelling spokesman for peace. At least for the time being, despite all his loyalty to Caesar, Lepidus also became willing to compromise, and indeed a compromise was worked out on 17 March. On some level, one can think of peace and compromise as a project of the old Lepidani as a whole from that particular day onwards, including not just Cinna, Paullus, Lepidus and Brutus, but also Brutus' mother Servilia – who was also Lepidus' mother-in-law.[65] She remembered perfectly well the fate of her husband, the supporter of Lepidus killed by Pompey.

Self-conscious efforts at preventing civil war were a notable feature of the months that followed the Senate meeting on 17 March in 44. Lepidus continued to insist that preserving peace was his policy.[66] Later in 44, he helped to negotiate a settlement with Sextus Pompey, for which he received on the proposal of Cicero a gilt equestrian statue on the Rostra (Cass. Dio, 45.10.6; Cic., *Phil.* 5.38–41; 13.7–13). In March of 43, he wrote to the Senate from Gaul urging that peace be negotiated with Mark Antony. (Cic., *Fam.* 10.27, SB369; *Phil.* 13,7).[67] In responding to this in the *Thirteenth Philippic*, Cicero cleverly tried to turn

Lepidus' family history against him, much as he had done with Brutus before the Ides. Lepidus, Cicero said, owes the *res publica* a great deal: 'the whole range of offices, the most elevated priesthood, and many adornments to Rome that commemorate him, his brother, and their ancestors'.[68]

In his speech Cicero hinted that Lepidus was already contemplating making an alliance with Antony and turning against the Senate (Cic., *Phil.* 13.13–14). To do so, Cicero said, would be dishonourable; Lepidus must remember that he is 'M. Lepidus, *pontifex maximus*, great-grandson of M. Lepidus, *pontifex maximus*'.[69] If he fails to remember this, if instead he treats the army as if it were his own, not the Senate's, he would be following 'examples from outside your family, and recent ones at that, rather than ancient and familial ones' (*alienis exemplis eisque recentibus ... quam et antiquis et domesticis*). In fact, as Cicero knew perfectly well, Lepidus would be acting just like his father. Ultimately, in May of 43 Lepidus did abandon the Senate and wrote that body a letter, arguing that under compulsion from his army he was championing the life of citizens, and the Senate must now put aside its 'private quarrels' and not treat his 'compassion' as a crime.[70] So perhaps by his lights he did become his father. He also was appealing to the 'crisis plot' that made destroying – and preserving – the lives of citizens the major issue for assessing political conflict.

As Caesarians – including Lepidus and Antony – came back into alignment and so grew stronger, the question of the purity of one's commitment to the *res publica* became more acute.[71] In response to his agreement with Antony, Lepidus was declared a public enemy, and the Senate also ordered that the brand-new equestrian statue of him be removed from the Rostra.[72] Lepidus' brother Paullus was the first to vote in favour of the decree, and this was no accident. (App., *B Civ.* 4.12). It demonstrated, like Cinna's speech on the Ides, that the *res publica*, and the Senate specifically, must come first. Lepidus repaid the favour when the triumviral proscription was announced: Paullus' name was the first on the list (App., *B Civ.* 4.12). Paullus escaped safely and joined M. Brutus, and after Brutus' death he remained in Miletus, even though he could have returned to Rome after the Misenum pact (App., *B Civ.* 4.37). In a sense, he had become his father too – challenging the tyranny based in Rome with Brutus at his side, just as their fathers had.

For brother to proscribe brother, though, could also be seen as the height of *impietas*, and the Aemilian survivors were left with a problem, especially the son of Paullus, the nephew of the triumvir. By 36, this younger Paullus had made his peace with the triumvirs and was fighting with Octavian in Sicily (Suet., *Aug.* 16.3). He was rewarded with a consulship for 34, in which year, after much delay, he dedicated his father's basilica, which henceforward would be called the

Basilica Paulli.⁷³ The accomplishment allowed him to bask in earlier Aemilian glory. And when, in 14 BCE, it burned down, Augustus gave money to help rebuild it (Cass. Dio, 54.24.2–3). By this point, Paullus was married to Augustus' niece Marcella and Augustus' granddaughter Julia the Younger was betrothed to Paullus' son. In publicly funding the new Basilica, Augustus was taking over the memory culture of the nobles – a process that would be carried a step further in the Augustan Forum.⁷⁴

This co-option by Augustus was one major shift in family history. A second was the publication of funeral speeches for those who could not actually receive a *laudatio* in the Forum. In the earlier Sullan war, the deaths of those on the losing side simply created gaping holes in family and communal memory. It is no coincidence that it was Brutus who confronted that problem directly, who also initiated the literary commemoration of those who died as 'enemies' of Rome. There was the series of works on Cato, and already in 49, we should note, he published a *laudatio* for his highly distinguished father-in-law Ap. Claudius Pulcher, who was fighting with the Pompeians in the East.⁷⁵ And then, after Brutus' death, memoirs of Brutus and Porcia were published by Porcia's son, Bibulus (Plut., *Brut.* 13.3). From Plutarch we know that these included the famous story of Porcia stabbing herself with a knife to prove her fortitude: 'I am Cato's daughter!' (Plut., *Brut.* 13.3–11). And there was the story of her breaking down into tears on seeing a painting of Hector and Andromache, upon which Brutus said he would not simply treat her like a subservient Greek wife: 'she is brave on behalf of her country, as we are' (Plut., *Brut.* 23.2–6). In the new commemorative literature, the focus increasingly was on moral qualities, including patriotism, service to the *res publica* – and not simply, or not even at all, on the objective achievements of triumphs, priesthoods and political offices that were so dominant in the older memory culture of the Republic.

New commemorative forms like eulogies for the Republican martyrs could, of course, lead to a fracturing of communal memory, for example by contradicting Augustus' version of events familiar to us from the *Res Gestae*. The eulogies might even help to inspire acts of violence that could escalate into civil war.⁷⁶ But by acknowledging the dead, they also had an important role to play in ending the first-century crisis of civil war. A story told by Macrobius suggests the canniness of Augustus here (Macrob., *Sat.* 2.4.18.1). Walking into a house where Cato had once lived, Augustus was treated to some Caesarian-style abuse of the dead man. To this, Augustus replied that anybody who opposed a change in the state – as Cato had – was a good citizen and a good man. Thus was Cato's patriotism honoured, and an extraordinary shift in politics masked.

4. Conclusion

Augustus' Cato stood for stability, not the values of a free republic. This was an effective version of Cato for the *princeps* because it acknowledged the past while burying its contentiousness. But well before Augustus, as we have shown, nobles were experimenting with new ways of presenting the histories of their family and, therefore, the history of the country. After Cinna returned from long years of exile or as Brutus and the Aemilii made their way into public life, they tried to find a means to reknit their families back into the political community. They did not bring to an end the ongoing struggle over the best means to govern Rome, and consciousness of their family's history might have heightened their own feelings of crisis at times. Later, civil war came to be more prominent in the stories families told of their past; finding ways to incorporate civil war into family history was a critical way to come to terms with civil war. If the great *pompa funebris* of the Middle Republic reflected Roman success abroad, the later array of family histories that arose mirrored a prolonged experience of internal conflict.

12

The Roman Family as Institution and Metaphor after the Civil Wars

Andrew Gallia
University of Minnesota

A mother had a son who wore the blue and another who wore the gray. Father and son have fought on either side. The dearest ties of blood and friendship stand suddenly separated and arraigned in deadliest enmity, and yet Nature will assert her sway at last; and should Death intervene to lay one low, as passionate, tender tears are shed as if the war had been a dream.
—A. Hunter, *Johnny Reb and Billy Yank* (1905: 177–8)

1. Grieving matrons in Lucan's *Civil War*

The second book of Lucan's *De Bello Civile* provides an apt introduction to the ways in which the trauma of civil war was refracted through the lens of family in Roman culture. The book opens with the terrible omens of war (*manifesta belli / signa*, 2.1–2) that reveal the gods' anger at the outbreak of the conflict between Caesar and Pompey. Lucan focalizes the religious dread that these signs provoke in Rome through the experience of the city's matrons, whose introduction into the narrative is mediated by an evocative simile:

> Then their complaining they suppressed, and deep voiceless
> grief pervaded all. Just so at the moment of death
> the stunned house falls silent – not yet is the body
> laid out and bewailed, not yet does the mother with loosened hair
> impel the slave-girls' arms to savage breast-beating –
> the moment when she hugs limbs stiffening as life flees,
> the inanimate features, eyes swimming in death.
> Fear is past and grief not yet arrived: distraught, she bends over him,

stunned by her loss. Their former finery the Roman matrons
laid aside and in grieving bands they fill the temples.

> tum questus tenuere suos, magnusque per omnes
> erravit sine voce dolor. sic funere primo
> attonitae tacuere domus, cum corpora nondum
> conclamata iacent, nec mater crine soluto
> exigit ad saevos famularum bracchia planctus,
> sed cum membra premit fugiente rigentia vita
> voltusque exanimes oculosque in morte minaces;
> necdum est ille dolor, nec iam metus: incubat amens
> miraturque malum. cultus matrona priores
> deposuit, maestaeque tenent delubra catervae.
>
> Luc., BC 2.20–29, transl. Braund

In her commentary on this passage, Elaine Fantham describes how 'the simile here uses private experience as both symbol of the collective grief and omen of future bereavement' (Fantham 1992: 83). The stunned silence that prevails at the onset of the public crisis is equated with the initial moments of emotional turmoil for a bereaved mother. This connection is underscored by the blurry rhetorical boundaries of the literary figure itself, as the *matrona* re-emerges as part of the main narrative in line 28 (after the simile has concluded) to put on mourning attire and fill the temples with grief.

The invocation of matronly bereavement in both private and public contexts serves to underscore the dual ways in which family matters are integral to the larger thematic concerns of Lucan's poem.[1] On the one hand, the family as a constitutive unit of Roman society is structured according to the same affective and moral principles that govern the community as a whole, such that a mother's grief can stand in for that of the Republic itself. On the other hand, the poet's move from public to private and back again in this passage also calls attention to the interdependency between these two realms in a more immediate way, as it suggests that Roman men and women would experience the horrors of the impending civil war as both a domestic and a civic crisis simultaneously. The public sorrow of a community riven by civil war is also the private sorrow of its citizens, and vice versa.

The two-sided nature of the connection between civic and domestic realms (*res publica* and *res privata*) reappears later in the same book of Lucan's epic, when the reader is confronted with the unconventional nature of Cato's family arrangements as he and Brutus contemplate how to respond to the looming conflict. In a startling display of his commitment to the principles of Stoicism,

Cato had divorced his wife Marcia so that she could be married to his friend Q. Hortensius and bear him legitimate children, only to remarry her upon Hortensius' death, in 49 BCE. (Plut., *Cato Min.* 25.4–5, 52, Fehrle 1983: 201–3). In the context of Lucan's narrative, the sudden reappearance of the recently widowed Marcia on Cato's doorstep threatens to upend, or at least complicate, the defence of partisan engagement with which the sage had been winning over the younger Brutus (Sannicandro 2007: 89). Cato, who had just finished analogizing his own devotion to the doomed Republic to that of a father grieving at a child's funeral pyre (2.297–301), is confronted by the mother of his children, hair and clothes dishevelled by mourning and grimy from the ash of an actual pyre, as she asks to be restored to her prior status as the wife of Cato (2.326–345).

Marcia is nevertheless aware of where such a private and personal appeal fits within the wider framework of Cato's public responsibilities, and she therefore proposes a different kind of marriage from the ones she had known before:

> As no partner in prosperity or joy do you receive me:
> into anxieties I come, to share your struggles.
> Allow me to accompany the camp. Why should I be left in peace and safety?
> Why should Cornelia be closer to civil war?
>
> non me laetorum sociam rebusque secundis
> accipis: in curas venio partemque laborum.
> da mihi castra sequi: cur tuta in pace relinquar
> et sit civili propior Cornelia bello?
>
> Luc., *BC* 2.346–349, transl. Braund

Having fulfilled the principal obligation of a Roman wife to bear offspring in not one, but two households, Marcia now seeks a different role for herself as wife, that of the devoted companion who will share in her husband's hardships. This rhetoric proves persuasive, and such is the marriage into which she is welcomed. The ceremony with which the couple resumed their vows was a private and solemn affair, with none of the festive elements typical of a Roman wedding. The renewed union is not consummated, as Cato denies himself even licit *amor* ('love') in his mourning for the fate of the world (379–380: *iusto quoque robur amori / restitit*).

These developments mark another way in which the family could be impacted by the trauma of civil war. The poet goes on to praise the unique features of Cato's home life as evidence of his rigid sense of honour and his devotion to the public good above all else, but it is also apparent that this radically unique (if ethically superior) form of marriage was only intelligible, if not conceivable, within the surrounding context of political crisis and civil war (Harich 1990, cf. Panoussi 2007: 120–4). Women do not usually have the opportunity to follow their husbands into harm's way in times of peace, and there is no need to eschew the conjugal joys of marriage unless the freedom of mankind is facing imminent doom. The fact that such a drastic reimagining of the marriage bond was possible (if only for someone like Cato) also suggests a more dynamic relationship between individual families and this surrounding context of civil war. Not only do families suffer when the polity is in crisis, their suffering also sometimes leads to the reaffirmation and re-articulation of bonds within the family, thereby filling the void left by the disintegration of analogous bonds in the public realm.

These insights into the impact of civil war on the family reflect deeply established tendencies in Roman discourses about crisis.[2] Rather than trace these strands back to the myths of the Sabine women (cf. Miles 1992) or Coriolanus' relationship with his mother Veturia (cf. Beltrami 1998: 123–74), this chapter surveys the historical literature of the Imperial period to explore how the experience of civil war shaped Roman ideas about the family, both as an institution and as a metaphor for other kinds of social relationships, in the context of generalized social collapse. As we have already seen in Lucan, the family was deeply enmeshed in Roman narratives of civil war. The material here examined reveals two contrary but related structures of thought, which may be labelled, *faute de mieux*, as 'optimistic' and 'pessimistic'. The first of these perspectives celebrates the family as a bulwark against the storm of civic disintegration, in which bonds of loyalty are tested and yet still endure. The latter perspective, meanwhile, emphasizes the breakdown of traditional family roles, which is understood as both a consequence and cause of the wider dissolution of public morality. After the crisis was over, official efforts to re-anchor a Roman concept of the family, as reflected in the Augustan family legislation, can be seen as responding to both of these perspectives simultaneously.

2. Exceptional cases

Marcia's willingness to share in Cato's anxieties and troubles points to the potential importance of the family as a source of resilience in the face of crisis. As the reference to Pompey's wife Cornelia indicates (Luc., 2.349, cf. 5.722–815, 8.33–108), this display of familial devotion was not an isolated occurrence in the Roman experience of civil war. Although it may seem unsurprising from a modern sociological perspective that individuals faced with the dissolution of shared patriotism and political harmony in a civil war would fall back to rely more heavily on the support of the family unit (McCubbin and Patterson 1982), such stories could be regarded as extraordinary according to the conventional frameworks of the Graeco-Roman mytho-historical tradition. In this regard, the Theban saga is perhaps the classic example of the imagined overlap between domestic and political instability. Among historians, Thucydides' descriptions of the effects of the plague in Athens (2.52–53) and especially the Corcyrean *stasis* (3.82–84) present breakdowns in public morality as pervading all aspects of life within a city. In Corcyra, factional loyalties τὸ ἑταιρικὸν supplanted those of family (τὸ ξυγγενὴς), as the capacity to trust in human connections 'was confirmed not so much by divine law as by the communication of guilt' (3.82.6: καὶ τὰς ἐς σφᾶς αὐτοὺς πίστεις οὐ τῷ θείῳ νόμῳ μᾶλλον ἐκρατύνοντο ἢ τῷ κοινῇ τι παρανομῆσαι, transl. Hobbes). Sallust similarly traced the societal collapse that underpinned the Catilinarian conspiracy to a class of depraved matrons who were expected either to suborn their husbands to the cause or kill them (*Cat.* 24–25). In contrast to such totalizing narratives of crisis, Roman Imperial historians sometimes sought to highlight the exceptions.

We may begin with Tacitus' *Histories*, which open with the author's reflections on the challenges of writing contemporary history under the Principate and an assessment of his own qualifications for the task. He explains that, while there is nothing to prevent him from writing about the present, he intends to leave the reigns of Nerva and Trajan for his old age and begin instead with the Flavian era and the civil wars of 69 CE. In contrast to the 'richer and safer material' of his own day, Tacitus specifies that the era covered in the present work represented a veritable horror show of calamities, involving natural disasters and devastating battles (in both civil and foreign wars), not to mention the reign of a tyrannical emperor, a kind of low-grade civil war, in which the fabric of Roman society was further rent apart by informers and terror (1.1.4–2.3). This history, while bleak, would not be unrelentingly so, however, as Tacitus goes on to clarify:

> Yet this age was not so barren of virtue that it did not also produce good examples. Mothers accompanied their fleeing children, wives followed husbands into exile, relatives were daring, sons-in-law steadfast, the fidelity of slaves was defiant even against torture.
>
> non tamen adeo virtutum sterile saeculum ut non et bona exempla prodiderit. comitatae profugos liberos matres, secutae maritos in exilia coniuges; propinqui audentes, constantes generi, contumax etiam adversus tormenta servorum fides.
>
> Tac., *Hist.* 1.3.1

Tacitus' concession to the virtue of such figures is still tinged with pessimism, of course, and in the context of his narrative the *bona exempla* of familial loyalty provide little respite from the pervasive tragic quality of the narrative as a whole (Ash 2007: 5–8).

Perhaps the most famous (and unsettling) case is the story of the Julii Mansueti, a Spanish father and son serving in opposing legions who came together at the second battle of Cremona, but only recognized one another after the son had mortally wounded his father. The grief-stricken son begs forgiveness for this unwitting parricide, protesting that 'the crime was a communal one, for what stake does one soldier have in such a multitude of civil arms?' (3.25.2: *publicum id facinus; et unum militem quotam civilium armorum partem?*). He then returns to his proper role as a dutiful son, fulfilling his private obligation by burying his father's corpse (3.25.3: *supremo erga parentem officio fungi*). This scene of battlefield recognition, a grotesque reworking of the meeting between Diomedes and Glaucus in Homer (*Il.* 6.120 ff.), is of course a well-known topos in the historiography of civil war (cf. Sisenna, *FRH* 26 F 132), but this likely made it more effective as an aspect of popular lore as well.[3]

Another event that may have its basis in a story that Tacitus would have heard of first-hand concerns the raiding of Otho's forces along the coast of Liguria. The mother of Tacitus' father-in-law, who owned property in the region, was also killed in the course of these raids (*Agr.* 7). Perhaps this connection explains how the historian came to hear of the 'brilliant example' (*praeclaro exemplo*) of an anonymous Ligurian woman who refused to reveal the whereabouts of her son, even under torture (*Hist.* 2.13). Her reply to the marauding soldiers emphasizes the primal nature of the obligation to her child: 'pointing to her womb, she said that he was hiding there' (*uterum ostendens latere respondit*). She presents her body as a physical manifestation of the maternal bond: just as she had sheltered her son during pregnancy, so would she continue to protect him with her womb.[4] Such a pointed and dramatic story of steadfastness (*constantia*) served to frame the trauma of civil war and the violent pressure it brought to bear on the immutable bonds of family as impinging upon the very laws of nature.

The Ligurian woman's refusal to reveal her son's hiding place is reminiscent of a somewhat happier story preserved by Valerius Maximus in a brief chapter of the *Memorable Deeds and Sayings* on the loyalty of wives to their husbands (*de fide uxorum erga viros*), in which a certain Turia shielded her husband Lucretius from the triumviral proscriptions by hiding him in the attic of her bedroom (6.7.2, cf. App., *B Civ.* 4.44). Some scholars have sought to link this Turia to the unnamed dedicatee of a fragmentary inscription in which a husband praises his wife, among other things, for rescuing him during these same proscriptions (Mommsen 1905: 415–17, cf. Gordon 1977). The husband recalls, 'how … I was saved by your counsel, how you did not suffer me to court disaster so rashly and unthinkingly, and by planning with more discretion prepared a secure hiding-place for me' (*CIL* 6.41062 = *ILS* 8393 2, 6–18: *ut … tuis consiliis cons[er]vatus sim? ut neque audac[i]us experiri casus | temere passa sis et mod[es]tiora cogitanti fida receptacula pararis*). The association remains uncertain, however, and the assumption that this was the only woman called upon to protect her husband in these uncertain times is certainly unjustified (Osgood 2014: 117–25).

Cassius Dio also records a similar story about Tanusia, who concealed her husband T. Vinius in a chest at a freedman's house until she could appeal to Octavian for clemency (47.7.4, cf. App., *B Civ.* 4.44, Suet., *Aug.* 27.2). Acilius' wife sacrificed her jewellery, just as the dedicatee of the inscription did, to purchase safe passage out of Italy for her husband (App., *B Civ.* 4.39). The wife of Ligarius, whose deeds are recorded by Appian (*B Civ.* 4.23), also attempted to hide her husband from the dangers of the proscriptions, but was unfortunately betrayed by a slave. After her husband was killed, she took her devotion further, demanding that the triumvirs condemn her as well for having sheltered a named enemy of the state. When they declined to punish her out of respect for her love for her husband (φιλανδρία), she starved herself to death instead as a mark of supreme devotion.

The list of examples could be extended. Appian provides an extensive catalogue of such cases, using stories of faithful wives, sons and slaves to counterbalance accounts of those who had betrayed their husbands, parents, or masters during the proscriptions (*B Civ.* 4.39–51, Gowing 1992: 259–62). He claims to have selected these anecdotes carefully, presenting only those that were 'most surprising and most likely to amaze' (4.16: ἀλλ' ὅσα παραλογώτατα ὄντα μάλιστα ἂν ἐκπλήξειε) from among the many stories that made up an extensive Roman literature on the subject. We might doubt whether Appian in fact bothered to consult multiple sources for his inventory (cf. Gabba 1956: 223–4), but his observations about the popularity of this theme in Imperial historiography ring true. As with the contemporary (and not unrelated) fashion for recounting the 'death scenes' (*exitus*, Plin., *Ep.* 5.5.3) of famous men, these accounts of families under stress accomplished what Lisa Hau has described as 'moralising through pathos' (Hau 2016a: 86, also in this volume). Because of the emotional impact that such stories imparted to the narrative, the framing of civil wars and proscriptions in terms of the extraordinary hardships imposed on the intimate and affective bonds of family served to highlight the essential nature of these crises. Like Tacitus, Appian makes sure to emphasize the difference between this bygone era of violent upheaval and the happiness of his own day (εὐδαιμόνισμα τῶν νῦν παρόντων, 4.16).

Within this broader discourse, the subset of 'optimistic' stories of familial devotion represent something more than a type of silver lining for Roman historians to impose upon the stormy and depressing narrative of civil war, however. Indeed, the final outcome of events was not always a cheerful one. But as the *Laudatio* inscription perhaps more than any other piece of evidence makes clear, these tales also give genuine insight into how many Romans would have framed their own experience of crisis. When the security of civil society was stripped away, the integrity of the family was tested in ways that had profound implications for individual survival (Hinard 1990). For the men and women who lived through the trauma of civil war and proscriptions, these experiences will have fundamentally reconfigured their sense of the value of the family and of its place in Roman society. Additionally, as a bond that could survive and even strengthen in the face of the collapse of political institutions, the familial devotion represented in these exemplary narratives also offered an anchor upon which to affix hopes for the restoration of a virtuous civil society in the aftermath of these crises. If the family could survive, so too could the *res publica*.[5]

This latter effort involved a form of metaphorical projection common in the history of Roman concepts, whereby the moral values that operate within one sphere of social life are treated as scalable, such that, for example, the dutifulness (*pietas*) of a child to a parent (itself derived from the reverence of a mortal to the gods) could be expanded to encompass the attitude of the subject toward the state (Roller 2001: 217–18, 249, cf. Schröder 2012). The overlapping domains of such concepts contributed to the tendency to view the family as a microcosm of the community at large and was used to establish frameworks whereby familial relationships could stand in for other social bonds. In this regard, much has been written about the title of *pater patriae* ('father of the fatherland'), and the explicit fashioning of the saviour of the state according to the role of a father (Alföldi 1971, Severy 2003: 158–60). Consideration of the experiences of Roman families in civil war helps us better to understand how this title became a powerful symbol for the likes of Cicero, Julius Caesar, Augustus and others who worked to rebuild after the crises that brought them to power.

As revealing as the self-representation of the dictator or emperor as a father-figure is, however, it is also perhaps too narrow a framework for assessing the impact of the familial experience of civil war, as it fails to account for an important dimension of so many of the above-cited cases – namely, the active role that women played, as mothers, daughters, wives and sisters, in preserving the integrity of their families during the crisis of civil war. While essential to the interpretation of these *exempla*, the gendered quality of these stories also ultimately calls attention to the fundamental asymmetry of the public and private spheres as normally conceived of in Roman culture. The extraordinary importance of women within the household, when held up against their conventional exclusion from the political realm, complicates any attempt to draw upon these scenes of familial devotion as a model for political reintegration.

Upon closer inspection, it is clear that a large part of what made these stories of mothers' and wives' (often anonymously commemorated) dedication to the interests of their sons and husbands exemplary is the paradoxical nature of the actions they undertook to protect their male kin. Rather than stay within the dependent position circumscribed for them within the household, these women were prompted by the crisis of civil war to take on roles traditionally reserved for men. This boundary-crossing is perhaps most evident in the long narrative of the elogium-inscription, where the husband praises his wife *inter alia* for providing for him financially (*CIL* 4.41062 2, 1: [*varia et ampla subsi*]*dia fugae meae praesitisti*), for her ingenuity and good advice (2, 4: [*nostrorum deceptis a*]*dversariorum custodibus*, 2, 17: *tuis consiliis cons*[*er*]*vatus sim*), and for her courage in publicly petitioning Lepidus for his safe return (2, 30: *quid hac virtute efficaciu*[*s*]). These narratives are thus as much a challenge to the conventional sexual order as a reassertion of the primary value of family within Roman society. As Josiah Osgood summarizes in his exemplary study of the *Laudatio*,

> Civil war was a defining experience for her, testing her in ways that she otherwise might not have been. Her achievements were most conspicuous then, and along with the achievements of other women, including Augustus' wife Livia, led to lasting changes in how women might comport themselves in public.
>
> Osgood 2014: 150

From the perspective of the author of this inscription, his wife's resourcefulness in taking on challenges that ordinarily were reserved for men prompts intense admiration and devotion. His view of women's capabilities (or at least that of his own wife) as well as his attitude toward the bond of marriage has therefore been 're-anchored' to a new standard that would have been different in significant respects from what typically prevailed among men of his class.

3. The burden of the *mos maiorum*

This was not, unfortunately, the final word on the subject. Against this point of view, we must also acknowledge that there were other powerful assumptions about gender roles within the family that continued to shape how such acts of heroism might be perceived. A woman who behaved like a man, even in the interest of her husband, was liable to be seen as a threat to the social order. Fulvia's conduct in the Perusine War, as characterized by Cassius Dio (48.3–14, esp. 48.10.4), is an extreme and therefore perhaps sufficient example of how a publicly engaged wife could be viewed as a dangerous 'she-man' (*virago*), dressing up in military attire and consumed with her own power over the men around her (Osgood 2006: 160). While over-the-top in its invective extremity, this image nevertheless serves to illustrate the anxieties aroused in a patriarchal society when women took advantage of opportunities for political agency such as those afforded them in times of crisis and civil war. For those Roman men who did not directly benefit from the lifesaving acts in question, it was perhaps easier to respond to these episodes of transgression with horror than to celebrate them with gratitude and respect.

In light of the hostile characterization of Fulvia's actions on behalf of her husband's interests in Italy, it is clear that one might also draw a very different set of conclusions about the relationship between the family and Roman society more broadly in the context of civil war. For those predisposed to see women's participation in the public realm as categorically dangerous and unsettling, it was possible to view the prominence of strong women during the civil wars as yet another cause of, rather than a resilient response to, the breakdown in the broader social order. By reversing the chain of causation in this way, the crisis playing out in the political realm became the manifestation of a deeper crisis in the ancestral tradition, through which both the state and the traditional bonds of family were undone.

This more reactionary way of thinking about the family in the context of civil war would find encouragement from another type of narrative, in which family members betrayed rather than protected one another. Appian's account of the proscriptions is rich in this material as well, and it is notable that he follows the exemplary story of Ligarius' wife (who starved herself after failing to keep her husband hidden from the bounty-hunters) with that of another unnamed woman, who not only arranged for her husband Septimius to be added to the proscription list, but also kept him at her house under the pretence of protecting him so that the executioners might take him more easily (*B Civ.* 4.23). The emotional devastation that this type of disloyalty inflicted upon a defenceless husband comes through most dramatically in the case of Salassus, who feared betrayal by the slave he had sent to inform his wife where he was hiding. Salassus had climbed up on the housetop to look for signs of trouble, when 'seeing not the porter, but his wife leading the murderers, he threw himself down from the roof' (4.24: ἰδὼν δὲ οὐ τὸν θυρωρόν, ἀλλὰ τὴν γυναῖκα τοῖς σφαγεῦσιν ἡγουμένην ἔρριψεν ἑαυτὸν ἀπὸ τοῦ τέγους). Once the protection of familial bonds is stripped away, no hope remains.

Such monstrous behaviour was not limited to the women within the family, of course. Tacitus likewise relates a story of outright fratricide, in which instead of being overcome by grief or horror (as the younger Mansuetus had been at the death of his father), the soldier who killed his brother had the audacity to request a special reward from his commanders (*Hist.* 3.51).[6] Appian also records the story of the proscribed Thuranius, who had hoped that his son might use his influence with Antony to appeal for his life, only to discover that this son had already denounced him (*B Civ.* 4.18). The most notorious connection between the breakdown of the family and the proscriptions involved the triumvirs themselves, however: Antony had placed his uncle L. Caesar on the lists, and Lepidus proscribed his own brother Paullus. As Cassius Dio comments:

> For in internecine warfare, which involves much time and many events, many have come into conflict even with their own kin according to the principles of factionalism.
>
> ἅτε γὰρ ἐν ἐμφυλίοις πολέμοις, καὶ πολλῷ μὲν χρόνῳ πολλαῖς δὲ καὶ πράξεσι γενομένοις, συχνοὶ καὶ τοῖς πάνυ συγγενέσι κατὰ τὸ στασιωτικὸν προσεκεκρούκεσαν
> Cass. Dio, 47.6.2, cf. App., *B Civ* 3.37

Thucydides' comments on the Corcyrean *stasis* and the all-pervasive corruption that accompanies civil strife had not lost their relevance. The roots of the crisis still extended into the institution of the family itself.

4. After the crisis

In the aftermath of civil war, the Romans had ready access to two radically different perspectives on the family: one which saw it as an institution in crisis just like every other institution suffering from the collapse of the ancient moral order, and another, more positive view, in which the family still endured as the final refuge against this collapse and a potential source of hope in a darkening world. Both of these perspectives reflected the realities of the ways in which the family had been forced to adapt under the strain of external crisis, particularly the increasing reliance on female relations who proved themselves capable of acting independently and exerting influence beyond the boundaries of the household. For some, this breach of traditional gender norms represented a disaster. The intervention of male relatives through institutions such as *patria potestas* (paternal authority) and *tutela* (male guardianship) had long been regarded as necessary checks against female mischief (Dixon 1984). For others, however, these developments represented an opportunity to revitalize the institution of marriage as a nurturing partnership founded on mutual affection and respect (cf. Veyne 1978).

This dual, or perhaps schizophrenic, narrative would seem to offer two very different starting points against which to reconstitute the larger social order in the aftermath of civil war. I think we can see these contradictions play out in the package of legislation often referred to as 'the Augustan marriage laws' (Treggiari 1991: 60–80, 277–91, Galinsky 1996: 128–33). These laws were in fact a part of a more encompassing programme of social legislation passed following Augustus' establishment of the principate as part of the run-up to the declaration of a 'new age' with the *Ludi Saeculares* in 17 BCE. As Beth Severy explains:

> By criminalizing adultery, encouraging marriage and childrearing, and regulating everything from seating in the theater to the private display of wealth, these new laws cast Augustus as a savior of the state in the context of Roman morality, thus adding to his status as a military and political restorer of the *res publica*.
>
> Severy 2003: 50

This was how Augustus himself characterizes these accomplishments in a familiar passage of his *Res Gestae*, in which he celebrates the restoration of 'many ancestral *exempla* that were already being erased' and the creation of 'new examples for posterity to follow' (*RG* 8: *legibus novi[s] m[e auctore l]atis m[ulta e]xempla maiorum exolescentia iam ex nostro [saecul]o red[uxi et ip]se multarum rer[um exe]mpla imitanda post[eris tradidi]*). The ideological purpose of these laws was to promote the renewal of the social order by enacting a restoration of values that were imagined as lost.

Ostensibly, these laws represented an attempt to correct the moral collapse within the family that the long era of crisis and civil war had laid bare. Adultery was criminalized, with penalties both for promiscuous women and for men who violated the sanctity of the marital bond (Suet., *Aug.* 34, McGinn 2003: 140–215). At the same time, marriage was encouraged, along with the traditional moral vision of this institution as an instrument for reproducing the civic community through the production and raising of children (Cass. Dio, 56.1.2–10.3, Treggiari 1991: 66–80). The importance of the family as a basic unit of the social order was also reinforced by means of regulations prohibiting intermarriage across certain social barriers (Treggiari 1991: 61–6).

In placing the family at the centre of his programme of moral reform, Augustus would appear to be siding with those who saw the breakdown of that institution as a cause of the crises that needed to be confronted in order to recover from civil war. And yet, there is also a reflection of the more 'optimistic' vision of the family in the system of incentives through which portions of this legal programme were meant to operate. The 'right of child-bearing' (*ius liberorum*) was a set of legal privileges bestowed upon couples who produced a sufficient number of children in the context of their marriage, which included, for matrons, the ability to inherit sums in excess of 100,000 HS (Cass. Dio, 56.10.2) and the right to conduct business without the intervention of a male guardian (Gai., *Inst.* 1.145). The laws thus confirmed a new, more positive vision of women's ability to act independently in the interests of the family, while also redirecting the substance of their familial devotion from the sorts of good offices that many had been called upon to perform during the civil wars to the peacetime task of reproduction.[7]

5. The imperial family

As domestic roles were being reconstituted and reconceptualized in this way, other changes were also taking place in the political structure of the *res publica*, of course. The overlap between this transformation and the Augustan reinvention of the family inevitably fostered an entirely new way of thinking about the connection between the family and the political community, in which the family of the *princeps* himself took centre stage. The genesis of this new concept is outlined in another anecdote from Cassius Dio:

> Meanwhile a clamor arose in the senate over the disorderly conduct of the women and of the young men, this being alleged as a reason for their reluctance to enter into the marriage relation; and when they urged him to remedy this abuse also, with ironical allusions to his own intimacy with many women, he at first replied that the most necessary restrictions had been laid down and that anything further could not possibly be regulated by decree in similar fashion. Then, when he was driven into a corner, he said: 'You yourselves ought to

admonish and command your wives as you wish; that is what I do.' When they heard that, they plied him with questions all the more, wishing to learn what the admonitions were which he professed to give Livia. He accordingly, though with reluctance, made a few remarks about women's dress and their other adornment, about their going out and their modest behaviour, not in the least concerned that his actions did not lend credence to his words.

Κἂν τούτῳ καταβοήσεως ἐν τῷ συνεδρίῳ περί τε τῆς τῶν γυναικῶν καὶ περὶ τῆς τῶν νεανίσκων ἀκοσμίας, πρὸς ἀπολογίαν δή τινα τοῦ μὴ ῥᾳδίως δι' αὐτὴν τὰς τῶν γάμων συναλλαγὰς ποιεῖσθαι, γενομένης, καὶ ἐναγόντων αὐτὸν καὶ ἐκείνην ἐπανορθῶσαι χλευασμῷ ὅτι πολλαῖς γυναιξὶν ἐχρῆτο, τὸ μὲν πρῶτον ἀπεκρίνατο αὐτοῖς ὅτι τὰ μὲν ἀναγκαιότατα διώρισται, τὰ δὲ λοιπὰ ἀδύνατόν ἐστιν ὁμοίως παραδοθῆναι, ἔπειτα δὲ ἐκβιασθεὶς εἶπεν ὅτι 'αὐτοὶ ὀφείλετε ταῖς γαμεταῖς καὶ παραινεῖν καὶ κελεύειν ὅσα βούλεσθε· ὅπερ που καὶ ἐγὼ ποιῶ.' ἀκούσαντες οὖν ταῦτ' ἐκεῖνοι πολλῷ μᾶλλον ἐνέκειντο αὐτῷ, βουλόμενοι τὰς παραινέσεις ἃς τῇ Λιουίᾳ παραινεῖν ἔφη μαθεῖν. καὶ ὃς ἄκων μέν, εἶπε δ' οὖν τινα καὶ περὶ τῆς ἐσθῆτος καὶ περὶ τοῦ λοιποῦ κόσμου τῶν τε ἐξόδων καὶ τῆς σωφροσύνης αὐτῶν, μηδ' ὁτιοῦν φροντίσας ὅτι μὴ καὶ τῷ ἔργῳ αὐτὰ ἐπιστοῦτο.

Cass. Dio, 54.16.3–5, transl. Cary

By placing so much emphasis on the reconstitution of the family as the basic unit of Roman society, Augustus invited more intensive scrutiny of his own activities as the head of his own household (*paterfamilias*). Not all of the attention would have been welcome, as the reference to Augustus' youthful peccadilloes suggests. The unusual circumstances of his marriage to Livia remained a source of potential embarrassment (Flory 1988), but the supposed misdeeds of their daughter Julia brought the most grief, however, as Augustus felt compelled to denounce her in a detailed letter that was read out before the Senate (Suet., *Aug.* 65.2, Fantham 2006: 81–8).

With the introduction of autocracy, the family of the emperor became a public institution. This merging of the domestic and the political under a system of dynastic monarchy found particular expression in the extraordinary position of authority attained by the empress Livia (Purcell 1986). Although the anonymous wife of the *Laudatio* inscription would have been ineligible for the privileges of *ius liberorum* because of the couple's inability to have children (*CIL* 6.41062 2, 42–50), Livia received these honours through an exceptional grant, despite the fact that she was the mother of only two sons (Cass. Dio, 55.2.6). Like Augustus' sister Octavia, she was also able to dedicate public buildings in her own name (Ov., *Fast.* 6.637–648). With the accession of Tiberius, Livia Augusta continued to accrue new honours as the mother of the reigning emperor and priestess of her deified husband's cult (Cass. Dio, 56.46.1, Severy 2003: 210–11). Her eventual deification, like that of other female members of the Imperial house, reflects (on an extraordinarily magnified scale) the changing nature of the Roman family and the position of women within it.

These developments were also arguably conditioned by the experience of the civil wars, insofar as the familial entanglements and especially the breakdown of marriage alliances among the leading combatants received special prominence in the common historical understanding of these conflicts. It was a generally accepted premise that the unravelling of the first triumvirate began not with the death of Crassus at Carrhae in 53 BCE, but in the previous year with the death of Pompey's wife (and Caesar's daughter) Julia, who was regarded as an essential moderating link between the two men (Vell. Pat., 2.47.2, Luc., *BC* 1.111–120).[8] Octavian and Antony's relationship similarly hinged, or so the sources suggest, on a sequence of unsuccessful marriage alliances. The climax of the Perusine War was marked by Octavian's divorce from Fulvia's young daughter Clodia (Suet., *Aug.* 62.1, Cass. Dio, 48.5.2), just as the battle of Actium was preceded by Antony's rejection of his rival's sister Octavia (Liv., *Per.* 132, Cass. Dio, 50.3.2).

By reframing the crisis of civil war as a matter of domestic rather than civic turbulence, these narratives reveal how the metaphorical relationship between these two domains had begun to collapse in on itself as everything depended upon the personality of a few powerful *principes*. With the emergence of the imperial household (*domus Augusta*) as the sole locus of power, the integrity of the family was no longer simply a metaphor for that of the civic community: the two had converged into a single institution. Thereafter, the situation became the one we find documented in Tacitus' *Annals* and Suetonius' biographies, in which dynastic politics were the only politics that mattered.

Notes

Chapter 1

1. Armitage (2017: 31–45) draws a sharp distinction between *stasis* and *bellum civile* as concepts. While it is true that the two terms do not map onto each other neatly, because citizenship was viewed differently in the Greek *polis* and in Rome, they do overlap in meaningful ways, shown perhaps most clearly by the fact that Greek authors consistently use the word *stasis* to describe the Roman civil wars.
2. Although Tiberius 'opened the fountain', Appian marks out Sulla as having a central role in the history of Roman *staseis*: his march on Rome in 88 BCE was a turning point in terms of scale and violence, a new kind of *stasis* with the *patris* at stake as a prize (*B Civ.* 1.7.55).
3. *Stasis* is far from the only candidate for Greek crisis-terminology. Plutarch, for instance, uses the term *ta eskhata*, 'the extremes', repeatedly to describe major upheavals, see *Ti. Gracch. Synkr.* 5.4; *Sulla* 29.4; *Cato* 53.5; *Ant.* 69.3; *Mor.* 814d. Another important term is *metabolē*, 'transition', on this see Whitmarsh in this volume. On *stasis* in Thucydides see Price (2001); on *stasis* in Aristotle see Skultety (2009); on the term *stasis* in Greek thought broadly see Loraux (1995).
4. On *stasis* in Appian see also Price (2015).
5. Ancient sources on the conspiracy: Cic., *Cat.*, *Mur.*, *Flac.*, *Fam.*, *Att.*, *Cons.*; Sall., *Cat.*; Plut., *Cic.*; App., *B Civ.* 2.1–7; Cass. Dio, 37. 42. Modern judgements on the significance of the conspiracy include Yavetz (1963: 485–99); Seager (1964: 338–47); Waters (1970: 195–215), Phillips (1976); Wiseman (1994).
6. Sall., *Cat.* 21.2; Cic., *Cat.* 4.11–12, cf. 4.2.
7. Powell (2013) notes that the further historians are removed in time from the events they are narrating, the less likely they are to leave room for possible, alternative outcomes. With time, it seems, historiography grows more static and overdetermined.
8. See e.g. Berliner (2005); Grigoropoulos et al. (2017).

Chapter 2

1. The essay as a whole is reprised as de Man (1983: 3–19).
2. E.g. Baechler (1975), Hobsbawm (1986).

3 See esp. Baker (1990); Figes and Kolonitskii (1999).
4 Syme (1939), building in part on Mommsen's platform (Finley 1986: 48).
5 Emphasis in the original.
6 Veyne (1984 [1971]: 132–3), attacking what he calls the 'historical concept' of revolution: such concepts are 'composite representations that give the illusion of intellection, but in reality are only kinds of generic images'. Ober (2007), explicitly using the language of revolution for Athenian democracy, marks a rare exception to this trend.
7 Leach 1953 (which focuses closely on archaic Greece), 1955; the influence of contemporary classicists is acknowledged more obviously in the 1961 reprints, see the references to Martin Nilsson and Hermann Fränkel on 128–9; Moses Finley is acknowledged at 124.
8 Exceptions include Finnish, Welsh, Icelandic and Hungarian.
9 '[The revolution] no longer returned to given conditions or possibilities but has, since 1789, led forward into an unknown future' (Koselleck 1985: 46). Contrast Hill (1990), arguing that the semantic shift took place well before 1688. An alternative tradition identifies the roots of the 'progressivist' conception of time in Jewish and Christian thought, as against the 'cyclical' conception of pagan antiquity: see esp. Bann (1990: 77–8).
10 Parker (1999: 119), an important discussion of the creative role played by 'the revolutionary narrative' in structuring experience phenomenologically in the midst of modernity. 'The revolutionary narrative has a quite specific function for the modern consciousness of human beings: it enables people to translate the threat of change into a possibility of deliberate improvement' (120).
11 Cole (1967); Edelstein (1967); Dodds (1973: 1–25) argues (wrongly, I think) that ideas of progress were largely limited to classical Athens.
12 Timotheus, *Persae* 203 (cf. 211–212) Hordern; LeVen (2014).
13 Osborne (2007); Spawforth (2011); cf. Goldhill and Osborne, eds (2006).
14 Osborne (2006). The only surviving account of the events surrounding Cleisthenes' reforms is at Arist, *Ath. Pol.* 20–2.
15 Cf. Hdt., 6.109.3, 8.142.3, 9.45.2, 9.60.1, etc.
16 Thuc., 1.122.3; on this theme see more generally Scanlon (1987).
17 Mills (1997: 87–128, noting on p. 89 the use of *epitaphios* motifs: see below). See also Isoc., *Panath.* 126–9.
18 Isoc., *Panath.* 148. Isocrates' bizarre warping of history depends upon (a) a lack of specificity about when exactly democracy began in Athens, and (b) the representation of Pisistratean tyranny as a cancerous malfunction of democracy (i.e. the people only wanted him to drive out the oligarchic faction).
19 Brock (2009: 156): 'the pattern of Athenian policy did not form any very uniform picture, and indeed, was not uniform even locally'; 161: 'the dominant consideration was pragmatism'.

20 See Hornblower (1991: 308), arguing (correctly I think) that Thucydides/Pericles sees Athens as a political, not a cultural, model for emulation.
21 A vexed sentence: I have followed Hornblower (2008: 651) for the syntax, but I have taken τὸ διάφορον as 'discord' (LSJ *s.v.* II.3) rather than 'the difference between them' (of which I cannot make sense).
22 Monarchies are distinguished from *politeiai* (*Pol.* 1310b), presumably because they are founded not in any social contract aimed at producing justice but in the will and desire of individuals.
23 A charge also levelled at him by pro-democratic factions: Lys., 12.62–78.
24 On Athenian responses to these see Shear (2011).
25 E.g. Lintott (1982: 51–2).
26 Serres (1995: 60–1, emphasis in the original).

Chapter 3

1 Other attestations reviewed in Instinsky (1952).
2 First attested on coinage on a Nero dupondius, RIC 1.405–7. Manders (2012: 209–10). Bill Welch's website offers a handy overview of *securitas* on coinage: http://www.forumancientcoins.com/moonmoth/reverse_securitas.html
3 Blössner (2007) provides an introduction and overview. Loraux (1997: 59–84) analyses *l'âme de la cité* ('soul of the city') in Freudian terms; Plato's analogy goes in both directions. Hershkowitz (1998: 8–9) stresses the implicit madness underlying Plato's depiction of *stasis* in the city. Spike Lee's film, 'Chi-raq' names both the central character and Chicago in its dysfunction. The state of soul and city are commensurate.
4 For *securus* meaning 'safe', see Hauser (1954: 55).
5 See Hamilton (2013: 51–8). Cicero links the absence of *cura* with tranquillity already at *Pro Murena* 55, delivered in 63 BCE. Cicero brings *securitas* into a wider pre-existing lexicon for emotional states. His dominant word for distress is *aegritudo*, literally 'sickness', which in the soul means grief, sorrow, or anxiety, and for peace of mind *tranquillitas*. Hadot (1995: 49–70) emphasizes agreement among the philosophical schools that peace of mind is a central aim in the blessed life. Graver (2002: xvii–xxvii) outlines the schools' positions on the emotions.
6 The blessed life becomes available once we are free from cares: Cic., *Off.* 1.13.
7 Cic., *Tusc.* 5.14.42; *Off.* 1.21.69. Mental or spiritual *aegritudo*: OLD 2.
8 See Rimell (2015: 7) for the 'paradox of enclosure as secure yet terrifying, walled yet penetrable space' (also 15, 18).
9 The modern meaning elides the psychic reaction to focus on actions taken in response to objective dangers, e.g. Waever (1993: 23): 'security is broadly about the pursuit of freedom from threat'.

10 Adjectives typically attaching to *cura* in its negative sense are *acris, aegra, anxia, assidua, dura, gravis, maesta, molesta, pavida, sollicita, tristis,* and *vigil,* see Fuchs (1948: 165–6).
11 Gill (2006: 109–10) considers the negativity entailed in *ataraxia* and Cicero's critique of the removal of pain. For other related philosophical negations (*aponia, akataplexia, adiaphora, astathemeta, anekrita*), see 124–5.
12 The negative orientation of *securitas* is further complicated by the double positive and negative meanings of the root *cura*, namely tending and anxiety. On the 'two fundamental but conflicting meanings' of *cura*, see Reich (1995: 319). He identifies four basic meanings of English 'care', which derives from Middle High German *kari*, itself from Common Teutonic *caru* ('trouble' or 'grief'): anxiety, anguish, or mental suffering; basic concern for people, ideas, institutions; solicitous, responsible attention to tasks; attentive care to a person (329). Hamilton (2013: 10–12) outlines the crisscrossing double negatives of security.
13 Schmitzer (2011: 199) on loyalty.
14 For the conflation of Tiberius' return to Rome (2 CE) and adoption (4 CE), see Woodman (1977: 130).
15 For the body politic imagery here, see Woodman (1983 *ad loc.*); Schmitzer (2011: 189–90).
16 Woodman (1983) *ad loc.* daggers the passage. I translate according to the reading of the Rhenanus.
17 Kantorowicz (1957). At Velleius 2.124.2–3: Augustus splits into his component parts at death. His physical body is buried and his numen receives divine honours.
18 Weber in Eisenstadt (1968).
19 For accession literature, see Braund (2012: 97–108); Hoffer (2012).
20 Hardie (1993: 93) on the succession problem in the *Aeneid*.
21 Woodman (1977) and (1983) consistently underscores that panegyric does not necessarily mean that the account is not based in fact. Independent sources frequently back up Velleius' topoi.
22 Bloomer (2011: 108–10) sees the ostensibly projected fuller work as a 'rhetorical foil' or 'mode' that highlights the unique importance of his subject. While he stresses Velleius' haste in writing (102), and Lobur (2011: 204) haste in the context of recitation, both see Velleius' rhetoric as a strategy of legitimation whereby he signals his willing participation in the Imperial system.
23 Gaius' death in 4 CE in Lycia was a tragedy for the Imperial family, but posed no threat to the Empire beyond the succession crisis, which Tiberius' adoption resolved.
24 Italian usefully distinguishes between *rappresentazione* (semiotic) and *rappresentanza* (political).
25 For the conventional emphasis on restoration in marking a new regime and debate about criticism of Augustus here, see Woodman (1977: 234, 238–40) and (1983: 252). Schmitzer (2011: 190) explains the repetition in positivistic terms: real conditions had declined from their illustrious beginning.

26 Fowler (1995) argues against Horatian panegyric here. Whatever the authorial intentions, the poetry puts the elements of the ideology on display.
27 Du Quesnay (1995: 172) notes the similarity of the link between the safety of the state and of the *princeps* to inscriptions of this type: *senatus consulto ob rempublicam cum salute imperatoris Caesaris Augusti conseruatam*; Fedeli and Ciccarelli (2008: 285). For panegyric conventions here, see Syndikus (2001: 322–3).
28 Woodman (1983: 255) collects further parallels for the panegyric topos, but also insists on Velleius' discernment, since he omits it in the similar account of Tiberius.
29 For the distinction between the political and the pastoral leader, see Foucault (2007) *passim*, esp. 147–253. By virtue of his position, Augustus organizes community beyond strict governance, but the lack of the self-sacrificial dimension of the Judeo-Christian tradition limits the parallel. For Augustus as a symbol, see Kennedy (1992).
30 Fuller discussion of this poem's rhetorical strategies is in Lowrie (1997: 343–52) and (2010). Freudenburg (2014) analyses parallels between refusals by poets and by statesmen.

Chapter 4

1 Research for this chapter has been made possible partly by the Alexander von Humboldt Foundation, which granted me a senior research fellowship to be spent at the University of Heidelberg in the academic year 2017–18, and partly by my home institution, the University of Glasgow, which granted me leave to take up this offer. I want to thank Jonas Grethlein and Matthew Fox for reading drafts of the chapter and sharing their thoughts with me. Translations in the chapter are my own unless otherwise attributed.
2 Hau (forthcoming a). The argument in that article proceeds partly on the basis of a theoretical discussion in the fragments of Agatharchides of Cnidus, to which I shall return below, and partly by analogy with the present-day historiographical movement of experientialism, which is also briefly touched on below. That article and this one are in many ways companion pieces. The issues touched on in both papers will be further explored in a forthcoming monograph: Hau (forthcoming b).
3 Schwartz (1896, 1903, and 1905). The theory was developed by, among others, Scheller (1911), von Fritz (1956), Zegers (1959), Brink (1960) and Fornara (1983).
4 The first sustained arguments against it were Walbank (1955) and (1960). His arguments have since been expanded by a.o. Fromentin (2001), Marincola (2003 and 2013), and Schepens (2005).
5 E.g. Walbank (1990), Meister (1990: 95–101), Luce (1997: 119–22), Gehrke (2001: 299), Zangara (2007: 76–7).
6 E.g. Schepens (2005), Kebric (2015), Baron (2016 and 2017).

7   Hau (forthcoming a).
8   On the subjectivity of crisis, see Klooster and Kuin in this volume.
9   General scholarship on Duris: Kebric (1977), Pédech (1989), Landucci Gattinoni (1997), Knoepfler (2000), Pownall (n.d.), Baron (2016), Naas and Simon (2016).
10 For Duris' biography see Landucci Gattinoni (1997: 9-38). For shorter versions, see Shipley (1987: 179-81) and Pownall (n.d.). Duris was once thought to have been a pupil of Theophrastus, thus creating a firm link with the Peripatetics. This assumption rests on Ath., *Deipn*. 4.1.128a = Duris *FGrH* 76 T1. The connection between Duris and Theophrastus, however, rests on an emendation of the text; without it, Athenaeus either states that Duris' brother, Lynceus, was a pupil of Theophrastus, or that the completely unrelated Hippolochus had that honour; see Dalby (1991) and Baron (2011). Knoepfler (2016: 21-2) casts serious doubts on our supposed knowledge about Duris' father.
11 *FGrH* = *Die Fragmente der griechischen Historiker*, the magnum opus of Felix Jacoby and the basis for all scholarship on Hellenistic historiography. Many of these fragments have now been re-published online in the *BNJ* (*Brill's New Jacoby*); the Duris fragments in *BNJ* have translations and commentary by F. Pownall (n.d.). For a perspicacious discussion of the delimitation of some of the Duris fragments and their implications for our understanding of this historian, see Baron (2011).
12 For readings of Thucydides which see him as portraying the downward spiral of the Athenians' moral degeneration, see e.g. Cornford (1907), Hunter (1973), Crane (1998 *passim*, e.g. 258), Hau (2016a: 200-2).
13 Pownall (n.d.) *ad loc.*; Stadter (1989) *ad loc*; Shipley (1987: 116-17); Landucci Gattinoni (1997: 228-33).
14 E.g. Plut., *Per.* 3, συντετάχαμεν τὸν Περικλέους βίον καὶ τὸν Φαβίου Μαξίμου τοῦ διαπολεμήσαντος πρὸς Ἀννίβαν περιέχον, ἀνδρῶν κατά τε τὰς ἄλλας ἀρετὰς ὁμοίων, μάλιστα δὲ πραότητα καὶ δικαιοσύνην ('I arraign side by side the life of Pericles and that of Fabius Maximus who continuously fought Hannibal, men similar in their virtues, and particularly in mildness and justice.) and 17, τοῦτο μὲν οὖν παρεθέμην ἐνδεικνύμενος αὐτοῦ τὸ φρόνημα καὶ τὴν μεγαλοφροσύνην ('this I have said in order to demonstrate his intelligence and greatness of thought.'), and all of the final chapter, 39.
15 I use 'social memory' in the sense set out clearly by Steinbock (2013: 7-19). Social memory is less institutionalized than cultural memory (see e.g. Assmann 2008, 2011) and more flexible than collective memory (Steinbock 2013: 8-13). For the relationship between Samos and Athens, see Shipley (1987) and Knoepfler (2016).
16 Shipley (1987: 138-43 and 161-4). The inscriptions which honour those men across Greece who helped the Samians in their exile are now collected in *IG* XII,6.I as numbers 17-41. For an overview of literary sources for the occupation see Knoepfler (2016: 25-6).
17 For social memory and collective memory, see n 15.

18 For evidence of slaves thus tattooed, see Stadter (1989: 249–50).
19 The story is believed by Plutarch, although he switches the symbols around so the Samians are tattooed with a samaina and the Athenians with owls (*Per.* 26.4), and by Aelian (*VH* 2.9). Pownall (n.d. *ad* Duris F66) and Stadter (1989 *ad* Plut., *Per.* 26.4) think that it may well be based on a kernel of truth.
20 E.g. Schwartz (1905), Scheller (1911: 68–71), Jacoby (1926b *ad loc.*), von Fritz (1956), Zangara (2007). Strasburger (1982) and Fornara (1983) argue that we should take Duris' theory of history seriously as a plausible alternative to the Thucydidean ideal. Note, however, that even Thucydides and Polybius expect the reading of their works to be pleasurable to some degree, alongside being educational: the comparative in Thucydides' καὶ ἐς μὲν ἀκρόασιν ἴσως τὸ μὴ μυθῶδες αὐτῶν ἀτερπέστερον φανεῖται (1.22.4) implies as much, as does Polyb., 1.4.10–11, διὸ παντελῶς βραχύ τι νομιστέον συμβάλλεσθαι τὴν κατὰ μέρος ἱστορίαν πρὸς τὴν τῶν ὅλων ἐμπειρίαν καὶ πίστιν. ἐκ μέν τοι γε τῆς ἁπάντων πρὸς ἄλληλα συμπλοκῆς καὶ παραθέσεως, ἔτι δ' ὁμοιότητος καὶ διαφορᾶς, μόνως ἄν τις ἐφίκοιτο καὶ δυνηθείη κατοπτεύσας ἅμα καὶ τὸ χρήσιμον καὶ τὸ τερπνὸν ἐκ τῆς ἱστορίας ἀναλαβεῖν. See also Walbank (1990).
21 Gray (1987). See also Veloso (2016).
22 This has been well argued by Baron (2016: 73–82), who also notes that *hedone* and similar expressions are typical of the way ancient readers describe the quality of Herodotus.
23 Hau (2016b) with references to earlier scholarship.
24 For the term emplotment, see White (1973 and 1980) and Klooster and Kuin in this volume.
25 Pelling (2016). He notes that life sometimes seems to imitate art, and that Antony's life lent itself particularly well to a tragic plotline.
26 The concept of emplotment in historiography was pioneered by H. White (1973), but I use it here in a looser sense because I believe that there are more possible ways to emplot historical events than the four (comedy, tragedy, satire, romance) explored by White.
27 As the fragments of Phylarchus are generally of lesser quality than those of Duris (the longest ones coming from polemical sources), so scholarship on Phylarchus is scarcer and more speculative. General scholarship on Phylarchus: Kroymann (1956), Africa (1960 and 1961), Pédech (1989), Landucci Gattinoni (n.d.). Good discussions of the Phylarchus fragments preserved by Athenaeus are Stelluto (1995) and Schepens (2007).
28 But for an attempt at a reconstruction, see Africa (1961).
29 For a persuasive argument that Phylarchus' account was the accepted authority on this time period until Polybius, see Schepens (2005).
30 Marincola (2013). For untruthfulness being the essence of Polybius' criticism see also Walbank (1960), Eckstein (2013), Hau (forthcoming b).
31 With thanks to L. Huitink, R. Waterfield and N. Wiater for useful discussion (in the two latter cases by email) of Polybius' use of *tropos*.

32 This has been forcefully argued by Marincola (2003).
33 One is reminded of the sentiment of some modern historians that too much explanation can seem to 'explain away' atrocities. See e.g. the introduction to one of the most acclaimed historical works about the Holocaust in recent years, by S. Friedländer (2007: xxvi): 'this photograph triggers disbelief. Such disbelief is a quasi-visceral reaction, one that occurs before knowledge rushes in to smother it. "Disbelief" here means something that arises from the depth of one's immediate perception of the world, of what is ordinary and what remains "unbelievable". The goal of historical knowledge is to domesticate disbelief, to explain it away. In this book I wish to offer a thorough historical study of the extermination of the Jews of Europe, without eliminating or domesticating that initial sense of disbelief.' See also Megill (2002: 116–17): 'There is an ethical closing of the eyes here, a strange complacency. It is a complacency deeply rooted within the historical discipline, already visible in Ranke (...). In "realist" international relations and related fields, including history, human-generated death is simply the price that states have to pay for the maintenance and extension of their power.'
34 For two opposed views of the historicity of Polybius and Phylarchus respectively, see Schepens (2005) and Eckstein (2013).
35 Polybius' bias in favour of the Achaeans who destroyed Mantinea was first pointed out by Walbank (1960), and his arguments have since been accepted by the majority of scholars (and taken to extremes by some) with a few exceptions. See e.g. Schepens (2005). *Pace* Eckstein (2013), who mentions some extreme examples of scholars accusing Polybius of bias and argues that they exaggerate.
36 For Polybius' life see Eckstein (1995: ch. 1) and McGing (2010: ch. 1).
37 There are 85 other fragments of Phylarchus, but they are all very brief, and although they give us a sense of a historiographer who was fond of marvels and liked an anecdote with a good punchline, this may simply be because those were the kind of passages most likely to be quoted or paraphrased. On the unrepresentativeness of the preserved fragments of a given work of historiography for the original complete work, see Brunt (1980), Lenfant (1999 and 2013), Pelling (2000). See also Schepens (2007) and Hau (forthcoming b) on the Phylarchus fragments in Athenaeus.
38 In the case of Mantineia, Polybius, as an Achaean, certainly sympathizes with the victors. In most of the rest of his *Histories*, which recount the Roman conquest of the known world including Achaea and the rest of Greece, he was not technically among the victors; but he was close friends with one of their greatest generals and writes much of his *Histories* from a point of view sympathetic to Rome. This does not mean that he never criticizes Rome, simply that, overall, he is an admirer of and sympathizer with Rome. For a good discussion of his position, see Eckstein (1995).
39 For Agatharchides, see Woelk (1966), Fraser (1972: 539–50), Strasburger (1982: 1006–10), Burstein (1989 and n.d.), Marcotte (2001), Ameling (2008).

40 For this expression (to designate the texts in which 'fragments' or earlier texts are preserved), see Schepens (1997).
41 Translations of the Photius and Diodorus passages are conveniently printed side by side in Burstein 1989. All Agatharchides fragment numbers are from that work (the fragments of *On the Red Sea* do not figure in either *FGrH* or *BNJ* as Jacoby considered the work a geography rather than a history). For the Greek text, one must consult Photius and Diodorus directly. Vivid descriptions of suffering: F24–29 = Phot. cod. 250. 24 447b–29 449a and D.S. 3.12.2–14.5; F53 = Phot. cod. 250.53 452b and D.S. 3.26; F59 = Phot. cod. 250.58 453a–b and D.S. 3.29.1–7; F84b = D.S. 3.39.3–9; F85 = Phot. cod. 250.83 456b–457a and D.S. 3.40. I compare some of the Photius and Diodorus passages in Hau (2019).
42 Schwartz (1894), Fraser (1972: 546–8), Strasburger (1982: 1006–10).
43 ὅτι πολλοὶ, φησί, καὶ τῶν πολιτικῶν ἀνδρῶν καὶ τῶν ποίημα γεγραφότων διηπορήκασι πῶς τὰς ὑπερβαλλούσας ἐνίοις ἀκληρίας τὸν ἐκτὸς τῶν κινδύνων κείμενον πρεπόντως ἐξαγγελτέον, Agatharchides F21 = Phot. cod. 250.21 445b39–41.
44 I discuss these passages in more detail in Hau (forthcoming a).
45 E.g. M. Becker (2002: 58): 'It strikes me that one problem with conventional history writing is that in a variety of ways, and for many reasons, it creates a fence between whatever happened historically and the reader. In other words, it shields readers from experience. (...) To encourage readers to re-experience the empathy I feel toward my characters, and the experiences of these characters themselves, the article includes many elements of the worlds of my characters. It is full of descriptions of color, sound, and food; it is full of descriptions of sadness, jealousy, emotionality, longing. (...) The intention is to allow its readers and listeners to experience what its writer, and perhaps its subjects, experienced.' For the theoretical background see Ankersmit (2005), Runia (2006) and Carr (2014). See also Klooster and Kuin in this volume.
46 For a discussion see Hau (2016a: 97–102, and forthcoming a).
47 See e.g. principles 3 and 7 in the list of twelve principles listed by Griffith (2011: 2), of which he says 'none of these twelve principles (...) should be controversial. Several of them, indeed, may well strike many readers as being banal and too obvious to need stating.'
48 For communal trauma, see Eckert in this volume.

Chapter 5

1 There is extensive scholarship on Polybius; note in particular Pédech (1964), Walbank (1972), Eckstein (1995), Champion (2004) and McGing (2010).
2 For the problems of defining 'crisis' see in this volume in particular Klooster and Kuin as well as Eckert.

3   Erskine (2012). On crises and temporal frames see in this volume Klooster and Kuin as well as Whitmarsh.
4   This is explored in detail in Maier (2012). On imagining alternative outcomes in Lucan see Ambühl in this volume.
5   For the translation of this phrase see Parmeggiani (2014).
6   All translations are my own unless otherwise indicated.
7   On Polybius' introductory remarks, Miltsios (2013: 7–8).
8   Educational importance: Thuc., 1.22.4, cf. Isoc., *ad Nic.* 35, Arist., *Rh.* 1368a29 for value of knowledge of the past. For the distinctiveness of Polybius' approach, Skidmore (1996: 11–12), cf. later Diod. Sic., 1.1, Philip of Pergamum *BNJ* 95F1. Polybius repeats the theme of coping at 12.25b3 and for the general usefulness of history note 1.35.6–10, 3.118.11, 11.19a, on which Walbank (1990).
9   Marincola (2013: 86–8), quoting the fourth century comic poet Timocles on the experience of watching tragedy: 'for in thinking about all the calamities greater than his own which have happened to others, he [the spectator] groans less at his own misfortunes' (ἅπαντα γὰρ τὰ μείζον' ἢ πέπονθέ τις ἀτυχήματ' ἄλλοις γεγονότ' ἐννοούμενος τὰς αὐτὸς αὑτοῦ συμφορὰς ἧττον στένει, F6, lines 1–7, 17–19 (K-A), trans. Marincola), cf. also Halliwell (2005) on ancient responses to tragedy in general, including those of Timocles and Aristotle in his *Poetics*.
10 On his audience, Walbank (1972: 3–5), McGing (2010: 66), although, as both note, Polybius also expects at least some Roman readers, 31.22.8.
11 Cf. Grethlein (2013) on teleology in historiography, with 224–40 on Polybius.
12 For instance, Roveri (1956), Pédech (1964: 331–54), Walbank (2007), Hau (2011), Brouwer (2011).
13 Cf. Hau (2011: 205) arguing that 'the pervasive presence of *tyche* in the discourse brings the point of view of the readers in line with that of the characters caught in the midst of bewildering events'.
14 Polyb., 1.35, cf. 38.4.8.
15 For the role of hindsight in historiography see in particular Powell (2013).
16 See Klooster and Kuin and Eckert on Vierhaus' concept of a 'historical crisis' in this volume.
17 See Klooster and Kuin in this volume, section 2.
18 See further Erskine (2000: 176–81).
19 Erskine (2013: 233–4), Champion (2004: 75).
20 Plut., *De glor. Ath.* 347a, Marincola (2003).
21 This re-experiencing of the past is explored in Grethlein (2013), who argues that the more teleological a history is, the less experiential it is. For him Polybius' emphasis on teleology limits his capacity to re-create the past as present but does not exclude it (224–67).
22 Polyb., 1.35.7–9, on this passage and its application to the Romans, Moore (2017: 146–8).

23 Polybius' account of the making of the alliance is lost, so we must rely on Livy, 26.24; a broken inscription recording the part of the text of the alliance also survives, Schmitt, *Staatsverträge* 3.536; Moretti, *ISE* 2.87.
24 Polyb., 5.104 (Agelaus of Naupactus); 9.32.3–39 (Lyciscus, an Acarnanian ambassador); 11.4.1–6.8 (an unnamed Greek ambassador).
25 Polyb., 9.37.7–8 (enslavement); 9.39.1–3 (capture of cities); 9.37.10 (cloud from the West).
26 On this barbarian behaviour see Erskine (2000) and Champion (2000).
27 For the capture of Aegina, Polyb., 9.42.5.
28 The language here reflecting Polyb., 3.6.6–9 on the *aitia* and *archē* of a war, cf. Derow (1994, esp. 86–9).
29 Hdt., 5.97.3, Thuc., 2.12.3 (spoken by a Spartan envoy), on which Hornblower (1991: 250). Walbank (1967: 276–7) notes the echo of Herodotus in Polybius, but suggests its use might be proverbial, cf. Polybius' later use of the phrase at 18.39.1. On Polybius' familiarity with Herodotus and Thucydides see McGing (2010: 52–61), McGing (2012) (Herodotus) and Rood (2012) (Thucydides).
30 On authenticity, Pédech (1964: 259–76), Walbank (1965), Champion (2000: 436–7); Wiater (2010) looks at the role of the speeches in the narrative. Although the three speeches play off each other the second is also responding directly to another speech by the Aetolian Chlaeneas (Polyb., 9.29–31).
31 For Polybian speeches as vehicles for counterfactual reflection, Maier (2013: 155–7), see also Maier (2012: 73–208) for a full discussion of Polybius' concern with contingency and alternative paths. Similarly Grethlein (2013: 45) notes how speeches illustrate 'the openness of the past when it was still the present' (with reference to Thucydides), cf. p. 255 on Polybius.
32 Often identified as the Rhodian Thrasycrates, Walbank (1967: 274–5), who seems to accept the identification while expressing some scepticism.
33 Cf. later Philopoemen warning against the increasing threat of slavery, Polyb., 24.13.
34 Compare its use at Polyb., 3.94.7, 9.16, 28.7.8.
35 Cf. Grethlein (2013: 258–60).
36 Polyb., 24.13, cf. also Polybius' father Lycortas, 28.6
37 For the *Histories* as a weapon in political debate, see Thornton (2013: 38–42, esp. 40).
38 Translation from Derow (1979: 4).
39 Polyb., 27.1–2, 28.2–7, cf. too 30.6.5, where Thessaly is included.
40 Cf. Welles *RC* 61 (letter of Attalus II, c. 159), *IOSPE* I² 402, lines 22–31 (treaty between Chersonesos and Pharnaces I of Pontus, 155).
41 Derow (1989: 316–19); almost every state was affected by these changes, Polyb., 30.6.2.
42 Cf. Polyb., 29.19; on Roman anger, Erskine (2015).
43 Polyb., 30.31.14, 30.31.20, Livy, 45.10.13–14. Despite this, one of the leading pro-Macedonians Polyaratus, after a failed attempt to flee, was taken to Rome on the

instructions of the Roman commander L. Aemilius Paullus, Polyb., 30.9.18–20. His fate there is unknown, Walbank (1979: 430).

44 Polyb., 30.13, Livy, 45.31, Paus., 7.10.7–12, cf. Erskine (2012) on Polybius' detention in Rome.

45 Cf. Polyb., 30.7.5–8; for Polybius on his own actions and position at the time, 28.3.7–9, 28.6, 28.12–13, 29.23–25.

46 For the praiseworthy, Polyb., 30.7.1–4 (naming certain Molossians). Among the contemptible were some Coan and Rhodian politicians, Polyb., 30.7.9–10; Polybius' scorn is particularly directed at the cowardice of two Rhodians, Deinon and Polyaratus (30.8–9), see n43 above.

47 Polyb., 3.4.2–3 (trans. Derow), on which Derow (1979: 4–6).

48 Polyb., 38.18.8, cf. 38.10.6.

49 Ferrary (1988: 289–90) dates the decision to shortly after 145; Walbank (1977) prefers a later date, perhaps even after the death of Scipio Aemilianus in 129. Note Polyb., 38.1–4 on the importance of giving a full account of the terrible events of the 140s.

50 For περίστασις as crisis, see the translation of Henderson (2001: 47), along with Polybius' use of the term at 3.112.9 (quoted above, section 2) and 4.33.12.

51 Polyb., 38.1, completion of *atychia*, cf. 38.11.1, 3.5.6.

52 Polyb., 38.1–3 reviews all earlier Greek disasters, on which Henderson (2001: 47–8).

Chapter 6

1 See Flor., 2.9.24 for the total of 70,000 slain near Sacriportus and the Colline Gate. Both Sulla's memoirs and the testimony of Claudius Quadrigarius give a figure of about 20,000 casualties for the Battle of Sacriportus alone. For Sulla, see *FRHist* 22 F25 (= Plut., *Sull*. 28.8) and for Quadrigarius, see *FRHist* 24 F88 / *FRH* 14 F85 (= Oros., 5.20.6). During the Battle of the Colline Gate, 40,000 Samnite troops and Sulla's four legions nearly annihilated each other (Vell. Pat., 2.27.1–3; Plut., *Sull*. 29.7; Plut., *Crass*. 6.6). This is consistent with Florus' figure for the total number of slain near Sacriportus and at the Colline Gate, as well with Appian's report on the death toll of 50,000 soldiers for the Battle of the Colline Gate alone (App., *B Civ*. 1.93).

2 Plut., *Sull*. 27.4–5 (Mount Tifata) and Vell. Pat., 2.28.1 (Clusium, Faventia, Fidentia).

3 Diod. Sic., 37.29.5; App., *B Civ*. 1.103. For the other authors, see n1 and n2 above.

4 Beloch (1886: 348 and 352) provides a figure of nearly one million Roman citizens for the census of 86/85 BCE. Cf. Brunt (1987: 92–7). De Ligt (2012: 118) arrives at similar figures for the census of 70/69 BCE. See also Eckert (2016a: 149n64).

5 See Flor., 2.9.25 regarding the episode with Fufidius. We know of a praetor named Fufidius in 81 BCE who was *propraetor* in Hispania Citerior in 80 BCE. Cf.

Broughton MRR II (1968: 76 and 81). Plut., *Sull.* 31.1–6 indicates that either Fufidius or a certain Metellus brought forward a proposal in the Roman Senate to stop the arbitrary killings that had begun after the massacre in the Villa Publica. Both Florus and Plutarch agree that, in the end, Sulla decided to stop the indiscriminate slaughter and introduced the proscriptions. See also Eckert (2016a: 139n2).

6   Flor., 2.9.5. See n1 above.
7   Heftner (2006) was the first to convincingly demonstrate that a time of anarchy lay between the massacre in the Villa Publica and the beginning of Sulla's proscriptions. See also Eckert (2016a: 140).
8   Florus' brief notes on the time of indiscriminate slaughter after the Villa Publica event indicate that the death toll caused by Sulla's marauding soldiers and followers in Rome was at least as high as the figure of 4,000 slain in the Villa Publica. Hence, the numbers given by Florus add up to at least 10,000 victims: 4,000 slain in the Villa Publica, a minimum of another 4,000 killed in the period of anarchy and 2,000 victims of the Sullan proscriptions. Casualties from the destruction of Sulmo need not be taken into account for this conservative estimate.
9   For the death toll of 100,000 soldiers in the civil war battles of 83/82 BCE, see n3 and n4 above. For a detailed analysis why the number of victims (i) due to the massacre in the Villa Publica, (ii) during the time of anarchy in Rome, (iii) due to the massacre after the surrender of Praeneste and (iv) during the Sullan proscriptions probably totalled to more than 30,000 Roman citizens, see Eckert (2016a: 139–44); cf. Eckert (2018: 288n25). The relevant sources are Livy, *Per.* 88 (8,000 victims in the Villa Publica), Oros., 5.21 (9,000 slain in Rome during the time of anarchy after the Villa Publica), Plut., *Sull.* 32.1 (12,000 slain near Praeneste) and Val. Max., 9.2.1 (4,700 proscribed Romans were listed in the Roman State Archive). According to Dionysius of Halicarnassus, Sulla ordered the execution of 40,000 soldiers after they had surrendered (Dion. Hal., *Ant. Rom.* 5.77.5).
10 For the date of the trial against Sextus Roscius, see Dyck (2010: 4).
11 Hölkeskamp (2009a); Meyer, Patzel-Mattern and Schenk (2013); Golden (2013); Gillhaus et al. (2016).
12 See Koselleck (1982); Koselleck (2006) and Klooster and Kuin in this volume.
13 Meier ([1966] 1980: XLIV). Flower (2010: IX) disputes Meier's 'crisis without end'.
14 Vierhaus (1978: 314–5 and 320–1).
15 Vierhaus (1978: 322–3). According to Vierhaus, a historical crisis cannot be the direct result of a natural disaster but can be the consequence of the economic effects of such an event.
16 Vierhaus (1978: 321, 323 and 329) referring to 'Teilkrisen', 'krisenhafte Vorgänge' and 'Systemkrisen'; Meier ([1966] 1980: XLIV); Beck (2009: 66); Jehne (2009: 148); Sawilla (2013: 151); Gillhaus (2016: 12).

17 Vierhaus (1978: 321 and specifically 328-9) for 'Krise ist ein Prozess'. While, according to Vierhaus, historical crises can be processes extending over longer periods of time, Harriet Flower would like to confine the term 'crisis' to the occurrence of 'acute events'. See Flower (2010: IX–X and 117–8).
18 Vierhaus (1978: 328–9); for the loss of authority of social norms, see Vierhaus (1978: 323).
19 Vierhaus (1979: 81); Bücher (2009: 99) referring to 'Instabilität', 'Labilität' and 'Unsicherheit'; Jehne (2009: 148): 'Untergang [...] ebenso wie Restabilisierung [...]': Gillhaus (2016: 12). See also Koselleck (2006: 357), who points out that the meaning of 'crisis' in ancient Greece encompassed the notion of a 'choice between stark alternatives'. Vierhaus and other scholars state that 'feelings of crisis' expressed by contemporaries of historical events are not sufficient to prove the existence of a historical crisis. See Vierhaus (1978: 322); Vierhaus (1979: 81); Hölkeskamp (2009b: 8); Sawilla (2013: 160–1); Gillhaus (2016: 12).
20 Vierhaus (1978: 314–5 and 320–1); Meyer, Patzel-Mattern and Schenk (2013: 10–12).
21 Cic., *Phil.* 12.27, 13.1; Diod. Sic., 38.16.1; Sall., *Hist.*, 1.28, 1.81; Livy, *Per.* 85; Vell. Pat., 2.25.2–3; Plut., *Sert.* 6.1–3; Plut., *Sull.* 28.1–6; App., *B Civ.* 1.85–86; Cass. Dio, F107.2–3.
22 Diod. Sic., 37.29.5; App., *B Civ.* 1.103, cf. n3.
23 Strab., 5.4.11; Val. Max., 9.2; Sen., *Clem.* 1.12.2.; Flor., 2.9.24. Cf. Hölkeskamp (2004: 109, 132–3).
24 Plut., *Sull.* 31; Flor., 2.9.23–25; App., *B Civ.* 4.10.; Cass. Dio, F109.
25 Plut., *Sull.* 32.1.
26 Livy, *Per.* 89; Val. Max., 9.2.1; Vell. Pat., 2.28.4; Lucan, 2.148f.; Plut., *Sull.* 31.
27 Cf. Cic., *Caecin.* 96, 101–2; Sall., *Hist.* 1.48.6 (McGushin); Plut., *Sull.* 31.
28 Social mediation in Alexander's process of cultural trauma is facilitated by the existence of modern mass media. Cf. Alexander (2004), Alexander (2012). Yet, social mediation is also discernible in pre-modern societies, which did not have such means of mass communication. Here, more time and effort had to be invested for social mediation, which mostly occurred through face-to-face communication. For Alexander's concept of cultural trauma cf. also Eckert (2014) Eckert (2016a: 146–8), Eckert (2016b).
29 It is important to note that collective terms such as 'Roman society (at large/as a whole)' employed in this chapter have to be understood as 'majority terms' in the sense of 'a (large) majority of the members of Roman society'. In a similar manner, 'Roman social identity' or 'Roman cultural identity' should be understood as the body of norms, values, ideas and corresponding symbolic representations shared by a (large) majority of the members of Roman society. Approaching sociological concepts from a 'majority term' perspective avoids the pitfalls of essentialism (not a society, but only its members can be the agents) and over-generalization (not all members of a society feel that they have been subjected to a horrendous event or associate themselves with a shared cultural identity).

30 For the date of the trial and Cicero's speech cf. Dyck (2010: 4); for the date of Sulla's abdication, see Vervaet (2018).
31 Cic., *Caec.* 96-97. See Crawford (1984: 33-4).
32 Sall., *Hist.* F1.48 (McGushin); Gran. Lic., 36.35-37 (Criniti); Flor., 2.11.3 and 2.11.5-8. For the relevance of Sallust's *Historiae* with respect to Sulla's legacy cf. Rosenblitt (2019a) and Rosenblitt (2019b).
33 [Q. Cic.], *Comment. pet.* 2; Cic., *Brut.* 317; Vell. Pat., 2.43.3; Val. Max., 8.9.3; Asc., 26, 74 and 84 (Clark); Plut., *Caes.* 4.1-2; Suet., *Iul.* 4.1 and 55.1. See for the Dolabellae also Thein (2019).
34 Sall., *Hist.* F2.45, 3.34 (McGushin); Asc., 78 (Clark). Cf. Kunkel and Wittmann (1995: 658).
35 Cic., *Leg.* 3.22 and 3.26; Sall., *Cat.* 38.1; Livy, *Per.* 97; Vell. Pat., 2.30.4; Asc., 76 (Clark); App., *B Civ.* 1.121. Cf. Kunkel and Wittmann (1995: 658).
36 Asc., 78 (Clark).
37 Steel (2014: 336).
38 Cic., *Cluent.* 117-134; [Q. Cic.], *Comment. pet.* 8; Cic., *Dom.* 124; Sall., *Cat.* 23.1; Sall., *Hist.* 4.53 (McGushin).
39 Cic., *Verr.* 2.1.37 and 2.1.123-124.
40 Cic., *Verr.* 2.3.81. For the relation between emotions and cultural trauma, see Eckert (2016b).
41 Cic., *Cluent.* 94; Cic., *Mur.* 42; Asc. 73 (Clark).
42 Asc., 90-1 (Clark); Cass. Dio, 37.10.2.
43 Asc., 84, 87 and 89-90 (Clark). For Catilina's leading role in the assassination of M. Marius Gratidianus, see [Q. Cic.], *Comment. pet.* 10; Sall., *Hist.* F1.36 and F1.48.14-15 (McGushin).
44 Sall., *Cat.* 16.4 and 37.6.
45 Quint., *Inst.* 11.1.85. For Cicero's speech *De proscriptorum liberis* cf. Crawford (1994: 205-11) and Eckert (2019: 167-71).
46 Plut., *Caes.* 37.1-2; Suet., *Iul.* 41; Cass. Dio, 41.18.2, 43.50.1-2 and 44.47.4. Cf. for the *lex Antonia de proscriptorum liberis* Rotondi (1962: 416).
47 Vell. Pat., 2.41.2; Plut., *Caes.* 1.1-3; Suet., *Iul.* 1.1-2 and 74.1.
48 Cic., *Att.* 8.3.7 (19 Feb 49 BCE); 8.7.1 (21 Feb 49 BCE); 8.8.2 (23 Feb 49 BCE) and 8.14.1-2 (2 March 49 BCE); Caes., *B Civ.* 1.15-23; Plut., *Caes.* 34; Suet., *Iul.* 34.1 and App., *B Civ.* 2.38.
49 Suet., *Iul.* 75.2; Flor., 2.13.50.
50 Caes., *B Civ.* 3.99; Livy, *Per.* 111; Vell. Pat., 2.52; Plut., *Caes.* 44-46; Plut., *Pomp.* 68-73.
51 Suet., *Iul.* 75.1-5; Cass. Dio, 43.50.1-2.
52 Plut., *Caes.* 48-51; Plut., *Pomp.* 79-80.
53 For Sulla's auctions of the goods of proscribed Roman citizens, see Cic., *Verr.* 2.3.81. Cicero refers again to Sulla's and Caesar's auctions of the property of civil war enemies in Cic., *Off.* 2.27, yet names only Sulla directly.

54 Cic., *Phil.* 2.64–69; Plut., *Ant.* 10.2–3 for Antony seizing Pompey's goods. See Cic., *Fam.* 13.8.1–3 and Cic., *Phil.* 2.103–104 for statements regarding Caesar auctioning the goods of civil war enemies. Cf. Cic., *Off.* 1.43 where Cicero addresses the unjust auctions of the property of civil war enemies by both Sulla and Caesar.
55 Cic., *Marc.* 27 (46 BCE) illustrates that even Caesar's dictatorship of ten years provoked memories of Sulla in Roman society, though Cicero still hoped that Caesar would restore the Republic. Cf. Eckert (2016a, 173–4).
56 App., *B Civ.* 1.99. According to Appian, the assembly of the Roman people ratified the *Lex Valeria*, the legal basis for Sulla's dictatorship, under compulsion.
57 Cic., *Phil.* 1.3, 2.91, 2.115; App., *B Civ.* 3.25 and 3.94; Cass. Dio, 44.51.2.
58 According to Velleius Paterculus, Sulla styled himself *Felix* after the suicide of his fiercest enemy Marius the Younger and the subsequent surrender of Praeneste in November or December 82 BCE. Cf. Vell. Pat., 2.27.5. The *Fasti Capitolini* record Sulla as *Sulla Felix dictator* for the year 82 BCE. Cf. Degrassi (1954: 74). Appian's translation of the proscription edict of 43 BCE indicates that Sulla had his surname *Felix* confirmed by a decree of an assembly of the Roman people. Despite the seemingly innocent wording of the triumvirs (whom you [the Roman people] named *Felix* on account of his success), we may safely assume that this decree of the Roman people in 82 BCE was ratified under compulsion in an atmosphere of terror and fear. See n56 for the ratification of the *Lex Valeria*. Cf. Eckert (2018) for the wider implications of Sulla's surname *Felix*.
59 For a telling remark on the absence of proscriptions in the civil war of 69 CE, see Tac., *Hist.* 2.62.1.

Chapter 7

1 Henderson (1998) best represents the deconstructivist approach. In her study of Lucan's unreliable narrator, Kimmerle (2015) convincingly demonstrates the untenability of one-sided ideological readings of his epic, be they Republican, anti-Caesarian or anti-Neronian. For brief overviews of the history and recent tendencies of Lucan scholarship see also Walde (2005) and Ambühl (2015: 1, 11–14).
2 On Lucan's narrator see Schlonski (1995) and Effe (2004: 61–72), on character focalization Ludwig (2014). Nill (2018) analyses the representation of violence in Lucan with the help of narratological and sociological methods; cf. also Backhaus (2019).
3 Christine Walde (2011 and forthcoming) identifies features of postmemory and trauma literature in the *Bellum Civile*; this approach has first been developed in the Basel Lucan project directed by her in 2001 to 2005, from which my own habilitation project also took its starting point (now Ambühl (2015)); therefore

some overlap of our approaches is inevitable, although I do not specifically rely on trauma theory here. For other applications of trauma theory to Lucan cf. Day (2013); Thorne (2016); on Sulla's proscriptions as a 'cultural trauma' see Eckert (2016a) and Eckert in this volume. On the *Bellum Civile* as an 'epic of the defeated' see Quint (1993: 131–57), on Lucan's counter-memory Gowing (2005: 67–101, esp. 82–96); Thorne (2011); similarly Roller (2001: 17–63).

4   Nesselrath (1992: 92–106) concludes that all of the nine 'Beinahe-Episoden' in Lucan which he discusses occur at crucial turning points. For delay as a favourite strategy of Lucan's narrator see also Masters (1992).

5   For similar speculations in Plutarch's *Lives* see Pelling (2013: 4–6).

6   E.g. Ferguson (1998); Salewski (1999); Cowley (2001); Roberts (2004). For methodological problems inherent in this approach and its epistemic value cf. Demandt ([1984] 2011); Kiesewetter (2002); Evans (2013).

7   See the volume edited by Brodersen (2000) (especially the introduction by Weber (2000)). Cf. also Pelling (2013).

8   Caesar's murder and the ensuing civil war between Octavian and Antony seem to be more popular case studies: Demandt (2011: 94–7) poses the question what would have happened if Brutus had won at Philippi in 42 BCE, but also in this case opts for the eventual instalment of a monarchy as an almost inevitable result (for related scenarios cf. 139, 141–2); for alternative outcomes of Actium see Pelling (2013: 16–18). Sonnabend (2000) argues that even in the fictive case of Augustus' early death in 23 BCE the principate would have been stable enough to be continued by his successor Agrippa, rather than having to return to the Republic and thereby risk a new civil war.

9   See the edited collections by Powell (2013) on hindsight and by Lianeri (2016) on future time in Greek and Roman history and historiography, see especially the contribution by Grethlein (2016).

10 Koselleck (2004: 3): 'The testimony of numerous witnesses from Antiquity to the present ... answers to the problem of how, in a concrete situation, experiences come to terms with the past; how expectations, hopes, or prognoses that are projected into the future become articulated into language. ... how, in a given present, are the temporal dimensions of past and future related?'

11 On contingency and counterfactuals in Polybius see Maier (2012 and 2013); for narrative strategies aimed at creating suspense and involving the audience in Livy see Pausch (2011) (cf. also Morello (2002) on the counterfactual Alexander digression in 9.17–19 and Domainko (2018) on uncertainty in Livy and Velleius); on virtual or alternative history in Tacitus see O'Gorman (2006) and Riedl (2010), cf. her monograph on alternatives in Tacitus and Ammianus in the context of civil wars: Riedl (2002: 157–70, 319–28); cf. Waddell (2016) on Appian. For other historians see the respective contributions in the volumes cited in n 9 above. Suerbaum, who in his 1997 article discusses cases of alternative history in Roman historians, in another article (1998) studies alternative scenarios in Vergil's *Aeneid*.

12 See the more detailed discussion in § 2 below. This poetics appeals to engaged readers, cf. Leigh (1997); D'Alessandro Behr (2007).
13 For strategies of coping in the aftermath of a civil war see Börm, Mattheis and Wienand (2016). Cf. also Armitage (2017) on the Roman civil wars and their conceptual legacy.
14 Demandt (2011: 94) and Grethlein (2013: 353–4) criticize Meier's 'retrospective fallacy'. For a critical review of the concepts of crisis, contingency and alternative history as applied to the end of the Roman Republic cf. the volume edited by Hölkeskamp (2009a), especially the contributions by Hölkeskamp (2009b), Walter (2009) and Jehne (2009); cf. also the relevant sections in Franchet d'Espèrey et al. (2003). For the implications of the term 'crisis' in general see Klooster and Kuin in this volume, for an attempt to identify notions of crisis in Lucan § 2 below.
15 Cf. Koselleck (2006: 370): 'the semantic quality of the concept of crisis, which always admits alternatives pointing not just to diametrically opposed possibilities, but also to those cutting across such opposites.'
16 Cf. e.g. O'Higgins (1988); Masters (1992: 91–149, 179–215); Quint (1993: 135–6); Day (2013: 93–105).
17 See Eigler (2012); Walde (2012); cf. also Nesselrath (1992: 92–4).
18 The use of the future tense by the narrator corresponds with his (partial) perspective as a contemporary and eyewitness of the events he narrates. Cf. Schlonski (1995: 32, 45–6, 161) ('historisch-prophetisches Futur'); Leigh (1997: 325–9) on the future tense in Latin epic, who demonstrates that in Lucan the 'contingent future' is crucial, for it 'suggests that the final outcome is still open and that significant choices remain to be made' (329).
19 In all the quotes from Lucan, the Latin text is taken from Shackleton Bailey (1997), the translation from Braund (1992). On Lucan's ignorant narrator who shares the characters' perspective and can only guess about the gods' motives and the meaning of events see Feeney (1991: 269–301, esp. 279–81 on this passage); cf. also Erler (2012).
20 On the identification of this augur with a Gaius Cornelius known from other sources and the poetics of this passage see Leigh (1997: 6–40).
21 Allan, de Jong and de Jonge (2017) view the ancient concept of *enargeia*, 'the power of bringing the things that are said before the senses of the audience', as a forerunner of the modern notion of immersion; they adduce the Homeric epics as prime examples for increasing the mimetic quality of the narrative text by means of a covert narrator, whereas Lucan's very visible narrator here achieves a similar effect by self-consciously highlighting and at the same time breaking the mimetic illusion.
22 Grethlein in his discussion of narrative re-experience and focus as historiographic strategies for 'making the past present' briefly adduces this very passage from Lucan as an example of the 'epic aspiration to presence' (2013: 22). Walde (2011: 297) defines it as a symptom of traumatic time collapse, Nauta (2013: 239–40) as a

23 Cf. Demandt (1978: 27, 80, 441), who argues that the modern collective use of the term is derived from its application to individual patients in ancient medicine but that originally it was also used by ancient historiographers in the sense of 'decision'. For the medical connotations see also Koselleck (2006: 360–1).

24 Cf. Raaflaub (1974: 192–200, 296–7) on the slogans used by the civil war parties; Ambühl (2015: 197–211).

25 For the state of the debate, its presuppositions and its (non)sense see Walde (2017). Masters (1992: 216–59) argues for a deliberate break-off that precisely by 'pointing ... to its own inconclusiveness' preserves 'evil without alternative, contradiction without compromise, civil war without end' (259). Moreover, Lucan's epic ends at about the same point as Caesar's own civil war *Commentaries*; on the related issue of their 'ending without the end' see Grillo (2012: 167–74, 184–5).

26 For the problem and some examples cf. Walde (2017: 180–1 n37, 185).

27 Cf. Lapidge ([1979] 2010) (a Stoicizing reading); Day (2013: 73–6).

28 Cf. Seneca's *Apocolocyntosis* 3 on Claudius, who made all the foreigners Roman citizens so that Clotho has to save a few of them as a 'seed' for the future, and later Juvenal's third satire. One might even see in Lucan an intertextual echo of the *Cypria* from the epic cycle, where the goddess Earth's complaint about the overpopulation leads to the Trojan war as a drastic relief measure. Tracy's (2014: esp. 274–9) view of Lucan as an advocate of cultural diversity in a globalized world seems a bit too postmodern to me.

29 On *metus Gallicus* and *Punicus* see Schrijvers (1988: 342–4), on the Parthians in Lucan see Tracy (2014: 15–30).

30 This phrase is an intratextual verbal quotation from Caesar's prayer to the apparition of Rome at the Rubicon (*BC* 1.200), another crucial turning point.

31 Cato: *BC* 2.304–319; Pompey: 7.117–120, 356–360, 647–672. Caesar employs this counterfactual motif in order to end the mutiny of his soldiers (5.320–321) and to motivate them to fight to the end (7.308–310).

32 On Republican duels and *devotiones* in Livy see Feldherr (1998: 82–111), on their inversion in Lucan Ambühl (2015: 223–7).

33 Cf. Schmitt (1995) on the speeches of the masses and Gall (2005) on the role of the soldiers and the people.

34 On the fraternization at Ilerda in *BC* 4 see e.g. Masters (1992: 70–90), on the mutiny in *BC* 5 Fantham (1985), on both episodes Nesselrath (1992: 95–9).

35 In the *Bellum Civile* the term *clementia* never occurs in this sense but is paraphrased (cf. e.g. 9.1066–1068, quoted above), as it is also in Caesar's *Commentaries* (see Grillo (2012: 78–105) and Grillo in this volume). On the *clementia Caesaris* in the historical civil war context cf. Raaflaub (1974: 293–307) and Konstan (2005), on its ambiguity in Lucan see Masters (1992: 78–87) and Kimmerle (2015: 232–55); cf.

also Roller (2001: 182–93). Interestingly, from a retrospective perspective of the 40s BCE, Sallust in his *Bellum Catilinae* incorporates an alternative view to the historical execution of the conspirators in 63 BCE by having Caesar propose clemency, 50.4–53.1; cf. Grethlein (2013: 278–98 and 2016: 68–73).

36 In Ambühl (2015: 259–76), I discuss the scene against the background of tragic intertexts.
37 Again, the terms *proscribere* and *proscriptio* do not occur in Lucan in contrast to other authors such as Cicero or Suetonius. Generally on the proscriptions see Hinard (1985).
38 This strategy was also employed in the actual civil war propaganda, cf. Grillo (2012: 151–7).
39 According to Suetonius (*Iul.* 85), Cinna was beheaded and his head carried around on a pike.
40 For the various sources and the symbolism of the act cf. Butler (2002: 1–2, 123). In Lucan and other civil war writers images of decapitation abound (e.g. Cinna in the preceding note; according to Suet., *Aug.* 13.1, after Philippi Octavian sent Brutus' head to Rome to be placed at the feet of Caesar's statue; cf. the use of Crassus' head as a prop in Plut., *Crass.* 33; generally see the comparative study by Kristensen (2016)), but still the detail of the rostra establishes a specific link to Cicero's fate. Interestingly, Cassius Dio's notice (47.8.3–4), that Antony's wife Fulvia pierced Cicero's tongue with hairpins before the head was publicly displayed, parallels the mutilation of Marius Gratidianus, whose hands and tongue were cut off by Sulla's henchmen (*BC* 2.181–182).
41 Finally, in his speech to the mutineers in book 9, Cato provocatively exhorts them to hand over his severed head to the 'tyrant' Caesar for a reward (9.279–283).

Chapter 8

1 From Ariminum to Brundisium.
2 Letters by Cicero have much to contribute to this information, but they focus on the relation between Domitius and Pompey and say nothing about the events that took place within the town, Shackleton Bailey (1968: 448–59), Von Fritz (1942: 145–80) and Burns (1966: 74–95).
3 App., *B Civ.* 2.38: 'At Corfinium Caesar came up with and besieged Lucius Domitius, who had been sent to be his successor in the command of Gaul, but who did not have all of his 4,000 men with him. The inhabitants of Corfinium captured him at the gates, as he was trying to escape, and brought him to Caesar. The latter received the soldiers of Domitius, who offered themselves to him, with kindness, in order to encourage others to join him, and he allowed Domitius to go unharmed wherever he liked, and to take his own money with him …' (trans. White, Loeb).

4. Cass. Dio, 41.10–11: 'He set out next against Corfinium, because this place, being occupied by Lucius Domitius, would not join his cause, and after conquering in battle a few who met him he shut up the rest and besieged them. Now Pompey, inasmuch as these followers were being besieged and many of the others were falling away to Caesar, had no further hope of Italy, and resolved to cross over into Macedonia, Greece, and Asia ... with this purpose, therefore, he himself [Pompey] set out for Brundisium and bade Domitius abandon Corfinium and accompany him. And Domitius, in spite of the large force that he had and the hopes he reposed in it, inasmuch as he had courted the favour of the soldiers in every way and had won them over by promises of land (as one of Sulla's veterans he had acquired a large amount under that régime), nevertheless obeyed orders. He, accordingly, was making preparations to evacuate the town with some degree of safety; but his associates, when they learned of it, shrank from the journey abroad, because it seemed to them a flight, and they attached themselves to Caesar. So, these joined the invader's army, but Domitius and the other senators, after being censured by Caesar for arraying themselves against him, were allowed to go and came to Pompey' (trans. Cary and Foster, Loeb).

5. In this respect, Appian's account departs from Caesar's, for whom Domitius is captured by the soldiers, not by the inhabitants of Corfinium.

6. Suetonius and Plutarch have little to add on the internal *stasis*: according to Plutarch, Domitius asked for some poison to commit suicide, but was given a sleeping drug, and having heard of Caesar's clemency turned himself in (Plut., *Caes.* 34.6–8, with Pelling (2011: 326–8)); according to Suetonius, Caesar took Domitius prisoner and set him free (Suet., *Iul.* 34.1).

7. For Cicero's letters, I use the traditional numbering, which Shackleton Bailey calls 'vulgate'.

8. I accept the dating suggested by Shackleton Bailey, according to which Cicero attaches these letters from Pompey in writing to Atticus on 27 and 28 February.

9. A couple of passing and euphemistic remarks coming from either side cast no more light on the episode: early in March, in a letter to Oppius and Cornelius, Caesar elegantly hints at 'the deeds at Corfinium' (*quae apud Corfinium sunt gesta*, 9.7c.1); and toward the end of February Cicero employs similar tact not to offend his addressee, Pompey: 'I have heard about what happened at Corfinium' (*simul audivimus et quae Corfini acta essent et ...*, *Att.* 8.11d.3).

10. Roman historians have analysed these letters in detail and focused on what happened around Corfinium, in the attempt to reconstruct Pompey's strategy at the opening of the war: Napoleon (*Précis* 9.47) and Clausewitz (*On War* 4.11) endorsed Cicero's view that abandoning Italy was a fatal mistake. Rice Holmes (1923: 3.12–15), instead, thought that Cicero misunderstood the situation, and Pompey did the right thing, but lost because of the stupidity of his republican senators or,

according to Syme (1939: 43–7), thanks to their disunity and conflicting interests. Scholars of the *BCiv.*, instead, have used the other sources to measure the extent of Caesar's distortion, or *Tendenz*: e.g. Rambaud (1953: 135–9).

11 Other letters demonstrate that Corfinium remained a paradigm of Caesar's *clementia* (e.g. *Att.* 9.16.1) and that this *clementia* won popularity (cf. *Att.* 8.9a.1, 8.15a.3 and 9.7c.1), perhaps contrary to Pompey's hope that a massacre by Caesar would make for good propaganda for himself (*sive, ut quidam putant, meliorem suam causam illorum caede fore putavit, Att.* 8.9a1).

12 During Caesar's march Cicero exclaimed 'what amazing speed!' (*o celeritatem incredibilem! Att.* 7.22.1). On 25 February, two days after learning about the capitulation at Corfinium, bitter, Cicero wrote: 'what is more miserable than the fact that of the two the one winning approval has the most reproachable cause, while the one winning unpopularity has the best cause?' and Cicero continues 'one is considered the saviour of his enemies, and the other the betrayer of his friends' (*alterum existimari conservatorem inimicorum, alterum desertorem amicorum, Att.* 8.9a.1).

13 See e.g. Cic., *Att.* 8.9a.1, 8.15a.3, 9.7c.1, 9.13.7 and 9.16.1. For Appian and Cassius Dio, see n3 and n4.

14 Conveniently summarized in Burns (1966: 75–8).

15 On the limits and characteristics of literary *exaedificatio* in historiography, see the classic treatment by Woodman (1988: 81–95). On Domitius, Von Fritz (1942: 162–5) and Burns (1966: 88–9) have already pointed out that no sources apart from Caesar give a negative account of Domitius' conduct.

16 Raaflaub (1974: 165–74), Batstone and Damon (2006: 94–5) and Grillo (2012: 136–43).

17 Cf. Batstone and Damon (2006: 64–9) and Grillo (2012: 131–6).

18 In the same address to his troops, Caesar uses *secessio* a second time, to compare the past times of civil turmoil with the current situation and with the beginning of the civil war, when 'no secession took place' (*nulla secessio facta, BCiv.* 1.7.7).

19 *Dissensio* is twice accompanied by the adjective *civilis* (*in civili dissensione*, 1.67.3 and *bella et civiles dissensiones* 3.1.3) and once it occurs without qualification but still meaning civil war: mentioning the two legions he handed down by the Senate's order, 'at the beginning of the conflict', Caesar writes *legiones duae traditae a Caesare initio dissensionis ex senatus consulto* (*BCiv.* 3.88.2).

20 On Caesar's *elegantia* see now Krebs (2018: 123–8) and Pezzini (2018: 186–7).

21 For Caesar's imitation of Thucydides, see Kraus, who has found some echoes of Thucydides in Caesar's description of the battle of Massilia (Kraus 2007: 371–8); Krebs, who has shown that there are some echoes also in the description of the siege of Avaricum in the *BGall.* (Krebs 2016: 1–11); Pitcher, who considers broadly Caesar's debt to Greek historians, including Thucydides (cf. n23); and especially Reggi, who

carefully analyses Caesar's debt to Greek historians (especially Thucydides and Polybius) in his technical vocabulary of naval battles (Reggi 2002: 71–103).
22 On the importance of differences as well as of similarities in Caesar's use of Greek historians see Pitcher (2018a: 245–7).
23 *Factio* is another rare noun, which scores only two occurrences in the *BCiv.*, 1.22.5 and 3.35.2.
24 Cf. Pitcher (2018a: 240): 'In general, there is much that is reminiscent of Greek historiography in the *BG* and the *BC*. What we often see happening in Caesar, however, is not so much systematic allusion to a single model as dipping into a grab-bag of narrative possibilities which Greek historiography in the round has established.'
25 On the resemblances between the benevolent reception of Italian towns in Book 1 and of Greek towns in Book 3 of the *BCiv.*, see Grillo (2012: 132–6).
26 In the life of Nero (2.3), Suetonius stresses Domitius' indecision and lack of resolve at Corfinium (cf. Sen., *Ben.* 3.24 and Pliny, *HN* 7.186); and Caesar may have built on this.
27 This famous line has been differently interpreted: for Edmunds (1975), Thucydides, true to traditional ethical thought, presents *stasis* as a pattern of inversions and implicitly endorses Spartan ethics; against the traditional interpretation that partisans change the meaning of words they use, Hogan (1980: 140) has argued that, according to Thucydides, in *stasis* people forget normal estimations and designate 'foul deeds by fair names (or vice versa)'; Wilson (1982), Nussbaum (2001: 404–5 and n24, 507–8) and most scholars now accept Hogan's interpretations; for a push back, see Orwin (1994: 177n11). More recently Piovan returns to this line about the manipulation of language, which he sees as a typical characteristic of *stasis* and totalitarian regimes (Piovan 2017, with updated bibliography).
28 For convenient summaries of the debate, see Raaflaub (2009: 182–3) and Grillo (2012: 178–80).
29 For a more detailed analysis of the historical context, see Batstone and Damon (2006) and Grillo (2012).
30 Plut., *Caes.* 57.4 and *LTUR* s.v. *Clementia Caesaris, aedes*, 1.279–80.
31 For this concept and terminology, see Klooster and Kuin, and on *clementia*, see Eckert, both in this volume.
32 App., *B Civ.* 1.46 and 1.52, with Gabba (1994: 121–4).
33 Pompeius Strabo was defeated around Ausculum and found refuge at Firmum; and Marius won an engagement by the Fucine Lake; cf. Gabba (1994: 120–1). L. Iulius Caesar, consul in 90, and Sex. Iulius Caesar also led Roman armies in the Social War, but they were only loosely related to Caesar.
34 Of course, Caesar mentions various *gentes* from Italy (e.g. the Marrucini and Frentrani at *BCiv.* 1.23.5 and the Lucani and Bruttii at *BCiv.* 1.30.4), but once

soldiers are enrolled (e.g. *BCiv.* 1.30.4), he does not indicate their native region. The Marsi and the Paeligni are the only exceptions, and tellingly, Caesar consistently calls these soldiers 'Marsians' and 'Paelignians' from the moment they are recruited by Domitius (1.15.7) until the time when, having joined Caesar's army, they serve under Curio in Africa (*BCiv.* 2.27.1 and 2.29.3).

35 Cf. Grillo (2012: 160–4).
36 Cf. e.g. Gruen (1974: 112–8 and 460–1).
37 See also Plut. *Caes.* 29.2 and Cic. *Att.* 5.11.2.
38 Cf. Grillo (2012: 131–40).
39 Cf. Plut., *Dion Brut. synkr.* 3.4.
40 On the reception of Caesar, see Wyke (2006); see in particular the opening essay by Pelling (2006: 3–15), who shows how different ways, ancient and modern, to tell Caesar's story call for different beginnings and ends; on the ambivalent personality of Brutus and its controversial reception, see Tempest (2017).
41 As a rule, Caesar's allusions to his literary models remain understudied, perhaps also because of our limited grasp of the genre of the *Commentarii*, which is somewhat borderline historiography, for a long time, scholars found models for the *Commentarii* especially in personal memoirs, political pamphlets or dispatches to the Senate (Chassignet 2018: 249–61). In fact, Caesar seriously engaged the Greek historiographical tradition; cf. n20.
42 Loraux (2002: 145–69 and 259–64).

Chapter 9

1 Civil *war* is a subcategory of the broader phenomenon of war (cf. Melander 2016: 203).
2 Lange (2016: 20–1); *contra* Bispham (2007: 40): '... the transition from an Italy at war with itself in 91 to an Italy formally united against an external enemy in 31 ...' The first part of the argument is to the point, the second (the external enemy Cleopatra) not only misunderstands the (civil) war between Antonius and Young Caesar, but also underestimates the impact of civil war altogether. On this, see now Price (2001); Osgood (2006; 2014); Breed et al. (2010); Welch (2012); Wienand (2012); Börm et al. (2016); Havener (2016); Lange (2016); Lange and Vervaet (2019), etc.); the underlying conflicts of the civil war and underlying constitutional issues and tensions: Brunt (1988); Osgood (2006); Flower (2010: 80–96), with reservations in Lange (2016: esp. 15–16).
3 This does of course not discount the fact that the Augustan regime heavily emphasized victory. See Gruen (1985); Havener (2016: 193–252); *contra* Rich (2016). Regarding peace, see Rich (2003); Cornwell (2017); Harris (2016): in the 50s

the Romans start to question their wars and talk of *pax*. He claims that Rich (2003) overstates his case (55 and note 102). But Harris seems to misinterpret the relationship between internal and external peace.

4 Kalyvas (2006: 18–19). Some features of ancient civil wars were in fact regular features of any civil war, particularly in terms of the dynamics of factions, the impact on society and participants, the numerous levels of justifications, and violence (see also Börm et al. (2015): this volume's primary importance is that it gives us an opportunity to view such civil wars as part of *la longue durée*; cf. Armitage (2017)). Factors positively relating to our, modern as well as ancient, knowledge of civil war: (1) Family ties are important, so are personal animosities (Kalyvas 2006: 389): 'For the many people who are not naturally bloodthirsty and abhor direct involvement in violence, civil war offers irresistible opportunities to harm everyday enemies.'; (2) Violent infighting is central (Kalyvas 2006); (3) Individual conflict and factions/dynasts ('Factionalism' – according to Thucydides a flaw in human nature – is a central theme of Thucydides' Corcyra description (3.81–5; cf. 4.46–8)).

5 Adding to problems, negotiated settlements constitute a high risk for renewed civil war (Mason and Mitchell (2016: 8)), but the longer a peace, the less likely it is to fail (9).

6 App., *B Civ.* 4.2; 4.9; 5.43; *RG* 1.4; see Lange (2009: 18–26) with more evidence.

7 App., *B Civ.* 5.65; Cass. Dio, 48.28.4; Lange (2009: esp. 29–33).

8 Unless otherwise stated, all translations are those of the Loeb Classical Library, with minor adaptations.

9 Degrassi (1947: 86-7, 569); *Fasti Barb.*: Degrassi (1947: 342–3).

10 On violence: Lange (2019); Lintott (1999) takes the view that Rome was inherently violent; see now Riess and Fagan (2016).

11 Thuc., 3.82.8; cf. Arist., *Ath. Pol.* 8.5; Cic., *Att.* 10.1.2; cf. Cass. Dio, 52.19.3.

12 Cf. Sulla and post-war terror see Osgood (2015: 1684-6): 'But even horrific battles were not enough to end civil war, as hostilities could resume under new leadership' (1685).

13 Liv., 1.19; *Per.* 133; Vell. Pat., 2.88.1 etc.; Lange (2009: 73–9; 90–3), with more evidence.

14 52.1.1; 50.1.2; 51.1.1–2; 56.30.5; 56.40.4, end of civil war.

15 53.17.1, 19.1; see Rich (1990: 14, 149).

16 Sense of an ending: Westall (2014); the joint ovation of 40 BCE is revealing: *Imp. Caesar Divi f. C. f. IIIvir r(ei) p(ublicae) c(onstituendae) ov[ans, an. DCCXIII] quod pacem cum M. Antonio fecit [---]* ('While Imp. Caesar Divi f. C. f. IIIvir r p c celebrated an ovation because he made peace with Antonius'), Degrassi (1947: 86-7, 568; cf. 342–3), *Fasti Barb.*

17 Lange (2016: 82, 119, 139–41, 146–7, 151–5).

18 For a more developed argument, see Lange (2016: esp. 139).
19 The best overview is found in Millar (1973); cf. Judge (1974); Rich (2012: 106–11).
20 Lange (2009); Rich (2010; 2012).
21 See Lange (2009: esp. 18–38, 181–8, 198); Rich (2010; 2012).
22 Tac., *Ann.* 3.28.1–2; Cass. Dio, 53.2.5; 53.2.6–22.5, suggests a single act.
23 *EJ*, 45; *RG* 13; Woodman (1983: 251); Lange (2009: 140–8).
24 See Lange (2016: esp. 121–3, 129–33); see above.
25 According to Woodman (1983: 219), Velleius Paterculus means the civil war that began in 49 BCE, whereas Suetonius means 43 BCE (Suet., *Aug.* 9.1: Mutina). As for 29 BCE, it works due to the triumphs, even if they were awarded for foreign wars in principle.
26 Degrassi (1963: 489); *EJ* 49; 'Public Holiday by decree of the Senate because on that day Imperator Caesar, son of the god, liberated the republic from the gravest danger'; cf. Arch of Augustus, Forum Romanum (*CIL* VI 873 = *EJ* 17): RE PUBLICA CONSERVATA ('for having preserved the *res publica*').
27 Macrob., *Sat.* 1.12.35 = *EJ* 37; Cass. Dio, 55.6.6; Suet., *Aug.* 31.2; Liv., *Per.* 134.
28 Brunt (1971: 326–44); Keppie (1983: 58–82); for impact, see mainly Osgood (2006: 108–51).
29 For Caesar's settlement programmes 47–44 BCE, see Keppie (1983: 49–58).
30 Keppie (1983: 58–82); Cass. Dio, 49.12.4 emphasizes that the freeborn soldiers of Sextus Pompeius were incorporated into the legions of Young Caesar.
31 It becomes even more evident that there are campaigns and there are wars. Surprisingly, Actium is mentioned as a local campaign (*in hac regione*) on the Victory Monument at Nicopolis/Actium (Lange 2016: 141–53, esp. 148–9). The war, however, ended at Alexandria, even if the most important battle was Actium (and thus two triumphs were awarded). The reason for this is that the war was declared on Cleopatra, Queen of Egypt.
32 Also involving L. Antonius and Fulvia; App., *B Civ.* 5.14; Cass. Dio, 47.14.4; Keppie (1983: 59); Kearsley (2013: 831).
33 Cass. Dio, 48.2.2; App., *B Civ* 5.3, 13, 17 (problems with the soldiers; Gowing (1992: 80)).
34 The civil war was ended, see above; App., *B Civ.* 5.129 (soldiers who had fought at Philippi and Mutina); Cass. Dio, 49.14; Vell. Pat., 2.81.2.
35 Cass. Dio, 51.4.5; Keppie (1983: 74); an inscription for an Antonian veteran returning to his home town has recently been published (*AE* 1996: 679); *contra* Hyginius (177F), saying that Young Caesar did not differentiate between his and Antonius' soldiers; Keppie (1983: 75).
36 He is right in suggesting that this was not an amount given at the actual triumph, but in the colonies.
37 Cass. Dio, 51.27.7 suggests that this may have been extra money paid out.
38 He also points to epigraphic evidence suggesting that they remained in Italy.

Chapter 10

* I warmly thank the editors of this volume for their numerous useful corrections, splendid observations and valuable suggestions made on an earlier draft of this chapter.
1 Unless indicated otherwise all references in this chapter are to the *Roman History* of Cassius Dio. Furthermore I will refer to Octavian Augustus as 'Octavian', and to Julius Caesar as 'Caesar'. Dio refers to both as 'Caesar'.
2 Although Dio's version of the debate on Antony in the Senate between Cicero and Calenus (45.18–46.28) is even longer.
3 See for instance Ruiz (1982: viii, cf. 273–468), Roddaz (1984: 210) and Reinhold (1988: 165).
4 For discussions of Maecenas' speech, see Meyer (1891), Hammond (1932), Bleicken (1962: 446–67), Millar (1964: 106–18), Van Stekelenburg (1971: 111–16), Manuwald (1979: 21–5), Bering-Staschewski (1981: 129–34), Ruiz (1982: 47–58), Zawadzki (1983: 296–316), Schmidt (1999: 109–17), Ziegler (2007: 87–96), Kuhlmann (2010). Smith argues that the speech has relevance within its historical context, but most others agree that its content primarily relates to Dio's own time. Observe, in this respect, that Ruiz (1982: 31) and Kuhlmann (2010: 110 n 2) are slightly unfair to Hammond, who in fact comes to the same conclusion (1932: 101).
5 Cf., e.g. Hammond (1932: 89), Berrigan (1968: 43), Roddaz (1984: 211, 215).
6 Van Stekelenburg (1971: 107–8, with n 9) and Reinhold (1988: 167) point at a contemporary parallel in Philostr., *VA* (5.32–37), where several trustees give constitutional advice to Vespasian. Van Stekelenburg also mentions some less known earlier texts: The constitution of Romulus in the *Roman Antiquities* of Dionysius Halicarnassus (2.7–29), Pseudo-Sallustius' *Epistulae ad Caesarem senem*, Dio Chrysostom's περὶ βασιλείας and Plinius' *Panegyricus*.
7 For a discussion of Dio's possible allusions (also on a structural level) to Herodotus in the debate, see Kuhlmann (2010: 112–8).
8 Compare, in this respect, the debate in Herodotus, where the historiographer insists that speeches of this kind were really delivered (3.80.1 and 6.43.3, cf. McKechnie (1981: 154)). Such assurances are lacking in the case of Dio's debate. Thucydides' speeches are almost exclusively held in a public setting, which creates a sense of accountability that is compatible with his methods (cf. Thuc., 1.22). In Dio's work we find various significant speeches that are delivered in private, such as Philiscus' consolatory speech to Cicero (38.18–29), Portia's speech to Brutus (44.13.3–4) and Octavian Augustus' discussion with Livia (55.14–21). On this partial omniscience and omnipresence of the narrator of the *Roman History*, see Hidber (2004: 196).
9 See e.g. Millar (1964: 104) and Zawadzki (1983: 275). Berrigan makes a distinction between the fictional content of the speeches and their historical setting, which he

believes to be 'real' (1968: 43; cf. Schmidt 1999: 107–8). Kuhlmann argues, however, that the historical circumstances would have made a debate by these specific actors and on these specific topics implausible in 29 BCE (2010: 110). For more scholarship on the debate's possible historical antecedents, see Manuwald (1979: 22 n 60).

10 Compare Pelling's observations in relation to Herodotus' debate on constitutions (2002: 129), of which the historicity is generally rejected.

11 There is a lacuna at the end of Agrippa's speech, which includes the introduction to and opening words of Maecenas' speech. For the Greek terminology, see Ruiz (1982: 63–84), who claims that Dio uses 'democracy' (δημοκρατία) for the Republican constitution, and 'oligarchy' (δυναστεία/ὀλιγαρχία) for Rome under the triumvirates (compare Sion-Jenkins 2000: 43–6). Kuhn-Chen argues that Agrippa's idea of democracy does not entirely match that of Dio himself, who focuses more on 'free speech' (παρρησία) as an essential criterion of democracy (2002: 195–201).

12 This lack of attention has been pointed out by Ruiz (1982: 33), Roddaz (1984: 211), Fechner (1986: 72) and Adler (2012: 477 n 3).

13 A rhetorical set-piece less relevant than the subsequent speech: Hammond (1932: 90), Gabba (1984: 72), Millar (1964: 105), Van Stekelenburg (1971: 110–11), McKechnie (1981: 150), Zawadzki (1983: 283, but see 276) and Kuhlmann (2010: 118); a speech complementary to the subsequent one by Maecenas: Bleicken (1962: 458–60), Ruiz (1982: 99, cf. 87–92), Fechner (1986: 73–83), Reinhold (1988: 170) and Adler (2012). Exceptional (and provocative) is Berrigan, who singles out Agrippa's speech as 'strong and majestic', in contrast to the 'sorry stuff' of Maecenas (1968: 45).

14 McKechnie (1981: 151–3); Aalders (1986: 283–95) argues that Dio's viewpoints are essentially Roman, but singles out his speeches as passages where his allegiance with the Greek historiographical tradition surfaces. An example in Agrippa's speech is the phrase 'Greeks and non-Greeks' (Ἕλληνες καὶ βάρβαροι, 52.10.2). Cf. Millar (1964: 191). Furthermore, Hammond (1932: 90) and Zawadzki (1983: 285–6) point at the Platonic colouring of the speech. Kuhlmann analyses the numerous parallels between Agrippa's speech and the pro-democracy speech of Otanes in Herodotus' *Histories* and argues that Dio's allusions to this passage account for its presumed Greekness (2010: 114–15). *Contra* Adler (2012: 513).

15 E.g. Roddaz (1984: 213). Compare also Zawadzki's surprise at the conclusion of Agrippa's speech (1983: 295).

16 The same line of thought is followed by Reinhold and Swan (1990: 161).

17 I focus upon books 36–53 of the *Roman History*, which roughly cover the second half of the civil wars, beginning with Pompey's war against the pirates and ending with Octavian's consolidation of power. Books 22–35, which deal with the earlier stages (e.g. the Gracchi, Sulla and Marius), are only known via a limited set of fragments.

18 Pitcher (2018b: 225). For Thucydides' judgments see De Bakker (2013) and Rood (2018).

19 Pitcher (2018b: 235), arguing that Dio in his characterization works according to the 'show, don't tell' principle (Pitcher 2018b: 227), although admitting that Dio adds narratorial assessments on character aspects in the case of some prominent Romans, like Pompey, Cato the Younger, Antony and Octavian, and also embeds statements upon the characters of others in some of his speeches.
20 Baragwanath's 2008 study of motivation in Herodotus' *Histories* has been seminal in this respect.
21 Compare De Temmerman and Van Emde Boas (2018: 22–3), who define words, deeds and thoughts as 'metonymical characterization' (with references to further scholarship in notes 73–5) and their comparison with those of other characters as 'metaphorical characterization'.
22 Compare 37.39.3, and, for salient examples 39.6.1 (Pompey recalling Cicero); 41.4 (Titus Labienus betraying Caesar); 48.24.6 (Quintus Labienus setting up the Parthians against Rome).
23 Observe also Dio's statements about the intentions of the triumvirs (41.54.1–3). Cf. Pelling (2006b: 261) on their disingenuousness.
24 Concrete examples in the narrative are numerous: 37.45 (Caesar refuses to charge Clodius); 37.58.1 (Caesar conceals his agreement with Pompey, pretends that they are still hostile); 38.1.6–7 (Caesar exempts himself from a committee for redistribution of the land); 38.8.3–5, 41.17.3 (Caesar pursues his interests by appointing allies, not introducing new laws by himself); 40.32.5 (Caesar pretends that he moves to Cisalpine Gaul for strategic reasons but in reality wishes to be closer to Rome); 42.52–54 (Caesar cleverly quells a mutiny). Observe that stealth, secrecy and pretension are also a familiar ingredient of Caesar's wars. He keeps the Helvetians at peace until he is ready to fight them (38.31.4), fools the Belgians in battle (39.2.1) and orchestrates a ruse for the Aduatuci (39.4.3–4).
25 E.g. 42.8.1–3: the Romans ridicule Caesar for lamenting Pompey's death; 42.44: the Romans see through fake matrimonial arrangements so that Caesar can live with Cleopatra.
26 For Octavian's strategic reticence when informed about Antony's dealings against him, compare 46.35.6–7; 48.46.4; 49.8.3–4. Timely restraint also features later in Octavian's career. When open war threatens between him and Antony after the death of Sextus Pompeius, Octavian stays outside Rome on some pretext to avoid the impression of taking the initiative (50.2.4).
27 Octavian breaks off the marriage (48.5.3), but later he betroths his sister Octavia to Antony (48.31.3) and the two men cement further family ties after another reconciliation (48.54.3–5). Caesar had acted similarly by betrothing his daughter to Pompey (38.9.1).
28 For the greediness of Octavian's soldiers observe also the note on which Dio ends his description of the battle of Actium: Octavian's men, lusting for the spoils,

approach the burning remains of Antony's fleet with an eye to plundering them, but fall victim to the flames (50.35.5–6).

29 Another interesting point of comparison is the difference in attitude between Caesar and Octavian towards the private archives of their opponents. Dio relates how Caesar, upon finding Cato's letters, did not read them, but burned them all (43.13.2), whereas Octavian kept most of Antony's correspondence (52.42.8) and also, against the laws, opened his will and read it out before the Senate (50.3.4–5).

30 Other examples of disingenuous speech: Ariovistus' treaty with Rome (38.44), Labienus tricking the Treveri by way of a speech to his own men in which he announces a hasty retreat (40.31), Litaviccus' speech that makes the Aedui revolt against Caesar (40.37.2), Curio's speeches against Caesar, whom he secretly supports (40.61.2–3).

31 The other triumvir, Crassus, is given an absurd harangue to his troops that discourages rather than stimulates them (40.19). The subsequent campaign against the Parthians falters, mainly due to Crassus' lack of foresight.

32 Reinhold 1988, *Comm. ad* 49.4.1–4, referring in particular to Septimius Severus and Caracalla.

33 The potential danger in Agrippa's position recurs as a theme when Octavian has become emperor, and appoints Agrippa as administrator of the city during his absence, compelling him to divorce his wife and marry his daughter Julia. This was all advised by Maecenas, who, according to Dio, is told to have jested: 'You have made him so great that he should either become your son-in-law or be murdered' (54.6.5).

34 For Menas, Sextus Pompeius' freedman, see 48.30.4–8 (attack upon Italy and capture of Sardinia on Sextus' behalf), 48.45.5–9 (desertion to Octavian), 48.54.7 (return to Sextus), 49.1.3–5 (second desertion to Octavian), 49.37.6 (killed whilst fighting on Octavian's behalf in Pannonia).

35 Pitcher (2018b: 233) observes that there are only a few statesmen whose deaths are accompanied by a judgement on character and that it is lacking, for instance, in the case of Caesar. With the exception of Antony (51.15.1–3) all these judgments are positive (Catulus 37.46.3; Pompey 42.5.1; Cato Uticensis 43.11.6; Maecenas 55.7.1–6), but none of them so much as Agrippa's (54.29.1).

36 Dio notes that only Agrippa and Maecenas are allowed to read the letters that Octavian sends to the Senate and change whatever they deem right; they are furthermore entitled to carry a ring with Octavian's seal (51.3.5–6).

37 Pelling (2006a: 106).

38 Perhaps Dio was also familiar with ancient theory on 'veiled speech' (*oratio figurata*), such as found in the works of pseudo-Demetrius and Quintilian. See Breij (2010).

39 A parallel is found in Herodotus' *Histories*, when Mardonius praises Xerxes' intention to march against Greece (Hdt., 7.9). There as well, the debate takes place

within the private setting of a court, and between an absolute monarch (Xerxes), a first adviser (Mardonius) whose interests are in the military, and a second adviser (Artabanus) who fulfils a less prominent role.

40 Cf. Hose (1994: 392) and Sion-Jenkins (2000: 148). In this respect Agrippa's speech resembles Herodotus' debate on constitutions, with Otanes weighing the ideal of democracy against tyranny in its worst aspects (Hdt., 3.80) and Darius cleverly obfuscating the difference between the freedom that the Persians gained in defeating their Median overlords and the freedom that is curtailed in a monarchy (Hdt., 3.82.5). Cf. Pelling (2002).

41 Observe in this respect Caesar's claim that he has taken upon himself the negative reputation that results from levying taxes, thereby preventing the Senate from being hated (43.18.3).

42 Cf. Bleicken (1962: 458–60).

43 Compare the speech that Dio ascribes to Catulus (36.31–36), who responds to the command offered to Pompey to fight the pirates. He refers to the danger that this position will overburden the one who holds it (36.35) and points out that elected generals will perform with more zeal than those appointed by a dictator (36.36).

44 Again Herodotus' debate on the Persian constitution offers itself as a parallel, with Otanes saying that the very position of a king forces even the most excellent man to 'stand aside from his usual soundness of mind.' (Hdt., 3.80.3)

45 Roddaz (1984: 213).

46 This mainly seems to be caused by Dio's abhorrence of democracy (typical of the imperial age), as can be seen in his discussion in 44.2, where he points out that democracies only flourished for brief periods, and would often quickly disintegrate. In his further narrative he points at the 'stupidity of the mob' to underline his argument, for instance in its assassination of Helvius Cinna (44.50.4), the wrong target instead of Cornelius Cinna. He also observes that the mob will by its nature always support the oppressed, which makes democracy unworkable (45.11.3–4). In the battle of Philippi, Dio reports that freedom and free speech were at stake (47.39.1–3), but explains that monarchy (restrictions upon παρρησία included) was the only natural outcome for the governance of an empire of such an enormous size (47.39.4–5). For a later reconfirmation of this, compare 54.6.1, where Dio takes the quarrels about the election of the consuls as evidence that democracy could not have succeeded in Rome. See also Gabba (1984: 71–3), Roddaz (1984: 209–10), Rich (1989: 95) and Hose (1994: 390–9), who turns against the arguments of Berrigan and Fechner (see above, notes 9 and 13).

47 See also the observations of Pelling (1997: 128–9) in relation to this passage and the earlier debate.

48 For the immediate context: Bringmann (1976); for the wider context: Lateiner (1989: 163–86, cf. 172–9) and Pelling (2002).

49 Another instructive parallel is Thucydides' Nicias, who spoke and voted against the Sicilian expedition in the Athenian democratic assembly, but took up the command nonetheless in accordance with the outcome of the meeting (Thuc., 6.8-26).

Chapter 11

1 We wish to thank the editors of this volume as well as an anonymous reviewer for helpful comments on earlier versions of this chapter. We also note that translations are based on previously published versions, especially those in the Loeb Classical Library.
2 Gotter (2000: 330). This whole paragraph is greatly indebted to Gotter (2000: 330-1) as well as two other major studies of the *pompa funebris* and related cultural practices, Flaig (1995) and Flower (1996) and also the more general statement by Flower (2006: 51-5). We also note here that Gotter (2000) (an article on M. Iunius Brutus) has been a major source of inspiration for this whole chapter. For a discussion of family history in the age of Augustus that complements this chapter see Osgood (2019).
3 Cic., *Brut.* 62 (*falsi triumphi, plures consulatus*). See the study by Ridley (1983) for the inflation of familial accomplishments. Another strategy was to create mythological or divine genealogies, discussed by Wiseman (1974), Flaig (1995:134-46), and Hölkeskamp (2004: 199-217, reprinting Hölkeskamp [1999]).
4 But of course there were other Roman pasts. See, e.g. Wiseman (2009) for efforts to disinter an alternative 'people's history' of Rome.
5 Flower (2006: 67-98) offers a groundbreaking discussion, with 86-98 especially important for this paragraph. Also valuable is her discussion in Flower (2010: 117-34).
6 In addition to Flower (2006: 90-93), see the foundational study of Hinard (1985).
7 Flower (2006: 96-7). For the memoirs see Cornell (2013 *FRH* no. 22, L. Cornelius Sulla) and a number of the papers in Smith and Powell (2009).
8 For brief reflections on this, see Osgood (2015: 1684-7). Analysis of the 70s BCE in particular was long focused on the career of Pompeius; for a welcome shift away from this approach, with reassessments of M. Aemilius Lepidus (cos. 78), discussed at length in the next section of our chapter, see the papers by Rosenblitt (2014), Santangelo (2014) and Burton (2014).
9 See now especially the studies by Rosenblitt (2014) and Burton (2014). Older studies of value are Hayne (1972), Gruen (1974: 12-17) and Syme (2016: 93-110).
10 E.g. in the venerable textbook of Scullard (1982), claiming Lepidus 'soon [after entering his consulship] found a chance to promote trouble'. The relevant section in *CAH* (2nd edn) Volume 9 is revealingly called 'The Revolt of Lepidus'.

11 Oros., 5.22.18 (*Sulla mortuo Lepidus, Marianae partis adsertor, adversus Catulum Sullanum ducem surgens redivivos bellorum civilium cineres suscitavit.*).
12 App., *B Civ.* 1.105 (ἄρτι δ' ἀποστάντος αὐτοῦ, Ῥωμαῖοι φόνου καὶ τυραννίδος ἀπαλλαγέντες ἡσυχῇ πάλιν ἐπὶ στάσεις ὑπερριπίζοντο ἑτέρας).
13 Flor., 2.11.1 (*Marco Lepido Quinto Catulo consulibus civile bellum paene citius oppressum est quam inciperet: sed quantulacumque fax illius motus ab ipso Sullae rogo exarsit*).
14 'Fiery war': Polyb., 35.1.1. For the fire of civil war, Hor., *Carm.* 2.1.7–8 is a *locus classicus*; see the parallel evidence cited by Nisbet and Hubbard (1978 *ad loc*).
15 It is worth noting that Q. Sertorius' breakaway state in Spain, harbouring men proscribed by Sulla, was at the peak of its power. Spann (1987: esp. 40–90) gives a good discussion, and also consult Konrad (1994).
16 On this and the next point see especially the discussion of Rosenblitt (2014), noting the significance of Cic., *Rosc. Am.* 152–3.
17 Santangelo (2014: 5–10) discusses the issue of the tribunate in the 70s, not entirely convincingly in our view.
18 The account of Granius Licinianus p. 33–4 Flemisch is important on this (esp. *verum ubi convenerunt tribuni plebis, consules uti tribuniciam potestatem restituerunt*).
19 Again, see especially Granius Licinianus p. 34 Flemisch.
20 For this and the sequence of events that follows see the careful chronology with references to the sources assembled by Burton (2014: 406–8).
21 Granius Licinianus p. 34 Flemisch; App., *B Civ.* 1.107.
22 Plin., *NH* 7.186.
23 Cinna: Suet., *Iul.* 5; see further below. Brutus: Val. Max., 6.2.8; Liv., *Ep.* 90; Plut., *Pomp.* 16.2–5, *Brut.* 4.1–3; Oros., 5.22.17. On Brutus see Treggiari (2019: 74–87).
24 See Oros., 5.22.17, 5.24.16 with the full discussion by Rosenblitt (2014: 417–23).
25 *Hostes publici*: Konrad (1988: 255).
26 Suet., *Iul.* 3 (*et Lepidi quidem societate, quamquam magnis condicionibus invitaretur, abstinuit, cum ingenio eius diffisus tam occasione, quam minorem opinione offenderat*).
27 The key source is Suet., *Iul.* 5. (*L. etiam Cinnae uxoris fratri, et qui cum eo civili discordia Lepidum secuti post necem consulis ad Sertorium confugerant, reditum in civitatem rogatione Plotia confecit habuitque et ipse super ea re contionem*).
28 Cic., *Verr.* 2.5.153; Plut., *Pomp.* 20.3–4, *Sert.* 27.3–4; App., *B Civ.* 1.115.
29 Hinard (1985: 162–86) gives a full discussion, with which we are broadly in agreement. The law is usually dated to 70, but Badian (2009: 19–20) argues for 71.
30 Cass. Dio, 44.47.4 is a key piece of evidence for this; see the discussion of Hinard mentioned in the previous note.

31 Cic., *Verr.* 2.5.152 (*civilis enim dissensionis et seu amentiae seu fati seu calamitatis non est iste molestus exitus, in quo reliquos saltem civis incolumis licet conservare*).
32 See Plut., *Cat. Min.* 17.45, with discussion by Hinard (1985: 204–7), and Eckert in this volume.
33 Quoted by Gell., *NA* 13.3.5 (*repperi tamen in oratione C. Caesaris, qua Plautiam rogationem suasit, 'necessitatem' dictam pro 'necessitudine', id est iure adfinitatis. Verba haec sunt: 'Equidem mihi videor pro nostra necessitate non labore, non opera, non industria defuisse.'*) The use of *necessitas* (in place of the more common *necessitudo*) may help Caesar emphasize his point.
34 The key sources are Suet., *Iul.* 5.1; Plut., *Caes.* 5.2–5. Flower (2006: 104–5) provides helpful analysis.
35 This is an important point in the biography of Brutus by Gotter (2000: 331–2).
36 Plut., *Brut.* 1.1–4 (cf. 1.6–8), with additional sources cited below.
37 Plut., *Brut.* 1.5, with additional sources cited below.
38 See Shackleton Bailey (1976: 129–31) and Treggiari (2019: 146–9).
39 Family tree: Atticus' book: Nep., *Att.* 18.3 (*fecit hoc idem separatim in aliis libris, ut M. Bruti rogatu Iuniam familiam a stirpe ad hanc aetatem ordine enumeraverit, notans, qui a quoque ortus quos honores quibusque temporibus cepisse*).
40 Quint., *Inst.* 9.3.95 quotes from a speech of Brutus *de dictatura Cn. Pompei*: 'For it is better to rule nobody than to be enslaved to anybody: since one may live with honour without ruling, whereas life is no life for the slave' (*praestat enim nemini imperare quam alicui servire: sine illo enim vivere honeste licet, cum hoc vivendi nulla condicio est*).
41 See, e.g. Quint., *Inst.* 3.6.93 and Ascon., p. 37 C.
42 Wiseman (1998: 106–20) (reprinting Wiseman 1993) is an important study that informs our discussion here. For a complementary discussion of the Aemilii, see Osgood (2019).
43 Plin., *NH* 35.12–13. He also adorned with similar shields his lavish house, the finest of its day in Rome (Plin., *NH* 36.49, 109) – another bid at enhancing the family's prestige.
44 Cic., *Att.* 4.16.8 (SB 89) (*Paulus in medio foro basilicam iam paene texerat isdem antiquis columnis. illam autem quam locavit facit magnificentissimam*).
45 See the passage in the previous note beginning *illam autem*...
46 On the experience of crisis, see Klooster and Kuin in this volume.
47 Quoted at Cic., *Att.* 9.7C.1 (SB 174C) (*haec nova sit ratio vincendi ut misericordia et liberalitate nos muniamus*).
48 Suet., *Iul.* 41.3; Plut., *Caes.* 37.2; Cass. Dio, 41.36.2 (with Hinard (1985: 217–19)).
49 *Att.* 9.14.2 (SB 182) (*atque eum loqui quidam αὐθεντικῶς narrabat Cn. Carbonis, M. Bruti se poenas persequi omniumque eorum in quos Sulla crudelis hoc socio fuisset*).

50 Suet., *Iul.* 75.4; Plut., *Caes.* 57.3; Cass. Dio, 42.18.2, 43.49.1.
51 Plut., *Brut.* 4.1 (... ἀξιῶν δὲ τὰ κοινὰ τῶν ἰδίων ἐπίπροσθεν ποιεῖσθαι καί τὴν Πομπηΐου νομίζων ὑπόθεσιν βελτίονα πρὸς τὸν πόλεμον εἶναι τῆς τοῦ Καίσαρος ἐκείνῳ προσέθετο).
52 It is invoked by Caesar (*BCiv.* 1.8.3) and for a discussion of it in Cicero's writings in the early 40s, including his letters, see Brunt (1986). See also the discussion below of the *Thirteenth Philippic*.
53 Plut., *Brut.* 4.3 (ὅτε καί φασι Πομπήϊον ἡσθέντα καί θαυμάσαντα προσιόντος αὐτοῦ καθεζόμενον ἐξαναστῆναι καί περιβαλεῖν ὡς κρείττονα πάντων ὁρώντων).
54 Welch (1995) gives a good discussion of Lepidus at this point in his career; see also Weigel (1992: 26–43).
55 Cic., *Att.* 14.7.1 (SB 361), 14.8.1 (SB 362); *Phil.* 13.3.
56 E.g. Cic., *Brut.* 331 (*tibi favemus, te tua frui virtute cupimus, tibi optamus eam rem publicam in qua duorum generum amplissimorum renovare memoriam atque augere possis*).
57 Cic., *Orat.* 35, *Att.,* 12.21.1 (SB 260), 13.46.2 (SB 338); Plut., *Brut.* 13.3. See further Treggiari (2019: 175–82).
58 This is the main theme of Gotter (2000).
59 Cic., *Phil.* 10.14 (*noster est Brutus semperque noster cum sua excellentissima virtute rei publicae natus, tum fato quodam paterni maternique generis et nominis*).
60 Sen., *Clem.* 1.9.3; Cass. Dio, 55.14.1. She had previously been married to Sulla's son Faustus.
61 Val. Max., 9.9.1; Suet., *Iul.* 85; Plut., *Brut.* 18.13; App., *B Civ.* 2.121; Cass. Dio, 44.50.4.
62 Note especially Val. Max., 9.9.1.
63 See esp. App., *B Civ* 2.126 for this episode.
64 Welch (2012: 121–30) gives a good overview of the politics of the aftermath of the Ides of March.
65 For fuller discussions of Servilia in this period: Osgood (2014: 47–52) and Treggiari (2019: 183–210).
66 Weigel (1992: 44–66) discusses Lepidus' politics during this time.
67 Cic., *Fam.* 10.27 (SB 369), *Phil.* 13.7.
68 Cic., *Phil.* 13.8 (*omnes honores, amplissimum sacerdotium, plurima urbis ornamenta, ipsius, fratris maiorumque monumenta*).
69 Cic., *Phil.* 13.15 (*haec si cogitas, est M. Lepidus, pontifex maximus, M. Lepidi, pontificis maximi, pronepos; sin hominibus tantum licere iudicas, quantum possunt, vide ne alienis exemplis eisque recentibus, uti quam et antiquis et domesticis malle videare*).
70 The letter is preserved at Cic., *Fam.* 10.35 (SB 408).

71 Cf. Welch (2012: 147) arguing (from a different perspective) that 'The Thirteenth Philippic traces the moment when a competition between public and private duty took root in civil war rhetoric.' I would say this moment represented more an intensification of earlier rhetoric.
72 Cic., *Fam.* 12.10.1 (SB 425); Vell. Pat., 2.64.4; App., *B Civ* 3.96; Cass. Dio, 46.51.4.
73 Cass. Dio, 49.42.2. For recent work on the building, see Tomei (2010).
74 Flower (1996: 224–46) gives a discussion. See also Osgood (2019).
75 *Laudatio* for Ap. Claudius Pulcher: Diom. *GL* I p. 367.26.
76 See the classic discussion by MacMullen (1966: 1–45).

Chapter 12

1 The issue of family in the epic is too pervasive and too complex for me to provide an adequate treatment here. Note especially the apparition of Julia's ghost at the beginning of Book 3, which concludes with a curse, *abscidis frustra ferro tua pignora: bellum / te faciet ciuile meum* (3.33–34: 'it is pointless for you to sever these pledges with arms: civil war will make you mine'). On the importance of the bond between Pompey and Caesar as *gener* and *socer*, see below and also Ambühl, this volume.
2 The connection between family and civic crisis is in fact a common one, which can be traced with benefit through other periods of history. Narratives about the American Civil War in particular have consistently been framed according to the terms of Lincoln's (antebellum) invocation of Matthew 12:25 ('A house divided against itself cannot stand', Lincoln 1989: 426). See, e.g. the epigraph to this chapter.
3 Tacitus explicitly invokes the authority of Vipstanus Messala when introducing the episode into his account of the battle, which I take as an indication that the historian felt the testimony of an eyewitness was necessary for a story that seemed too good to be true in its juxtaposition of public and private concerns to create a metonymic encapsulation of the horrors of civil war (both moral and real) through their impact on an individual family. Compare Syme (1958: 177).
4 Compare Agrippina's invocation of her motherhood through a similar gesture to the centurion sent to kill her in *Ann.* 14.8.5: *protendens uterum 'ventrem feri' exclamavit*; Ash (2007: 114).
5 Compare here Alexander's arguments (2012) about collective responses to cultural trauma, discussed by Eckert in this volume.
6 Tacitus goes on to compare this soldier's shamelessness with the fiercer *paenitentia* recorded in Sisenna's account of the Marian civil wars, in which a soldier killed himself after realizing that he had committed a similar crime.

7   To suggest another modern analogy, the situation is evocative of the evolution of gender roles in the United States following the Second World War, in which women's increased participation in the labour force (born of necessity as part of the mobilization for war) continued in the face of a renewed emphasis on domesticity and the demands of motherhood: Hartmann (1982: 77–95), cf. May (2008).
8   See Ambühl in this volume.

Bibliography

Aalders, G.J.D. (1986), 'Cassius Dio and the Greek World', *Mnemosyne* 39.3–4: 282–304.

Adler, E. (2012), 'Cassius Dio's Agrippa-Maecenas Debate: An Operational Code Analysis', *AJPh* 133: 477–520.

Africa, T.W. (1960), 'Phylarchus and the Gods: The Religious Views of a Hellenistic Historian', *Phoenix* 14: 222–7.

Africa, T.W. (1961), *Phylarchus and the Spartan Revolution*, Berkeley.

Alexander, J.C. (2004), 'Toward a Theory of Cultural Trauma', in J.C. Alexander, R. Eyerman, B. Giesen, N.J. Smelser, P. Sztompka (eds), *Cultural Trauma and Collective Identity*, 1–30, Berkeley.

Alexander, J.C. (2012), *Trauma: A Social Theory*, Malden, MA.

Alföldi, A. (1971), *Der Vater des Vaterlandes im römischen Denken*, Darmstadt.

Allan, R. J., I. J. F. de Jong, C. C. de Jonge (2017), 'From *Enargeia* to Immersion: The Ancient Roots of a Modern Concept', *Style* 51 (1): 34–51.

Alston, R. (2015), *Rome's Revolution: Death of the Republic and Birth of the Empire*, New York.

Ambühl, A. (2015), *Krieg und Bürgerkrieg bei Lucan und in der griechischen Literatur: Studien zur Rezeption der attischen Tragödie und der hellenistischen Dichtung im Bellum civile*, Berlin.

Ambühl, A. (2019), '*Venturi me teque legent* (Lucan, *Bellum civile* 9.985): Self-fulfilling prophecies in der lateinischen Dichtung als Reflexionsfiguren einer Rezeptionsästhetik', in A. Gerok-Reiter, A. Wolkenhauer, J. Robert, S. Gropper, (eds), *Ästhetische Reflexionsfiguren in der Vormoderne*, 133–57, Heidelberg.

Ameling, W. (2008), 'Ethnography and Universal History in Agatharchides', in T.C. Bennan, H.I. Flower (eds), *East & West. Papers in Ancient History Presented to Glen W. Bowersock*, 13–59, Cambridge, MA.

Ando, C. (2008), 'Decline, Fall, and Transformation', *Journal of Late Antiquity* 1/ 1: 31–60.

Ankersmit, F. (2005), *Sublime Historical Experience*, Stanford.

Armitage, D. (2017), *Civil Wars. A History in Ideas*, New York.

Ash, R. (2007), *Tacitus, Histories Book II*, Cambridge.

Assmann, J. (2008), 'Communicative and Cultural Memory', in A. Erll, A. Nünning (eds), *Cultural Memory Studies. An International and Interdisciplinary Handbook*, 109–18, Berlin.

Assmann, J. (2011), *Cultural Memory and Early Civilization: Writing, Remembrance, and Political Imagination*, Cambridge.

Bacevich, A.J. (2016), 'Ending Endless War. A Pragmatic Military Strategy', *Foreign Affairs*: 36–44.
Backhaus, M. (2019), *Mord(s)bilder: Aufzählungen von Gewalt bei Seneca und Lucan*, Berlin.
Badian, E. (2009), 'From the Iulii to Caesar', in M. Griffin (ed.), *A Companion to Julius Caesar*, 11–22, Malden, MA.
Baechler, J. (1975), *Revolution*, 2nd edn, Oxford.
Baker, K.M. (1990), *Inventing the French Revolution*, Cambridge.
Bakker, M.P. de (2013), 'Character Judgments in the *Histories*: their Function and Distribution', in A. Tsakmakis, M. Tamiolaki (eds), *Thucydides between History and Literature*, 23–40, Berlin.
Bann, S. (1990), *The Inventions of History: Essays on the Representation of the Past*, Manchester.
Baragwanath, E.M. (2008), *Motivation and Narrative in Herodotus*, Oxford.
Baron, C. (2011), 'The Delimitation of Fragments in Jacoby's *FGrHist*: Some Examples from Duris of Samos', *Greek, Roman, and Byzantine Studies* 51: 86–110.
Baron, C. (2016), 'Duris of Samos and a Herodotean Model for Writing History', in J. Priestley and V. Zali (eds), *Brill's Companion to the Reception of Herodotus in Antiquity and Beyond*, 59–82, Leiden.
Baron, C. (2017), 'Comedy and history, theory and evidence in Duris of Samos', in E. Baragwanath, E. Foster (eds), *Clio and Thalia: Attic Comedy and Historiography*, *Histos* Supplement 6, 211–39.
Batstone, W., C. Damon (2006), *Caesar's Civil War*, Oxford.
Beck, H. (2009), 'Die Rolle des Adligen und die Krise der römischen Republik', in K.-J. Hölkeskamp (ed.), *Eine politische Kultur (in) der Krise*, 53–71, Munich.
Becker, M. (2002), 'Talking Back to Frida: Houses of Emotional Mestizaje', *History and Theory* 41: 56–71.
Beloch, J. (1886), *Die Bevölkerung der griechisch-römischen Welt*, Leipzig.
Beltrami, L. (1998), *Il Sangue degli antenati: Stirpe, adulterio e figli senza padre nella cultura romana*, Bari.
Berdal, M., D.H. Ucko, eds (2009), *Reintegrating Armed Groups After Conflict: Politics, Violence and Transition*, New York.
Bering-Staschewski, R. (1981), *Römische Zeitgeschichte bei Cassius Dio*, Bochum: Brockmeyer.
Berliner, D. (2005), 'The Abuses of Memory: Reflections on the "Memory Boom"', *Anthropological Quarterly* 78: 197–211.
Berrigan, J.R. (1968), 'Dio Cassius' Defense of Democracy', *CB* 44: 42–5.
Bispham, E. (2007), *From Asculum to Actium: The Municipalization of Italy from the Social War to Augustus*, Oxford.
Blair, W.A. (2015), 'Finding the Ending of America's Civil War', *AHR* 120/5: 1753–66.
Bleicken, J. (1962), 'Der politische Standpunkt Dios gegenüber der Monarchie', *Hermes* 90: 444–67.

Bloomer, W.M. (2011), 'Transit Admiratio: Memoria, Invidia and the Historian', in E. Cowan (ed.), *Velleius Paterculus: Making History*, 93–119, Swansea.

Blössner, N. (2007), 'The City-Soul Analogy', in G.R.F. Ferrari (ed.), *The Cambridge Companion to Plato's Republic*, 345–85, Cambridge.

Börm, H., M. Mattheis, J. Wienand, eds (2016), *Civil War in Ancient Greece and Rome: Contexts of Disintegration and Reintegration*, Stuttgart.

Börm, H. (2018), 'Stasis in Post-Classical Greece: The Discourse of Civil Strife in the Hellenistic World', in H. Börm, N. Luraghi (eds), *The Polis in the Hellenistic World*, 53–83, Stuttgart.

Braund, S. (1992), *Lucan: Civil War*, New York.

Braund, S. (2012), 'Praise and Protreptic in Early Imperial Panegyric', in R. Rees, *Oxford Readings in Classical Studies: Latin Panegyric*, Oxford.

Breed, B.W., C. Damon, A. Rossi, eds (2010), *Citizens of Discord: Rome and its Civil Wars*, Oxford.

Breij, B.M.C. (2010), 'Oratio Figurata', in G. Ueding (ed.), *Historisches Wörterbuch der Rhetorik*, vol. 10, 1297–1302, Tübingen.

Bringmann, K. (1976), 'Die Verfassungsdebatte bei Herodot 3,80–82 und Dareios' Aufstieg zur Königsherrschaft', *Hermes* 104: 266–79.

Brink, C.O. (1960), 'Tragic History and Aristotle's School', *PCPS* 6: 14–19.

Brock, R. (2009), 'Did the Athenian Empire Promote Democracy?', in J. Ma, N. Papazarkadas, R. Parker (eds), *Interpreting the Athenian Empire*, 149–66, London.

Brodersen, K., ed. (2000), *Virtuelle Antike: Wendepunkte der Alten Geschichte*, Darmstadt.

Broughton, T.R.S. (1968), *The Magistrates of the Roman Republic Vol. 2 99BC–31BC*, Atlanta.

Brouwer, R. (2011), 'Polybius and Stoic Tyche', *Greek, Roman and Byzantine Studies* 51: 111–32.

Brunt, P.A. (1971), *Italian Manpower 225 B.C. – A.D. 14*, Oxford.

Brunt, P.A. (1980), 'On Historical Fragments and Epitomes', *CQ* 30: 447–94.

Brunt, P.A. (1986), 'Cicero's *officium* in the Civil War', *JRS* 76: 12–32.

Brunt, P.A. (1988), *The Fall of the Roman Republic and Related Essays*, Oxford.

Burns, A. (1966), 'Pompey's strategy and Domitius' stand at Corfinium', *Hist.* 15: 74–95.

Burstein, S.M. (1989), *Agatharchides of Cnidus on the Erythraean Sea*, London.

Burstein, S.M. (n.d.), 'Agatharchides of Knidos (86)', in I. Worthington (ed.), *Brill's New Jacoby*, Leiden.

Burton, P. (2014), 'The Revolt of Lepidus (cos. 78 BC) Revisited', *Hist.* 63: 404–21.

Butler, S. (2002), *The Hand of Cicero*, London.
Carr, D. (2014), *Experience and History: Phenomenological Perspectives on the Historical World*, New York.
Cartledge, P. (1998), 'Writing the History of Archaic Greek Political Thought', in N. Fisher, H. Van Wees (eds), *Archaic Greece: New Approaches and New Evidence*, 379–99, London.
Champion, C. (2000), 'Romans as ΒΑΡΒΑΡΟΙ: Three Polybian Speeches and the Politics of Cultural Indeterminacy', *CPhil*. 95: 425–44.
Champion, C. (2004), *Cultural Politics in Polybius's Histories*, Berkeley.
Chassignet, M. (2018), 'Caesar and Roman Historiography Prior to the *Commentarii*', in L. Grillo, C. Krebs (eds), *The Cambridge Companion to the Writings of Julius Caesar*, 249–62, Cambridge.
Christia, F. (2012), *Alliance Formation in Civil Wars*, Cambridge.
Clausewitz, C. von. (1942), *Principles of War*. Translated by H.W. Gatzke, Harrisburg, Pa.
Cole, T. (1967), *Democritus and the Sources of Greek Anthropology*, Cleveland.
Cooley, A.E. (2009), *Res Gestae Divi Augusti: Text, Translation, and Commentary*, Cambridge.
Cornell, T.J., ed. (2013), *The Fragments of the Roman Historians*, 3 vols, Oxford.
Cornford, F.M. (1907), *Thucydides Mythistoricus*. London.
Cornwell, H. (2017), *Pax and the Politics of Peace: Republic to Principate*, Oxford.
Cowan, E., ed. (2011), *Velleius Paterculus: Making History*, Swansea.
Cowan, R. (2010), 'Virtual Epic: Counterfactuals, Sideshadowing, and the Poetics of Contingency in the *Punica*', in A. Augoustakis (ed.), *Brill's Companion to Silius*, 323–51, Leiden.
Cowan, R. (2018), 'Sideshadowing Actium: Counterfactual History in Lollius' *Naumachia* (Horace, *Epistles* 1.18)', *Antichthon* 52: 90–116.
Cowley, R., ed. (2001), *The Collected What If? Eminent Historians Imagine What Might Have Been*, New York.
Crane, C.C. (2005), 'Phase IV Operations: Where Wars are Really Won', *Military Review*: 27–36.
Crane, G. (1998), *Thucydides and the Ancient Simplicity: The Limits of Political Realism*, Berkeley.
Crawford, J.W. (1984), *M. Tullius Cicero. The Lost and Unpublished Orations*, Göttingen.
Crawford, J.W. (1994), *M. Tullius Cicero. The Fragmentary Speeches*, Atlanta.
Csapo, E. and M. Miller (1998), 'Democracy, Empire, and Art: Towards a Politics of Time and Narrative', in D. Boedeker, K. Raaflaub (eds), *Democracy, Empire and the Arts in Fifth-Century Athens*, 87–125, Cambridge, MA.
D'Alessandro Behr, F. (2007), *Feeling History: Lucan, Stoicism, and the Poetics of Passion*, Columbus.
D'Angour, A. (2011), *The Greeks and the New: Novelty in Ancient Greek Imagination and Experience*, Cambridge.
Dalby, A. (1991), 'The Curriculum Vitae of Duris of Samos', *CQ* 41: 539–41.

Dart, C.J. (2014), *The Social War, 91 to 88 BCE: A History of the Italian Insurgency against the Roman Republic*, Farnham.
Day, H.J.M. (2013), *Lucan and the Sublime: Power, Representation and Aesthetic Experience*, Cambridge.
De Jong, I.J.F. (2004), *Narrators and Focalizers: The Presentation of the Story in the Iliad*, 2nd edn, London.
Degrassi, A. (1947), *Inscriptiones Italiae vol. 13/1, Fasti Consulares et Triumphales*, Rome.
Degrassi, A. (1954), *Fasti Capitolini*, Turin.
Degrassi, A. (1963), *Inscriptiones Italiae 13/2, Fasti Anni Numani et Iuliani*, Rome.
Demandt, A. (1978), *Metaphern für Geschichte: Sprachbilder und Gleichnisse im historisch-politischen Denken*, Munich.
Demandt, A. (2011), *Ungeschehene Geschichte. Ein Traktat über die Frage: Was wäre geschehen, wenn . . .?*, Göttingen.
Derow, P.S. (1979), 'Polybius, Rome, and the East', *JRS* 69: 1–15
Derow, P.S. (1989), 'Rome, the Fall of Macedon and the Sack of Corinth', *Cambridge Ancient History* 8: *Rome and the Mediterranean to 133 BC*, 2nd edition, 290–323, Cambridge.
Derow, P.S. (1994), 'Historical Explanation: Polybius and His Predecessors', in S. Hornblower (ed.), *Greek Historiography*, 73–90, Oxford.
Dixon, S. (1984), '*Infirmitas sexus*: Womanly Weakness in Roman Law', *Tijdschrift voor Rechtsgeschiedenis* 52: 343–71.
Dodds, E.R. (1973), 'The Ancient Concept of Progress', in E.R. Dodds, *The Ancient Concept of Progress and Other Essays on Greek Literature and Belief*, 1–25, Oxford.
Domainko, A. (2018), *Uncertainty in Livy and Velleius: Time, Hermeneutics, and Roman Historiography*, Munich.
Du Quesnay, I. M. Le M. (1995), 'Horace, *Odes* 4.5: *Pro Reditu Imperatoris Caesaris Divi Filii Augusti*', in S.J. Harrison (ed.), *Homage to Horace*, 128–87, Oxford.
Dyck, A.R. (2010), *Cicero: Pro Sexto Roscio*, Cambridge.
Eckert, A. (2014), 'Remembering Cultural Trauma. Sulla's Proscriptions, Roman Responses and Christian Perspectives', in: Becker, E.-M., J. Dochhorn, E.-K. Holt, Trauma and Traumatization in and beyond biblical Literature, 262–74, Göttingen.
Eckert, A. (2016a), *Lucius Cornelius Sulla in der antiken Erinnerung: Jener Mörder, der sich Felix nannte*, Berlin and Boston.
Eckert, A. (2016b), '"There is no one who does not hate Sulla": Emotion, Persuasion and Cultural Trauma', in E. Sanders, M. Johncock (eds), *Emotion and Persuasion in Classical Antiquity*, 133–46, Stuttgart.
Eckert, A. (2018), 'Good Fortune and the Public Good: Disputing Sulla's Claim to be *Felix*', in H. van der Blom, C. Gray, C. Steel (eds), *Institutions and Ideology in Republican Rome. Speech, Audience, Decision*, 283–98, Cambridge.
Eckert, A. (2019), 'Reconsidering the Sulla Myth', in A. Eckert and A. Thein (eds), *Sulla: Politics and Reception,* 159–72, Berlin and Boston.

Eckert, A. (forthcoming 2020), 'Sulla's Dictatorship "rei publicae constituendae" and Roman Republican Cultural Memory', in M.T. Dinter and C. Guerin (eds), *Cultural Memory in Republican and Augustan Rome*, Cambridge.

Eckstein, A.M. (1995), *Moral Vision in the Histories of Polybios*, Berkeley.

Eckstein, A.M. (2013), 'Polybius, Phylarchus, and Historiographical Criticism', *CPhil.* 108: 314–38.

Edelstein, L. (1967), *The Idea of Progress in Classical Antiquity*, Baltimore.

Edmunds L. (1975), 'Thucydides' ethics as reflected in the description of stasis (3.82–83)', *HSPh* 79: 73–92.

Effe, B. (2004), *Epische Objektivität und subjektives Erzählen: 'Auktoriale' Narrativik von Homer bis zum römischen Epos der Flavierzeit*, Trier.

Eigler, U. (2012), '*Fama, fatum* und *fortuna*: Innere und äussere Motivation in der epischen Erzählung', in T. Baier (ed., with the assistance of F. Stürner), *Götter und menschliche Willensfreiheit: Von Lucan bis Silius Italicus*, 41–53, Munich.

Eisenstadt, S.N., ed. (1968), *Max Weber: On Charisma and Institution Building*, Chicago.

Erler, M. (2012), 'Der unwissende Erzähler und seine Götter: Erzählperspektive und Theologie bei Lukan und in Vergils *Aeneis*', in T. Baier (ed., with the assistance of F. Stürner), *Götter und menschliche Willensfreiheit: Von Lucan bis Silius Italicus*, 127–40, Munich.

Erskine, A. (2000), 'Polybios and Barbarian Rome', *Mediterraneo Antico* 3: 165–82.

Erskine, A. (2012), 'Polybius among the Romans: Life in the Cyclops' Cave', in C. Smith, L. Yarrow (eds), *Imperialism, Cultural Politics and Polybius*, 17–32, Oxford.

Erskine, A. (2013), 'How to Rule the World: Polybius book 6 Reconsidered', in B. Gibson, T. Harrison (eds), *Polybius and His World: Essays in Memory of F.W. Walbank*, 231–46, Oxford.

Erskine, A. (2015), 'Polybius and the Anger of the Romans', in D. Cairns, L. Fulkerson (eds), *Emotions between Greece and Rome*, 105–27, London.

Esposito, R. (2011), *Immunitas: The Protection and Negation of Life*, trans. A. Hanafi, Cambridge, MA.

Evans, R. J. (2013), *Altered Pasts: Counterfactuals in History*, Lebanon, NH.

Fantham, E. (1985), 'Caesar and the Mutiny: Lucan's Reshaping of the Historical Tradition in *De bello civili* 5.237–373', *CPhil.*, 80 (2): 119–31.

Fantham, E. (1992), *Lucan, De bello civili. Book II*, Cambridge.

Fantham, E. (2006), *Julia Augusti: The Emperor's Daughter*, London.

Fearon, J.D. (2007), 'Iraq's Civil War', *Foreign Affairs*: 2–15.

Fechner, D. (1986), *Untersuchungen zu Cassius Dios Sicht der Römischen Republik*, Hildesheim.

Fedeli, P., I. Ciccarelli, I., eds (2008), *Q. Horati Flacci, Carmina Liber IV*, Florence.

Feeney, D.C. (1991), *The Gods in Epic: Poets and Critics of the Classical Tradition*, Oxford.

Fehrle, R. (1983), *Cato Uticensis*, Darmstadt.

Feldherr, A. (1998), *Spectacle and Society in Livy's History*, Berkeley.

Ferguson, N., ed. (1998), *Virtual History: Alternatives and Counterfactuals*, London.
Ferrary, J.L. (1988), *Philhellénisme et impérialisme: Aspects idéologiques de la conquête romaine du monde hellénistique*, Rome.
Figes, O., B. Kolonitskii (1999), *Interpreting the Russian Revolution: The Language and Symbols of 1917*, New Haven.
Finley, M. (1986), 'Revolution in Antiquity', in R. Porter, M. Teich (eds), *Revolution in History*, 47–60, Cambridge.
Flaig, E. (1995), 'Die Pompa funebris. Adlige Konkurrenz und annalistische Erinnerung in der römischen Republik', in O.G. Oexle (ed.), *Memoria als Kultur*, 115–48, Göttingen.
Flory, M. (1988), 'Abducta Neroni uxor: The Historiographical Tradition on the Marriage of Octavian and Livia', *TAPA* 118: 343–59.
Flower, H.I. (1996), *Ancestor Masks and Aristocratic Power in Roman Culture*, Oxford.
Flower, H.I. (2006), *The Art of Forgetting: Disgrace and Oblivion in Roman Political Culture*, Chapel Hill.
Flower, H.I. (2010), *Roman Republics*, Princeton.
Fornara, C.W. (1983), 'II. The Theoretical Foundations of Greco-Roman Historiography and their Application', in C.W. Fornara, *The Nature of History in Ancient Greece and Rome*, 91–142, Berkeley.
Foucault, M. (1988), *The Care of the Self: The History of Sexuality, vol. 3*, tr. R. Hurley, New York (orig. publ. Paris 1984).
Foucault, M. (2007), *Security, Territory, Population: Lectures at the Collège de France 1877–78*, tr. G. Burchell, New York (orig. publ. Paris 2004).
Fowler, D.P. (1995), 'Horace and the Aesthetics of Politics', in Harrison (1995): 248–66; reprinted in M. Lowrie, (ed.) (2009), *Oxford Readings in Classical Studies: Horace's Odes and Epodes*, Oxford: 247–70.
Franchet d'Espèrey, S., V. Fromentin, S. Gotteland, J.-M. Roddaz, eds (2003), *Fondements et crises du pouvoir*, Bordeaux.
Fraser, P.M. (1972), *Ptolemaic Alexandria I-III*, Oxford.
Freudenburg, K. (2014), 'Recusatio as Political Theatre: Horace's Letter to Augustus', *JRS* 104: 105–32.
Friedländer, S. (2007), *The Years of Extermination. Nazi Germany and the Jews 1939–1945*, London.
Fritz K., von (1942), 'Pompey's policy before and after the outbreak of the civil war of 49 B.C.', *TAPA*: 145–80.
Fritz, K. von (1956), 'Die Bedeutung des Aristoteles für die Geschichtschreibung', in L. Pearson (ed.), *Histoire et Historiens dans l'Antiquité*, 85–145, Vandoeuvres-Genève.
Fromentin, V. (2001), 'L'Historie Tragique, a-t-elle existé?', in A. Billault (ed.), *Lectures Antiques de la Tragédie Grecque*, 77–92, Paris.
Fuchs, H. (1948), *Rückschau und Ausblick im Arbeitsbereich der lateinischen Philologie*, Basel.

Gabba, E. (1956), *Appiano e la storia delle guerre civili*, Florence.
Gabba, E. (1984), 'The Historians and Augustus', in F. Millar, E. Segal (eds), *Caesar and Augustus. Seven Aspects*, 61–88, Oxford.
Gabba, E. (1994), 'Rome and Italy: The Social War', in J. Crook, A. Lintott, E. Rawson (eds), *The Cambridge Ancient History* Vol. 9. 104–28, Cambridge.
Galinsky, K. (1996), *Augustan Culture: An Interpretative Introduction*, Princeton.
Gall, D. (2005), 'Masse, Heere und Feldherren in Lucans Pharsalia', in C. Walde (ed.), *Lucan im 21. Jahrhundert – Lucan in the 21st Century – Lucano nei primi del XXI secolo*, 89–110, Munich.
Gehrke, H.-J. (1985), *Stasis: Untersuchungen zu den inneren Kriegen in den griechischen Staaten des 5. und 4. Jahrhunderts v. Chr*, Munich.
Gehrke, H.-J. (2001), 'Myth, History, and Collective Identity: uses of the past in ancient Greece and beyond', in N. Luraghi (ed.), *The Historian's Craft in the Age of Herodotus*, 286–313, Oxford.
Gelzer, M. (1968), *Caesar: Politician and Statesman*, trans. P. Needham, Cambridge, MA.
Gill, C. (2006), *The Structured Self in Hellenistic and Roman Thought*, Oxford.
Gillhaus, L., S. Kirsch, I. Mossong, F. Reich, S. Wirz (eds) (2016a), *Elite und Krise in antiken Gesellschaften*, Stuttgart.
Gillhaus, L. (2016b), 'Krise und Elite. Einführung in die Thematik', in L. Gillhaus, S. Kirsch, I. Mossong, F. Reich, S. Wirz (eds), *Elite und Krise in antiken Gesellschaften*, 11–31, Stuttgart.
Ginsberg, L.D. (2017), *Staging Memory, Staging Strife. Empire and Civil War in Octavia*, Oxford.
Golden, G.K. (2013), *Crisis Management during the Roman Republic*, Cambridge.
Goldhill, S., R. Osborne, eds (2006), *Rethinking Revolutions through Ancient Greece*, Cambridge.
Gordon, A.E. (1977), 'Who's Who in the *Laudatio Turiae*', *Epigraphica* 39: 7–12.
Gotter, U. (2000), 'Marcus Iunius Brutus – oder: die Nemesis des Namens', in K.-J. Hölkeskamp, E. Stein-Hölkeskamp (eds), *Von Romulus zu Augustus: grosse Gestalten der römischen Republik*, 328–39, Munich.
Gowing, A.M. (1992), *The Triumviral Narratives of Appian and Cassius Dio*, Ann Arbor.
Gowing, A.M. (2005), *Empire and Memory: The Representation of the Roman Republic in Imperial Culture*, Cambridge.
Graver, M., ed. and trans. (2002), *Cicero on the Emotions: Tusculan Disputations 3 and 4*, Chicago.
Gray, J. (2018), *Seven Types of Atheism*, London.
Gray, V. (1987), 'Mimesis in Greek Historical Theory', *AJPhil*. 108: 467–86.
Grethlein, J. (2010), *The Greeks and Their Past: Poetry, Oratory and History in the Fifth Century BCE*, Cambridge.
Grethlein, J. (2013), *Experience and Teleology in Ancient Historiography: 'Futures Past' from Herodotus to Augustine*, Cambridge.

Grethlein, J. (2016), 'Ancient Historiography and "Future Past"', in A. Lianeri (ed.), *Knowing Future Time in and through Greek Historiography*, 59–77, Berlin.

Griffith, M. (2011), 'Twelve Principles for Reading Greek Tragedy', in D.M. Carter (ed.), *Why Athens? A Reappraisal of Tragic Politics*, 1–7, Oxford.

Grigoropoulos, D., V. Di Napoli, V. Evangelidis, F. Camia, D. Rogers, S. Vlizos (2017), 'Roman Greece and the "Mnemonic Turn". Some Critical Remarks', in T.M. Dijkstra, I.N.I. Kuin, M. Moser, D. Weidgenannt (eds), *Strategies of Remembering in Greece Under Rome (100 BC–100 AD)*, 21–35, Leiden.

Grillo, L. (2012), *The Art of Caesar's Bellum Civile: Literature, Ideology, and Community*, Cambridge.

Grillo, L. and C. Krebs (2018), *The Cambridge Companion to the Writings of Julius Caesar*, Cambridge.

Groß, D. (2013), *Plenus litteris Lucanus: Zur Rezeption der horazischen Oden und Epoden in Lucans Bellum Civile*, Rahden.

Gruen, E. (1974), *The Last Generation of the Roman Republic*, Berkeley.

Gruen, E. (1985), 'Augustus and the ideology of war and peace', in R. Winkes (ed.), *The Age of Augustus*, 51–72, Louvain-la-Neuve.

Hadot, P. (1995), *Philosophy as a Way of Life: Spiritual Exercises from Socrates to Foucault*, Oxford.

Halliwell, S. (2002), *The Aesthetics of Mimesis: Ancient Texts and Modern Problems*. Princeton.

Halliwell, S. (2005), 'Learning from Suffering: Ancient Responses to Tragedy', in J. Gregory (ed.), *A Companion to Greek Tragedy*, 394–412, Oxford.

Hamilton, J.T. (2013), *Security: Politics, Humanity, and the Philology of Care*, Princeton.

Hammond, M. (1932), 'The Significance of the Speech of Maecenas in Dio Cassius, Book LII', *TAPA* 83: 88–102.

Hardie, P. (1993), *The Epic Successors of Virgil: A Study in the Dynamics of a Tradition*, Cambridge.

Harich, H. (1990), 'Catonis Marcia: Stoisches Kolorit eines Frauenporträts bei Lucan (II 326–350)', *Gymnasium* 97: 212–23.

Harris, W.V. (2016), *Roman Power: A Thousand Years of Empire*, Cambridge.

Harrison, S.J., ed. (1995), *Homage to Horace*, Oxford.

Hartmann, S.M. (1982) *The Homefront and Beyond: American Women in the 1940's*, Boston.

Hartzell, C.A. (2016), 'Negotiating Peace: Power Sharing in Peace Agreements', in T.D. Mason, S.M. Mitchell (eds), *What Do We Know About Civil Wars?*, 121–37, Lanham.

Hau, L.I. (2011), 'Tychê in Polybios: Narrative Answers to a Philosophical Question', *Histos* 5: 183–207.

Hau, L.I. (2016a), *Moral History from Herodotus to Diodorus Siculus*, Edinburgh.

Hau, L.I. (2016b), 'Truth and Moralising: The Twin Aims of the Hellenistic Historiographers', in I. Ruffell, L. I. Hau (eds), *Truth and History in the Ancient World. Pluralising the Past*, 226–49, London.

Hau, L.I. (forthcoming a), 'Pathos with a Point: Reflections on "Sensationalist" Narratives of Violence in Hellenistic Historiography in the Light of 21st-Century Historiography', in J. Grethlein (ed.), *Experience in Ancient Narrative*, Oxford.

Hau, L.I. (forthcoming b), *From Tragic to Immersive History: Duris, Phylarchus, Agatharchides*, Edinburgh.

Hau, L.I. (2019), 'Diodorus' use of Agatharchides' description of Africa', in M. Coltelloni-Trannoy, S. Morlet (eds), *Histoire et géographie chez les auteurs grecs (République et Empire)*, 27–42, Paris.

Hauser, M. (1954), *Der römische Begriff Cura*, Winterthur.

Havener, W. (2016), *Imperator Augustus. Die diskursive Konstituierung der militärischen persona des ersten princeps*, Stuttgart.

Hayne, L. (1972), 'M. Lepidus (cos. 78): A Re-appraisal', *Hist.* 21: 661–8.

Heftner, H. (2006), 'Der Beginn von Sullas Proskriptionen', *Tyche* 21: 33–52.

Hegel, G.W.F. (1956), *The Philosophy of History*, trans. J. Sibree, New York.

Henderson, J. (1998), 'Lucan: The Word at War', in J. Henderson, *Fighting for Rome: Poets and Caesars, History and Civil War*, 165–211, Cambridge.

Henderson, J. (2001), 'From Megalopolis to Cosmopolis: Polybius, or there and back again', in S. Goldhill (ed.), *Being Greek under Rome: Cultural Identity, the Second Sophistic and the Development of Empire*, 29–49, Cambridge.

Hershkowitz, D. (1998), *The Madness of Epic: Reading Insanity from Homer to Statius*, Oxford.

Hidber, T. (2004), 'Cassius Dio', in I.J.F. de Jong, R. Nünlist, A. Bowie (eds), *Narrators, Narratees, and Narratives in Ancient Greek Literature*, 187–99, Leiden.

Hill, C. (1990), 'The Word "Revolution"', in C. Hill, *A Nation of Change and Novelty: Radical Politics, Religion and Literature in Seventeenth-Century England*, 82–101, London.

Hinard, F. (1985), *Les proscriptions de la Rome républicaine*, Rome.

Hinard, F. (1990), 'Solidarités familiales et ruptures à l'époque des guerres civiles et de la proscription', in J. Andreau, H. Bruhns (eds), *Parenté et stratégies familiales dans l'antiquité romaine*, 555–70, Rome.

Hobsbawm, E. (1986), 'Revolution', in R. Porter, M. Teich (eds), *Revolution in History*, 5–46, Cambridge.

Hoffer, S.E. (2012), 'Divine Comedy? Accession Propaganda in Pliny *Epistles* 10.1–2 and the *Panegyric*', in R. Rees, *Oxford Readings in Classical Studies: Latin Panegyric*, Oxford, 194–220.

Hogan, J.T. (1980), 'The ἀξίωσις of words at Thucydides 3.82.4', *GRBS* 21: 139–49.

Holguin, S. (2015), 'How Did the Spanish Civil War End? ... Not So Well', *AHR* 120/5: 1767–83.

Hölkeskamp, K.J. (1999), 'Römische gentes und griechische Genealogien', in G. Vogt-Spira and B. Rommel (eds), *Rezeption und Identität: die kulturelle Auseinandersetzung Roms mit Griechenland als europäisches Paradigma*, 3–21, Stuttgart.

Hölkeskamp, K.J. (2004), *Senatus Populusque Romanus: die politische Kultur der Republik: Dimensionen und Deutungen*, Stuttgart.
Hölkeskamp, K.J., ed. (2009a), *Eine politische Kultur (in) der Krise? Die ‚letzte Generation' der römischen Republik*, Munich.
Hölkeskamp, K.J. (2009b), 'Eine politische Kultur (in) der Krise? Gemäßigt radikale Vorbemerkungen zum kategorischen Imperativ der Konzepte', in K.J. Hölkeskamp (ed.), *Eine politische Kultur (in) der Krise? Die 'letzte Generation' der römischen Republik*, 1–25, Munich.
Holmes, T.R. (1923), *The Roman Republic and the Founder of Empire* (3 vols.), Oxford.
Hornblower, S. (1991), *A Commentary on Thucydides, vol. 1: books 1–3*, Oxford.
Hornblower, S. (2008), *A Commentary on Thucydides. vol.3: Books 5.25–8.109*, Oxford.
Hose, M. (1994), *Erneuerung der Vergangenheit. Die Historiker im Imperium Romanum von Florus bis Cassius Dio*, Stuttgart.
Howard, M. (1962, Feb.), 'The Use and Abuse of Military History (lecture)', *Royal United Services Institution, Journal* 107: 4–8.
Hunink, V. (1992), 'Deserta Stamus in Urbe: Het beeld van Italië in Lucanus' Bellum Civile', *Hermeneus*, 64: 198–204.
Hunter, A. (1905), *Johnny Reb and Billy Yank*, New York.
Hunter, V.J. 1973. *Thucydides: The Artful Reporter*, Toronto.
Hutchison, E. and R. Bleiker (2015), 'Grief and the Transformation of Emotions after War', in L. Åhäll and T. Gregory (eds), *Emotions, Politics and War (Interventions)*, 210–21, London.
Instinsky, H.U. (1952), *Sicherheit als politisches Problem des römischen Kaisertums*, Baden-Baden.
Jacoby, F. (1926a), *Die Fragmente der Griechischen Historiker (FGrH) IIA*, Berlin.
Jacoby, F. (1926b), *Die Fragmente der Griechischen Historiker (FGrH) IIC, Kommentar zu Nr. 64–105*, Berlin.
Jehne, M. (2009), 'Caesars Alternative(n). Das Ende der römischen Republik zwischen autonomem Prozess und Betriebsunfall', in K.J. Hölkeskamp (ed.), *Eine politische Kultur (in) der Krise? Die 'letzte Generation' der römischen Republik* 141–60, Munich.
Judge, E.A. (1974), '"Res Publica Restituta". A Modern Illusion?', in J.A.S. Evans (ed.), *Polis and Imperium. Studies in honour of Edward Togo Salmon*, 279–311, Toronto.
Kalyvas, S.N. (2006), *The Logic of Violence in Civil War*, Cambridge.
Kantorowicz, E.H. (1957), *The King's Two Bodies: A Study in Mediaeval Political Theology*. Princeton.
Kathman, J.D., Shannon, M. (2016) 'Ripe for Resolution: Third Party Mediation and Negotiating Peace Agreements', in T.D. Mason and S.M. Mitchell (eds), *What Do We Know About Civil Wars?*, 109–20, Lanham.
Kearsley, R. (2013), 'Triumviral Politics, the Oath of 32 BC and the Veterans', *CQ* 63/2: 828–34.

Kebric, R.B. (1977), *In The Shadow of Macedon: Duris of Samos*, Wiesbaden.
Kebric, R.B. (2016), 'Caesar, Douris of Samos, and the death of "Tragic History"', in V. Naas, M. Simon (eds), *De Samos à Rome: personnalité et influence de Douris*, 341–60, Paris.
Kennedy, D. (1992) '"Augustan" and "Anti-Augustan": Reflections on Terms of Reference', in Powell (1992): 26–58.
Keppie, L. (1983), *Colonisation and Veteran Settlements in Italy 47–14 BC*, London.
Kiesewetter, H. (2002), *Irreale oder reale Geschichte? Ein Traktat über Methodenfragen der Geschichtswissenschaft*, Herbolzheim.
Kimmerle, N. (2015), *Lucan und der Prinzipat: Inkonsistenz und unzuverlässiges Erzählen im Bellum Civile*, Berlin.
Knoepfler, D. (2000), 'Trois Historiens Hellénistiques: Douris de Samos, Hiéronymos de Cardia, Philochore d'Athènes', in J. Leclant, F. Chamoux (eds), *Histoire et Historiographie dans l'Antiquité. Actes du IIe colloque de la Villa Kérylos à Beaulieu-sur-Mer les 13 et 14 octobre 2000*, 25–44.
Knoepfler, D. (2016), 'Douris et l'histoire d'Athènes: les connexions oropo-samiennes', in V. Naas, M. Simon (eds), *De Samos à Rome: personnalité et influence de Douris*, 17–35, Paris.
Konrad, C.F. (1988), 'Metellus and the Head of Sertorius', *Gerión* 6: 253–62.
Konrad, C.F. (1994), *Plutarch's Sertorius*, Chapel Hill.
Konstan, D. (2005), 'Clemency as a Virtue', *CPhil.*, 100: 337–46.
Koselleck, R. (1982), 'Krise', in R. Koselleck, O. Brunner, W. Conze (eds), *Geschichtliche Grundbegriffe. Historisches Lexikon zur politisch-sozialen Sprache in Deutschland* Vol. 3, 617–50, Stuttgart.
Koselleck, R. (1985), 'Historical Criteria of the Modern Concept of Revolution', in R. Koselleck, *Futures Past: On the Semantics of Historical Time*, trans. K. Tribe, 39–54, Cambridge, MA.
Koselleck, R., (2004), *Futures Past: On the Semantics of Historical Time*, trans. and with an introduction by K. Tribe, New York.
Koselleck, R. (2006), 'Crisis', trans. M.W. Richter, *Journal of the History of Ideas*, 67 (2): 357–400.
Kraus, C. 2007, 'Caesar's account of the Battle of Massilia (BC 1.34–2.22): Some Historiographical and Narratological Approaches.' in J. Marincola (ed.): *A Companion to Greek and Roman Historiography*, 371–8, Malden, MA.
Krebs, C. (2016), 'Thucydides in Gaul: The Siege of Platea as Caesar's Model for his Siege of Avaricum', *Histos* 10: 1–14.
Krebs, C. (2018), 'A Style of Choice', in L. Grillo, C. Krebs (eds), *The Cambridge Companion to the Writings of Julius Caesar*, 110–30, Cambridge.
Kristensen, T.M. (2016), 'Maxentius' Head and the Rituals of Civil War', in H. Börm, M. Mattheis and J. Wienand (eds), *Civil War in Ancient Greece and Rome: Contexts of Disintegration and Reintegration*, 321–46, Stuttgart.
Kroymann, J. (1956), 'Phylarchos', *RE Suppl VIII*: 471–89.

Kuhlmann, P. (2010), 'Die Maecenas-Rede bei Cassius Dio: Anachronismen und intertextuelle Bezüge', in D. Pausch (ed.), *Stimmen der Geschichte: Funktionen von Reden in der antiken Historiographie*, 109–21, Berlin.

Kuhn-Chen, B. (2002), *Geschichtskonzeptionen griechischer Historiker im 2. und 3. Jahrhundert n. Chr. Untersuchungen zu den Werken von Appian, Cassius Dio und Herodian*, Frankfurt a. M.

Kunkel, W., R. Wittmann (1995), *Staatsordnung und Staatspraxis der römischen Republik. Die Magistratur* (HdAW Abt. 10, Teil 3, Band 2, Abschnitt 2), Munich.

Landucci Gattinoni, F. (1997), *Duride di Samo*, Rome.

Landucci Gattinoni, F. (n.d.), 'Phylarchos (81)', in I. Worthington (ed.), *Brill's New Jacoby (BNJ)*.

Lange, C.H. (2009), *Res Publica Constituta: Actium, Apollo and the Accomplishment of the Triumviral Assignment*, Leiden.

Lange, C.H. (2011), 'The Battle of Actium: a Reconsideration', *CQ* 61/2: 608–23.

Lange, C.H. (2016), *Triumphs in the Age of Civil War: the Late Republic and the Adaptability of Triumphal Tradition*, London.

Lange, C.H. (2017), '*Stasis* and *Bellum Civile*: A Difference in Scale?', *Critical Analysis of Law* 4/2: 129–40.

Lange, C.H. (2019), 'Cassius Dio on Violence, Stasis, and Civil War: the Early Years', in C. Burden-Strevens, M. Lindholmer (eds), *Cassius Dio's Forgotten History of Early Rome*, 165–89, Leiden.

Lange, C.H., F.J. Vervaet, eds (2019), *The Historiography of Late Republican Civil War*, Leiden.

Lapidge, M. ([1979] 2010), 'Lucan's Imagery of Cosmic Dissolution', in C. Tesoriero (ed.), *Lucan. Oxford Readings in Classical Studies*, 289–323, Oxford.

Lateiner, D. (1989), *The Historical Method of Herodotus*, Toronto.

Leach, E. (1953), 'Cronus and Chronos', *Explorations* 1: 15–23.

Leach, E. (1955), 'Time and False Noses', *Explorations* 5: 30–5.

Leach, E. (1961), *Rethinking Anthropology*, London.

Leigh, M. (1997), *Lucan: Spectacle and Engagement*, Oxford.

Lenfant, D. (1999), 'Peut-on se fier aux "fragments" d'historiens? L'exemple des citations d'Hérodote', *Ktèma* 24: 103–21.

Lenfant, D. (2013), 'The Study of Intermediate Authors and its Role in the Interpretation of Historical Fragments', *Anc. Soc.* 43: 289–305.

LeVen, P.A. (2014), *The Many-Headed Muse: Tradition and Innovation in Late Classical Greek Lyric Poetry*, Cambridge.

Lianeri, A., ed. (2016), *Knowing Future Time in and through Greek Historiography*, Berlin.

De Ligt, L. (2012), *Peasants, Citizens and Soldiers. Studies in the Demographic History of Roman Italy 225 BC – AD 100*, Cambridge.

Lincoln, A. (1989), *Speeches and Writings 1832–1858*, edited by R.P. Basler, New York.

Lintott, A. (1982), *Violence, Civil Strife and Revolution in the Classical City, 750–330 BC*, London.
Lintott, A. (1999, 2nd edn), *Violence in Republican Rome*, Oxford.
Lipschutz, R.D., ed. (1995), *On Security*, New York.
Lobur, J. A. (2011), 'Resuscitating a Text: Velleius' History as Cultural Evidence', in E. Cowan, E., ed. (2011), *Velleius Paterculus: Making History*, Swansea, 203–18.
Loraux, N. (1986), *The Invention of Athens: The Funeral Oration in the Classical City*, trans. A. Sheridan, Cambridge, MA.
Loraux, N. (1995), 'La guerre civile grecque et la représentation anthropologique du monde à l'envers', *Revue de l'histoire des religions* 212.3: 299–326.
Loraux, N. (1997), *La cité divisée: l'oublie dans la mémoire d'Athènes*, Paris.
Loraux, N. (2002), *The Divided City: On Memory and Forgetting in Ancient Athens.* trans. C. Pache with J. Fort, New York.
Lowrie, M. (1997), *Horace's Narrative Odes*, Oxford.
Lowrie, M. (2010), 'Horace, *Odes* 4', in *Blackwell's Companion to Horace*, G. Davis, ed., 210–30, Chichester.
Luce, T.J. (1997), *The Greek Historians*, London.
Ludwig, K. (2014), *Charakterfokalisation bei Lucan: Eine narratologische Analyse*, Berlin.
MacMullen, R. (1966), *Enemies of the Roman Order: Treason, Unrest, and Alienation in the Roman Empire.* Cambridge, MA.
Maier, F.K. (2012), *'Überall mit dem Unerwarteten rechnen': die Kontingenz historischer Prozesse bei Polybios*, Munich.
Maier, F.K. (2013), 'How to Avoid Being a Backward-looking Prophet – Counterfactuals in Polybius', in A. Powell (ed.), *Hindsight in Greek and Roman History*, 149–70, Swansea.
Man, P. de (1967), 'The Crisis of Contemporary Criticism', *Arion* 6: 38–57.
Man, P. de (1983), *Blindness and Insight: Essays in the Rhetoric of Contemporary Criticism*, 2nd edn, London.
Manders, E. (2012), *Coining Images of Power: Patterns in the Representation of Roman Emperors on Imperial Coinage, A. D. 193–284*, Leiden.
Manuwald, B. (1979), *Cassius Dio und Augustus. Philologische Untersuchungen zu den Büchern 45–56 des dionischen Geschichtswerkes*, Wiesbaden.
Marcotte D. (2001), 'Structure et caractère de l'oeuvre historique d'Agatharchide', *Hist.* 50: 385–435.
Marincola, J. (2003), 'Between Pity and Fear: the Emotions of History', *Anc. Soc.* 33: 285–315.
Marincola, J. (2010), 'Aristotle's *Poetics* and "Tragic History"', in S. Tsitsiridis (ed.), *Parachoregema. Studies on Ancient Theatre in Honour of Professor Gregory M. Sifakis*, 445–60, Heraklion.
Marincola, J. (2013), 'Polybius, Phylarchus, and "Tragic History": a Reconsideration', in B. Gibson, T. Harrison (eds), *Polybius and his World: Essays in Memory of F.W. Walbank,* 73–90, Oxford.

Mason, T.D., S.M. Mitchell, eds (2016), *What Do We Know About Civil Wars?*, Lanham.
Masters, J. (1992), *Poetry and Civil War in Lucan's Bellum Civile*, Cambridge.
May, E.T. (2008), *Homeward Bound: American Families in the Cold War Era*, 2nd revised edn, New York.
McCubbin, H.I., J.M. Patterson (1982), 'Family Adaptation to Crises', in H.I. McCubbin, A.E. Cauble, J.M. Patterson (eds), *Family, Stress, Coping, and Social Support*, 26–47, Springfield.
McGing, B. (2010), *Polybius' Histories*, Oxford.
McGing, B. (2012), 'Polybius and Herodotus', in C. Smith, L. Yarrow (eds), *Imperialism, Cultural Politics and Polybius*, 33–49, Oxford.
McGinn, T. (2003), *Prostitution, Sexuality, and the Law in Ancient Rome*, 2nd edn, Oxford.
McKechnie, P. (1981), 'Cassius Dio's Speech of Agrippa: A Realistic Alternative to Imperial Government?', *G&R* 28: 150–5.
Megill, A. (2002), 'Two Para-Historical Approaches to Atrocity', *H&T* 41: 104–23.
Meier, C. (1997), *Res publica amissa: Eine Studie zu Verfassung und Geschichte der späten römischen Republik*, Frankfurt a.M.
Meier, C. ([1966] 1980), *Res publica amissa. Eine Studie zu Verfassung und Geschichte der späten römischen Republik*, Frankfurt a.M.
Meister, K. (1990), *Die griechische Geschichtsschreibung*, Stuttgart.
Melander, E. (2016), 'Gender and Civil Wars', in Mason, T.D., S.M. Mitchell (eds), *What do We Know about Civil Wars?*, 197–214, Lanham.
Meyer, C., J.G Patzel-Mattern, K. Schenk,(eds) (2013), *Krisengeschichte(n). Krise als Leitbegriff und Erzählmuster in kulturwissenschaftlicher Perspektive*, Stuttgart.
Meyer, P. (1891), *De Maecenatis oratione a Dione ficta*, Berlin (diss.).
Miles, G.B. (1992), 'The First Roman Marriage and the Theft of the Sabine Women', in R. Hexter and D. Selden (eds), *Innovations of Antiquity*, 161–96, New York.
Millar, F. (1964), *A Study of Cassius Dio*, Oxford.
Millar, F. (1973), 'Triumvirate and Principate', *JRS* 63: 50–67.
Mills, S. (1997), *Theseus, Tragedy, and the Athenian Empire*, Oxford.
Miltsios, N. (2013), *The Shaping of Narrative in Polybius*, Berlin.
Moles, J. (1996), 'Herodotus Warns the Athenians', in F. Cairns, M. Heath (eds), *Papers of the Leeds Latin Seminar. Ninth Volume: Roman Poetry and Prose, Greek Poetry, Etymology, Historiography*, 259–84, Leeds.
Mommsen, T. (1905), *Gesammelte Schriften*, Vol. 1, Berlin.
Moore, D.W. (2017), 'Learning from Experience: Polybius and the Progress of Rome', *CQ* 67: 132–48.
Morello, R. (2002), 'Livy's Alexander Digression (9.17–19): Counterfactuals and Apologetics', *JRS*, 92: 62–85.
Naas, V., M. Simon (eds) (2016), *De Samos à Rome: personnalité et influence de Douris*, Paris.
Napoleon Ier (1870), *Précis des guerres de Jules César: écrit à Sainte-Hélène par Marchand sous la dictée de l'empereur*, Paris.

Nauta, R. (2013), 'Metalepsis and Metapoetics in Latin Poetry', in U.E. Eisen, P. von Möllendorff (eds), *Über die Grenze: Metalepse in Text- und Bildmedien des Altertums*, 223–56, Berlin.

Nesselrath, H.-G. (1992), *Ungeschehenes Geschehen: ‚Beinahe-Episoden' im griechischen und römischen Epos von Homer bis zur Spätantike*, Stuttgart.

Neufeld, M. (2015), 'From Peacemaking to Peacebuilding: The Multiple Endings of England's Long Civil Wars', *AHR* 120/5: 1709–23.

Nill, H.-P. (2018), *Gewalt und Unmaking in Lucans Bellum Civile: Textanalysen, aus narratologischer, wirkungsästhetischer und gewaltsoziologischer Perspektive*, Leiden.

Nisbet, R.G.M., M. Hubbard (1978), *A Commentary on Horace: Odes, Book II*, Oxford.

Nussbaum, M. (2001), *The Fragility of Goodness: Luck and Ethics in Greek Tragedy and Philosophy*, Cambridge.

O'Gorman, E. (2006), 'Alternative Empires: Tacitus's Virtual History of the Pisonian Principate', *Arethusa* 39 (2): 281–301.

O'Higgins, D. (1988), 'Lucan as *Vates*', *Cl. Ant.* 7 (2): 208–26.

Ober, J. (2007), '"I Besieged That Man": Democracy's Revolutionary Start', in K.A. Raaflaub, J. Ober, R.W. Wallace (eds), *Origins of Democracy in Ancient Greece*, 83–104, Berkeley.

Orwin, C. (1994), *The Humanity of Thucydides*, Princeton.

Osborne, R. (2006), 'When was the Athenian democratic revolution?', in S. Goldhill, R. Osborne (eds), *Rethinking Revolutions through Ancient Greece*, 10–28, Cambridge.

Osborne R., ed. (2007), *Debating the Athenian Cultural Revolution: Art, Literature, Philosophy, and Politics, 430–380 BC*, Cambridge.

Osborne, R. (2010), *Athens and Athenian Democracy*, Cambridge.

Osgood, J. (2006), *Caesar's Legacy: Civil War and the Emergence of the Roman Empire*, Cambridge.

Osgood, J. (2014), *Turia. A Roman Woman's Civil War*, Oxford.

Osgood, J. (2015), 'Ending Civil War at Rome: Rhetoric and Reality (88 BCE – 197 CE)', *AHR* 120/5: 1683–95.

Osgood, J. (2019), 'Family History in Augustan Rome', in I. Gildenhard, U. Gotter, W. Havener, L. Hodgson (eds), *Augustus and the Destruction of History: the Politics of the Past in Early Imperial Rome*, 135–44, Cambridge.

Panoussi, V. (2007), 'Threat and Hope: Women's Rituals and Civil War in Roman Epic', in M. Parca and A. Tzanetou (eds), *Finding Persephone: Women's Rituals in the Ancient Mediterranean*, 114–34, Bloomington.

Parker, N. (1999), *Revolutions and History: An Essay in Interpretation*, Cambridge.

Parmeggiani, G. (2014), 'On the Translation of Polybius 1.1.2', *Histos* 8: 180–8.

Paton, W.R. (1922), *Polybius. Histories*, Cambridge, MA.

Pausch, D. (2011), *Livius und der Leser: Narrative Strukturen in Ab urbe condita*, Munich.

Pédech, P. (1964), *La méthode historique de Polybe*, Paris.

Pédech, P. (1989), *Trois Historiens Méconnus: Théopompe, Duris, Phylarque*, Paris.

Pelling, C. (1997), 'Cassius Dio and the Early Principate', in M.J. Edwards and S. Swain (eds), *Portraits: Biographical Representation in the Greek and Latin Literature of the Roman Empire*, 117–44, Oxford.

Pelling, C. (2000), 'Fun with Fragments. Athenaeus and the Historians', in D. Braund and J. Wilkins (eds), *Athenaeus and his World*, Exeter.

Pelling, C. (2002), 'Speech and Action: Herodotus' Debate on the Constitutions', *PCPS* 48: 123–58.

Pelling, C. (2006), 'Judging Julius Caesar', in M. Wyke (ed.), *Julius Caesar in Western Culture*, 3–26, Malden.

Pelling, C. (2006a), 'Speech and Narrative in the *Histories*', in C. Dewald, J. Marincola (eds), *The Cambridge Companion to Herodotus*, 103–21, Cambridge.

Pelling, C. (2006b), 'Breaking the Bounds: Writing about Julius Caesar', in B. McGing, J. Mossmann (eds), *The Limits of Ancient Biography*, 255–80, Swansea.

Pelling, C. (2011), *Plutarch Caesar. Translated with an Introduction and Commentary*, Oxford.

Pelling, C. (2013), 'Historical Explanation and What Didn't Happen: The Virtues of Virtual History', in A. Powell (ed.), *Hindsight in Greek and Roman History*, 1–24, Swansea.

Pelling, C. (2016), 'Tragic Colouring in Plutarch', in J. Opsomer, G. Roskam, F.B. Titchener (eds), *A Versatile Gentleman. Consistency in Plutarch's Writing*, 113–33, Leuven.

Pezzini, G. (2018), 'Caesar the Linguist: The Debate about the Latin Language', in L. Grillo, C. Krebs (eds), *The Cambridge Companion to the Writings of Julius Caesar*, 173–92, Cambridge.

Phillips, E.J. (1976), 'Catiline's Conspiracy', *Hist.* 25: 441–8.

Piovan, D. (2017), 'The Unexpected Consequences of War. Thucydides on the Relationship between War, Civil War and the Degradation of Language 1', *Araucaria* 19.37: 181–97.

Pitcher, L. (2018a), 'Caesar and Greek Historians', in L. Grillo, C. Krebs (eds), *The Cambridge Companion to the Writings of Julius Caesar*, 237–48, Cambridge.

Pitcher, L. (2018b), 'Cassius Dio', in K. de Temmerman, E. van Emde Boas (eds), *Characterization in Ancient Greek Literature*, 221–35, Leiden.

Porter, R., M. Teich, eds (1986), *Revolution in History*, Cambridge.

Powell, A. (1992), *Roman Poetry and Propaganda in the Age of Augustus*, London.

Powell, A. (ed.) (2013), *Hindsight in Greek and Roman History*, Swansea.

Pownall, F. (n.d.), 'Duris of Samos (76)', in I. Worthington (ed.), *Brill's New Jacoby*.

Price, J.J. (2001), *Thucydides and Internal War*, Cambridge.

Price, J.J. (2015), 'Thucydidean *stasis* and the Roman Empire in Appian's interpretation of history', in K. Welch (ed.), *Appian's Roman History: Empire and Civil War*, 45–63, Swansea.

Purcell, N. (1986), 'Livia and the Womanhood of Rome', *PCPS* 32: 78–105.

Quint, D. (1993), *Epic and Empire: Politics and Generic Form from Virgil to Milton*, Princeton.

Raaflaub, K. (1974), *Dignitatis contentio: Studien zur Motivation und politischen Taktik im Bürgerkrieg zwischen Caesar und Pompeius*, Munich.

Raaflaub, K. (2009), '*Bellum Civile*', in M. Griffin (ed.), *A Companion to Julius Caesar*, 175–91, Malden.

Rambaud, M. (1953, 2nd edn 1966), *L'art de la déformation historique dans les Commentaires de César*, Paris.

Reggi, G. (2002), 'Cesare e il racconto delle battaglie navali sotto Marsiglia', *RIL* 136: 71–108.

Reich, W.T. (1995), 'History of the Notion of Care', in W.T. Reich (ed.), *Encyclopedia of Bioethics*, rev. edn, 5 vols, 319–31, New York.

Reinhold, M. (1998) *From Republic to Principate: An Historical Commentary on Cassius Dio's Roman History, Books 49-52 (36-29 BC)*, Atlanta.

Reinhold, M., P.M. Swan (1990), 'Cassius Dio's Assessment of Augustus', in K.A. Raaflaub, M. Toher (eds), *Between Republic and Empire. Interpretations of Augustus and His Principate*, 155–73, Berkeley.

Rich, J.W. (1989), 'Dio on Augustus', in A. Cameron (ed.), *History as Text: The Writing of Ancient History*, 87–110, Chapel Hill.

Rich, J.W. (1990), *Cassius Dio. The Augustan Settlement (Roman History 53-55.9)*, Warminster.

Rich, J.W., J.H.C. Williams (1999), '*Leges et Iura P.R. Restituit*: A New Aureus of Octavian and the Settlement of 28–27BC', *The Numismatic Chronicle* 159: 169–213.

Rich, J.W. (2003), 'Augustus, War and Peace', in L. De Blois, P. Erdkamp, O. Hekster (eds), *The Representation and Perception of Roman Imperial Power. Proceedings of the Third International Network Impact of Empire (Roman Empire, c. 200 B.C.–A.D. 476)*, 329–57, Amsterdam.

Rich, J.W. (2010), 'Deception, Lies and Economy with the Truth: Augustus and the Establishment of the Principate', in A. J. Turner et al. (eds), *Private and Public Lies. The Discourse of Despotism and Deceit in the Graeco-Roman World*, 167–91, Leiden.

Rich, J. W. (2012), 'Making the Emergency Permanent: *auctoritas*, *potestas* and the Evolution of the Principate of Augustus', in Y. Rivière (ed.), *Des réformes augustéennes*, 37–121, Rome.

Rich, J.W. (2016), 'Review of Havener, *Imperator Augustus: die diskursive Konstituierung der militärischen persona des ersten römischen Princeps*', *BMCR* 2016.11.49.

Ridley, R.T. (1983), '*Falsi triumphi, plures consulatus*', *Latomus* 42: 372–82.

Riedl, P. (2002), *Faktoren des historischen Prozesses: Eine vergleichende Untersuchung zu Tacitus und Ammianus Marcellinus*, Tübingen.

Riedl, P. (2010), 'Alternatives Geschehen in Tacitus' Historien', *Millennium*, 7: 87–132.

Riess, W., G.G. Fagan, eds (2016), *The Topography of Violence in the Greco-Roman World*, Ann Arbor.

Rimell, V. (2015), *The Closure of Space in Roman Poetics*, Cambridge.

Roberts, A., ed. (2004), *What Might Have Been: Imaginary History from Twelve Leading Historians*, London.

Roddaz, J.-M. (1984), *Marcus Agrippa*, Rome.
Roller, M.B. (2001), *Constructing Autocracy: Aristocrats and Emperors in Julio-Claudian Rome*, Princeton.
Rood, T. (2012), 'Polybius, Thucydides, and the First Punic War', in C. Smith and L. Yarrow (eds), *Imperialism, Cultural Politics and Polybius*, 50–67, Oxford.
Rood. T. (2018), 'Thucydides', in K. de Temmerman, E. van Emde Boas (eds), *Characterization in Ancient Greek Literature*, 153–71, Leiden.
Rosenblitt, A. (2014), 'The Turning Tide: the Politics of the Year 79 BCE', *TAPA* 144: 415–44.
Rosenblitt, A. (2019a), *Rome after Sulla*, London, New York, Oxford, Sydney.
Rosenblitt, A. (2019b), 'Sulla's Long Shadow. Sallust in Tacitus and Tacitus in Sallust', in: A. Eckert and A. Thein (eds.) (2019), *Sulla. Politics and Reception*, 125–142, Berlin and Boston.
Rotondi, Giovanni (1962), *Leges publicae populi Romani*, Hildesheim.
Roveri, A. (1956), 'Tyche in Polibio', *Convivium* 24: 275–93.
Ruffell, I. and L.I. Hau (2016), 'Introduction', in I. Ruffell, L.I. Hau (eds), *Truth and History in the Ancient World. Pluralising the Past*, 1–12, London.
Ruiz, U.E. (1982), *Debate Agrippa - Mecenas en Dion Cassio: Respuesta senatorial a la crisis del Impero Romano en época severiana*, Madrid (diss.).
Runia, E. (2006), 'Presence', *H&T* 45.1: 1–29.
Runia, E. (2010), 'Inventing the new from the old – from White's "tropics" to Vico's "topics"', *Rethinking History* 14.2: 229–41.
Salewski, M., ed. (1999), *Was Wäre Wenn. Alternativ- und Parallelgeschichte: Brücken zwischen Phantasie und Wirklichkeit*, Stuttgart.
Sannicandro, L. (2007), 'Per uno studio sulle donne della *Pharsalia*: Marcia Catonis', *MH* 64: 83–99.
Santangelo, F. (2014), 'Roman Politics in the 70s BC: a Story of Realignments?', *JRS* 104: 1–27.
Sawilla, J. M. (2013), 'Zwischen Normabweichung und Revolution – Krise in der Geschichtswissenschaft', in C. Meyer, K. Patzel-Mattern, G J. Schenk (eds), *Krisengeschichte(n). Krise als Leitbegriff und Erzählmuster in kulturwissenschaftlicher Perspektive*, 145–72, Stuttgart.
Scanlon, T.F. (1987), 'Thucydides and Tyranny', *Cl. Ant.* 6: 286–301.
Scheidel, W. (2015), *State Power in Ancient China and Rome*, Oxford.
Scheller, P. (1911), *De Hellenistica Historiae Conscribendae Arte*, Leipzig (diss.).
Schepens, G. (1997), 'Jacoby's *FGrHist*: Problems, Methods, Prospects', in G.W. Most (ed.), *Collecting Fragments/Fragmente sammeln*, Göttingen.
Schepens, G. (2005), 'Polybius' Criticism of Phylarchus', in G. Schepens, J. Bollansée (eds), *The Shadow of Polybius: intertextuality as a research tool in Greek historiography*, 141–64, Leuven.
Schepens, G. (2007), 'Les fragments de Phylarque chez Athénée', in D. Lenfant (ed.), *Athénée et les Fragments d'Historiens*, 239–61, Paris.

Schlonski, F. (1995), *Studien zum Erzählerstandort bei Lucan*, Trier.

Schmidt, M.G. (1999), 'Politische und persönliche Motivation in Dios Zeitgeschichte', in M. Zimmermann (ed.), *Geschichtsschreibung und politischer Wandel im 3. Jh. n. Chr*, 93-117, Stuttgart.

Schmitt, A.W. (1995), *Die direkten Reden der Massen in Lucans Pharsalia*, Frankfurt a.M.

Schmitzer, U. (2011), 'Roman Values in Velleius', in Cowan (2011): 177-202.

Schrijvers, P.H. (1988), 'Deuil, désespoir, destruction (Lucain, La *Pharsale* II 1-234)', *Mnemosyne*, 41: 341-54.

Schröder, B.-J. (2012), 'Römische "pietas": kein universelles Postulat', *Gymnasium* 119: 335-58.

Schwartz, E. (1894), 'Agatharchides', *RE* 1: 739-40.

Schwartz, E. (1896), *Fünf Vorträge über den Griechischen Roman*, Berlin.

Schwartz, E. (1903), 'Diodoros von Agyrion', *RE* V 1: 663-704.

Schwartz, E. (1905) 'Duris von Samos', *RE* 2: 1853-6.

Scullard, H.H. (1982), *From the Gracchi to Nero: a History of Rome 133 BC to AD 68*, (5th edn), London.

Seaford, R. (2003), 'Tragic Tyranny', in K. Morgan (ed.), *Popular Tyranny: Sovereignty and its Discontents in Ancient Greece*, 95-116, Austin.

Seager, R. (1964), 'The First Catilinarian Conspiracy', *Hist.* 13: 338-47.

Serres, M. with B. Latour (1995), *Conversations on Science, Culture and Time*, trans. R. Lapidus, Ann Arbor.

Severy, B. (2003), *Augustus and the Family at the Birth of the Roman Empire*, New York.

Shackleton Bailey, D. ed. (1968), *Cicero's Letters to Atticus vol. IV*, Cambridge.

Shackleton Bailey, D. (1976), *Two Studies in Roman Nomenclature*, New York.

Shackleton Bailey, D. ed. (1997), *M. Annaei Lucani De bello civili libri X*, editio altera.

Shear, J.L. (2011), *Polis and Revolution: Responding to Oligarchy in Classical Athens*, Cambridge.

Shipley, G. (1987), *A History of Samos 800-188 BC*, Oxford.

Shuckburgh, E.S. (1889), *Histories. Polybius*, London.

Sion-Jenkins, K. (2000), *Von der Republik zum Prinzipat. Ursachen für den Verfassungswechsel in Rom im historischen Denken der Antike*, Stuttgart.

Skidmore, C. (1996), *Practical Ethics for Roman Gentlemen: the Work of Valerius Maximus*. Liverpool.

Skultety, S. (2009), 'Competition in the best of cities', *Political Theory* 37.1: 44-68.

Sluiter, I. (2017), 'Anchoring Innovation: A classical research agenda', *European Review* 25: 20-38.

Smith, C. and A. Powell (2009), *The Lost Memoirs of Augustus and the Development of Roman Autobiography*. Swansea.

Sonnabend, H. (2000), 'Augustus - wird nicht alt', in K. Brodersen (ed.), *Virtuelle Antike: Wendepunkte der Alten Geschichte*, 103-15, Darmstadt.

Spann, P.O. (1987), *Quintus Sertorius and the Legacy of Sulla*, Fayetteville.

Spawforth, A.J. (2011), *Greece and the Augustan Cultural Revolution*, Cambridge.
Stadter, P.A. (1989), *A Commentary on Plutarch's Pericles*, Chapel Hill.
Steel, C. (2014), 'The Roman Senate and the Post-Sullan Res Publica', *Hist.*, 63 (3): 323–39.
Steinbock, B. (2013), *Social Memory in Athenian Public Discourse: Uses and Meanings of the Past*, Ann Arbor.
Stekelenburg, A. V. van (1971), *De redevoeringen bij Cassius Dio*, Leiden (diss.).
Stelluto, S. (1995), 'Il motivo della τρυφή in Filarco', in I. Gallo (ed.), *Seconda Mescellanea Filologica*, 47–84, Naples.
Stockt, L. van der (2005), '"Πολυβιάσασθαι"? Plutarch on Timaeus and "Tragic History"', in G. Schepens and J. Bollansée (eds), *The Shadow of Polybius*, 271–305, Leuven.
Strasburger, H. (1982 [1966]), 'Die Wesensbestimmung der Geschichte durch die Antike Geschichtsschreibung', in *Studien zur Alten Geschichte* vol. 2: 963–1016.
Suerbaum, W. (1997), 'Am Scheideweg zur Zukunft: Alternative Geschehensverläufe bei römischen Historikern', *Gymnasium*, 104: 36–54.
Suerbaum, W. (1998), 'Si fata paterentur: Gedanken an alternatives Handeln in Vergils Aeneis', in A.E. Radke (ed.), *Candide Iudex: Beiträge zur augusteischen Dichtung. Festschrift für Walter Wimmel zum 75. Geburtstag*, 353–74, Stuttgart.
Syme, R. (1939), *The Roman Revolution*, Oxford.
Syme, R. (1958), *Tacitus*, Oxford.
Syme, R. (2016), *Approaching the Roman Revolution: Papers on Republican History*, (edited by F. Santangelo), Oxford.
Syndikus, H.-P. (2001), *Die Lyrik des Horaz*, vol. 2, 3rd edn, Darmstadt.
Teegarden, D.A. (2014), *Death to Tyrants! Ancient Greek Democracy and the Struggle Against Tyranny*, Princeton.
Temmerman, K. de and E. van Emde Boas (2018), 'Character and Characterization in Ancient Greek Literature: an Introduction', in K. de Temmerman, E. van Emde Boas (eds), *Characterization in Ancient Greek Literature*, 1–23, Leiden.
Tempest, K. 2017, *Brutus the Noble Conspirator*, New Haven and London.
Thein, A. (2019), 'Dolabella's naval command', in A. Eckert, A. Thein, *Sulla. Politics and Reception*, 71–88, Berlin and Boston.
Thorne, M. (2011), '*Memoria Redux*: Memory in Lucan', in P. Asso (ed.), *Brill's Companion to Lucan*, 363–81, Leiden.
Thorne, M. (2016), 'Speaking the Unspeakable: Engaging Nefas in Lucan and Rwanda 1994', in A. Ambühl (ed.), *War of the Senses – The Senses in War: Interactions and Tensions between Representations of War in Classical and Modern Culture, thersites. Journal for Transcultural, Presences and Diachronic Identities from Antiquity to Date* 4: 77–119.
Thornton, J. (2013), 'Oratory in Polybius' Histories', in C. Kremmydas, K. Tempest (eds), *Hellenistic Oratory: Continuity and Change*, 21–42, Oxford.
Tomei, M.A., ed., (2010), *Memorie di Roma: gli Aemilii e la basilica nel Foro*, Rome.

Tracy, J. (2014), *Lucan's Egyptian Civil War*, Cambridge.
Treggiari, S. (1991), *Roman Marriage: Iusti Coniuges from the Time of Cicero to the Time of Ulpian*, Oxford.
Treggiari, S. (2019) *Servilia and Her Family*, Oxford
Ucko, D.H. (2009), 'Militias, tribes and insurgents: the Challenge of Political reintegration in Iraq', in M. Berdal and D.H. Ucko (eds), *Reintegrating Armed Groups After Conflict. Politics, Violence and Transition*, 89–118, London.
Veloso, C.W. (2016), '*Mimèsis* et historiographie chez Aristotle et chez les historiens des époques hellénistique et impériale: quelques réflexions', in V. Naas, M. Simon (eds), *De Samos à Rome: personnalité et influence de Douris*, 195–208, Paris.
Ven, H. van de (1995), 'The Emergence of the Text-Centred Party', in T. Saich, and H. van de Ven (eds), *New Perspectives on the Chinese Communist Revolution*, 5–32, Armonk, NY.
Vervaet, F, (2018), 'The Date, Modalities and Legacy of Sulla's Abdication of his Dictatorship: A Study in Sullan Statecraft', *Historia Antigua* 36: 31–82.
Veyne, P. (1978), 'La famille et l'amour sous le haut-empire romain', *Annales E.S.C.* 33: 35–63.
Vierhaus, R. (1978), 'Zum Problem historischer Krisen', in K.G. Faber and C. Meier (eds), *Historische Prozesse. Beiträge zur Historik*, 313–29, Munich.
Vierhaus, R. (1979), 'Politische und historische Krisen. Auf dem Weg zu einer historischen Krisenforschung', *Jahrbuch der Max-Planck-Gesellschaft*, 1979: 72–85.
Waddell, P. (2016), '*Carthago Deleta*: Alternate Realities and Meta-History in Appian's *Libyca*', in V. Liotsakis, S. Farrington (eds), *The Art of History: Literary Perspectives on Greek and Roman Historiography*, 241–52, Berlin.
Waever, O. (1993), 'Societal Security: The Concept', in Waever et al., 17–40.
Waever, O., Buzan, B., Kelstrop, M., and Lemaitre, P., eds (1993), *Identity, Migration and the New Security Agenda in Europe*, London.
Walbank, F.W. (1955), 'Tragic History: A Reconsideration', *BICS* 2: 4–14.
Walbank, F.W. (1957), *A Historical Commentary on Polybius I*, Oxford.
Walbank, F.W. (1960), 'History and Tragedy', *Hist.* 9: 216–34.
Walbank, F.W. (1965), *Speeches in Greek Historians*, Oxford (reprinted in *Selected Papers: Studies in Greek and Roman Historiography*, 242–61, Cambridge 1985).
Walbank, F.W. (1967), *A Historical Commentary on Polybius*, vol. 2, Oxford.
Walbank, F.W. (1972), *Polybius*, Berkeley.
Walbank, F.W. (1979), *A Historical Commentary on Polybius, vol. 3*, Oxford.
Walbank, F.W. (1977), 'Polybius' last ten books', in *Historiographia Antiqua: Commentationes Lovanienses in honorem W. Peremans septuagenarii editae*, 139–62, Leuven (reprinted in *Selected Papers: Studies in Greek and Roman Historiography*, 325–43, Cambridge 1985).

Walbank, F.W. (1990), 'Profit or Amusement: some thoughts on the motives of Hellenistic Historians', in H. Verdin, G. Schepens and E. de Keyser (eds), *Purposes of History: Studies in Greek Historiography from the 4th to the 2nd centuries BC*, 253–66, Leuven (reprinted in *Polybius, Rome and the Hellenistic World*, 201–22, Cambridge, 2002).

Walbank, F.W. (2007), 'Fortune (tychê) in Polybius', in J. Marincola (ed.), *A Companion to Greek and Roman Historiography*, 349–55, Oxford.

Walde, C. (2005), 'Einleitung', in C. Walde (ed.), *Lucan im 21. Jahrhundert – Lucan in the 21st Century – Lucano nei primi del XXI secolo*, vii–xix, Munich.

Walde, C. (2011), 'Lucan's *Bellum Civile*: A Specimen of a Roman "Literature of Trauma"', in P. Asso (ed.), *Brill's Companion to Lucan*, 283–302, Leiden.

Walde, C. (2012), 'Fortuna bei Lucan – Vor- und Nachgedanken', in T. Baier (ed., with the assistance of F. Stürner), *Götter und menschliche Willensfreiheit: Von Lucan bis Silius Italicus*, 57–74, Munich.

Walde, C. (2017), '*Tu ne quaesieris scire nefas quem finem . . . di dederunt . . .*: Reflexionen zur Debatte um das Ende von Lucans *Bellum Civile*', in C. Schmitz, J. Telg genannt Kortmann, A. Jöne (eds), *Anfänge und Enden: Narrative Potentiale des antiken und nachantiken Epos*, 169–98, Heidelberg.

Walde, C. (forthcoming), *Am Beispiel von Lucan: Explorationen in die römische Literaturgeschichte*.

Walter, U. (2009), 'Struktur, Zufall, Kontingenz? Überlegungen zum Ende der Römischen Republik', in K.-J. Hölkeskamp (ed.), *Eine politische Kultur (in) der Krise? Die 'letzte Generation' der römischen Republik*, 27–51, Munich.

Waterfield, R. (2010), *Polybius: The Histories, translated by Robin Waterfield; introduction and notes by Brian McGing*, Oxford.

Waters, K.H. (1970), 'Cicero, Sallust and Catiline', *Hist.* 19.2: 195–215.

Weber, G. (2000), 'Vom Sinn kontrafaktischer Geschichte', in K. Brodersen (ed.), *Virtuelle Antike: Wendepunkte der Alten Geschichte*, 11–23, Darmstadt.

Weigel, R.D. (1992), *Lepidus: the Tarnished Triumvir*, London.

Welch. K. (1995), 'The Career of M. Aemilius Lepidus', *Hermes* 123: 443–54.

Welch, K. (2012), *Magnus Pius. Sextus Pompeius and the Transformation of the Roman Republic*, Swansea.

Westall, R. (2014), 'Triumph and Closure: Between History and Literature', in C.H. Lange, F.J. Vervaet (eds), *The Roman Republican Triumph: Beyond the Spectacle*, 33–52, Rome.

White, H. (1973), *Metahistory. The Historical Imagination in Nineteenth Century Europe*, Baltimore.

White, H. (1980), 'The Value of Narrativity in the Representation of Reality', *Critical Inquiry* 7: 5–27.

Whitmarsh, T. (2005), *The Second Sophistic*, Oxford.

Whitrow, G.J. (1988), *Time in History*, Oxford.

Wiater, N. 2010, 'Speaker and Narrator: Speeches and Historical Narrative in Polybius's Histories', in D. Pausch (ed.), *Stimmen der Geschichte. Funktionen von Reden in der antiken Historiographie*, 69–107, Berlin.

Wienand, J. (2012), *Der Kaiser als Sieger. Metamorphosen triumphaler Herrschaft unter Constantin I*, Berlin.
Wilson J. (1982), 'The customary meaning of words were changed. Or were they? A note on Thucydides 3.82.4', *CQ* 32: 18–20.
Wiseman, T.P. (1974), 'Legendary Genealogies in Late-Republican Rome', *G&R* 21: 153–64.
Wiseman, T.P. (1993), 'Rome and the Resplendent Aemilii', in H. D. Jocelyn, H. Hurt (eds), *Tria Lustra: Essays Presented to John Pinsent*, 181–92, Liverpool.
Wiseman, T.P. (1994), 'The Senate and the Populares', in J.A. Crook, A. Lintott, E. Rawson (eds) *Cambridge Ancient History* 9, 327–67, Cambridge.
Wiseman, T.P. (1998), *Roman Drama and Roman History*, Exeter.
Wiseman, T.P. (2009), *Remembering the Roman People: Essays on Late-Republican Politics and Literature*, Oxford.
Woelk, D. (1966), *Agatharchides von Knidos: Über das Rote Meer, Übersetzung und Kommentar*, Freiburg.
Woodman, A. ed. (1977), *Velleius Paterculus: The Tiberian Narrative, 2.94–131*, Cambridge.
Woodman, A. ed. (1983), *Velleius Paterculus: The Caesarian and Augustan Narrative (2.41–93)*, Cambridge.
Woodman, A. (1988), *Rhetoric in Classical Historiography: Four Studies*, Portland.
Wyke, M., ed. (2006), *Julius Caesar in Western Culture*, Malden.
Yavetz, Z. (1963), 'The Failure of Catiline's Conspiracy', *Hist.* 12, 1963: 485–99.
Zangara, A. (2007), *Voir l'histoire. Théories anciennes du récit historique*, Paris.
Zartman, I.W. (1995), 'Introduction: Posing the Problem of State Collapse', in I.W. Zartman (ed.), *Collapsed States: The Disintegration and Restoration of Legitimate Authority*, 1–12, Boulder.
Zawadzki, R. (1983), 'Die Konzeption der römischen Staatsverfassung in der politischen Doktrin des Cassius Dio', *Analecta Cracoviensia* 15: 271–318.
Zegers, N. (1959), *Wesen und Ursprung der tragischen Geschichtsschreibung*, Cologne (diss.).
Ziegler, R. (2007), 'Zeitkritik und Krisenempfinden bei Cassius Dio', in H. Scholten (ed.), *Die Wahrnehmung von Krisenphänomenen. Fallbeispiele von der Antike bis in die Neuzeit*, 83–96, Cologne.

Index

Achaea 58–61, 65–6, 71, 76–81, 147
Achaean League 57, 60, 76, 78, 80
Actium 109, 137, 139, 141–2, 146–9, 156–7, 161, 197
Aetolia 71–3, 76
Agatharchides 59, 62–4
Agrippa 151, 153, 156, 158–65
Alexander, Jeffrey C. 91
Alexandria 62, 98, 116, 139, 141, 146, 149
allusion 72, 124–33
amnesty 27, 116–17, 172
ancestors 107, 169, 174–80
anchoring, re-anchoring 10–12
Andriscus 78, 79
Ankersmit, Frank 10–11
annona 40, 43
Antonius, Marcus 6, 87, 99, 115–17, 138–42, 145, 147, 149, 151, 154–8, 161, 179, 180, 193, 197
Appian 5, 6, 9, 32, 85, 99, 121, 122, 124, 138, 170, 189, 190, 192, 193
Aristophanes 19, 21, 52
Aristotle 19, 24, 25, 26, 27, 50, 51, 52, 53, 57, 62, 106, 140
Arretium 93, 94
Athenaeus 70
Athens 12, 15, 19–25, 27–9, 50–3, 55, 61–2, 72, 125, 163, 187
audience, readership 3, 8, 49, 53, 56, 58–9, 60, 64, 67–8, 71, 73, 74–5, 79, 81, 85, 104, 105, 107–9, 126, 129, 154, 156–7, 164
Augustus, *see* Octavian

Basilica Aemilia 175–6
bias 52, 54, 56, 60, 61, 117
body politic 4, 31, 36, 41–2, 44–6
Boeotian League 76
Brundisium 85, 90, 121, 138
Brutus, M. Junius 14, 104, 133, 142, 155, 171–82, 184–5

Caesar, Julius 8, 13–14, 34, 41, 43–6, 87–8, 94–100, 103–5, 107–9, 111–18, 121–34, 135–40, 142–9, 154–8, 161, 164–5, 172–3, 176–9, 183, 190
Cannae, battle of 69–71, 75, 77, 94, 104
Carthage 71, 79
Catiline 7–9, 38, 96, 158, 187
Cato the Younger 96, 108–9, 112, 117, 133, 154, 158, 178, 181–2, 184–6
characterization 25, 52, 61, 68, 70, 74, 79, 98, 112, 123–4, 127, 151, 153–5, 192, 194
Christianity 4, 16–17
Cicero 7–10, 31–3, 38–9, 51, 87, 90–1, 93–6, 98, 116, 121–4, 129, 133, 140, 154–5, 157–8, 160, 169, 172–5, 177–80, 190
Cat. 38, 99, 187
Fam. 7–8, 9–10, 179–80
Prosc. lib. 96
Rosc. Am. 90–1, 93–4, 171
Tog. cand. 96
Verr. 95–6, 172–3
Cinna 14, 116, 171–3, 177, 179–80, 182
civil war 9, 12, 14, 36, 43–4, 46, 103–5, 108–9, 111, 113–14, 117–18, 125, 135–40, 143–4, 146, 149, 154–5, 173, 182–92, 194
American 138–41
endings of 13–14, 35–6, 43, 119, 131, 135–49, 172
Roman 9, 13–14, 31–2, 35–6, 37, 85–7, 89–91, 93–4, 96–100, 103–13, 115–17, 121, 125, 129, 131–3, 135–46, 148–9, 151–2, 154, 157, 162, 169–73, 176–9, 181–95
clementia (clemency) 87, 97–8, 100, 109, 115, 117, 124, 129, 133, 140, 149, 156, 164, 189
Cleopatra 104, 135–6, 139, 143, 145–6, 149, 151, 156, 158, 161

Colline Gate 85–7, 90, 93
comedy 21, 56
Commodus 14, 152
community 3, 5, 7, 11–12, 14, 21, 27, 32, 52–3, 64, 76, 92, 128, 130, 141, 169, 182, 184, 190, 195, 197
conservatism 16, 18
Corfinium 13, 97–8, 121–34
Corinth 74, 78, 125
Cornelia 173, 176, 185–6
crisis 3–6, 7, 9, 11–15, 50, 65–70, 73, 75–7, 80, 81, 87, 91, 92, 96, 99, 106, 109, 114, 122–5, 128, 129, 152, 165, 170, 172, 180, 184, 186, 192, 194
    consequences of 11–14, 76, 91, 93–100, 176–7, 184, 186, 190–2
    coping with 11–13, 29, 64, 75, 77, 79, 85, 93, 99–100, 105, 153, 171, 177, 179, 182, 186, 190, 193–4
    definition of 4–5, 7, 11–12, 15, 65, 68, 73, 88, 89, 106, 108, 151
    etymology of 4
    historical 4–7, 67, 87–90, 110
    narrative of 5–10, 12, 14, 68–70, 95, 106, 108, 128–33, 151–3, 173, 184, 187, 197
    recovery from 3, 11–13, 70, 93, 96–7, 100, 161, 181, 186, 190,
Critias 25, 28
Critolaus 78
Cynoscephalae, battle of 74

Darius 152, 165
De Jong, Irene 104, 106
De Man, Paul 15–16
defeat 22, 49–50, 61, 64, 69–70, 73, 76, 80, 94, 97–8, 103–4, 107–9, 111, 113–14, 131, 140–1, 144, 155, 158–60, 171–2, 174, 175, 178
democracy 19–24, 27–9, 125, 151, 153, 162–3
Democritus 32–3
didacticism 62–4
Dio, Cassius 14, 122, 124, 139, 141, 145, 147–8, 151–65
dissensio (disagreement) 125, 128, 131, 133–4, 153, 172–3
Dolabella, Cn. Cornelius 95
Drusus 42
Duris 13, 49–56, 61–2, 64

economy 4, 9, 17–18, 35, 41–2, 89, 91, 110, 136
emotion 6, 13, 20, 25, 35, 42, 46, 51, 59–64, 68–70, 74, 80, 90, 96, 107, 184, 189, 193
emplotment 6, 8, 10, 11, 55, 61, 104, 129, 133
enargeia (vividness) 63–4, 70
'end of the world' 109, 112, 117
Esposito, Roberto 33
Euripides 19, 22
exaedificatio (structure) 6, 10, 37, 67, 76, 104, 123–5, 131, 138
experience, re-experience 3, 9–15, 17–19, 28, 57, 60, 64–5, 67–70, 73–5, 77, 80–1, 93, 96–7, 105, 107, 141, 148, 158–9, 177, 179, 182–4, 186, 190–1, 197

faction(s), factionalism 26, 86, 123, 125–8, 137, 140, 144, 187, 193
family 14, 39, 42, 93–4, 112, 114, 169–70, 172–97
    history 14, 169–70, 172–4, 177–82
fathers, paternal authority 39, 41–2, 112, 174, 178–9, 185, 188, 190, 193
Finley, Moses 16–17
fire 72, 109, 170–2, 176
First Mithridatic War 94–5
Flamininus 71, 75
Florus 45, 85–7, 170
Foucault, Michel 46
fraternisation 112, 114, 117
freedom 21, 27, 38, 71, 73, 75–7, 153, 158, 162, 186
Fufidius 86
Fulvia 192, 197
funerals 22–3, 51, 152, 169–71, 173–74, 176, 181, 185,
'futures past' 105

Germany 37, 41, 110
gnomic wisdom 162
Golden Age 21, 40
Gracchi 5–6
Gratidianus 96
Greece 3, 13, 17, 23, 73, 76–7, 79, 95, 126, 155
    under Rome 13, 65, 71–3, 76–7, 79
Grethlein, Jonas 8, 11, 22, 105
grief 33, 183–4, 188, 193, 196

Index

Hannibal 69–71, 73–5, 94, 104–5, 111
Hegel, Friedrich 6–7
Herodotus 14, 21, 54, 72, 106, 152, 160–1, 163–5
hindsight 8, 68, 73, 81, 105, 172
historiography 6, 7, 11, 50, 51, 54, 56, 57, 61, 70, 105, 152, 154, 188–9
Hellenistic 11, 13, 49, 54
history 4–7, 9–11, 13–14, 17–20, 23, 40, 49–52, 56, 59–62, 64–70, 76–81, 85, 87–8, 94–5, 101, 103–6, 111, 125, 131–2, 135, 137–8, 149, 151–4, 156, 158, 162–3, 165, 169–170, 172–4, 177–8, 180–2, 187, 190
   counterfactual 13, 104–5, 109–12, 114–17
   experiential 10, 13, 49, 64
   phenomenology of 11, 15, 16, 28
   teleology of 6–8, 67, 78, 105
   tragic 49, 53, 56–7, 62
Hölkeskamp, Karl-Joachim 88–9
Horace 10, 40–4, 46, 105, 110
Hybrida, Antonius 95

imaginary 31, 110, 118
imperialism 13, 19, 21, 23, 31–2, 34, 36, 38, 44, 77, 137
injustice, social 9
intertextuality 14, 17, 105, 110
Isocrates 22
isonomia (equality before the law) 26, 162, 165
Isthmian Games 71, 74–5
ius liberorum (Augustan marriage laws) 194–5

Julia 104, 173, 176, 181, 196–7

Kantorowicz, Ernst 42
Koselleck, Reinhart 4, 88, 105–6, 108

language 4, 11, 15–19, 72, 121, 124–5, 127–8, 131, 133–5, 137, 178
   distortion of 160–1
laudatio (eulogy) 173, 179, 181, 190–1, 196
Laudatio Turiae 14, 142
Lepidani 14, 169–70, 173
Lepidus, M. Aemilius 14, 87, 94, 99, 154, 156, 170–2, 175, 178–80, 191, 193
Lex Aurelia de tribunica potestate 95

Lex Aurelia Iudicaria 95
Lex Cornelia de proscriptione 90, 96
Livia 156, 191, 196
Lucan 13, 103–18, 183–6
Lucceius 7–9
Lysias 22

Macedon 60, 65–7, 71, 73–81, 147, 175, 178
Maecenas 151–3, 156, 160–1, 163–5
Marcia 185–6
Marius 13, 115, 117, 130, 149, 173
marriage 22, 34–5, 179, 185–6, 191, 194–7
masks, ancestor 169, 174
Meier, Christian 88, 106
memory 18, 38, 39, 100, 103, 169, 170, 175
   collective/social 13, 27, 43, 52, 53, 61, 64, 143, 169, 176, 181
   history and 10, 66
mimesis (imitation) 54–5, 62
monarchy 14, 31, 79, 141, 143, 149, 153, 160–5, 196
mothers, maternal bond 41, 179, 183–8, 191, 196

Naupactus, peace of 71
Nero 109, 111
Nerva 46, 187
Nesselrath, Heinz-Günther 104

Octavian Augustus 6, 14, 31, 32, 34–43, 45, 87, 99–100, 104, 115, 117, 135–7, 140–9, 151–65, 180–2, 189, 190–1, 194–7
oligarchy 23–5, 27, 125–6
Orosius 87, 170–1
Otanes 165

pace parta terra marique (peace on land and sea) 142
parrhesia (frankness of speech) 153, 157–8, 160
peace 19, 21, 27, 31–7, 39–41, 43, 46, 71, 73, 77, 87, 90, 109, 112–14, 129, 131–2, 135–40, 142–5, 148–9, 151, 153, 160, 178–80, 185–6, 195
Peripatetics 50, 53, 57
Perseus of Macedon 75–8, 175
Pharsalus 98, 104, 107–8, 110, 112, 115, 127, 177–8
'phase IV' operations 135, 149

Philip V of Macedon 60, 71, 73–5,
Philiscus 154–5, 158, 160
Philopoemen 75
Photius 49–50, 52–4, 62–3
Phylarchus 13, 49–50, 56–64
Plato 32
Pliny 46, 100
Plutarch 49–53, 55, 58, 61, 70, 87, 116, 176, 178, 181
Polybius 13, 49–50, 56–63, 65–81, 105, 135, 152
Pompey, Cn. 8, 13, 87, 97–101, 104–5, 107–9, 111–13, 115–17, 121–4, 126–7, 129–30, 133, 157, 163–5, 172, 174, 177–9, 183, 186, 197
Pompey, S. 108, 178–9
Praeneste 86, 90, 146
principate 36, 104, 109, 117, 137, 143–4, 151–3, 165, 187, 194
pronoia (foresight) 73, 132, 134, 151
proscriptions, Sullan 13, 86–8, 90–1, 93–4, 96, 115, 164, 169, 173
    triumviral 87–8, 99–101, 115, 140, 156, 158–9, 162–3, 180, 188–90, 192–3
Pydna, battle of 71, 73, 75–8

reconciliation 10, 97, 109, 112–14, 117, 140, 149
res publica 8, 86, 88, 136, 138–40, 144–5, 170–1, 173, 177–81, 184, 190, 194–5
revenge 87, 100, 109, 111, 114–15, 117, 138, 170, 174, 177, 178
revolution 5, 7–8, 12, 15–29, 51–3, 55, 61, 72, 111, 155, 158, 170
Rhodes 73, 76–7
Roman Republic 6, 9, 14, 31–4, 36, 38–9, 45–6, 88–9, 91, 103–4, 112, 117, 123, 134–8, 140, 151, 153, 160–2, 164, 179, 181–2, 184–5
    Late 106, 114, 135–8, 141, 143–4, 149, 152
Rome 5, 9, 39, 60, 65, 69–70, 77–8, 80, 86–7, 90, 93, 97–100, 110–11, 115, 121, 141, 144, 146–7, 155–8, 162, 165, 171–2, 174, 177, 180, 183
Rome, constitution of 14, 32, 70, 142, 151–4, 161
Runia, Eelco 10–11

Sacriportus 85, 90
Sallust 9, 158, 187
salus (salvation, well-being) 32–4, 45, 114
Scipio Aemilianus, P. Cornelius 6, 79
secessio (secession) 125, 128, 130
securitas (state security) 12–13, 31–46
self-portrayal 129, 134
senate 35, 37–9, 70, 90, 93, 95, 129–30, 132, 139, 142–3, 145–6, 152, 161, 163–4, 171–2, 179–80, 195–6
Seneca the Younger 44–5, 100, 116
sensationalism 49–50
Sertorius 172
settlements, negotiated 40, 74, 135, 137–8, 140–4, 146–9, 179
Severi 14
side-shadowing 105
Social War 71, 129–32, 134
soldiers 49, 85–7, 90, 93–4, 97–9, 104, 109, 111–12, 114–16, 121–6, 128, 130–2, 144, 146–9, 156–9, 172, 188, 193
stasis (civil strife) 5–6, 13, 26, 122, 124–32, 134, 136, 138, 140, 187, 193
succession 21, 34–7, 39–40, 50
suffering 27, 46, 49, 52, 55–6, 59–61, 63–4, 69–70, 72, 91–4, 104, 159, 186, 189, 193
suicide 60, 109, 112, 133, 156, 158, 178
Sulla 13, 85–101, 115–17, 140–1, 164, 169–73, 176–7, 179, 181
Syracuse 23–24

Tacitus 105, 145, 149, 187–8, 190, 193, 197
temple of Janus 43, 142, 145, 149
Thucydides 5, 9, 14, 21, 23–4, 51–2, 57, 67, 70, 72, 125–9, 132, 138, 140, 152, 154, 187, 193
Tiberius 5–6, 32, 34, 36, 38–9, 42, 100, 196
time, temporality 12, 17–19, 21–3, 28–9, 42, 64–5, 74, 89, 105
tragedy 20, 29, 49–50, 56–8, 61, 64, 67, 126
trauma 10, 77, 87, 103, 183, 185, 188, 190
    collective 13, 27, 54
    cultural 91–3, 97–101
triumph 35, 139, 141–9, 158, 169, 181
triumvirate 87–8, 99–101, 104, 136, 138–40, 143–5, 147–8, 154–7, 162–3, 165, 175, 180, 188–9, 193, 197
tyche (fortune) 65–8, 68, 77, 79–80, 108, 111

tyranny 20–5, 27, 104, 157, 160–2, 173, 178–80, 187

Ungeschehenes Geschehen (if-not situations) 104

Velleius Paterculus 31–2, 34–41, 145–6
Vergil 43, 105
veterans 116–17, 146–7, 149, 171
victory 10, 13, 33, 49–50, 52, 61, 64, 71, 76, 80, 85–7, 90, 96–8, 108, 112, 115, 117, 133, 135–7, 140–9, 151, 159, 172, 177–8
Vierhaus, Rudolf 87–9, 91

Villa Publica massacre 86, 90, 93
violence 5, 12, 26–8, 52, 57–8, 60, 64–5, 87, 89–91, 93–4, 97, 99–101, 128, 135, 140–1, 144, 156, 163, 169–71, 181, 188, 190
Volaterrae 93

Weber, Max 36
White, Hayden 6–8, 10–11, 55, 104, 129
women, wives 14, 38, 56–7, 60, 64, 90–1, 98, 104, 156, 173, 181, 184–97

Xenophon 25, 27–8

www.ingramcontent.com/pod-product-compliance
Lightning Source LLC
Chambersburg PA
CBHW050324020526
44117CB00031B/1695